Kathryn Artingstall has applied her decades of direct investigative experience to fashion a superb contribution to the literature on factitious illness—whether it is applied to oneself or inflicted upon another. This meticulously researched volume is packed with practical knowledge—including diagrams, case examples, and practical tools—that will assist anyone looking for comprehensive information on the web of deceit that characterizes illness deception in all its forms.

—Marc D. Feldman, MD
Clinical Professor of Psychiatry and Behavioral Medicine
The University of Alabama
Tuscaloosa, Alabama

Munchausen by Proxy and Other Factitious Abuse provides an in-depth study into what is a frequently difficult to recognize criminal behavior that has a lasting, debilitating effect on the victims and defendants in the criminal justice system—a vital, *tour de force* resource on this complex subject.

—Judge Marc L. Lubet
Ninth Judicial Circuit
Orlando, Florida

Munchausen by Proxy
and Other Factitious Abuse

Practical and Forensic Investigative Techniques

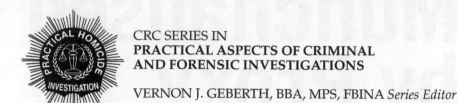

CRC SERIES IN
PRACTICAL ASPECTS OF CRIMINAL AND FORENSIC INVESTIGATIONS

VERNON J. GEBERTH, BBA, MPS, FBINA *Series Editor*

Practical Homicide Investigation: Tactics, Procedures, and Forensic Techniques, Fifth Edition
Vernon J. Geberth

Practical Homicide Investigation Checklist and Field Guide, Second Edition
Vernon J. Geberth

Munchausen by Proxy and Other Factitious Abuse: Practical and Forensic Investigative Techniques
Kathryn Artingstall

Practical Analysis and Reconstruction of Shooting Incidents, Second Edition
Edward E. Hueske

Gunshot Wounds: Practical Aspects of Firearms, Ballistics, and Forensic Techniques, Third Edition
Vincent J. M. DiMaio

Informants, Cooperating Witnesses, and Undercover Investigations: A Practical Guide to Law, Policy, and Procedure, Second Edition
Dennis G. Fitzgerald

Practical Military Ordnance Identification
Tom Gersbeck

Practical Cold Case Homicide Investigations Procedural Manual
Richard H. Walton

Autoerotic Deaths: Practical Forensic and Investigative Perspectives
Anny Sauvageau and Vernon J. Geberth

Practical Crime Scene Processing and Investigation, Second Edition
Ross M. Gardner

The Counterterrorism Handbook: Tactics, Procedures, and Techniques, Fourth Edition
Frank Bolz, Jr., Kenneth J. Dudonis, and David P. Schulz

Practical Forensic Digital Imaging: Applications and Techniques
Patrick Jones

Munchausen by Proxy

and Other Factitious Abuse

Practical and Forensic Investigative Techniques

Kathryn Artingstall

CRC Press
Taylor & Francis Group
Boca Raton London New York

CRC Press is an imprint of the
Taylor & Francis Group, an **informa** business

CRC Press
Taylor & Francis Group
6000 Broken Sound Parkway NW, Suite 300
Boca Raton, FL 33487-2742

Printed on acid-free paper
Version Date: 20160311

International Standard Book Number-13: 978-1-4987-3221-5 (Hardback)

Library of Congress Cataloging-in-Publication Data

Names: Artingstall, Kathryn, author.
Title: Munchausen by proxy and other factitious abuse : practical and forensic investigative techniques / Kathryn Artingstall.
Other titles: CRC series in practical aspects of criminal and forensic investigations.
Description: Boca Raton : CRC Press/Taylor & Francis Group, 2017. | Series: CRC series in practical aspects of criminal and forensic investigations | Includes bibliographical references and index.
Identifiers: LCCN 2016011289 | ISBN 9781498732215 (alk. paper)
Subjects: | MESH: Munchausen Syndrome by Proxy | Child Abuse--prevention & control | Forensic Psychiatry--legislation & jurisprudence | Criminals--legislation & jurisprudence
Classification: LCC RC569.5.M83 | NLM WA 325 | DDC 616.85/8223--dc23
LC record available at http://lccn.loc.gov/2016011289

Visit the Taylor & Francis Web site at
http://www.taylorandfrancis.com

and the CRC Press Web site at
http://www.crcpress.com

Printed and bound in the United States of America by Publishers Graphics, LLC on sustainably sourced paper.

For voices that have not been heard, voices that remain silent, and the hope that knowledge bestows lessened victimization upon humankind.

Contents

Series Editor

The Series Editor for *Practical Aspects of Criminal and Forensic Investigations* is Lieutenant Commander (retired) Vernon J. Geberth, New York City Police Department, who was the commanding officer of the Bronx Homicide Task Force, which handled more than 400 homicides a year. Geberth has been president of P.H.I. Investigative Consultants, Inc., since 1987. He has more than 40 years of law enforcement experience and has conducted homicide investigation seminars for more than 60,000 attendees from more than 7,500 law enforcement agencies.

He is an author, educator, and consultant on homicide and forensic investigations. He has published three best-selling books in this series, *Practical Homicide Investigation, 4th edition, Sex-Related Homicide and Death Investigation: Practical and Clinical Perspectives,* and *Practical Homicide Investigation: Checklist and Field Guide.*

He created, edited, and designed this series of more than 40 publications to provide contemporary, comprehensive, and pragmatic information to the practitioner involved in criminal and forensic investigations by authors who are nationally recognized experts in their respective fields.

He welcomes the opportunity to review new proposals for books covering any area of criminal and forensic investigation and may be reached through his email, vernongeberth@practicalhomicide.com.

Series Editor

The Series Editor for *Practical Aspects of Criminal and Forensic Investigations* is Lieutenant Commander (retired) Vernon J. Geberth, New York City Police Department, who was the commanding officer of the Bronx Homicide Task Force, which handled more than 400 homicides a year. Geberth has been president of P.H.I. Investigative Consultants, Inc., since 1987. He has more than 40 years of law enforcement experience and has conducted homicide investigation seminars for more than 67,000 attendees from more than 8500 law enforcement agencies.

He is an author, educator, and consultant on homicide and forensic investigations. He has published three best-selling books in this series, *Practical Homicide Investigation*, 4th edition, *Sex-Related Homicide and Death Investigation: Practical and Clinical Perspectives*, and *Practical Homicide Investigation Checklist and Field Guide*.

He created, edited, and designed this series of more than 40 publications to provide contemporary, comprehensive, and pragmatic information to the practitioner involved in criminal and forensic investigations by authors who are nationally recognized experts in their respective fields.

He welcomes the opportunity to review new proposals for books covering any area of criminal and forensic investigation and may be reached through his email, vernongeberth@practicalhomicide.com.

Preface

Let's begin by way of introduction as the author of this book. Please be aware that I am not a physician, psychiatrist, or social worker; I am a police officer with nearly 35 years of experience and have an investigative specialty concerning criminal and civil violations with a factitious factor. The contents of this book represent my knowledge, research, and personal experience as it relates to all aspects of factitious disorder (FD) and factitious disorder by proxy (FDP; formerly Munchausen by Proxy) from a victim protection platform.

Victimization of vulnerable populations (children and the elderly) prompted my initial research into FD and FDP nearly 20 years ago because there was a fundamental lack of knowledge, outside the medical realm, regarding the deviant methodology of the FDP offender upon the tiniest victims—children. Through the venue of successful prosecution, child abuse and child homicide cases with an FDP factor were difficult to identify/understand, more difficult to effectively investigate, and most difficult to effect meaningful child protection within. I felt a responsibility to learn more and asked why an offender would victimize in the manner of FDP. Answers arrived in the form of casework, research, and an alliance with an extraordinary FBI agent, Larry Brubaker, who happened to be on the same research mission.

Casework provided relative and practical understanding of difficult concepts relating to FD and FDP as knowledge grew. This knowledge was shared in the first edition of this text titled *Practical Aspects of Munchausen by Proxy and Munchausen Syndrome Investigations*, because crime doesn't just happen in our own backyards and knowledge is power. Understanding why, recognizing patterns of response/action, and acquiring the knowledge that atrocities don't always happen somewhere else make an investigator, prosecutor, child protective specialist, physician, and psychiatrist a formidable weapon as a child advocate. There is no greater or more rewarding role than the ability to make a positive difference within someone's life—even if the path is a most difficult one!

The application of modern criminal justice processes involves crossovers or partnerships with varied professional disciplines, including clinical, psychosocial, social service, and privatized service providers, with each entity viewing victimization from unique perspectives centering on a singular core element—the victim. Law enforcement cannot work alone to provide an effective intervention in an abuse case with a factitious element without involving medical, psychological, and prosecutorial disciplines. Abusive situations with a factitious element are covert and generally occur via an unaware third-party delivery system.

While standards of custodial arrest in criminal cases with a factitious factor remain at the level of probable cause for law violations, identification of an underlying pattern of indirect victimization (via a covert root cause) is needed to understand the methodology of victimization. When criminal conduct has a factitious factor, the investigative process requires interdisciplinary collaboration. Victims may be individual people, businesses, socialized programs, families, or others. The criminal justice process is complicated when crimes are well defined; it is complicated with confusion when recognition and prosecution of (criminal) behavior is clouded with deception. When the behavior is further complicated with the tentacles of medical and psychological pathology, we then ask ordinary citizens to understand these complexities and render judgment and confusion results. Education and understanding is the underlying criminal and civil justice platform for all cases with a factitious element. This book is a resource toward attaining understanding. It will not cover every situation nor answer every question because criminal behavior is an ever-changing entity, but it will broaden your understanding.

There is power in thinking big. The concept of victimization with a factitious factor is a grand scheme of fraud utilizing a generally unaware proxy or proxy that is ineffective, unable to intervene within the scheme, or sometimes naïvely contributory. Power attained by a criminal perpetrator within a factitious victimization scheme comes directly from another's unrecognized knowledge of the deception. Intangible perpetrator benefit surrounding external response to address the effect(s) of root cause action(s) is often difficult to see as the abuser harms the victim directly or through the indirect action(s) of caregiver(s). The process of victimization with a factitious element also spins secondary (financial) victimization within systems, provider, and privatized (insurance) entities.

Although the concept of FD or the victimization found with FDP originated within a medical context of self-abuse or child abuse, application of a *factitious element* has expanded into a multitude of investigative areas including the homicide of children, elder abuse, systematic medical fraud, domestic litigation, and financial crimes. The concept of FD or FDP has become a defensive posture in certain criminal cases and there have been attempts to link FD/FDP as a defense in criminal case conviction appeals. Hospital risk managers and legal firms either representing business or individuals have seen the factitious element on both the defensive and offensive planes. The factitious concept has also been utilized as a means to understand and identify self-induced criminal victimization or falsified heroic event reporting.

When there is a revelation of knowledge or discovery surrounding behavior, disease, or criminal activity and that revelation is amplified through media coverage, word may spread quickly among individuals or groups. When FDP cases began to seriously be identified, investigated, and recognized as always the "media sensation" during the 1990s, the amount of cases (often in particular geographic areas) increased. Rather suddenly, the behavioral factor of FDP was reportedly seen in avenues of criminal offenses, civil domestic litigation, medical fraud, animal abuse, and others. There was a lack of definitive understanding regarding the singularities found within FDP behavior and an uneasiness regarding how FDP sequencing affected the bottom line to criminal prosecution of criminal acts. There was also an understanding on a civil level that unprosecuted actions of individuals may not necessarily rise to the required threshold of a crime. Some asked if those actions were circumstantially linked to other activities such as exploitation of the elderly or estate manipulation. Then came the inevitable defense angle from the wrongly accused as the incarcerated learned of a new behavioral discovery and sought to establish appeal grounds for their convictions. Law enforcement and prosecutors struggled with how to sufficiently explain FDP within the context of a person on trial for child abuse, aggravated child abuse, murder, abuse of the elderly, and others. Simultaneously, the civil aspect of criminal convictions with the FDP factor renewed the potential for financial recovery.

Understanding FD and FDP within the complicated world in which we live provides a traditional base knowledge and a modern concept application of distorted behavior regarding how people bend acceptable societal norms. This understanding is founded in an international language seen through worldwide victimization pathways. So the journey begins.

Acknowledgments

A researcher or a caseworker who investigates the complicated and often emotional subject of victim abuse cannot emerge from that experience intact without support. I am thankful to many people for their support during this journey of discovery spanning 35 years.

I wish to acknowledge Vernon Geberth, series editor, for his inspiration, guidance, and stellar example of what it means to do the right thing by making a difference in the lives of victims, one case at a time.

I wish to thank Retired FBI Agent Larry Brubaker for his collaborative insight that transcended traditional agency singularity and facilitated the sharing of information and training to law enforcement agencies nationally.

The professionals I have met during this journey have provided an invaluable resource of critical refinement as challenges regarding process and innovation prevailed. To the men and women I have had the privilege of working with in the field of national, local, and state law enforcement and criminal prosecution, I salute you and your critically important work. To the medical professionals I have had the honor to assist, thank you for your tireless dedication, incredible insight, and caring on behalf of victims.

To my family, who has continuously supported me through unspoken tolerance during required dedicated work time after normal business hours, your understanding and encouragement are appreciated.

Author

Kathryn A. Artingstall, BS, CAHSO, CHSSO, is currently the security manager for Florida Hospital–Winter Park. She serves as the chairperson for the Florida Hospital Security Safe Environment Committee and provides support for security subcommittees on Security Operations/Standards, Emergency Management/Safety and Training. She is the current chairperson for the International Association of Healthcare Safety and Security (IAHSS), Central Florida East Chapter, and a member of ASIS International. She earned a BS in interdisciplinary social science from Florida State University.

Kathryn has an extensive background in law enforcement. She is a retired Orlando police officer with more than 35 years of law enforcement experience and is presently an administrative deputy sheriff for the Orange County, Florida Sheriff's Office. During her law enforcement career, she was a patrol officer, detective, and court deputy. She is the recipient of numerous law enforcement awards of excellence.

Her previous book *Practical Aspects of Munchausen by Proxy and Munchausen Syndrome Investigations* (CRC Press, 2004) received acclaim as an innovative, formative, investigative resource relating to FDP as a criminal element. Her work has been published in the FBI Law Enforcement Bulletin, *Law and Order Magazine* and *Fire Engineering Magazine*. She has appeared in numerous local, national, and international media programs educating the public on the subject of factitious disorder by proxy as an abuse delivery system.

Kathryn is an accomplished researcher, lecturer, educator, consultant, and author and has provided FDP criminal and civil case analysis nationally. She is a highly motivated advocate of victim protection and previously qualified as an expert witness on the subject of child abuse.

1 Merging Understanding amid Worlds

The most incomprehensible thing about the world is that it is comprehensible.

Albert Einstein

History of Factitious Disorder by Proxy

Factitious disorder (FD) imposed upon another or factitious disorder by proxy (FDP) is not a newly established idea or recognition of behavior. Some of the earliest described situations associated with FDP date back to the eighteenth century when the German baron Von Munchausen (1720–1797) entertained friends and neighbors with stories, which over the years became more and more exaggerated and finally quite unbelievable.[1]

When the baron, at the age of 74, married a 17-year-old girl, his wedding night was spent alone and it is said that his bride "danced with another." Shortly thereafter, the baron's wife gave birth to a son who was named Polle. It was whispered at that time "the life of the Munchausen child will likely be short." The child died under suspicious circumstances before he reached his first birthday.[2]

Unusual behavioral patterns among young men gained notoriety in the writings of Charcot, who in 1877 described adults who attempted to gain hospitalization and treatment for self-inflicted injuries or falsified medical documentation. The term "mania operative passive" was coined as a result of this recognized condition.[3]

In 1951, Dr. Richard Asher described a similar pattern of abuse whereby people fabricated illness and traveled from doctor to doctor—inventing false stories or illness causation, which led to complex medical investigations and hospital procedures, including surgeries. Asher coined the term Munchausen syndrome and applied it to this behavior.[4]

In 1977, Dr. Roy Meadow, a British pediatrician, described an extreme form of child abuse in which mothers deliberately induced or falsified reported illness in their children and referred to this behavior as Munchausen syndrome by proxy. Meadow described cases of children who were unnecessarily treated for numerous medical problems that were falsified by their mothers.[5]

Dr. Donna Rosenberg bolstered awareness of Munchausen by Proxy (MBP) with the authoring of *Web of Deceit* in 1987. Dr. Rosenberg's research included a review of 117 cases of MBP child abuse and provided intuitive foresight into the potential application of MBP within modern medicine.[6]

During the 1990s, a crossover occurred from the medical profession into the criminal justice system for criminally investigated cases involving an FDP (then known as

Munchausen [syndrome] by proxy) factor. The concept of FDP was virtually unknown within criminal justice circles although recognition and documentation of the behavior had been occurring regularly within the medical field up to that point. Confusion surrounded the concept of FDP, and it largely centered on the descriptor that FDP behavior was a *syndrome* accompanied with a perception of illness and inferred lack of accountability for a person's actions. Spirited deliberation occurred as members of the criminal justice system sought criminal prosecution when FDP behavior crossed the threshold into specified willful victimization covertly executed through an unknowing third-party delivery system. Munchausen by Proxy (MBP) dropped the term "syndrome" from the official description of behavior. Initial criminal cases of child abuse and child homicide utilizing the mode of FDP provided understanding that FDP is a delivery system of inflicted harm but it is also a confusion factor for juries. FDP was utilized (ineffectively) as a defense within trial as defendants were portrayed as innocent due to their *illness*. Substantive charges of criminal victimization acts were muddied with the notion that purported mental illness seen within MPB absolved the defendant of accountability. Over time, the choice was to divest a criminal case of the primary inference upon the delivery system (FDP) of the criminal act and try a case based upon the identified crime. What this did was open the door to further use of FDP as a criminal defense, and prosecutors found that although they may have elected to not introduce FDP, they needed to counter prepare for FDP being raised as a criminal defense. Criminal cases involving an FDP factor were always media sensations, and this is accurate today.

Initially, the behavior of FDP was seen as a medical (only) diagnosis. Medical cases originating in England and specifically the publication and works of Roy Meadow and David Southall opened the door internationally by providing knowledge that FDP behavior may not be isolated or as rare as previously described.

The numbers of worldwide cases studied, identified and published, gave rise to allegations of false reporting. Some people cried, "witch hunt" and falsification or improper diagnostic labeling as physicians concluded FDP behavior when diagnostic means failed to discover identifiable causes of a person's illness. At times, FDP was accurate but sometimes it was not. What a deplorable situation for medical staff—continue testing in search of the cause of a person's illness within a normal medical investigatory realm or give weight to the suspicion of FDP as a causation factor and take necessary steps to prove this medically aligned causation theory? Acknowledgment of the possibility of FDP as a causation factor is also acknowledgment that the medical profession is an unwilling causation instrument of medical harm. Liability rests on both sides of this quandary but, more importantly, the life of the victim hangs in the balance. The behavior of FDP was likely a criminal act, and this understanding forged an investigative union between physicians, police, prosecutors, psychiatrists, and (child) protective professions. The interdisciplinary team was assembled.

Understanding and defining FDP on a psychological level was limited to the understanding contained within the *Diagnostic and Statistical Manual of Mental Disorders Fourth Edition* and the specifics of FDP were sketchy. Dr. Marc Feldman began publishing on research pertaining to cases involving FD and FDP factors and embraced the connective element of the interdisciplinary team. Issues of both FD and FDP are psychologically complex. Defining behavior, associative treatment pathways, and acceptable professional standardization of how a behavior is viewed is difficult. The inference that rests within presently accepted understanding of FDP is that the behavior may be viewed as a criminal act, and it is referenced in the *Diagnostic and Statistical Manual of Mental Disorders Fifth Edition* (DSM-V).

As the world changed into the new millennium in 2000, knowledge, publication, and recognition of FDP as a factor in abuse cases continued to evolve. Policing agencies called to investigate child abuse with an FDP element worked the cases as straightforward abuse situations but were required to understand the delivery factor of FDP. The concept of abuse with an FDP factor was identified in greater detail within other vulnerable populations—specifically the elderly. The proxy element found within all FDP cases was recognized within other categories including pets.

Secondary victims to the FDP abuse methodology were recognized, often within financially related genres, and this understanding began to spin off litigation within a civil court realm. Secondary victims may include the following: hospitals, hospital systems, privatized and governmental medical insurance entities, and specified physicians. Secondary victimization perspective is gained by recognizing that FDP abuse methodology is often a chronic series of criminal covert abuse actions and a highly organized scheme to defraud.

The behavior of FDP—not the diagnosis—was recognized not only by interdisciplinary professionals but by the general public as well. All cases involving the FDP cases were and continue to be media sensations and the public takes note. People came forth and expressed concern that their relative(s) may be victims of FDP behavior at the hands of someone they knew; suddenly, what could never be explained seemed to make perfect sense! Cases involving use of the elderly for monetary gain (tangible gain) while also providing the caregiver with belonging, nurturing, and other intangible gain were described. If the elderly person died, was this murder? Were these alleged behaviors and FDP abuse process, malingering by proxy or other deviant pathways with a singular goal of inheritance? Were any of these actions criminal, and who could be tasked with such complex investigations?

Search for Understanding Behavior

In 2012, the U.S. Department of Health and Human Services documented 686,000 cases of child abuse and neglect. This was a rate of 9.2 per 1000 children. In 2012, 22 out of every 1000 children younger than 1 year were victims of abuse or neglect, and 2.2 per 100,000 were known to have died as a result of abuse or neglect. It is believed that many more deaths were unreported.[7]

FDP was once considered vanishingly rare. Many experts now believe it is more common, with a reported annual incidence of 0.4/100,000 in children younger than 16 years, and 2/100,000 in children younger than 1 year. The perpetrator typically inflicts physical harm; although occasionally, she may simply lie about symptoms or tamper with laboratory samples.[8] Early studies indicated that FDP is a behavior in which the offender is often the mother (94%–99%). The most common methods of inflicting harm are poisoning and suffocation and overall mortality is 6%–9%.[9,10] FDP is considered a form of abuse.

It is estimated that every health official is likely to encounter at least one FDP child abuse case (fabricated illness) during their career.[11] Physicians that are less than sure that FDP abuse is at the center of a patients' illness are often reluctant to report their suspicions. The failure to consider the possibility of FDP in the differential diagnosis is the most common reason for failing to link FDP as the cause of a patients' illness.[12,13] Illness that is fabricated by a caregiver is an international problem and transcends cultural divides.[14]

Mental Illness Defined

Mental illness is defined as any of various disorders characterized by impairment of an individual's thoughts, emotions, or social functioning, including schizophrenia and mood disorders such as bipolar disorder.[15]

There is general public presumption that people afflicted with mental illness during the commission of a crime lack the ability to control their actions. This generalized public understanding is amplified when crimes are egregious and offend the sensibility of people. It is often argued that persons thought to have mental illness may not be capable of differentiating between right and wrong behavior. People believed to have a mental illness are sometimes not prosecuted for their actions if a judge or jury believes that the mental illness either prevented the person from refraining from the criminal act or promoted the behavior.

A person who utilizes another as a proxy for purposes other than measurable (often monetary) gain, thereby invoking an FDP behavioral pattern, may be commonly viewed as mentally ill. This general premise becomes problematic in the overall criminal justice process of holding people accountable for their actions. It would be an error to assume that all who perpetuate FDP behavior are to be considered mentally ill just as it would be an error to assume the same for those perpetuating pedophilia, child abuse, child homicide, or other behaviors considered to be disorders.

Factitious Disorder

FD has historically been known as Munchausen syndrome. Current practice finds that the general descriptor of this behavior publicly attaches the label of Munchausen syndrome while the authoritative term used is FD. The clinical description of FD is found in the DSM-V[16] and is listed as a recognized mental illness. FD is a self-imposed behavior that occurs when a person falsifies physical or psychological signs or symptoms or induces injury or disease by deception. The person presents themselves to others as if ill, impaired, or injured assuming the role of someone who is sick. The deceptive behavior isn't dependent upon the presence of external rewards and cannot be explained by the presence of another mental disorder (such as delusional or psychotic disorder).

Diagnostic features of FD include the following:

- Falsification of medical or psychological signs and symptoms in oneself.
- Seeking medical treatment following induction of injury or disease.
- The diagnosis of FD requires demonstrating that a person is taking covert actions to misrepresent, simulate, or cause signs or symptoms of illness or injury in the absence of obvious external rewards.

- Illness may be falsified and may include exaggeration, fabrication, simulation, and induction.
- Preexisting genuine conditions may be enhanced causing people to view the individual as more ill or impaired than they actually are, which leads to excessive clinical intervention.

Individuals who are aligned with the self-inflicted behavior of FD were initially identified within the medical literature and aligned with repetitive hospitalizations geared toward treating either self-inflicted injury or falsified illness. FD may be limited to one or more brief episodes, but it is usually a chronic, lifelong pattern of successive hospitalizations or sought-after medical treatment.

Within the arena of criminal investigations, FD has been linked to repetitive false reporting incidents as alleged crime victims are found to either have verbally fabricated their victimizations or self-victimized through induction methods to support their self-perpetuating role as a crime victim. The degree of both inflicted and verbalized (only) victim injury appears to escalate as victimization allegations repeat. FD may be limited to singular episodes within the victimization realm contained in a criminal setting. It is also possible to manifest itself on a repetitive level—seen as a series of unresolved cases with one victim and unknown singular or multiple offenders.

The issue of involuntary commitment for FD offenders who refuse to accept the notion of psychological treatment when behaviors are life threatening has produced some amount of ethical dilemma.[17] The decision to use an emergency psychiatric commitment for an individual's protection when FD self-harming is present is guided by local statutes. Discussion regarding the dangerousness level needed for commitment when persons refuse to voluntarily admit has been discussed.[18] It has been cited that individuals with FD have self-injurious behaviors that might lead to death because being a medical patient is a goal.[19]

Each situation should be evaluated based upon the merits of total case presentation. Review of historical records and other criteria is generally necessary for qualified medical/psychiatric staff to render decisions regarding involuntary commitment.

Many medical specialties have noted FD trends within cases encountered. Hemoptysis (coughing up blood from the lungs[20]) is the most common type of pulmonary FD generally caused by self-inflicted wounds or deliberately biting one's own tongue.[21] This technique has also been used to simulate blood loss within an FDP victim.

FD affects adults and children alike. A study by Jaghab, Skodnek, and Padder categorized 30 cases of FD involving children as patients who had fabricated their own symptoms. Self-mutilation and suicide attempts were common in these individuals.[22] Self-fabrication/inducement of illness or symptoms seen as a continuance of FDP abuse in the form of collusion is always possible and should be addressed whenever adolescent FD victims are identified. Looking closely into the history of a child's apparently self-falsified illness(es) is warranted.

FD Case Examples

- A 21-year-old female went to a gastroenterologist complaining of diarrhea and abdominal discomfort and was diagnosed with celiac disease. She was placed on a diet and her symptoms resolved. The female moved out of her parents' home when she was 22 and resumed her previous diet. She went back to the gastroenterologist complaining of excessive (20) watery daily bowel movements and was placed back on the restrictive diet, but the symptoms did not subside and a host of medical testing and hospitalization occurred. The female maintained throughout the course of her medical treatment and she did not consume any over-the-counter medications or supplements. After testing, the females' symptoms did not appear in concert with the testing results.

Although the female denied using over-the-counter medicines, when confronted in front of her family, the female's mother stated that she found a receipt for two large bottles of milk of magnesia that was purchased on the day the female was admitted to the hospital for dehydration. The female then admitted utilizing laxatives. The female was weaned from medications and underwent counseling and her symptoms resolved completely.[23]

- The notion of being both a patient and a criminal simultaneously presented. On August 30, 2010, in Washington, a woman threw acid in her own face and then sought help stating that she had been attacked by an African-American woman that had approached her asking if she wanted something to drink. The alleged attacker then reportedly threw a cup of acid into the victim's face, disfiguring her. After surgery, a news conference occurred and the victim was booked as a guest on *The Oprah Winfrey Show*, but canceled the appearance.

  The woman was later diagnosed with body dysmorphic disorder that causes an obsession with minor or imagined physical flaws. The woman pleaded guilty to lying to the police and was charged with three counts of second-degree theft after going on a shopping spree with donation money intended for her recovery.[24] The theft charges were later dismissed after the money was repaid. The woman spent 1 year at a mental health treatment facility in Washington.[25] Professionals surmise that this was a combination malingering and FD case because notoriety and financial gain occurred.[26]
- On October 14, 1999, Wendy Scott died of cancer. Prior to her death, she had resided in London traveling for years from hospital to hospital, pretending to be ill so that she could become a patient. Admission to hundreds of hospitals and 42 operations (nearly) all of them unnecessary occurred.[27] Ms. Scott's "legitimate medical problem was misunderstood to be further evidence of FD" following 650 hospitalizations.[28]
- A patient injected talcum powder under her skin, creating nodules. The substance entered the patient's bloodstream, traveled to her lungs, and killed her (in the ER bathroom).
- A woman was pepper-sprayed by the police when she resisted going to a psychiatric hospital. For several years after that, the woman scabbed and scarred her face as an alleged scratching reaction to the spray and sued the police and pepper spray manufacturer. The woman admitted that she later drilled a hole into her skull and sprayed week-old urine and saliva into her brain creating an abscess. The woman had been seeing 21 different doctors at the time of her death. The combination of prescribed medicines from multiple physicians was a factor in her death.[29]
- A 14-year-old female died following multiple hospitalizations for mercury poisoning and related illness/injury. The subsequent investigation revealed the mercury

exposure occurred from inhalation of mercury contained within (broken) thermometers. The female was diagnosed with Munchausen syndrome.[30]
- A patient found to be applied blue textile die to her fingers to simulate Raynaud's syndrome.[31]
- Another patient decorated her skin with pigment mimicking purpura (skin rash caused by internal bleeding from small vessels[32]).[33]

Factitious Disorder Imposed on Another

FD imposed on another is also known as FDP and historically known as MBP. Researching the behavior associated with FDP almost always links within the phrase MBP. For understanding, FDP will be the term utilized within this text to describe FD imposed on another. FDP is defined in the DSM-V[34] as FD imposed on another and is listed beneath the umbrella of somatic symptom and related disorders. FDP is a deception associated with the falsification of medical or psychological signs and symptoms in others. Inducing injury or disease in another then presenting the person to others as if they are actually ill, impaired, or injured may be present, and the deceptive behavior is evident absent the presence of obvious external rewards.

Diagnostic features of FDP include the following:

- Falsified physical or psychological signs or symptoms or induction of injury or disease in another, associated with deception.
- A person presents another person (victim) to others as ill, impaired, or injured.
- Deceptive behavior is present even in the absence of external rewards.
- The behavior is not better explained by another mental disorder.

Diagnostic features of FD also apply to FDP with clarification that when someone falsifies illness in someone or something, they create a victimization association between themselves and their object. When the victimization produces an obvious tangible gain (such as money), the action is not considered FDP; it may be considered malingering by proxy with purpose and criminal behavior may also attach. If the victimization produces intangible gain (notoriety, praise, verification of self-worth, sense of environmental/situational belonging, and others), the perpetrator is clinically labeled with FDP and the object (used in the process [generally a child, elderly person, or pet]) is deemed a victim.

In cases involving the FDP factor, the actions of the offender are viewed as deliberate acts of intentional abuse as FDP offenders utilize other persons, or things, that they have control over. Children have been identified as the largest category of victims in FDP cases, and biological mothers have been identified as the largest category of offenders.

Hospitalists who suspect FDP should consult psychiatry. FDP is a diagnosis of exclusion often based on circumstantial evidence. Social services may aid in suspected FDP vulnerable adult or child abuse especially when the victim lacks capacity (see Chapter 8).

Case Examples

- Shortly after Victim A was born, he was placed into the custody of his paternal grandparents. From the age of approximately 2 months to 7 years, Victim A was continually taken by the grandmother to numerous doctors who performed a myriad of tests including endoscopies, sonograms, barium enemas, colostomy, and feeding tube placement. The grandmother claimed the child suffered from *unremitting celiac disease*, severe diarrhea, cerebral palsy, seizures, brain atrophy, bladder dysfunction, and disruptive behavior. Celiac disease is also known as gluten-sensitive enteropathy or celiac sprue. It is a chronic intestinal disorder caused by intolerance to protein found in grains.[35]

With approval of the grandfather, Victim A was withheld from public school. When home schooling was arranged with state-mandated supervision, the grandmother told the sponsor that Victim A's death was imminent and, on one occasion, convinced a clergy to pray with Victim A to accept his upcoming fate (death).

The grandmother lied about her education and claimed to be a nurse. At times, Victim A would actively collude by faking his own symptoms when prompted.

The state assumed custody of Victim A and removed him from the grandparents' custody. It was discovered that Victim A had none of the alleged illnesses the grandmother claimed; he was weaned from medication, feeding tube was removed, colostomy was reversed, and no evidence of seizure or other abnormalities were noted.

There was a confirmation that Victim A had surreptitiously been fed laxatives. Expert opinion related the grandmother had deliberately fabricated Victim A's problems and grandfather had quietly acquiesced as well as being active deceptive. Victim A's FDP abuse was identified as physical abuse and emotional/educational/physical neglect. It appeared that both grandparents shared a common goal of keeping Victim A from his birth parents and undermining/punishing the birth mother. The grandmother delighted in attention and sympathy received by the medical treatment of Victim A.

All rights were terminated regarding the grandparents' custody of Victim A, and he was placed with foster parents, enrolled in school, and thrived. Although the grandmother had denounced religion previously, she dismissed the sudden improvement of Victim A as "a miracle performed by God."[36]

- During June 2008, an ad was placed in newspapers located in India seeking the safe return of a missing child that had been violently kidnapped by his noncustodial mother. Newspapers reported that the child's mother suffered from MBP and cautioned medical facilities that the mother may seek medical services for fictitious disease or bogus medical conditions. Physicians were warned not to subject the missing child to any type of heroic or elective surgery or medical intervention without first informing his father.[37]
- During December 2008, a 35-year-old woman from Kyoto, Japan, was arrested for allegedly attempting to kill her 1-year-old daughter by injecting contaminated water (via syringe) to the child's intravenous drip. The 1-year-old was the woman's fifth child; the woman's second, third, and fourth daughters all died of unknown illness by the age 4.

  Hospital staff consulted police after suspecting that the 1 year old was being poisoned and found the suspected woman possessed a syringe. She also had mixed a sports drink with water in her possession and apparently waited until the liquid went bad before using it as an injectable poison. A surveillance camera, set up in the ICU, recorded the mother injecting the drink into the IV drip of the victim.[38]

- In Aschaffenburg, Germany, a 6-month-old girl experienced eight hospital admissions within 5 months. Symptoms of vomiting repeatedly, bloody diarrhea, and acute life-threatening events were never substantiated. Blood in diapers and napkins presented by the mother was shown to be of maternal origin. When confronted, the mother agreed to psychiatric admission. Following 5 months of treatment, her mental state stabilized and she entered supported living. She remained separated from the child, who was given to the father and developed normally.[39]
- A Tennesseean woman said for years that her babies died of sudden infant death syndrome (SIDS). In 1991, 3-month-old Victim A died of apparent SIDS. Three years later, 7-month-old Victim B died, causing the coroner to change the cause of death regarding Victim A. The woman gave birth to a third child who was removed from her custody when he was 3 weeks old; he lived. The state moved for termination of parental rights and was opposed by the mother.
- The mother was charged with the murder of Victim A and Victim B. Munchausen syndrome was thought to be a factor in the death of the victims that "caused her to suffocate her children." The mother pleaded no contest to reckless homicide and received 12 years of probation. Her plea agreement also required her to undergo a sterilization procedure and prohibited her from having contact with any children under the age of 5.[40,41]

Many FDP cases have been identified in the literature. Boyd, Ritchie, and Likhari describe eight particular dermatological cases that in summary provide the following statistics:

Victim age range: 15 months to 23 years.
Victim sex: 50% male and 50% female.
Illness causation: Brodifacoum, multiple surgeries, and skin grafts, presumed fecal injection of an immunization site, household cleaner containing lye, presumed forceful nail avulsion, and presumed contact with a curling iron or other multiple agents.
Outcome: The mother was admitted for psychological evaluation and the child was recovered. The mother was confronted and committed suicide. The child required skin grafting, the child had a severe loss of blood from an oral ulceration, and the child was removed from the mother's custody. The parents were evaluated and found to be "normal," were confronted, and became distraught. Victim contact was limited and the daughter was recovered.[42]

Suspicion Factors for the Presence of FDP (Fabricated Illness)[43]

See Figure 1.1.

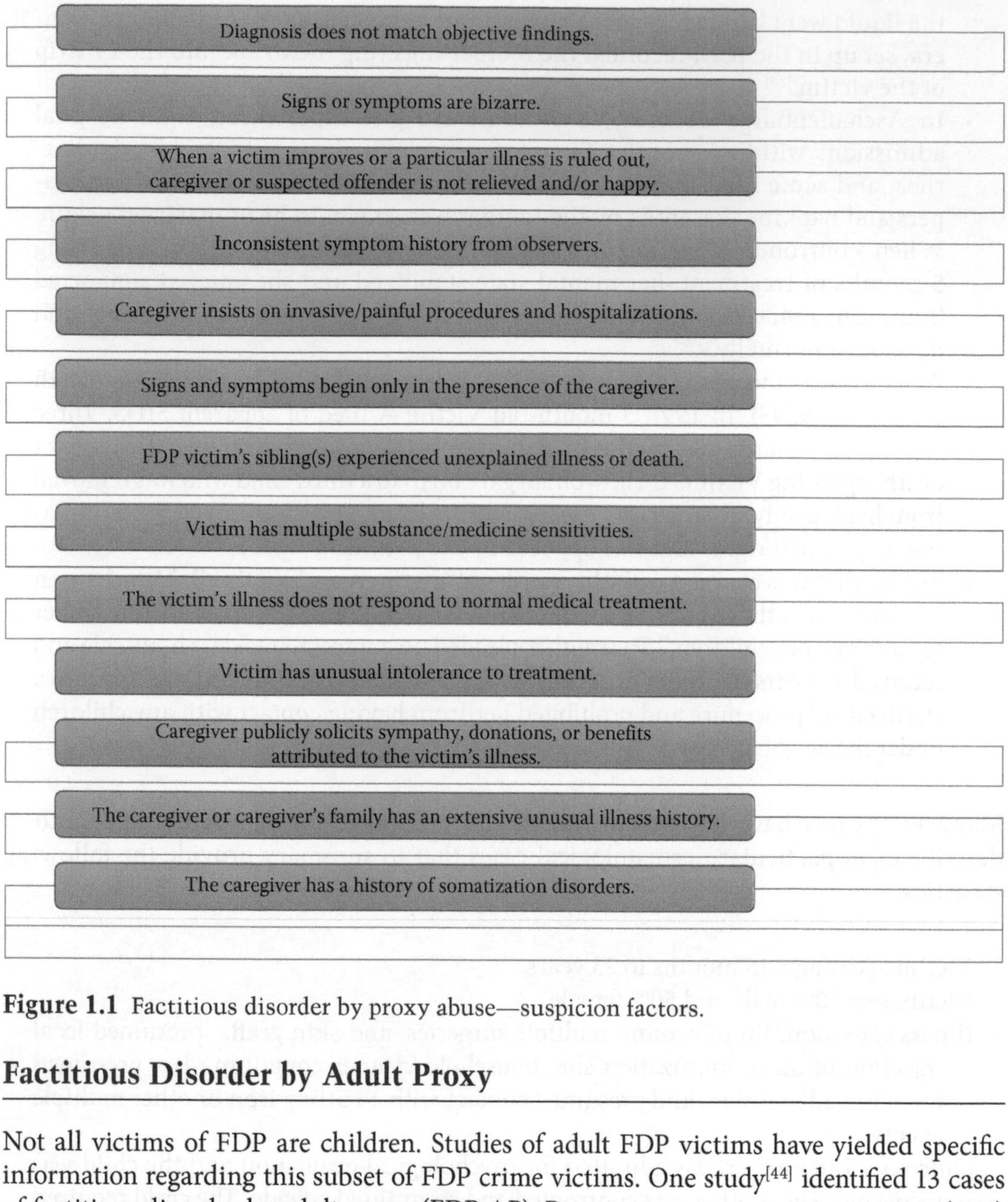

Diagnosis does not match objective findings.
Signs or symptoms are bizarre.
When a victim improves or a particular illness is ruled out, caregiver or suspected offender is not relieved and/or happy.
Inconsistent symptom history from observers.
Caregiver insists on invasive/painful procedures and hospitalizations.
Signs and symptoms begin only in the presence of the caregiver.
FDP victim's sibling(s) experienced unexplained illness or death.
Victim has multiple substance/medicine sensitivities.
The victim's illness does not respond to normal medical treatment.
Victim has unusual intolerance to treatment.
Caregiver publicly solicits sympathy, donations, or benefits attributed to the victim's illness.
The caregiver or caregiver's family has an extensive unusual illness history.
The caregiver has a history of somatization disorders.

Figure 1.1 Factitious disorder by proxy abuse—suspicion factors.

Factitious Disorder by Adult Proxy

Not all victims of FDP are children. Studies of adult FDP victims have yielded specific information regarding this subset of FDP crime victims. One study[44] identified 13 cases of factitious disorder by adult proxy (FDP-AP). Perpetrators were caregivers, most (62%) were women, and many worked in healthcare. The victim age range is 21–82 years. Most victims were unaware of the abuse. In two cases, the victim may have colluded with the perpetrator. Disease fabrication most often resulted from poisoning.

Study results included the following data:

Adult proxy (adult victims) (Figure 1.2)
Adult proxy (adult perpetrators) (Figure 1.3)

Geriatric and developmentally delayed individuals were particularly vulnerable to victimization. Thirty-eight percent of the victims were geriatric and one was

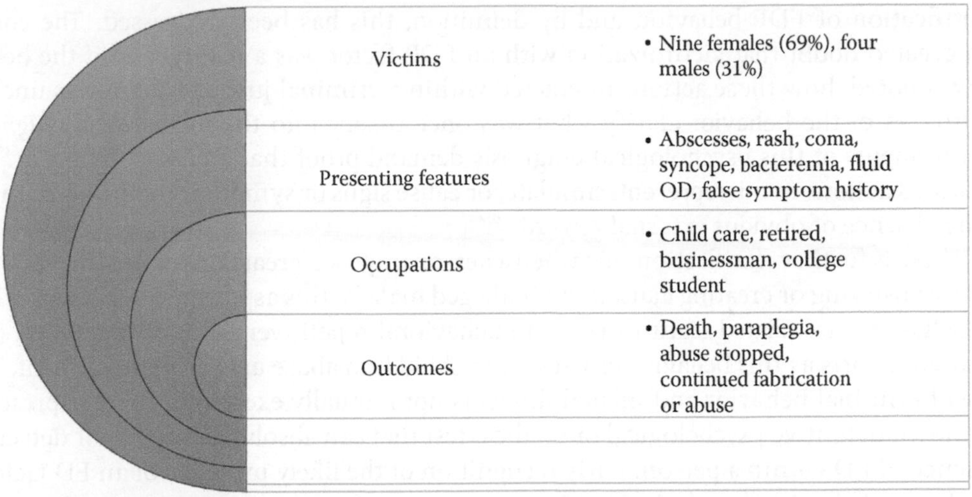
Victims
• Nine females (69%), four males (31%)
Presenting features
• Abscesses, rash, coma, syncope, bacteremia, fluid OD, false symptom history
Occupations
• Child care, retired, businessman, college student
Outcomes
• Death, paraplegia, abuse stopped, continued fabrication or abuse

Figure 1.2 Case study: factitious disorder by proxy adult victimization traits.

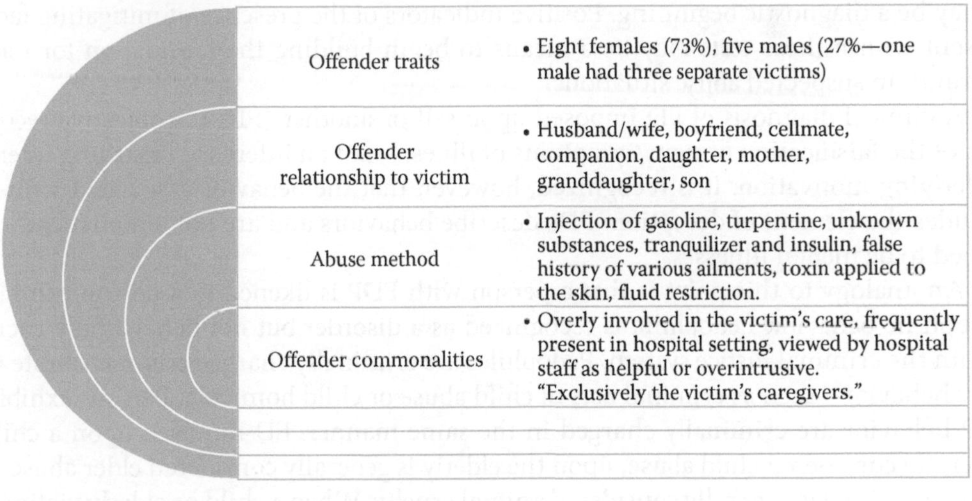
Offender traits
• Eight females (73%), five males (27%—one male had three separate victims)
Offender relationship to victim
• Husband/wife, boyfriend, cellmate, companion, daughter, mother, granddaughter, son
Abuse method
• Injection of gasoline, turpentine, unknown substances, tranquilizer and insulin, false history of various ailments, toxin applied to the skin, fluid restriction.
Offender commonalities
• Overly involved in the victim's care, frequently present in hospital setting, viewed by hospital staff as helpful or overintrusive. "Exclusively the victim's caregivers."

Figure 1.3 Case study: factitious disorder by proxy adult offender traits.

developmentally delayed. Suffocation was not reported in these adult victim cases, but poisoning was the most common method of disease fabrication. This study warns that advanced age does not preclude vulnerability in FDP victimization situations and may actually increase it.

FD/FDP Definitional Predicate

Behavior associated with FD and FDP has been more clearly defined in the DSM-V (published in 2013) than previously available. Problems associated with interventional interpretation of the offender's suspected behavior historically created confusion surrounding identification of FDP behavior, and by definition, this has been addressed. The confusion created doubt that victimization with an FDP factor was a reality, and if the behavior was noted, how those actions interacted within a criminal justice system was unclear. Hallmarks of the behavior clarify what was once theory into the format of a *diagnosis*. Requirements of this psychological diagnosis demand proof that a person is taking "surreptitious actions to misrepresent, simulate, or cause signs or symptoms of illness or injury in the absence of obvious external rewards."[45]

There is further clarification that when a person imposes, creates, or claims that another is ill by falsifying or creating causation for alleged malady, this aspect may represent criminal behavior. Associated features relate to behavioral repetitiveness and intentional concealment efforts as this behavior crosses a threshold into abuse and/or maltreatment. This type of criminal behavior and mental illness is not mutually exclusive. There is presently no known definitive psychological or medical test that can absolutely predict or detect the presence of FD within a person. Early recognition of the likely presence of an FD factor is based upon behavioral analysis.

Likely FDP-related factors collected by review and analysis of known FD cases have been identified and formulated into various awareness tools. Singular positive FDP indicators utilizing know suspicion standard tools isn't necessarily a firm diagnostic platform but is may be a diagnostic beginning. Positive indicators of the presence of mitigating factors present within these tests may be a means to begin building the foundation for modus operandi in suspected abuse situations.

A clinical diagnosis of FD imposed upon self or another (FDP) is objective recognition of the falsification of signs/symptoms of illness—not an inference regarding intent or underlying motivation. It is recognized, however, that the behavior associated with FDs includes the element of deception. FDs describe behaviors and are not automatically presumed to be mental illnesses.

An analogy to this point is that a person with FDP is likened to a person exhibiting pedophilic behavior. Pedophilia is recognized as a disorder but not behaviorally excused within the criminal justice system. Pedophiles are criminally charged commensurate with their behavior—seen as criminal acts of child abuse or child homicide. Persons exhibiting FDP behavior are criminally charged in the same manner. FD imposed upon a child is generally considered child abuse, upon the elderly is generally considered elder abuse, and upon an animal is generally considered animal cruelty. When a child or elderly victim dies as a result of abuse that is caused by the factitious behavior of the perpetrator, a homicide has occurred. The methodology or process of abuse is FDP, and it may be a combination of direct or indirect victim harming.

This indirectness entails others as unwilling/unaware secondary victims—caught within behavior of either FD or FDP perpetrators. Secondary victims are indirectly affected by the deception and innocent pawns utilized within the offender's behavioral pathway in the pursuit of intangible gain. Secondary victims regularly associated with both FD and FDP actions include medical staff or other service providers utilized in the deception, family members and friends, hospital systems, and insurance companies. Secondary victims are adversely affected by the actions of the offender often in psychological, reputational, or monetary ways.

Diagnostic criteria for both FD and FDP are identical with one exception: whenever an individual, regardless of whether afflicted with FD or not, utilizes another person in a replacement capacity for himself or herself for the purpose of assuming the sick role, the offensive action becomes FDP and is generally considered a criminal act of abuse. Determination of the presence or absence of FDP is often a chronic behavioral study of totality circumscribing a suspected victim. FDP offenders should not necessarily be considered mentally ill and thereby relieved of the responsibility for their actions or inactions as sophisticated deception, cover-up, and an often-staunch response to incontrovertible proof are often enhanced with their adamant denial.

This understanding is indirectly evidenced through the covertness of the FDP offender's criminal actions and premeditation thought to accompany chronic (serial) victimization. Premeditation and planning are required to effectively offend chronically. If FDP offenders lacked the capacity of understanding acceptable and unacceptable behavior, FDP abuse would not be perpetrated in such a disguised forum. Abuse with an FDP factor in a medical setting is a continuing infliction of victim pain. The prosecution of abuse with an FDP factor is a prosecution of more than one event—it is a serialized log of events and often difficult to recognize because it is covert and may be complicated with actual illness and changes. Victimization sequencing regulating duration, intensity, and the changing of mode is seen as the threat of discovery looms, loss of the proxy is threatened, or the relative medical need of the victim is seemingly met. Identification of victimization (of all types) is historically rare during the early stages of victimization pathways.

The behavior of FDP is an action or inaction by an offender toward or upon a person who is vulnerable and under the care or custody of another, and the behavior is not better accounted for by another mental disorder. The behavior associated with FDP is likened to the behavior seen in substance abuse disorders, eating disorders, impulse-control disorders, pedophilic disorder, and others.[46] The presence of a behavioral *disorder* does not relieve a person of behavioral responsibility when the action or behavior crosses the threshold into criminal activity. The threshold is where laws are found to protect the vulnerable victims and provide criminal justice application guidance.

In FDP abuse investigations, the majority of identified victims have been children. The frequently accessed substantive criminal charges with an FDP factor are child abuse, endangerment, or related offenses including homicide. FDP is a behavioral qualifier to a substantive statutory law violation—not a charge within itself. In cases of FDP, the perpetrator receives the diagnosis while the person or other living thing utilized by the perpetrator to attain an intangible goal or objective is deemed the victim. In some cases, the actions or inactions of the perpetrator of FDP represent maltreatment, abuse, or other (secondary) criminal acts such as fraud or theft. Criminal behavior and mental illness are not mutually exclusive.[47]

Child Abuse with an FDP Factor as Battered Child Syndrome Methodology

Abuse with an FDP factor upon a child is considered part of the battered child syndrome methodology. A child is thought to be a victim of battered child syndrome when he or she is repeatedly mistreated or beaten and, as a result, sustains a collection of injuries.[48] Only physicians are qualified to make a medical diagnosis of battered child syndrome. Police and prosecutors see the results of a person's behavior upon a child and call it child abuse. Recognizing an abused child when injuries are visible and direct is generally straightforward; recognizing a victim of child abuse when the abuse is delivered through a secondary delivery system, often in the name of medical treatment, is quite another situation.

Identified or suspected presence of FDP in any potential abuse case should incorporate multidisciplinary team integration within the investigatory process as the diagnosis of FDP remains assigned to the perpetrator of the action—not to the victim. The victim is assigned the diagnosis of abused.[49]

Nonmedical personnel (law enforcement, child protective workers, social workers, etc.) may express suspicion of the presence of FDP and work toward resolution of that suspicion in the same manner as other suspected abuse investigations but do so on a criminal investigative platform—not a medical or psychological diagnostic premise. The identification of the actions associated with FDP upon a child is also an identification of child abuse. The same criminal conduct seen within battered child syndrome is also present in FDP child abuse. Substantive criminal charges with an FDP factor include child abuse, endangerment, or related offenses including homicide.

FDP is distinctive from other known forms of child abuse because the testimony, cooperation, and conviction of medical personnel are often compulsory in establishing criminal proof of abuse through an FDP format, and medical conviction is often intertwined with the criminal investigatory product. As knowledge of FDP and FD grows within the criminal justice realm, it may be quite tempting for law enforcement or other nonmedical personnel to call behavior as they see it: abuse through the methodology of FDP. Nonmedical personnel often have intricate evidence gathering responsibilities within an abuse case involving an FDP factor. Sometimes, the medical diagnosis of FDP (perpetrator) and abuse (victim) becomes clear simultaneously in the process of developing probable cause of criminal activity. While custodial arrests of FDP suspects are not contingent upon a medical diagnosis of FDP, both are connected to the establishment and provability of evidence to support the theory of one another. Nonmedical personnel should refrain from assuming responsibility for labeling the existence of FD within a case investigation and allow a physician or psychiatrist to diagnose the behavior because they are licensed to do so. The team concept further explains the intricate role of team members within case management (see Chapter 9).

Abuse cases involving FDP are difficult to understand because the abuse that the victim endures is usually not clearly evident, the effect(s) of the abuse are often delayed, and the victim's injury is frequently perpetrated through the action of a person who historically is not viewed as a suspect (victim's caretaker). Medical professionals acting in good faith in the treatment of an apparently ill individual become an unwilling instrument of medical abuse caused by the direct actions of the FDP offender. Medical staff is unaware of the deception and their role contained within it. Suspicion of an FDP factor within a medical treatment pathway—designated to make a person well—involves a realization within the medical staff that their actions may be contributory toward the enhancement of illness within their patient. Medical staff is governed by the principles contained within the Hippocratic oath and medical pathways seeking to diagnose illness and the conviction/tenacity associated within that process. All within the goal of relieving suffering becomes the vehicle of choice the FDP offender uses for self-gain. The self-gain is covert and results in a desired effect of attention and verification of self-worth derived from either the abusive act or deception created around the victim.

The FDP factor in criminal investigations challenges conceptual standards or norms within the medical fields and within the criminal justice realm. FDP abuse is not a straightforward investigation of wrongdoing; it is a covert cloaked methodology of behavior with a concealed benefit afforded the perpetrator. Root causes for the abuse are hidden and sometimes masked within actual victim illness. The produced enhancement of that illness comes within the closed world of hospitalization and medicine.

Some abuse situations involving an FDP factor simultaneously or intermittently coincide with FD status within the offender. FD involves self-inflicted acts of harm and there can be a flip from one to the other, especially when the suspect is confronted with imminent prosecution. Such actions should be reviewed in the context and order, which they occur in relationship to FDP identification. Is FD self-perpetuated by a suspected FDP offender evidence of mental illness, or is it an escape mechanism to avoid detection and prosecution? Prosecution should be carefully weighed. A combined medical/psychological diagnosis and criminal investigative conclusion may offer differing opinions.

Part of the established criterion for a diagnosis of the FD behavior is that deceptive behavior is present even if there is no obvious external reward. There are many reasons why people either fail to tell the truth or fabricate something. People who lie about an abuse injury to protect themselves from only liability are not considered within the realm of FD. If, however, that same person's actions (lying, fabricating, inducing injury) extend beyond the need for immediate self-protection, the collective behavior is labeled within the scope FD, and upon evaluation, it may rise to the level of criminal conduct.

Child neglect either due to economic constraint or willful torture without a direct or indirect offender benefit in the form of increased attention or notoriety is not considered typical FDP. Overanxious parents of children, whose belief of illness existence emanates from fear without direct or indirect benefit, are not necessarily FDP offenders. People who simultaneously commit act(s) of child or other abuse whereby a pattern of FDP reward can be measured when examining methodology and then outwardly commit a directed act of physical abuse or other directed behavior resulting in victim death may be using the FDP mechanism but they are also murderers.

There are situations within the spectrum of FDP in which a victim dies as a result of treatment geared toward addressing an increased symptom caused by the actions of an FDP offender. The underlying cause of death is the action(s) of the offender not the treatment. Some situations involving FDP methodology may fall into the category of actual unintended death when the FDP offender goes a bit too far and the introduction of a facilitating factor supersedes the victim's bodily ability to cope causing death. The offender's intent regarding the achievement of victim death requires careful investigative process. It is for the courts to determine sanctions and prosecutors to assign charging. FDP is a behavioral understanding of a person's action or inaction evidenced through the recognition of secondary gain and murder is murder.

The behavior of FDP upon a child is sometimes viewed as a behavioral manifestation of unmet parental needs, a cry for help, or an attempt to secure external help in the overwhelming experience of child rearing. In some cases, the hospital is seen as a haven to escape abuse, neglect, or poverty.[50] Lack of parenting ability in FDP cases is often a factor, but not necessarily motivation.

The FDP or FD methodology factor has been seen within seemingly unresolvable criminal investigations involving sexual battery, kidnapping, robbery, home-invasion robbery, parental child abduction, arson, child endangerment, child abuse, attempted homicide and homicide, elder abuse, scheme to defraud, and medical fraud. Looking at criminal cases, applying known motivational factors and recognizing intangible gains associated with FD or FDP behavior may provide insight into cases that were historically unresolvable. Cold cases take on new resolvability factors when they are examined through the eye of an FD/FDP-educated and intuitive investigator. Current alleged repetitive case investigations, seemingly unresolvable, acquire new meaning when FD/FDP concepts are considered. Criminal investigations are fact based, and reasonable explanations for incomprehensible alleged victimizations are generally difficult to achieve. FD/FDP understanding bridged a previously unknown void answering-why and opened a door for effective victim intervention for many types of real or unreal criminalization patterns.

A police investigator educationally aware of FD/FDP understands that medical fields are not the only professions affected by people who utilize FD/FDP as a victimization platform. Policing agencies themselves have been identified as replacement hosts for the medical environment. Falsified reporting of various victimization crimes (often repeatedly) and instances of heroism, sometimes internally within policing agencies, falls under the specter of investigators armed with the knowledge of FD/FDP methodology. A greater understanding of fabrication origination enables law enforcement to recognize potential unseen FDP methodology as the motivational factors for fabrication or falsely reporting incidents identified through intangible reward identification. The very real answer to *why* someone would fabricate an illness, utilize victimization, or portray himself or herself as a *hero* is likely to center upon knowledge contained within the factitious world of victimization.

Innovative understanding and application of FD/FDP methodology continues to mutate as offenders grow in their ability to effectively offend without detection over prolonged time periods. The challenge within the multidisciplinary team remains constant as infiltration of the sphere of abnormal reason and conduct tests reasonableness between inherent knowledge of right versus wrong and the authenticity of gross mutation beneath falsified exteriors of not only mothering perfection, but portrayed exemplary human behavior, albeit false.

Pathological Lying Categories

Pathological lying seems to be a feature present in FD and borderline personality disorder. Malingering includes the presence of external incentives such as economic gain, avoiding legal responsibility, or improving physical well-being that is absent in FD.[51] "It is often difficult to determine whether the lies are an actual delusional distortion of reality or are expressed with the conscious or unconscious intent to deceive."[52]

Deception has been found in the following *conditions*: malingering, confabulation, Ganser's syndrome, borderline personality disorder, antisocial personality disorder, histrionic and narcissistic personality disorders, and factitious disorder, but not all have been associated with pathological lying. In FD, the intentional production of physical or psychological symptoms is solely for the purpose of assuming the role of a sick person. Appearing sick is not something that a pathological liar generally wants.[54]

Abnormal illness affirming behavior occurs when a person produces or amplifies signs and symptoms of an illness outside the scope of any biomedical disease that may also be present.[55] FDs and malingering are forms of abnormal illness—affirming behavior that include conscious production of signs or symptoms from varying platforms of production and motivation[56] (Table 1.1).

Table 1.1 Common Indicators of Factitious Disorder by Proxy (Child) Abuse[53]

- Parent or caretaker reports signs/symptoms not explained by any known medical condition and/or cannot be explained through diagnostic testing.
- When a particular health problem is resolved, the parent or caretaker suddenly begins reporting a new set of symptoms.
- Victim's daily activities are being limited far beyond the usual expectation of a person with that particular condition.
- Parent or caretaker seeks multiple opinions from a varied range of health professionals.
- Parent/caretaker may attempt to maintain a close and friendly relationship with medical staff but quickly become abusive or argumentative if views are challenged.
- The nonoffending parent has little or no involvement in the care of the child.
- The victim has a history of multiple hospitalizations and attending physicians that may occur when the child's treatment is challenged by medical staff.
- Parent or caretaker appears very attentive yet not worried about the child's health.
- Parent or caretaker exhibits vast medical knowledge and/or encourages tests and procedures upon the victim, even if it is invasive, painful, and permanently debilitating.
- When direct evidence that the child's symptoms are being fabricated is established.

FD and FDP Connective Theory

FD/FDP factors may be simultaneously present within a singular case investigation. Connective theory exists noting that multigenerational FDP abuse cycles may occur in much the same manner that domestic violence seems to transcend through a cycle of violence. Is FDP a learned behavior or does it proliferate as a threshold of acceptable conduct within a person? Within some identified cases of child abuse with the FDP factor seemingly present, offenders claim to have themselves been undiscovered FDP child abuse victims. A potential recidivism link in an abuse cycle involving FDP will require further scientific study for validity standards. The likelihood of scientifically establishing this link is isolated either due to the proliferation of unidentified cases (concealment) or the high-profile nature surrounding all cases that are identified. Identification of FDP factored cases remains difficult for many reasons including the knowledge of FDP/FD, the offender's ability to conceal actions, the serialization of criminal acts, and a reluctance on behalf of prosecutors to acknowledge the pattern of FDP behavior because it confuses juries and provides a basis of potential defense in criminal or civil trials.

Connective theory between FD as a mental illness and FDP as a methodology linked to a prosecutable crime does not mean that either identified perpetrator is absolved of civil responsibility attached to secondary victimization. An individual who victimizes a system through self-inflicted FD-patterned behavior or criminal FDP abuse isn't generally held harmless for secondary victimization damages. We see how financially tasking it is for medical insurance companies or hospital systems when a person utilizes FD or FDP behavioral patterns within those system and system resources (physicians, medical testing procedures, and hospitalization) as conduits for the behavioral objectives of offenders.

Victim Neglect within the Scope of Systematic Factitious Abuse

Evaluation of FDP within a criminal context originates from an understanding that FDP upon another may involve the utilization of a person or thing as means for the perpetrator to attain some measure of personal gain. This personal gain is not necessarily easily recognized or clearly visible. The actions of the perpetrator are fundamental to what is experienced by the victim and those experiences are of criminal nature in the form of abuse or neglect.

FDP abuse upon another often involves either a child or an elderly person as a victim of serialized or chronic sequencing. The sequencing may be a lifelong entity when the behavior is not stopped through recognition and intervention. All identified cases of FDP upon another, known to this author, have occurred in situations whereby offenders have been in either temporary or permanent custody or control over a victim. This usually indicates a parental/authoritarian role (child victims) or custodial/caretaker role (elderly victims).

Custody and control over another places an FDP offender in a strategically offensive advantage connected to unrestricted and unmonitored victim access. Victim accessibility may be raised as an issue of thwarted trust accountability when criminal cases are prosecuted. Parental or custodial duty is a position of trust that holds those entrusted to a standard of reasonable or prudent dependent care. Trustees who fulfill the role of parental or custodial control over another are expected to provide needed food, clothing, shelter, supervision, medical care, nurturance, and teaching.[57] Protection from preventable or induced harm is an inferred responsibility. When a trustee thwarts a parental or custodial role, neglect and/or abuse are often present.

Skill is required to actively commit abuse or neglect in plain sight especially on a repetitive or chronic basis. Skill is pervasive within the superficial environment of care and nurturing seemingly present in all known FDP cases because the reality of what is actually occurring is contrary to the offender's behavioral projection. This behavioral projection is what people may recognize as truth based but reality may be far from that inference. Understanding that FDP offenders possess skill necessary to commit cloaked abuse or homicide allows us to understand that it takes an equal or greater amount of investigatory skill to recognize abusive FDP behavior. Offender skill and required investigative skill to effectively intervene within the FDP world is ever changing.

The presence and subsequent criminal charging of neglect is often overlooked when FDP victimization is identified. Criminal charging of child abuse, elder abuse or related homicides take precedence over the other often-present behavior of various forms of neglect. Within the scope of the FDP offender in the role of abuser or murderer, as publicly projected parenting perfection is displayed, the obscured reality of severely neglected victims is present but remains obscured. The neglect is formulated and delivered in such a manner that the victim and those in positions of authority may not even be aware of it.

Child neglect either due to economic constraint or willful torture without a direct or indirect offender benefit in the form of increased attention or notoriety is not considered typical FDP abuse. Overanxious parents of children, whose belief of illness existence emanates from fear without direct or indirect benefit, are not necessarily FDP offenders. People who simultaneously commit act(s) of child or other abuse whereby a pattern of FDP reward can be measured when examining methodology and then outwardly commit a directed act of physical abuse or other directed behavior resulting in victim death may be using the FDP mechanism but they are also murderers.

Alternative Answers to Unexplained Behavior

The definition of anything is a combination of what it is and what it is not. FD imposed upon self or another (FDP) has diagnostic criteria, which labels the perpetrator, not the victim. Diagnostic criteria are clearly defined behavioral indicators but factitious disordered behaviors do not generally exist in a vacuum; therefore, an understanding of other potentially present conditions is needed on medical, psychological, and criminalistic levels.

There are several peculiar disorders/syndromes, which have inescapable similarities to the behavioral characteristics of FDP and FD. These disorders/syndromes have been used as articulate defenses when the presence of FDP or FD is questionable. In many cases, circumstantial evidence alone is present and absent a confession, and it is difficult to assess what has occurred and link that behavior to a directed offender action. When a governing body such as law enforcement enters the scenario, it is for the purpose of establishing or ruling out criminal conduct, and thus a fiduciary responsibility to understand and prove what has occurred on a platform of probable cause is presented. Within this context, alternative causes for unexplainable medical symptoms, which illuminate potential abuse with an FDP factor or false reporting likened to FD methodology, need to be eliminated within a reasonable degree of medical certainty by medical staff.

A general recognition that error is a potential human factor in all circumstances, including the identification and prosecution of FDP- and FD-based crime, empowers the relevancy of diminishing error. Managing the human error factor within the criminal side of FDP/FD is attained through knowledge and elimination of other reasonable explanations for that behavior. FDP and FD are not absolute answers for medically unexplainable symptoms in every potential case of abuse that law enforcement investigates, and this makes the recognition link from medical malady to criminal act all the more difficult and confusing.

Somatic Symptom Disorder

Somatoform disorder has been presented as alternative reasoning for the inability of medical professionals to accurately diagnose illness within a patient who is suspected of FDP activity. According to the DSM-V, somatoform disorders may feature the presence of physical symptoms that suggest a general medical condition that cannot be fully explained medically. The symptoms do not result from the effects of substances or from other mental disorders. If a person is afflicted with a somatoform disorder, the symptoms must cause significant distress or impairment in social, occupational, or other areas of functioning.

In somatoform disorder, the symptoms are real to the person afflicted and not produced under voluntary control. Symptoms are not intentionally simulated or created. It is possible that somatoform disorder and FD may be present within a person at the same time or they may be simultaneously inflicted upon another through the avenue of FDP while self-inducing FD methodologies and experiencing actual other medical illness. Somatoform disorder alone is not usually connected with abuse and not reported because it aligns itself within avenues of self-inflicted injury seen within FD cases. FDP (use of another person) is considered abuse and is reported to authorities in accordance with either mandatory child or other dependent (elderly, infirm, protected) abuse reporting laws. The reporting of abuse is not contingent upon confirmation of an abusive situation or ruling out the presence of other factors (illness or disorders). Mandatorily reporting abuse to authorities stems from known or suspected abusive situations.

Somatic system disorder is considered a chronic problem that may temporarily subside but rarely ever goes away completely. Features listed within the DSM-V include distressing somatic symptoms that may result in significant disruption of daily life; excessive thoughts, feelings, or behaviors that may be seen as unrealistic and persistent thoughts about the seriousness of the symptoms; and high level of anxiety or excessive time and energy devoted to health or symptoms.

A person with somatic symptom disorder is classified according to severity: mild, moderate, and severe. Pain is a commonly reported symptom. Somatic symptoms are real to the individual whether or not it is medically explained. These symptoms may exist with a concurrent medical aliment(s) and are not mutually exclusive. People with somatic symptom disorder excessively worry about their illness, think the worst about their health, and may allow medical treatment geared toward addressing symptoms to take on a central role in their lives becoming an identity feature or dominating interpersonal relationships. They may seek repeated care from multiple doctors for the same symptoms and seem unresponsive to medical treatments.[58] Most individuals that have somatic symptom disorder also have hypochondriasis. There are many other specified disorders, in which a person may have, including panic disorder, depressive disorder, illness anxiety disorder, dissociative disorder, and conversion disorder.

Malingering

To differentiate FDP from malingering, documenting the absence of tangible incentive for the behavior is needed. In both FDP and malingering, there is an intentional production of symptoms. Looking at why a person might create fabricated medical symptoms and the associated gain/reward helps clarify intent.

Malingering differs from somatic symptom disorder and FD (upon self or other) within the analysis of purpose. Malingering is defined as the act of pretending to be ill or injured in order to avoid work or duty.[59] There are external tangible gains that are primary motivators for a person to become a malingerer such as obtaining drugs, collecting medical (or other) payments, evading criminal prosecution, or avoiding responsibility. The attainment of intangible things such as attention/notoriety, perceived nurturance, a sense of belonging, and those often seen within FDP application are not prevalent goals when malingering alone is present. If a person malingers and their aim is to assume the sick role for monetary incentive alone, FD is not relevant.[60] Malingering, FD, and FDP are not mutually exclusive. Feigning of illness for disability compensation is a pervasive issue. In 2011, an estimated $20.2 billion was paid for malingering adult mental disorder issues through U.S. Social Security.[61]

Case Example

During 2010, a woman in New York faked cancer to allegedly obtain a discounted wedding.[62] During 2012, she was indicted on charges of fraud and grand larceny for falsely claiming she was dying of leukemia and accepting generous donations toward her wedding. She was sentenced to time and already served in jail as long as she paid restitution.

Malingering by Proxy

Fraud and child abuse have recently been recognized as forged malingering oddities when guardians have been caught coaching their children to misbehave or fake disabilities in order to secure or maintain supplemental security income (welfare) payments. Some critics believe that the practice of utilizing children as income resource vehicles has an added threat factor due to legislative enactment of the 1996 Welfare Reform Act.

Prior to 1996, children could qualify for benefits if they had impairments that seriously limited their inability to perform activities normal for their age. The Welfare Reform Act instituted by the U.S. government in 1996, however, required that children have "marked and severe functional limitation(s)" to be eligible for benefits. The definition of severity is unclear. There is concern that some parents may fabricate severe and permanent illness in their children as a means of maintaining or obtaining child welfare payment.

If the fabrication of such illness includes repeated hospitalizations and/or treatment, FDP association may also occur. Abuse by proxy for the explicit purpose of monetary compensation may straddle the debate line between clinical FDP child abuse and malingering by proxy. The qualitative labeling associated with this behavior should be diminutive as greater issues of child abuse and medical fraud take prominence. The distinction between financial frauds associated with FDP child abuse versus malingering by proxy is found within the offender's motivational origination and methodology.

Malingering by proxy is described in the literature as directing or pressuring one's child to exaggerate or feign symptoms to obtain financial assistance for the parent.[63]

Case Example

The mother of a 13-year-old eighth grader who was diagnosed with uncomplicated ADHD disagreed and insisted the child had bipolar disorder and be admitted to the hospital. In the hospital, the child was weaned off medications, and the mother was unhappy stating that she had applied for disability benefits for the child on the grounds of "chronic mental illness." The parents of this child had recently divorced and the mother was on a restricted income. The mother facilitated unnecessary medical intervention and medications for the child in order to maintain disability benefits (monetary income).[64]

Online FD/FDP Support Groups

Online support groups exist for both FD and FDP entities. Anonymity of people posting on these sites makes it difficult to determine if the postings are accurate. FD members on one site, however, described a conscious process of choosing an illness they wanted to feign, researching it to ensure realism, fantasizing about enacting FD and expected affection/attention. Members claimed to employ a variety of methods to obtain the "sick role" including self-harm, exaggeration, and lying.[65] *In 2015, there are 13,000,000 Internet sites regarding "Munchausen support."* Support is directed for those who are allegedly falsely accused, convicted, or incarcerated for abuse, victims of abuse, and families affected by the alleged abuse. Support originates from private and professional resources.

FD/FDP Category Grouping: Identification

Both FD and FDP have been categorized by multiple means. Libow and Schreier classified FDP into three categories: help seekers, active inducers, and doctor addicts according to the degree of harm upon the victim and taking into consideration why the FDP offender abused the victim. Help seekers infrequently produce symptoms in the victim; active inducers commit dramatic physical assaults on victims and; doctor addicts are personally convinced that their children are ill.[66]

Both FD and FDP administration may be categorized by methodology: (1) simulation (mild form) and (2) production (severe form).[67] Both categories contain the element of fabricated symptoms that secondarily provide an avenue of surreptitious personal gain for the offender. FD/FDP methodology can be a directed infliction of injury or injury obtained indirectly through (medical) treatment. Treatment response addresses fabricated conditions on all levels or actual conditions created within victim by the actions of the offender or medical staff.

Actual bona fide victim illness may originate from organic disease as a by-product of medical measures or from the direct/indirect actions of the FDP offender. Determining responsibility for a victim's injury/ailments rests within examination of purpose: medical staff acting in good faith to treat an apparent illness; FD/FDP offenders are creating illness that has voluntary root cause origins. When actual victim illness is a by-product of a voluntarily induced action or inaction of another (FDP), who is responsible for the situation? The FDP offender is! Accountability seems rather clear.

Simulation and production may occur simultaneously or intermittently, chronically or acutely, and the infliction may be on a consistent basis, or there may be breaks within the offense schedule. There are many mitigating factors that affect the selected timing of FD/FDP behavior. Simulation does not always precede production and vice versa.

Simulation

Behavior seen within FD/FDP simulation occurs when an offender fakes and illness by verbally presenting an untrue history for a nonexistent illness or condition. Simulation usually does not involve the direct self-infliction of physical abuse that is often seen within FD/FDP production situations. In medical situations, pretend illness or signs of pretend illness are illustrated in both FD/FDP methodologies evidenced by FD/FDP offenders who verbally claim the existence of illness symptoms. Sometimes, these claims are bolstered by nonintrusive actions such as an offender biting his or her own tongue and then wiping it into a child's diaper claiming that the origin of the blood is the child (FDP) or a person falsely claiming multiple victimizations to policing agencies to exact attention (FD). To justify the claim of illness or victimization, the victim is subjected to medical testing to explain created and presented symptoms. Tangible evidence of fabrication may be found in cases of simulation, but it is always concealed—often in plain sight.

Testimony of the FD/FDP offender combined with evidence may clearly illustrate how simulation occurs. Falsification of medical charts (offenders making their own entries) and the unexplained appearance of outside substances are characteristically found as seeds of deceptive origination in FD/FDP (medical) simulation cases. The foundational premise for simulating an illness or falsifying an alleged victimization is limitless and dependent upon the creativity and skill of the offender.

FDP offenders have been known to withhold medication or treatment from a genuinely ill child in order to exaggerative a legitimate preexisting condition requiring hospitalization. The action goes well beyond neglect when the reason for the behavior is to enhance illness within the victim to achieve attention, and sequencing within subsequent hospitalizations validates this theory. The cause/effect responsibility of an FDP offender performing exclusively in a simulation status is generally defined as "hands-off" application, resulting in physical or psychological abuse of another.

Production

FDP production is the actual infliction of harm by an offender onto a victim. The purpose of inflicted bodily intrusion is to intentionally create signs and symptoms of an illness. These symptoms would not otherwise be present if it were not for some action, in which the perpetrator directly inflicted on the victim. Methods of infliction such as suffocation to produce apnea or poisoning through the administration of nonauthorized medicine, toxins, or objects foreign to a person's body are commonly seen as FDP production vehicles. Producing sickness on internal and external manipulation is the most frequently recognized form of FDP. Although production is often considered the more severe form of FDP abuse, the lethality of FDP simulation is equal to that of FDP production in terms of potential victim demise.

When a person reaches an actionable place where he or she is responsible, directly or indirectly for inflicted harm or injury onto a victim, that person has crossed a threshold into deliberate measurable abuse. Whether the abuse is covert or blatant affects the likelihood of discovery. The offender's motivations are irrelevant when determining the existence of abuse but are seen as significant qualitative keys regarding the identification of abuse pathways in FDP cases. Qualitative keys (motivational aspects of FDP victimization) may be seen as FDP abuse suspicion factors but do not necessarily direct evidentiary collection means in every suspected case. Death usually arrives slowly for FDP abuse victims with considerable suffering during the process. If there were ever a creative fantasyland for those who choose to abuse others, FDP would be the forum. Multidisciplinary investigative abuse teams would be remiss to underestimate the ability of the FDP offender to originate or transform causes for either simulation or production FDP victimization formats.

Presentation of FDP Identified Illnesses

The causes for FDP simulation and production are limited only to the offender's imagination, and no listing of FDP abuse methods will ever be considered complete. FDP production cases have been identified as ipecac poisoning; manual suffocation; salt, insecticide, drug, and laxative poisoning caustics applied to the skin; poisoning by injection of liquid soap, gasoline, fecal bacteria, dirt, other blood containing bacteria such as *Escherichia coli*; injection of vegetable oil as nose drops causing aspiration pneumonia; and injection of other substances. Poisoning and suffocation are the primarily identified methods of FDP production and cause either immediate or primed effects seen as symptoms of illness within the victim.

Poisoning Cases

All criminal cases of suspected poisoning require cause determination that may include elemental issues of FD/FDP. Some reasons why poisoning occurs in children include

1. Accidental overdosage of prescription or over-the-counter drugs
2. Accidental ingestion of toxins or chemical reactions to other substances
3. Metabolic or environmental causes
4. Deliberate poisoning resulting in homicide, attempted homicide, suicide, aggravated child abuse, child abuse, or elder abuse

How Human Poisoning Occurs

Deliberate poisoning methodology may include an FD/FDP element and manifest itself as either an unintended consequence within the FD/FDP methodology or a directed pathway to end the life of a targeted victim when the risk of offending supersedes a sought-after reward benefit. Core factors associated with FD/FDP behavior must be applicable in order to assert an FD/FDP inference. Whether or not FDP is a component in a victimization sequence resulting in abuse or death, the action upon the victim is of criminal nature (Figure 1.4).

An identifiable secondary FD/FDP gain such as a commonly present attention need coupled with repetitive offender behavior (either within the repetitive victimization sequence of a singular victim or between multiple victims within a singular family) normally is present in authentic FDP poisoning cases. Singular poisoning instances within FDP victimization may indeed occur, but they are normally not recognized. Lack of recognition may be due to witness inability to discern or the death of the victim that causes case closure without detection. The death of a person either attributed to or interrelated with a poisoning factor without an established pattern of multiple hospitalizations, medical treatments, and emergency response service calls (EMS or police) would not normally be associated with FDP behavior. Poisoning deaths that omit these factors are generally considered either accidental or directed homicides.

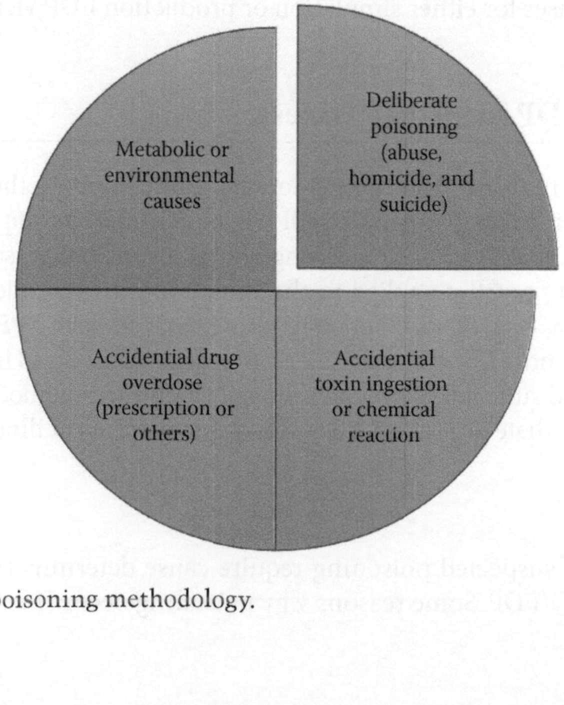

Figure 1.4 Human poisoning methodology.

Victim Suffocation

The methodology of suffocation within FDP production causes temporary or permanent cessation of breathing in a victim. The act of suffocation (real or feigned) may be difficult to medically determine if there is a lack of physically definitive bodily damage to the victim. Suffocations produce or suggest medical abnormality that instigates medical testing. In some cases of lethal suffocation, autopsy results either may fail to provide proof of suffocation or are inconclusive. Suffocation deaths may be mislabeled as SIDS, respiratory failure, or other causes not associated with homicidal asphyxia.

Suffocation involves cutting off a person's air intake. Inflicted FDP suffocation has been orchestrated through various means including plastic wrap over the victim's mouth, pillow over the victim's face, pressing the victim's face into the chest of the offender, the offender placing his or her hand over the mouth/nose of the victim, and the offender placing his or her body over the victim's body pushing the victim's face into a mattress.

The ability of an FDP offender to openly, effectively, and chronically offend upon a victim is a learned and graduated skill. As individual incidents of FDP increase in number and frequency on selected victims, the skill and boldness of the perpetrator increases proportionately. The ability of the perpetrator to mask the origin of the victim's illness may become more bizarre and creative with time.

Methods of infliction have been identified by direct infliction (production cases) or through more creative means found within simulation cases. In the simulation case type, an elaborate scheme involving removing apnea leads from the victim, placing the lead upon the offender (who holds his or her breath), and then quacking reattaches the leads onto the victim as medical assistance is summoned. Life support equipment attached to a victim has also momentarily been "turned off," causing the victim to stop breathing momentarily and then the equipment is turned back on. These actions produce abnormalities within medical monitoring systems and reignites victim medical treatment. In the process, attention is directly afforded to both the child and the caregiver of the child (offender).

Case Example

One of the first criminally prosecuted cases of abuse with an FDP factor occurred in the United Stated within Texas and may have set the predicate for the existence of FDP as an abuse delivery system. Criminal case protocol emerged with the introduction of covert child abuse methods not previously identified. Although it is believed other criminally prosecuted cases were in existence in the United States prior to the Reid case, media notoriety and the subsequent highly visible courtroom scrutiny of this case aroused awareness of the gross nature of FDP child victimization. Initial estimates of the quantity of FDP cases within the United Stated projected limited application. The numbers of later documented cases justified FDP as a causation index in criminal child abuse investigations. This case was aired on the *NBC News* show, Dateline, on January 5, 1993.

On February 7, 1984, Hereford, Texas, paramedics responded to a call for help. Upon arrival, paramedics found Tanya Reid performing CPR on her baby, Morgan. Morgan was transported to Northwest Texas Hospital, pronounced brain-dead, and died on February 8, 1984. An autopsy revealed that Morgan had damage to her brain caused by cardiorespiratory arrest. The cause of the cardiorespiratory arrest was unknown. The official autopsy conclusion was that child abuse had not been the cause of Morgan's death. Morgan was 8 months old at the time of her death. The Reid family relocated to Chicago, Illinois, after Morgan died and then moved once again to Iowa.

On May 2, 1985, Tanya gave birth to a health boy—Robert Reid—in Iowa. Twenty-six days later, Robert was rushed to the hospital after Tanya reported that Robert had turned blue and stopped breathing. This incident marked the beginning of 20 or more reported episodes of either Robert's breathing cessation or seizure that only Tanya witnessed. Repeated medical testing failed to identify a cause for Robert's alleged medical problems despite numerous hospitalizations, tests, drug therapies, and the best efforts of numerous physicians. When Robert was 34 months old, he was removed from the custody of his parents and placed into foster care. Robert's alleged seizures and breathing spells stopped.

Tanya was criminally charged and convicted of child endangerment after authorities presented a criminal case alleging that Tanya intentionally caused Robert to stop breathing. Issues relating to MBP (FDP) typology—including warning signs, offender traits, and common medical responses—were presented within the context of the criminal case. Tanya was given a 10-year prison sentence and released after serving 3 years.[68]

During 1993, Tanya Reid was once again placed on trial, this time for the death of Morgan (who died in 1984). A jury determined that Tanya Reid had indeed murdered her daughter, Morgan, during 1984, and had utilized a deadly weapon—her hands. Tanya Reid was convicted and sentenced to 62 years in prison and a fine of $10,000.00. Reid's lawyers appealed this ruling and obtained a sentence reversal. In 1996, Reid was retried for the murder of Morgan, reconvicted, and resentenced to 40 years in prison.[69]

During the course of the police investigations surrounding both cases, historical information concerning Tanya Reid indicated that, as a teenager, she revived an infant whom she had been babysitting and was earmarked a "hero" by the community for her phenomenal action in saving the child. This child had never experienced breathing difficulty prior to the incident with Tanya Reid and never reportedly had further episodes after Tanya's access to him was restricted. Tanya Reid was a licensed practical nurse.

The Tanya Reid case highlights child abuse and child homicide situations with an FDP factor and it piloted expansion of FDP understanding within law enforcement. During the 1990s, review of the rather large volume of FDP and smaller account of FD cases found within medical literature provided glimpses of variety and applied methodology deviancy. Within many of these publications, the issue of reality in terms of seeing what was actually occurring seemed elusive. Reality seemed to come into focus when there was an understanding that the behavior of FDP was criminal. *Reality* also became a premise for criminal defense.

Defining what constitutes abuse when an FDP methodology is utilized has been discussed at length. Those charged with investigating abuse cases with a potential FDP factor should be open-minded to allow adequate exploration of abnormal abuse or homicide case methodology. In FDP cases, there is strong potential and prevalent existence, the appearance is often not a true reflection of reality, and no one should automatically be placed above suspicion. There is generally a marked absence of other abuse forms such as physical injury or sexual abuse, but this is not an absolute.

FDP victims are not routinely identified by police in the direct way that physical or sexual abuse victims are. FDP victimization is commonly referred to police through intuitive medical personnel or citizens/family members that have been educated regarding FDP as a form of abuse. In some situations, the reporter may have a higher understanding level of an FD/FDP concept than the agency to which it is reported and become frustrated with a department's inaction on behalf of the allegation. The ever-increasing numbers of FDP cases, reported or suspected, within medical and law enforcement forums have taken mythical rarity to practical reality and in the process created awareness through public education. FDP/FD behavior as a qualifying factor in recognized alternative abuse methodology or victimization falsification commands law enforcement awareness and investigatory refinement.

FDP Warning Signs/Indicators

FD/FDP medical literature review provides an identification basis of classic warning indicators for probable FD/FDP abuse linkage. These factors may provide initial suspicion and recognition for criminal abuse cases with and FD/FDP delivery system. Criminal abuse cases, regardless of qualifiers, are built upon evidence. The presence of FD/FDP warning indicators, alone, are generally insufficient to establish probable cause "for arrest." Warning signs may provide an initial basis to initiate criminal investigations as evidence is sought to prove theoretical validity or irrelevance of FD/FDP behavior as a mode within criminal or civil investigations.

- Unexplained and prolonged illness that cannot be diagnosed by experienced physicians. Illness(es) are often described as so unique that the physicians remark that they have never seen anything like it before.
- Repeated hospitalizations and/or medical visits.
- Extensive medical tests that fail to produce a diagnosis.
- Symptoms that do not make medical sense.
- Persistent failure of the victim to respond to therapy.
- Signs and symptoms that dissipate when the victim is removed from the sole presence of the offender.
- Caretakers who do not seem worried about their child's illness but are constantly at the child's side while hospitalized.
- Mothers who have usually close relationships with the medical staff.
- A family history of SIDS.
- Mothers with previous medical or health-care experience who have a history of the same type of illness as their child.
- A parent who welcomes medical testing of the child, even if painful.
- Attempts to convince medical staff that the child is still ill when advised that the child is to be released from the hospital.
- A model family that normally would be above suspicion.
- A caregiver with a previous history of FD.
- A caregiver who adamantly refuses to accept the possibility that the illness source is nonmedical.
- Caregivers who speak about the child's illness as if it were their own.
- Caregivers who speak for their children when conversation is directed specifically to the child.

Behavior that interrelates to evidence gathering as either criminally or civilly based investigations are examined that have either a known or theoretical bases of the FDP/FD factor have provided a baseline platform of warning signs within specific case analysis. This platform is not absolute nor will it likely ever be complete, but it does provide guidance through experience. Warning signs provide insight when interviewing suspected offenders; they are technique tools, and identification of these signs within an investigatory process are usually hidden intangible entities.

FDP Behavioral Warning Signs

- Stalking FDP victims through covert domination for the purpose of direct control and manipulation of a victim's behavior and indirect medical status
- Manipulation of medical staff through power and control of the victim's treatment pathways
- Victim domination through isolationism
- Victim confusion index (usually seen in older FDP victims as active collusion)
- Control and punishment of authoritative figures (medical staff, law enforcement, prosecutors, judges, juries) through implementation of lawsuits, threats, or directed victimization events
- Actively accursing family members or others of victimization responsibilities
- Public display of emotional extremes or complete apathy
- An obsessive degree of punctuality for medical appointments (appointments are rarely missed unless a higher form of medical intervention is available)
- Insistence that the offender accompany the FDP victim to medical appointments
- Self-inflicted isolation from interfamilial contacts
- Networking with other FDP offenders
- Caretakers who refuse to accept medical diagnosis of their child(ren) being diagnosed as well as asking instead for more and more tests
- Parents who tell others that their child is "terribly ill" or "not expected to live" although informed by medical personnel that the child is not ill

FDP Abuse or Homicide: Family Screening

FDP behavior is not confined to specific groups. Prediction of FDP victimization is unlikely on a clinical level due to lack of diagnostic testing required to absolutely identify all causes of FD/FDP behavior. If this type of testing existed, it would likely be predicated upon the validity of offender disclosure coupled with warning signs and indicators based upon past behavior. The threshold of honesty, whether it is conscious or subconscious, within the FD/FDP offender seems to be based upon many things:

- Disclosures of actions, which generally affect public morality levels, are difficult to obtain. Recognition of hidden FDP family dynamics can be a potential line of sight into behavioral actuality when the primary subject of the suspected behavior (FD/FDP offender) is reluctant to be truthful.
- Nonoffending spouses of FD/FDP offenders may lack the capacity to recognize the behavior, even if it occurs within what normally is considered plain view.

- There is a stigma associated with disclosure of FD/FDP behavior, which is assigned not only by society but also by integral family members or friends of the FD/FDP offender. There is good reason why FD/FDP offenders, their nonoffending significant others, family members, and friends choose to not disclose either evidentiary or suspect concerns. What if they are wrong? How would disclosure affect the family or the victim? What would the rest of the world or community think?

Patterns of FD/FDP behavior may be revealed through the questioning of nonoffending spouses, family members, or friends. Behavioral signs and warning indicators known to exist within previously identified criminal or civil investigations of wrongdoing may emerge. If the nonoffending spouse of a suspected FD/FDP offender understands.

There is another factor that my enter into the pathway of a nonoffending spouse that twists the value of truth when disclosure of actual or fabricated FDP victimization is utilized as a leverage tool in pursuit of civil matters pertaining to divorce, child custody, probate, or other types of victimization. Careful examination of motive is warranted whether the actualization of FDP victimization is provable or contrived as a defense to an allegation of wrongdoing by the nonoffending spouse. Warning signs and indicators become critically important during the collection of evidence.

Suggested Screening Questions for FDP Nonoffending Parents, Family Members, or Others

- All children become ill at some point in their childhood. When your child gets sick, is the illness short term or does your child "never seem to get better?"
- Do you feel that your partner/spouse does an exceptional job caring for your child?
- Has your partner/spouse ever been the victim of an unresolved crime or been a patient with an illness whose cause could not be determined?
- Has our partner/spouse exhibited the same symptoms or illness(es) as your child? Have the causes of these illness(es) been determined?
- Have you ever seen your partner/spouse frequently giving medications or treatments to your child? Was the medication and/or treatment medically prescribed or initiated for other purposes such as prevention?
- Has your family ever been involved in a household fire?
- Is your partner/spouse jealous when you and he or she spend time apart?
- Do your personal activities or your employment responsibilities frequently separate you from your spouse? How often are you separated?
- Does your partner/spouse make it easier for you to spend time at work by supporting your efforts?
- Have you accepted monetary donations to help cover treatment costs for your child?
- Have you ever suspected that your child's illness was induced? Did you confront your partner/spouse regarding these suspicions? What was his or her response?
- How long have you known your partner/spouse? What was life like for him or her before you met? (establishment of residential and personal timeline)
- Do you consider yourself as supportive toward your partner/spouse? If yes, how is this accomplished?

- Do you believe that your partner/spouse has the ability to offend in the manner that he or she is accused?
- Do you understand that FDP abuse is an international problem that may affect more than one child within a family?
- What are your concerns?

Frequency and Reporting of Cases

In recent years, FDP case identification and associated identification factors have increased in reported frequency within the medical literature. Linking FDP behavior within criminal investigations has also increased, but the prevalence of FDP within criminal prosecution is minimized as substantive charging of primary offenses supersedes the FDP methodology quantifier. There have been criminal capital cases over the years involving homicides, which bridge this general premise, but in all criminal cases, FDP isn't the issue—the victimization is.

Historically, studies originating with the medical realm provided some insight into prevalence and behavioral observations within identified FD and FDP cases. Within these studies, prevalence was believed to be conservative. Victimizations with an FDP factor were thought to be far greater than reported. In terms of child abuse or child homicide victimization, reported victimizations with a recognized FDP factor were comparatively low to other child abuse/homicide methodologies.

International prevalence of FDP cases was initially documented in at least 16 different countries and thought to be present in many others during 1987. Findings in 1977–1997 reflected that 700 cases of FDP abuse were reported within the medical literature, and FDP cases were identified in 52 countries.[70]

A 2-year study conducted by researchers in England and the Republic of Ireland (1992–1994) produced epidemiology of FDP. Within this study, a total of 128 cases were identified and the following victim characteristics were noted:

Gender	60 boys (47%). 68 girls (53%).	
Mean age at diagnosis	20 months (heavily skewed toward children under age 2).	
Abuse methods	FDP fabrication.	55 victims
	Poisoning alone.	15 victims
	Suffocation alone.	15 victims
	Two or more abuse forms.	43 children
Offenders	109 biological mothers (85%). 6 biological fathers. 1 boyfriend. 11 undetermined.	
Homicide statistics	8 deaths due to FDP abuse (10%).	
Serial abuse	83 children. 18 children died prior to this study. They were siblings (of 15 children within this study). 5 children were diagnosed as SIDS (sudden infant death syndrome). Victims.[71]	

Another FDP-related study involved the serialized nature of FDP victimization. Multiple victims within singular families were identified. Five families with a cumulative total of 18 children were utilized in this study. Of the 18 children, 13 were known to be abuse victims via an FDP methodology. Five had no recognized FDP victimization histories. Siblings were found to have either the same or similar illness(es), and in each family, only 1 child was victimized at a time of the 13 identified child abuse victims, and 4 (31%) died.[72]

Reporting Tendencies

In generalized terms, FDP victimization tendencies may provide criminalization commonalities/insight as FDP is seen as an abuse delivery system. A study conducted by the U.S. Bureau of Justice Statistics reported that nearly two-thirds of all crimes are not reported to the police. The most common reasons for not reporting violent crime was that the offender was unsuccessful or that it was a private/personnel matter. This report indicated that victims reported violent crimes to the police in order to prevent further victimization (to others), to stop or prevent their own further victimization, and because they recognized the behavior was criminal.[73]

Historically, people who criminally abuse others through the avenue of FDP have been successful without detection. FDP abuse and FD actions are such private/personal and shameful matters for families that offenders rarely tell anyone of their actions. They even lie to themselves. FDP offender accountability via the criminal justice system places emphasis upon the consequence for victimization. Holding people accountable for their actions regarding abuse with an FDP factor highlights the difference between responsibility and excused behavior because of mental illness. Public awareness through publication and media activity almost always surrounds FDP abuse situations. This awareness has created public and professional education unmatched historically. From an FDP victimization platform, awareness is perhaps the greatest tool within victim protection venues. Knowledge transcends professional boundaries and even has the ability to infiltrate the often-closed world of the FDP/FD offender's family. Families who are aware of FDP may vocalize/report their concerns, even when these concerns are only unconfirmed suspicions. Please be aware, however, just as suspicions are reported on behalf of true concern regarding victimization, that same report may be a mechanism to divert an offender's own responsibility of criminal activity or utilized as a potential mechanism to leverage civil litigation. Although false reports of FDP does occur for personal reasons, the greatest motivation for reporting suspected FDP abuse appears to be the desire to stop or prevent further victimization from occurring.

Resource Reporting for Suspected Abuse with an FDP Factor

Medical Personnel

Reports of FDP/FD within literature has been an ongoing process since 1786.[74] Today, knowledge of FD/FDP within the medical realm is far greater than knowledge and recognition within criminal justice circles. There is an understanding within medical/psychological professions that FDP is a criminal act, and when such recognized behavior occurs to a victim, it must be reported to authorities as abuse within required mandated reporting structures.[75] The prevalence of FDP discerned through reported cases has risen from once solely medically recognized as a means to criminally catalog abuse delivery mechanisms within prosecuted primary offenses.

School Resources

Reports of suspected FDP abuse may also originate from school personnel. The likelihood of recognizing a potential FDP abuse situation within school systems is directly proportionate to educators' base knowledge of FDP existence. The correlation between excessive absenteeism and potential abuse in many forms is often real. School officials, like medical staff or law enforcement officers, are also considered mandated reporters of known or suspected child abuse within the United States.[76] Educators who have some knowledge of FDP abuse have recognized potential active collusion within their students and then associated suspected behavior of active collusion within the criminal behavior of FDP child abuse and initiated either a police report or a referral to child protective services.

Fire and Emergency Medical Team Personnel

The trained observational skill of fire and emergency medical team personnel has produced abuse concerns when repetitive service calls involving injury or illness in singular families occur. Again, knowledge of FDP/FD is key in recognizing potential abuse or false report patterns. This concern may initially be formally reported or informally transferred to law enforcement. If behavioral recognition is substantiated, FDP/FD identification may result.[77]

Guardians

Guardians are people who serve as advocates for wards (children or dependent adults). They are also a valuable resource for identification of potential FDP abuse cases. Guardians are entrusted by the state to comprehensively examine/monitor a person's living conditions. There are guardians entrusted with the physical/emotional care of a ward and those deemed "guardians of the estate" who look after a ward's property, money, and assets. Reporting instances of known or suspected abuse—direct or covert—is required.

Guardian *ad litem* (GALs) often represent the interests of minor children. They are also known as court-appointed special advocates or attorneys for the child. They are the voice of the child and may represent the child in court.[78] Since the inception of the *Child Abuse Prevention and Treatment Act in 1974*, every case involving an abused or neglected child that results in a judicial proceeding requires that a guardian *ad litem* be appointed to represent the child. When guardians are aware of the existence of FD/FDP, recognition of potential abuse patterns is possible.

Home Health-Care Staff and Administration

Abuse victims with an FDP factor or persons who self-inflict through the mechanism of FD often inhabit a world that is entwined with medical professionals. Sometimes, this world extends to the home, as home health-care workers are deployed to address continuing or unresolved medical need within an individual. When a home care worker is assigned to a home, he or she becomes an extension of the offender's control indirectly telling the victim that he or she is ill. The outside world looking in at the situation also concludes, "If the victim is gravely ill, then why else would home healthcare be ordered?" FDP offenders often resist attempts to discontinue nursing services, asking for extended support, as the victim remains dependent.

Children that are chronically ill and have home health-care services are not necessarily confined to their homes—some may be required to attend school. In this situation, clinical staff may be required to attend with the child. If the child illness(es) are being fabricated or induced or if there is active collusion, in the custodial absence of the offender, the nurse may become an extension of the offender's control. An FDP offender may easily become nervous when the victim is away in a school or other setting. The nurse is the compromise to seclusion while maintaining a link to the medical world. Extended seclusion for victims may arouse suspicion and threaten exposure.

If FDP behavior is suspected and home health-care personnel are in place, removal of a home health-care nurse without adequate alternative victim protection may lead to increased family flight risk or an increased scope of victim infliction (rate and lethality). Either action will produce a reaffirmation or renewal of victim dependence and foster the fantasy of illness.

Cost factors associated with managed care and liability may necessitate immediate removal of home health-care staff when suspicion or confirmation of FD/FDP is revealed. During the treatment process, it is also typical for services to be reduced on a set scale as constant patient evaluation looms. If the patient seems to be improving, services are likely to diminish. This is the same concept seen when a FD/FDP victim is seen within a hospital setting: patient improvement equates to less services/attention and becomes a catalyst for increased infliction.

It is important that police and social service providers realize that a covert FDP/FD factor within a criminal or civil investigation may quickly be affected by the external actions of health insurance companies. FD/FDP offender's actions are affected by the removal or lessening of available health-care services. An increase in the amount and severity of inflicted or fabricated symptoms may result in the withdrawal of health-care services as the offender's effort to regain intangible value derived from attention is sought. An offender may think, "You thought he or she wasn't ill, now see how ill he or she is!" Caution is warranted if a suspected FD/FDP offender's ability to access healthcare is impaired. Contingency plans and an understanding within health insurance companies regarding FD/FDP case protocol would be insightful in furtherance of victim protection. By understanding the (potential) role that home health-care workers assume within the scope of FD or FDP victimization, awareness is created on a recognition and preventative intervention scale within the abuse cycle.

Victimization Location Preferences

The majority of identified cases of FD and FDP have occurred within the confines of the medical realm. The primary location of treatment, geared toward addressing either fabricated or induced harm within a victim, is a hospital setting. The hospital setting becomes a crime scene in cases of FDP abuse. The treatment itself is considered an indirect part of victim abuse at the hands of an unwilling third-party participant (medical staff). Testing records, treatment billing, and the testimony of the medical staff is investigative product. Outpatient medical locations such as emergency rooms, walk-in clinics, private physician's offices, and health departments have also been identified as treatment locations for FD/FDP abuse methodologies. Within residential confines, bringing the health-care element into the home either reinforces the FD/FDP behavior or serves as a catalyst under certain conditions.

Criminal or civil cases involving the FD/FDP factor outside the scope of the medical realm have been identified. It is the behavioral pathway entailing identification of fabrication, lying, exaggeration, and falsification of victimization, financial manipulation, civil litigation, or heroism circumscribing a person's actions that reflects an FD/FDP behavioral pathway. Fire and police stations have been identified as "home bases" in criminal case investigations with an FD/FDP suspicion factor. Victimization falsification on any level draws professional service providers into close proximity to the alleged victim. Outside the scope of a medical setting, the conduit toward attainment of FD/FDP gratification shifts from medical staff onto alternative symbols of power: police or fire personnel.

FDP Case Resolution Factors

The investigation of crime or alleged criminal/civil misconduct with a suspected FD/FDP factor is an examination of deception. Victimization generally occurs chronically, over prolonged time periods, and involves more than one investigative segment. Periods of apparent nonactivity or rest periods between offending segments may give appearance that a case has resolved. Appearances can be deceiving. Within many chronic criminal actions, victimization fluctuates depending upon external and internal factors. This is true in situations involving an FD/FDP factor as well. Apparent periods of rest between offending segments may actually be a temporary reprieve for the victim, preparation time for the offender to select, and preparation of a new victim or simply a break because the offender's life is acceptable at that time. FDP offenders are generally not known to directly terminate FDP abuse altogether without other factors present such as

1. Age progression of the victim
2. Police intervention with public admissions or provability of criminal acts via FDP methodology
3. Victim's death (without access to other victims)

There are civil and criminal case investigations where a "suspected" FDP/FD factor is present. Not all suspect cases may absolutely have a sustainable link to this factor. Lack of evidence to validate a suspicion coupled with often-present vehement denial by the offender and/or the offender's family complicates the investigative process. The complexity of secondary victimization is also a factor in both recognition of an abusive sequence and the dogma that surrounds the medical professionals involved (Figure 1.5).

When the case falls short of criminal provability, dependency and civil issues are often at the forefront of judicial involvement. The criminality of FDP may not necessarily be directly addressed in dependency/civil court, but criminal investigative results may directly affect dependency court rulings. FDP is not a substantive charge—it is a qualifier or vehicle of understanding to further explain abuse or neglect methodology. Understanding the premise of FDP or FD as situations are examined upon the context of abuse or neglect may provide clarity and assist the court in understanding complicated methodology within cases where FD/FDP resides. Prosecuting criminal cases of abuse, neglect, fraud, and others or civil cases of dependency, divorce, probate issues, or others with a known or suspected inference of FDP/FD should be conducted within set prosecutorial and judicial standards. FDP child abuse or child homicide cases are child abuse/homicide cases with an FDP delivery system.

When criminal/civil cases with an FD/FDP factor are unfounded either on investigatory levels (law enforcement, social service inquiries), prosecutorial levels, or judicial

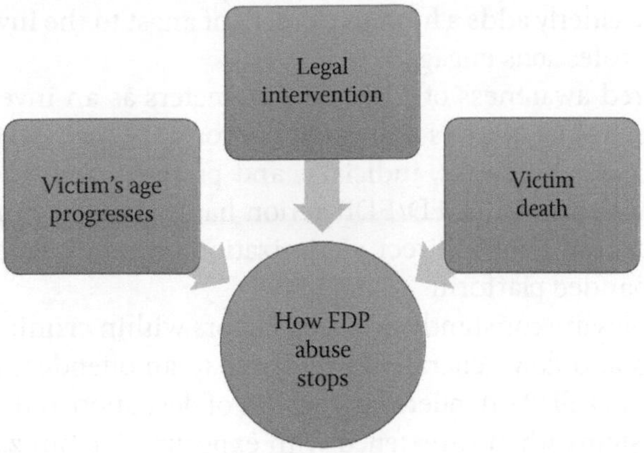

Figure 1.5 Factitious disorder by proxy abuse—victimization resolutions.

levels, the alleged offender is vindicated. If an FD/FDP factor is unrecognized or not proven within the medical realm, the alleged offender is empowered. Vindication may cast tremendous empowerment, if in error, by reinforcing denial and bolstering offender confidence enabling recidivism. The assessment and safety of victims and associated risk is very concerning in these situations.

Mobility Factors and Trends

Through analysis of identified FDP victimization and FD situations, a tendency for accused FD/FDP offenders to relocate, as a means of resolution to express or suggestive concern of FD/FDP is apparent. Relocation is a simple solution for an FD/FDP offender's disastrous problem presented if they are identified. Identification equates to a breakdown in the FDP/FD offender's shell of protection—carefully predicated upon deception and covertness. The life of an FD/FDP offender is an existence built upon lies—specifically feigned illness or situations that produce a measure of the value of life itself.

Relocation potential in FDP cases poses an extreme situation of threatened harm to victims. The apparent ability and willingness of the majority of FDP offenders to relocate rather than risk detection facilitates repeated undetected victimization at will. The location choice for relocation often occurs in unsuspecting community environment. Threatened harm and an understanding of the infliction scale in FD/FDP victimization sequences demonstrates the importance of immediate social service victim protection as intervention justification is achieved through evidence collection.

Conclusion

Concept, treatment, and understanding of FD/FDP have changed in format, name, and application over the years. Recognition of FDP as an abuse methodology opened the door of understanding within criminal and civil areas of victimization and improved professional response within protection ability. FD/FDP abuse methodology patterns remain covert, complex, and difficult to recognize and understand. The fact that victims are primarily either children or the elderly adds a human element of angst to the investigative/protective responsibility of all professions engaged.

There is a required awareness of FD/FDP parameters as an investigatory knowledge base within civil or criminal matters that extend beyond the medical profession into areas of law enforcement, social services, judiciary, and private enterprise. By definition, the concept of behavior found within FD/FDP action has expanded from a well-established medical/psychological entity of indirect victimization on multiple levels to indirect victimization on an expanded platform.

Learning principles are constantly evolving factors within criminal/civil investigatory processes, which ebb and flow generally in response to an offender's adaptation of criminalization pathways. FD/FDP offenders are masters of deception and really good at changing their delivery systems when threatened with exposure. Victimization reports are not always genuine nor are they always provable. When an FD/FDP factor is a potential presence within a criminal or civil investigation, casework complexity requires the analysis of indirect gain by all those involved. Just as the FD/FDP offender garners indirect intangible benefit from victimization, false reports of FD/FDP activity may garner that same indirect intangible benefit for the accuser or the accuser may simply be wrong.

FD/FDP factorization as a delivery mode in criminal/civil investigations is still considered a new and innovative application within old reliable investigatory standards. Knowledge of FD/FDP helps to expand the proficiency of modern policing and furtherance of victim protection through a partnership quest with medical, child protective, and legal personnel. Searching for truth in a world of deception as a victim's life hangs in the balance conveys the importance of understanding FD/FDP concepts as they apply to justice. Victimization occurs on multiple levels within FD/FDP behavioral applications, and indirectness permeates everything connected to this concept.

Notes

1. Jones, J.G., Butler, H.L., Hamilton, B., Perdue, J.D., Stern, H.P., and Woody, R.C., Munchausen syndrome by proxy. *Child Abuse and Neglect*, October 1986;10(1):33–40.
2. Burman, D. and Stevens, D., Munchausen family, *Lancet*, August 27, 1977;2(8035):456.
3. Signal, M., Gelkiph, M., and Levertov, G., Medical and legal aspects of Munchausen syndrome by proxy perpetrator. *Medical Law*, September 1990;9(1):739–749.
4. Asher, R., Munchausen's syndrome. *Lancet*, 1951;1:339–341.
5. Meadow, R., Munchausen syndrome by proxy: The hinterland of child abuse. *Lancet*, August 13, 1977;2(8033):343–345.
6. Rosenberg, D., Web of deceit: A literature review of Munchausen syndrome by proxy. *Child Abuse and Neglect*, 1987;11:547–563.
7. Children's Bureau, Child maltreatment 2012. Washington, DC: U.S. Department of Health and Human Services, Administration for Children and Families, Administration on Children, Youth and Families, 2013. http://www.acf-hhs.gov/programs/cb/research-data-technology/statistics-research/child-maltreatment.
8. McClure, R.J., Davis, P.M., Meadow, S.R., and Sibert, J.R., Epidemiology of Munchausen syndrome by proxy, non-accidental poisoning, and nonaccidental suffocation. *Archives of Disease Childhood*, 1996;75(1):57–61.
9. Rosenberg DA. Web of deceit: A literature review of Munchausen syndrome by proxy. *Child Abuse and Neglect*. 1987;11(4):547–563.
10. Schreier, H.A. and Libow, J.A., Munchausen syndrome by proxy: Diagnosis and prevalence. *American Journal of Orthopsychiatry*, 1993;63(2):318–321.

11. Fabricated or induced illness by careers: A complex conundrum. *Lancet*, 2010;375(9713):433.
12. Rosenberg, DA. Web of deceit: A literature review of Munchausen syndrome by proxy. *Child Abuse and Neglect*, 1987;11(4):547–563.
13. Squires, J.E. and Squires, R.H. Jr., Munchausen syndrome by proxy: Ongoing clinical challenges. *Journal of Pediatric Gastroenterology Nutrition*, 2010;51(3):248–253.
14. Feldman, M.D. and Brown, R.M., Munchausen by proxy in an international context. *Child Abuse and Neglect*, 2002;26(5):509–524.
15. The American Heritage®, *Dictionary of the English Language* (5th ed.). Boston, MA: Houghton Mifflin Harcourt Publishing Company.
16. American Psychiatric Association, *Diagnostic and Statistical Manual of Mental Disorders* (5th ed.). Washington, DC: American Psychiatric Association, 2013.
17. Ford, C.V. and Abernathy, V., Factitious illness: A multidisciplinary consideration of ethical issues. *General Hospital Psychiatry*, 1981;3:329–336.
18. Cleveland, S., Mulvey, E.P., Appelbaum, R.S., and Lidz, C.W., Do dangerousness-oriented commitment laws restrict hospitalization of patients who need treatment?—A test. *Hospital Community Psychiatry*, 1989;40:266–271.
19. Houck, C.A., Medicolegal aspects of factitious disorder. *Psychiatry in Medicine*, 1992;10:105–116.
20. http://en.wikipedia.org/wiki/Hemoptysis.
21. Mucha, S., Varghese, L., French, R., and Shade, D., Separating fact from factitious hemoptysis: A case report. *Critical Care Nurse*, August 2014;34(4):36–42.
22. Jaghab, K., Skodnek, K., and Padder, T., Munchausen's syndrome and other factitious disorders in children. *Psychiatry*, March 2006;3:46–55.
23. Keswanti, R., Sauk, J., and Kane, S., Factitious diarrhea masquerading as refractory celiac disease. *Southern Medical Journal*, 2006;99(3):293–295.
24. CNN Wire Staff, Woman in face acid attack charged with theft, http://www.cnn.com/2010/CRIME/09/20/washington.acid.hoax.charges/index,html. Accessed on October 1, 2014.
25. Online/newscast - abc news, http://abcnews.go.com/blogs/headlines/2013/02/acid-attack-hoaxer-bethany-storro-says-she-was-suffering-from-mental-illness-exclusive/. Accessed on November 1, 2013.
26. Maia Szalavitz In *Time Magazine*, http://healthland.time.com/2010/09/22/phony-cancers-and-self-inflicted-acid-attacks-a-national-outbreak-of-munchausens/. Accessed on November 1, 2013.
27. Denise Grady In *New York Times*, http://www.nytimes.com/1999/10/25/us/wendy-scott-50-who-faked-illness-for-attention.html. Accessed on November 1, 2013.
28. See Note 2.
29. See Note 2.
30. Lech, T., Case report ICP OES and CV AAS in termination of mercury in an unusual fatal case of long-term exposure to elemental mercury in a teenager. Institute of Forensic Research, Krakow, Poland.
31. Serinken, M., Karciouglu, O., Turkcuer, I., and Bukiran, A., Raynaud's phenomenon-or just skin with dye? *Emergency Medicine Journal*, 2009;26:21–22.
32. http://www.healthline.com/helath/purpura#Overview1.
33. Shirazi, A.R., Hougeir, F.G., DiCaudo, D.J., and Swanson, D.L., The diagnosis: Factitious purpura. *Cutis*, 2009;84:71, 105–106.
34. American Psychiatric Association, *Diagnostic and Statistical Manual of Mental Disorders* (5th ed.). Washington, DC: American Psychiatric Association, 2013.
35. Ciclitira, P.J., AGA technical review on celiac sprue. American Gastrointestinal Association. *Gastroenterology*, 2001;120:1526–1540.
36. Lasher, L. and Feldman, M., Celiac disease as a manifestation of Munchausen by proxy. *Southern Medical Journal*, 2004;97(1):67–69.
37. http://www.rescueaditya.org/mbproxy.html.

38. http://www.japantoday.com/category/crime/view/mother-arrested-for-attempted-murder-of-hospitalized-1-year-old-daughter-by-mixing-energy-drink-in-iv.
39. Klepper, J., Heringhaus, A., Wurthmann, C., and Voit, T., Expect the unexpected: Favorable outcome in Munchausen by proxy syndrome. *European Journal of Pediatrics*, September 2008;167(9):1085–1088.
40. https://groups.google.com/forum/#!topic/soc.men/Xz58QsVl74w.
41. http://www.freerepublic.com/focus/fr/637003/posts.
42. Boyd, A.S., Ritchi, C., and Likhar, S., Munchausen syndrome and Munchausen syndrome by proxy in dermatology. *Journal of American Academy of Dermatology*, August 2014;71(2):276–381.
43. Flaherty, E., MacMillan, H., and Committee on Child Abuse and Neglect, Caregiver-fabricated illness in a child: A manifestation of child maltreatment. *American Academy of Pediatrics*, September 2013;132(3):590–597.
44. Burton, M.C., Warren, M.B., Lapid, M.I., and Bostwick, J.M., Munchausen syndrome by adult proxy: A review of the literature. *Journal of Hospital Medicine*, January 2015;10(1):32–35.
45. American Psychiatric Association, *Diagnostic and Statistical Manual of Mental Disorders* (5th ed.). Washington, DC: American Psychiatric Association, 2013, p. 325.
46. See Note 45.
47. American Psychiatric Association, *Diagnostic and Statistical Manual of Mental Disorders* (5th ed.). Washington, DC: American Psychiatric Association, 2013, p. 326.
48. Meadow, R., Munchausen syndrome by proxy: The hinterland of child abuse. Lancet, 1977;II:343–345. Burman, D. and Stevens, D., Munchausen family, *Lancet*, 1977;II:456.
49. See Note 45.
50. Yorker, B., Covert video surveillance of Munchausen syndrome by proxy: The exigent circumstances exception. *Health Matrix: Journal of Law-Medicine*, Summer 1995;5(2):325–346.
51. American Psychiatric Association, *Diagnostic and Statistical Manual of Mental Disorders* (5th ed.). Washington, DC: American Psychiatric Association, 2013.
52. Snyder, S., Pseudologia fantastica in the borderline patient. *American Journal of Psychiatry*, 1986;143:1287–1289.
53. Cabral, R., Identifying cases of fabricated exaggerated or induced illness. *British Journal of School Nursing*, March 2014;9(2):78–82.
54. Dike, C.C., Baranoski, M., and Griffith E.E., Pathological lying revisited. *Journal of American Academy of Psychiatry and the Law*, 2005;33:342–349.
55. Pilowsky, I., A general classification of abnormal illness behaviors. *British Journal of Medical Psychology*, 1978;51:131–137.
56. Eisendrath, S.J., Factitious illness: A clarification. *Psychosomatics*, 1984;25:110–117.
57. Child Neglect and Munchausen Syndrome by Proxy-Portable Guides to Investigating Child Abuse, OJJDP, September, 1996.
58. American Psychiatric Association, *Diagnostic and Statistical Manual of Mental Disorders* (5th ed.). Washington, DC: American Psychiatric Association, 2013, pp. 311–312.
59. The American Heritage Dictionary (2nd ed.). Houghton Mifflin, 1985, pp. 641, 786.
60. American Psychiatric Association, *Diagnostic and Statistical Manual of Mental Disorders* (5th ed.). Washington, DC: American Psychiatric Association, 2013, p. 321.
61. Chafetz, M. and Underhill, J., Estimated costs of malingered disability. *Archives of Clinical Neurpsychology*, 2013;28:33–639.
62. http://www.cbsnews.com/news/jessica-vega-ny-woman-accused-of-faking-cancer-to-get-dream-wedding-is-charged/.
63. Chafetz, M. and Dufrene, M., Malingering-by-Proxy: Need for child protection and guidance for reporting. *Child Abuse and Neglect*, 2014;38:1755–1765.
64. Casser, J.R., Hales, E.S., Longhurst, J.G., and Weiss, G.S., Can disability benefits make children sicker? {Letter to the Editor}. *Journal of the American Academy of Child and Adolescent Psychiatry*, 1996;35(6):700–701.

65. Lawlor, A. and Kirakowski, J., When the lie is the truth: Grounded theory analysis of an online support group for factitious disorder. *Psychiatry Research*, 2014;218:209–218.
66. Libow, J. and Schreier, H., Three forms of factitious illness in children: When is it Munchausen syndrome by proxy? *American Journal of Orthopsychiatry*, 1986;56:602–610.
67. See Note 19.
68. State of Iowa vs. Tanya Reid. Criminal Case no. 40357.
69. Ibid.
70. See Note 19.
71. McClure, R.J., Davis, P.M., Meadow, S.R., and Sibert, J.R., Epidemiology of Munchausen syndrome by proxy, non-accidental poisoning and non-accidental suffocation. *Archives of Disease in Childhood*, 1996;75:57–61.
72. Alexander, R., Smith, W., and Stevensen, R., Serial Munchausen syndrome by proxy. *Pediatrics*, October 1990;86(4):581–585.
73. Bureau of Justice Statistics, Highlights from 20 Years of Surveying Crime Victims, 1973–1992.
74. Gudde, E. An American version of Munchausen. *American Literature*. 1942;13(4):372–390.
75. https://www.childwelfare.gov/.
76. http://www.ncsl.org/research/human-services/child-abuse-and-neglect-reporting-statutes.aspx.
77. http://www.legalmatch.com/law-library/article/guardianship-fiduciary-duties.html.
78. http://en.wikipedia.org/wiki/Legal_guardian.

2 Offenders and Victims

You have to learn the rules of the game. And then you have to play better than anyone else.

Albert Einstein

The Factitious Disorder by Proxy Offender

A person's profile is a biographical essay of noteworthy characteristics and achievements.[1] Criminal personality profiling is an educated guess at identifying specific offender characteristics for specific crimes.[2] For purposes of identifying FD/FDP behavior, profiling of general classification of offender personality is based upon observations of physical and psychological behavior coupled with recognition and interpretation of evidence. Alignment of anyone within a criminal profile grouping is not prima facie evidence of responsibility for criminal acts. Responsibility is proven through avenues of probable cause developed from evidence establishment. A profiler may combine brainstorming, intuition, and educated guesswork guided by practical experience to arrive at hypothetical formulations.[3]

FD/FDP behavior as it relates to the delivery system of criminal abuse, neglect, and homicide or the output of those primary offenses viewed as secondary victimization (fraud, monetary civil maneuverings, interpersonal influential strategies) is often an indirect behavioral pattern. The distinction between FD/FDP offender profile identification and that of other criminal personality profiling rests within the interpretation of commonly dismissed or unrecognized behavioral traits. These traits are generally not recognized as catalysts for criminal behavior because they are accepted behavior. FD/FDP offenders know this and hide in the periphery of what society accepts as baseline normal activity. These accepted actions/behaviors, however, serve the FD/FDP offender in a new way by formulating an exposed barrier that hides beneath it the reality of authentic abuse. FDP profiling is unique because the identity of the suspected offender is generally known and it is the offender's behavior or actions that are examined. These actions are guarded/cloaked in seemingly legitimate actions, and it is quite difficult to differentiate reality from feigned affect.

The *profiling effect* of FD/FDP behavior allows the creation of generalities involving FD/FDP family members. Organizational diversity within the FD/FDP offender's family certainly occurs, and professionals who attempt to intervene within are cautioned to guard against all forms of cultural blindness during case evaluation. Consideration of the melting pot theory in regard to stereotypical class identification of the FDP family should be scrutinized as all possible avenues of alternative explanation for legitimate illness or illicit victimization are considered.

FD/FDP offender profile generalizations are utilized as investigative recognition tools, which provide an understanding of underlying victimization methodology and a base for further case evaluation of potential criminal behavior (FDP cases) of falsified allegations of victimization or claims of heroism (FD cases). Interpretation of defined protocol characteristic must remain flexible to contemplate mutation adaptation. Investigative flexibility is attained by avoiding rigid FD/FDP interpretation as a justification for dismissal or furtherance of an FD/FDP element within a case review.

Basic criminal investigatory concepts apply to criminal cases with an FD/FDP element, but these cases require extended knowledge and skill to link an intangible gain system within a hidden delivery system to an often-inexact visible criminal act. Verification of the apparent existence of FD/FDP profile traits alone, without evidence, does not provide confirmation of the existence of FD/FDP factors. Evaluators are reminded that official diagnosis of FD/FDP is a medical entity and criminal or social investigatory professionals are generally not qualified to render such diagnosis. Many are, however, qualified to link behavioral patterns known to exist within FD/FDP situations as underlying causation of victimization then connect that link within the criminal investigatory process as motive understanding.

Recognition and Obstacles

Recognition of FD/FDP behavior usually requires analysis of a series of specific events, indirect fundamental causation of the events and the indirect/direct consequences of the event. This series of events, primarily seen within hospitalization/medical victimization as treatment pathways, is geared toward addressing signs/symptoms of illness and may occur over prolonged time periods. The series of events or abuse patterns may be divided into isolated sequences, present as continual progression of offensive actions toward a singular victim, extend to more than one victim in a family series, or manifest in a singular action repeated among multiple victims.

Event series linked to FD/FDP behavior occurring outside the primary medical scope of hospitalization has included other professions, specifically law enforcement, EMS/fire, and civil litigation. If medical staff are the conduit for an offender's intangible gain benefits (attention, belonging, verification of self-worth) and the medical setting (hospital, clinic, and physician's office) is the location of benefit procurement, there are parallels within nonmedical professions. FD/FDP cases that revolve around law enforcement seen through allegations of repeated (factitious) victimization place police officers into the conduit role that a physician plays in a medical setting. Multiple service calls either on EMS or firefighter response levels in which call origination is either fabricated or induced place EMS/firefighters into that same role. The interaction and subsequent actions that occur after a person alleges victimization or injects into a professional world seem to produce both a heightened sense of excitement and belonging within the offender.

Fundamental causation tends to change as the FD/FDP offender's developmental abilities expand becoming distinct and effectual. A constantly evolving base of potential alternative causation and amplification of accessible unsuspecting virgin medical professionals creates a potential infinite causation sphere through opportunity, assumed causation rationalization and the offender's evolving mastery of offense and concealment ability. The combination of these factors often renders recognition of FD/FDP patterns difficult.

It is generally difficult for people to believe the inhumane treatment we humans are capable of or demonstrate toward one another. This difficulty is amplified when people live in isolation of "real world" tendencies. If you are from a small town where crime is rare and prejudice is an unacceptable behavior, you are generally isolated by geography and culture from exposure. Mankind's demonstrated deviant capabilities and often-present personal desire to not view grave unpleasantness creates obstacles to identification and recognition of ability within criminal behavior. FDP as an abuse delivery system is heinous behavior that people who are sheltered have difficulty conceptualizing and believing as real. FD behavior as a self-abuse mechanism or victimization falsification base is equally bizarre, and therefore, the validity of its existence is questioned. Doubt of existence feeds the pretense of alleged offender innocence through naivety and creates a situation where justification for absolution is rarely needed because suspicion is either nonexistent, delayed, or dismissed.

Stereotypical abusive behavior and methodology that "should" be present and is what society expects when a person is abusing another, is often absent in FDP cases. The expression "seeing is believing" does not ring true within the world of abuse with an FDP delivery system. FDP pretense is a form of observable fractured reality that allows public view of the FDP offender/FDP victim to seem normal on the surface. Reality, often known only to the offender, seeps through behavioral surface cracks that are present but not generally detected at first glance. Reality of abuse through an FDP delivery mechanism reflects the hidden darker side of humanity—generally restricted from public view. Discovery of abuse with an FDP hidden delivery system may challenge the virtue of parenthood when victims are children and creates an atmosphere of guilt for witnesses once the abuse is exposed. Witnesses are victimized because they come to understand that abuse was happening in plain view or they were contributory toward that abuse yet they failed to see it. Accepting reality of FD/FDP existence may also cause people to question their own basic trust in appearance and personal ability to differentiate and recognize good and evil. FD/FDP verification or suspicion may easily turn any witness's world upside down.

"Great Pretender"

FDP offenders have been called the "great pretenders" and are often described as the last people you would suspect of being abusers. There have been quite a number of abuse cases identified with an FDP element and growing number of self-abuse or falsified criminal case reports involving an FD factor. From review of cases on both medical and law enforcement reporting levels, similarities have been identified for principal players within victimization pathways centered on FD/FDP. Examination of demonstrated behavior, including action or lack of interaction within families or external to families, provides overall profile generalizations for offenders, victims, and nonoffending parents, siblings to the victim, and secondary victims. These generalizations have been confirmed through the study of identified FD/FDP pathways seen within medically documented or criminally charged case investigations and serve as indicators (not rules) within criminal case investigations with a potential FD/FDP methodology factor. The labeling of FDP/FD remains assigned to the perpetrator of the action—not to the victim. The victim is assigned the diagnosis of abused.[4] FDP is generally derived as a medical diagnosis while FD is generally identified as a mental illness. This differentiation is seemingly defined within the fact that when a person chooses to inflict harm upon himself or herself, it is generally considered to be a mental defect, but when the infliction of harm is upon another, there is an element of directed imposed will and that is abuse. Detectives should guard against basing investigatory case conclusion upon medical labeling and work abuse or other cases with a suspected FD/FDP element as any other potential crime. If the FD/FDP element is proven to be present, it is a qualifier within the investigatory sequence and not necessarily reasoning for lack of prosecution. Each case must be evaluated upon its own individual merits.

Victim/Offender Roles

During the 1990s, law enforcement first became more cognizant of FDP as a causative factor in the index of identified abuse causes. The most readily identified offender who utilizes FDP, as a delivery mechanism for abuse, was the biological mother of child victim. Since that time, the identified pool of FDP offenders and victims has expanded as knowledge of FD/FDP has grown, but even with increased identification of victimology, the primary source pool of offenders remains biological mothers of child victims. From this understanding, an established profile of generalized FDP/FD offender traits is validated with an understanding that FD/FDP offenders can be anyone. The role of an FDP offender in custodial roles to a child victim has been associated with fathers, grandmothers, stepmothers, adoptive parents, and aunts.

There have been isolated cases in which offenders outside the victim's family unit have been identified. Offender to victim is linked within particular professions of medicine and childcare. The relationship between the offender and the victim within each case delineating from the norm (caretaker vs. child) is comparatively small in terms of total FDP abuse cases presently defined.

FDP as an abuse factor with adult victims has also presented. Within these cases, there was also an established dependency link between the offender and victim. Examination regarding tangible versus intangible offender reward produced by victimization was not necessarily monetarily motivated. Adult victims are generally geriatric with existing illness(es) that contribute toward their dependency and inability to communicate what is occurring to them (Alzheimer, dementia, etc.).

The role of perpetrator to oneself (FD cases) can also be anyone. These cases are generally linked to the medical/psychological treatment realm; law enforcement is generally unaware of their existence. The identified attention driver based within FD cases encountered in a medical setting is clinical staff who provide offender treatment but simultaneously provide much more to the FD offender: intangible gain defined by attention, a sense of belonging, nurturance, self-validation, verification of self-worth, and more. Within professions unrelated to the medical realm yet similar in scope as it pertains to providing services to people by trained professionals, law enforcement and firefighter staff have encountered situations that have FD elements within.

Offender Occupations

Occupations that identified abusers utilizing an FDP deployment have held include housewife, home helper, nurse, nurse trainee, nurse's aide, medical office worker, schoolteacher, baby food demonstrator, hospital worker, convenience store clerk, and day care workers.

Typical Offender Traits

The cataloging of FDP offenders is generally denoted as the biological mother unless otherwise explained within this text. Hundreds of recorded situations listed within the medical literature[5] combined with numerous case reviews of FDP offenders identified within criminal abuse cases provide a basic profile of typical offender traits. The generalization of both behavioral and physical actions of FDP offenders supports profile justification. Profile factors should be considered warning indicators in the assessment of a potential FD/FDP element within a criminal/civil investigatory process. Warning indicators may provide an investigatory suspicion base within investigatory hypothesis or theory establishment as the answer is sought regarding why a person has illness that cannot be identified or treated or in cases of unresolved repetitive alleged criminal victimizations. They may also be utilized as a suspicion index for arson or fires of undetermined origin cases. Theory alone is not sufficient to substantiate abuse with an FDP factor or falsified reporting with an FD/FDP factor. Proof is required through the gathering of evidence that is almost always a multidisciplinary delicate process.

When FDP offenders target children, they outwardly seem to be "perfectly attentive parents." Sometimes, they are viewed as martyrs because they are constantly at the sick child's bedside while projecting an outward façade of a truly devoted parent. Attentiveness and dedication toward an ill child is usually considered an attribute, but when FDP is present, this trait is a contradiction. An underground look at the situation may reveal concealment of hidden (offender) satisfaction derived from the attention gleaned from victimization. Attention directed toward an FDP offender may originate from many sources within FDP victimization: medical staff treating the victim, publicity regarding a victim's illness(es), support groups based upon defined illness, family members, or friends. Attention is an intangible item and entity that is often hiding in plain sight. It is almost ever easily seen or quickly identified but is always present in some form within an actual FD/FDP situation.

FDP offenders are often, but not always upper class, educated persons who have attained some degree of medical education. The attainment of this education is either collected through formal instruction or informally through self-initiated study/experience. In FDP cases, an underground review of this characteristic reveals that the sophisticated method employed by FDP offenders to victimize within the medical setting requires specialized knowledge of particular illness, treatments, and effects of specific types of abusive actions. In many cases, this knowledge is attained through testing infliction procedures on the victim. Skill, knowledge and planning are necessary to repeatedly victimize without arousing suspicion and/or experiencing detection.

Many medical professionals report that FDP offenders appear to be uncharacteristically calm in view of the victims baffling medical symptoms. Medical tests that are painful to the child victim and repetitive hospitalizations are welcomed without question. FDP offenders excessively praise the medical staff for their effort in helping a sick child. FDP offenders are often described as pleasant, medically sophisticated concerned individuals who not only encourage but also solicit medical procedures. An FDP offender's behavior has been described as making a career from false illness through the devotion of limitless time.[6]

FDP offenders may have a history of the same illness(es) as their children. A retrospective view of this trait sometimes reveals that the offender may exhibit a repetitive illness while pregnant with the FDP child victim or patterned illness may be present within the FDP offender prior to conception (seen as FD). A variation of an FDP offender's own illness may be reflected as a later pattern of victim infliction. The infliction variation may reflect the offender's tested knowledge of cause/effect according to the degree of victim injury.

FDP offenders typically shelter victims from outside activities such as school or play with other children. An FDP offender achieves isolation and victim control by limiting activity and controlling outside access to the victim. By restricting a victim's ability to interact with peers, especially in the developmental phase of childhood, an FDP victim associates whatever type of victimization is occurring as normal. An underground review of this FDP trait reveals that isolationism allows victimization opportunities and lessens the potential of outside interference, questioning, or suspicion by consistently creating a pattern of acceptable behavior for the victim.

When an FDP target child is hospitalized, it appears that the FDP offender attains personal satisfaction contentment and a renewed sense of control. An underground examination of this trait reveals that direct benefit may allow these inwardly held attributes to flourish. When a child is hospitalized, normal parenting tasks for FDP offenders are diverted as the responsibility for the child no longer rests solely upon the parent (offender). Some FDP offenders are thought to look upon a child victim's hospitalization as a vacation from the practicality of reality. The hospital setting quickly becomes a substitute for the atmosphere and desired ideal happiness of home, but the hospital is better than home because it's an antiseptic, perfect environment that replaces parental demand with parental attention.[7] Society generally attains personal satisfaction, contentment, and a renewed sense of control by taking time off from work for vacations. It appears that FDP offenders substitute the hospital setting as a stress-relieving alternative source of respite.

FDP offenders have been known to write notes thanking and encouraging primary physicians and comforting medical staff during a victim's treatment pathway as medical staff becomes frustrated due to patient setback or apparent ineffective treatment seen as lack of positive patient response.[8] It isn't illegal or even considered unusual for persons involved in public service to receive such "thank you" notes, but in FDP cases, such notes may serve alternative purposes. An underground review of this FDP trait reveals that direct correspondence between the offender and professionals is intended as encouragement in order to either sustain or further an FDP abusive cycle. The involvement of medical staff in an FDP abuse situation or law enforcement/firefighters in FD-based alleged victimizations is required for FD/FDP offenders to achieve their goals. Obviously, despite exhaustive efforts, chronic unresolved abuse and criminal or civil cases could result in professional's discouragement. In a contorted way, the FD/FDP offender may feel a sense of parental responsibility toward the professional and find it gratifying to personally extend support and encouragement from an authoritarian position. One must also question whether such communication is indirectly intended to solicit a reciprocal response of encouragement for the offender. It is possible that an offender is either attempting to open or maintain communication lines to evaluate suspicion level or encourage continuing professional involvement and/or interest by personalizing the professional–patient relationship.

Abusers Using FDP Methodology: Profile Characteristics

- Described as "great pretenders"—the last people you would suspect of being abusers of children or the elderly.
- Most often the biological mothers of child victims.
- Generally upper-class, educated persons.
- Uncharacteristically calm in view of the victim's baffling medical symptoms.
- Welcome medical tests that are painful to the victim.
- Excessively praise the medical staff.
- Seemingly knowledgeable about the victim's illness and may actively participate in the victim's care.
- Some degree of medical education (either formal or via self-initiated study/experience).
- May have a history of the same illness(es) as the victim.
- Shelter victims from outside activities (school or play with other children or senior activities).
- Publically maintains a high degree of attentiveness to the victim but privately may act otherwise.
- Seems to find emotional satisfaction when the victim is hospitalized. Medical staff may praise the FDP offender as recognition of exemplary caretaker ability is noted.

The average age of an FDP offender is gauged in accordance with the point in time that FDP behavior is detected. Chronic abuse patterns present in FDP/FD abuse cycles suggest that an offender's commencement age within the scale of infliction is far younger than most studies report. FD/FDP behavior is usually delayed for days to years due to lack of outside behavioral recognition. Covertness (of an abuse sequence involving FD/FDP as a delivery system) and offending skill factor into an outsider's ability to recognize abuse with an FDP/FD factor are factors affecting recognition.

Analysis of confirmed case reports of FD/FDP provides practical insight into behaviors and characteristics of FD/FDP offenders. Various studies provide a glimpse into generalized offender traits. One study identified 42 cases of child abuse with an FDP delivery system where offender's age ranged from 16 to 41 years with an average age of 28.3 at the time of detection. Offenders were identified in all social classes; however, upper-middle-class Caucasians were most frequently identified. FDP offenders were sometimes simultaneously involved in various stages of family violence or domestic unrest, and some offenders appeared to be afflicted with eating disorders such as obesity, anorexia, or bulimia.

Back to the Future

Relatively, new awareness within criminal or civil investigations of alleged wrongdoing entwined with either an FD or FDP factor challenges established investigatory and prosecutorial protocol. The historical lack of awareness of FD/FDP within investigatory realms provides understanding that criminal violations of law (abuse, neglect, fraud, homicide) and civil issues of (dependency and related monetary maneuvering) may have been missed as new understanding is applied to old or cold case review. The difficulty in establishing the FD/FDP factor within a historical case is that generally, victim abuse or offender action has temporarily or permanently ceased for various reasons. Verification of evidence is generally required by medical staff to formulate a conclusive diagnosis that is more than just a matter of expert opinion. Evidence is also required to establish that a crime has occurred but the factor of FD/FDP within that criminal progression is a qualifier—not a prerequisite. The evaluation of a potential FD/FDP historical situation that lacks current victimization progression may only be evaluated within the historical context of behavioral pathways that involves medical and behavioral record reviews.

It is rare that investigatory interviews involving a person suspected of historically utilizing FD/FDP behavior yield confessions. In strictly historical and therefore either undetected or unproven linkage of (criminal) behavior within FD/FDP delivery methodologies, there is a marked lack of incentive to confess bolstered by an empowerment derived from getting away with whatever wrongful actions resulted from within the FD/FDP delivery. When approaching a person suspected of wrongdoing, especially with an FD/FDP suspected methodology, expect to see a demonstrated right of the suspected offender to remain silent.

Historical FD/FDP cases, which transcend isolationism by coexistence with either continuing or prevailing application of FD/FDP victimization, create exposure windows through investigative opportunity seen within evidence-gathering procedures and interrogation platforms.

Case Study

Kate was 26 days old when she was admitted to a hospital for cessation of breathing. After 4 days in neonatal ICU and negative testing results, Kate was released home to her mother (Sandy). Kate was 40 days old when she was readmitted to the hospital for cessation of breathing. Medical testing results were negative and Kate was discharged home. When Kate was 50 days old, she was brought to the pediatric emergency room because of another alleged apneic attack and was hospitalized. In the hospital, Kate had multiple apneic attacks and was transferred to the pediatric intensive care unit (PICU) for 6 days. In PICU, Kate had no further apneic attacks and was transferred back to a regular hospital room. After one night in the regular hospital room, four apneic attacks occurred.

A multidisciplinary team consisting of child protection, social pediatrics, child psychiatry, and neurology participants convened. Kate's custody was transferred to paternal grandparents and Sandy was not allowed access to Kate; Kate's health improved and no further apneic episodes occurred. When confronted, Sandy stated that she had auditory and visual hallucinations and was afraid of hurting the baby. Sandy received counseling and later was allowed supervised visitation with Kate.

- Covert video surveillance was not utilized because of "technical" issues.
- Law enforcement was not part of the multidisciplinary team.
- Sandy was always the first to witness and report Kate's cessation of breathing.
- Medical staff found Kate cyanotic and limp.[9]

Categorization of FDP Offenders

Noted psychologists H. Schreier and J. Libow first categorized FDP offenders into groups: help seekers, active inducers, and doctor addicts. Looking at motivations within these FDP groupings provided differential clarity as follows:

1. *Help seeker*: Offenders are motivated by apparent communication of their own anxiety, exhaustion, depression, or inability to parent.
2. *Active inducer*: Offenders are motivated by secondary gain that includes controlling relationships with physicians and acknowledgement of outstanding caretaker status from medical staff.
3. *Doctor addict*: Offenders are motivated by their obsession to obtain medical treatment for nonexistent illnesses.[10]

Professional FDP Offenders

Study and increased recognition of FDP behavior has broadened the scope of potential FDP offenders to include nonfamily members and professionals. It is important that alibis be substantiated when considering the viability of any potential suspect. It appears that FDP offenders receive the gratification of attention, increased self-esteem, and a false (yet seemingly real) sense of belonging when FD/FDP is utilized within various settings. Such *endowments* are garnered when a person uses another as a target object (FDP) or when they utilize themselves in the role of victim (FD situations). A person who offends utilizing a FD/FDP delivery mechanism and holds a professional job role achieves personal gain within a professional setting through peer, social, and job-related acceptance. These benefits may be considered feasible catalysts as the offender maneuvers through his or her own professional culture eliciting unknowing professional participation in FDP/FD victimization.

The investigation of such cases is highly sensitive and has been perceived as relatively rare, but the potential remains that a professional's actions may relate to FDP responsibility on an intentional basis if circumstances are adept, secondary gain is exposed, and as rationality for infliction is connected to motive. The decision to trust or exonerate medical or other professionals suspected of FDP should be based upon the same standard of investigative analysis provided to nonprofessionals suspected of FD/FDP tendencies.

Accusation or suspicion of individuals holding professional occupations is commonplace in many investigations involving the FD/FDP factor. The FDP/FD offender, the FDP nonoffending parent, or family of FDP victims often initiates accusation or vocalized suspicion. FDP offenders utilize the tool of accusation to thwart suspicion and garner a reprieve from a perceived or real investigation. Investigations mean a risk of exposure equating to an interruption in the ability to offend with resulting loss of intangible secondary gain. Nonoffending FDP parents and family members may utilize an accusatory stance toward professional caregivers because of dynamics that are present that prevent them from initially believing that the FDP offending parent could actually be responsible for victimization. It is easier to blame the medical staff for administering unnecessary medical tests than accept that the testings/procedures were caused by the direct/willing actions of their apparently revered relative (FDP offender).

If a medical/professional is labeled or accused as a suspected offender of patient/victim harm, then known motivations for medical personnel to offend upon their patients must be explored. It is possible that anyone may be capable of inflicting FD/FDP within the scope of victimization and also possible that the killing of a patient, directly or indirectly by medical personnel, may be motivated by the following:

- Euthanasia (mercy killing)—killing for compassion
- Excitement or exhilaration when participating in life/death emergency procedures
- To justify the need for an intensive care unit[11]
- FDP-related activity or for other reasons

Victim Profile

The international majority of identified FDP victims have been children although some cases of adults victimizing other adults through an FDP methodology have been documented.[12] The identified age range for child victim ranges from the age of fetal gestation to adolescence.

The presentation of illness in FDP victims is extensive and continues to grow. Illness caused by the intentional actions of an FDP offender can be either simulated or produced and has been documented as the following: physical pain, appetite loss/diarrhea/vomiting, cessation of breathing (turning blue), infections, cystic fibrosis, skin abnormalities, bruising easily, abnormal blood pressure, apparent immunodeficiency, personality changes, excessive eating/urinating, seizures, shock, unconsciousness, weakness, weight loss, and other conditions.[13]

Effects of FDP child abuse upon the primary victim—the child—may be physical/psychological, direct/indirect, immediate/delayed, or acute/chronic. FDP child abuse is sometimes described as the victimization that may never end because it is intricate. Physical harm has been categorized into long (chronic) and short (acute) term. Long-term effects included destructive skeletal changes, limps, mental retardation, brain damage, blindness, death, and unnecessary removal of organs. Short-term effects range from mild infections to life-threatening illnesses.

Chronic adverse effects seen in surviving FDP victims include immaturity, symbiotic relationships with their mothers, separation problems, irritability, aggressiveness, and participating in the deception (active collusion). Psychological consequences included severe withdrawal, preoccupation of being poisoned/attached, mild emotional disturbances related to fear of bleeding and death, preoccupation with their maternal relationships, loss, death, aggression, vulnerability, and depression.[14]

Psychological effects are usually chronic and long-standing. The child often views the offender's love for them as dependent upon their illness so the child "helps" in the illness deception rather than risk parental abandonment. These children may also identify with their illness and use it as a means of expression and communication that allows them to become FDP participants.[15] The children may also view their illness(es) as punishment that alters their ego strength and self-esteem. Chronic sickness may impinge upon the child's ability to test reality.[16]

Children who are abuse victims through the avenue of FDP are characteristically seen as dependent upon the offending parent and display separation anxiety when apart from them. These children are often immature due to forced dependence and may enter into a symbiotic relationship with the offender (mother). Collusion with the offender is possible as the child seeks to stabilize family dynamics.[17]

When FDP offenders are alone with young child victims, there is no reason to pretend, hide inner feelings, or be covert—even during assaultive actions. Very young victims may not have speech capability or they may see what is happening to them as normal. Infliction of harm by FDP offenders onto a child is often direct while the child is awake and aware of what is happening. The manner in which an FDP offender directly or indirectly interacts with an FDP child abuse victim is often reflected within examination of the child's behavior. The effects of child maltreatment or elder abuse may be seen as a victim's demonstrated or omitted behavior when unable to communicate distress through verbalized means. Observing the interactive behavior between a victim and suspected FDP offender or other family members may provide observable investigative clues that, when recognized, should trigger a suspicion factor and encourage the observer to investigate further.

A child who is a victim of FDP abuse attains a certain tolerance level as the FDP offender's ticket into the medical world. FDP child victims learn quickly to passively tolerate medical procedures while in the presence of or under the control of the offender. A victim's reaction to medical procedures when removed from the presence/control of the offender may be totally opposite what is exhibited in the offender's presence. The true terror that an FDP victim endures within the medical realm as invasive tests are performed may surface when the offender is removed and the source of support, encouragement, and justification to the victim is changed.

Case Summary

Ben was always very happy with his father and didn't seem to be happy when Mom was around. Ben refused to be masked until Mom left. Usually, kids get used to it after a couple of times but Ben was always upset when Mom was present.

Ben would choke/cough up phlegm for Mom on command; his developmental ability to respond to Mom's commands was remarkable. This behavior was seen as a form of conditioning.

When Mom and Ben were separated, Ben's health improved. When Mom was told of the improvement, she stated that Ben would never tolerate this and will get sick again.

Victim Conditioning

As children mature, FDP infliction simplifies if the offender is able to convince the child that the illness or disability is real. Falsified illness, if deemed authentic by the victim (and bolstered by the medical community), becomes an accepted unquestioned entity. The often-restricted true behavior and activities of the victim may be repressed to the point that they are nearly eradicated. An active, but not necessarily conscious, collusion emerges. FDP offenders who are successful in attaining active collusion status of the victim lessen or eliminate suspicion and detection risk. A victim who is continually and consistently subjected to the performance of an FDP offender does not normally question the offender's actions and neither do witnesses—at least initially. If questions are asked, they are usually conveyed either directly or indirectly to the offender or to family members—not to victims. Questions of the offender's behavior are usually dismissed as irrelevant or rationalized as justified behavior and thus accepted by the victim as correct.

For the FDP victim, a presence of basic or real underlying medical conditions within the FDP may be interpreted that all ailments or symptom experiences are true organic illness. FDP victims often appear to be complacent because they believe that the procedures they endure are necessary to treat true illness—even if the illness cannot be identified. If victims are actively colluding with the offender, they may be aware of their role in an FDP deception. Victims generally do what offenders tell them to do. Offenders often make victim feel dependent and view the victims as their "baby." Victims learn to manipulate from mother's example and learn to like the attention level hospitalization provides.

Case Review

A 22-year-old was confined to a wheel chair because he was raised believing that he was unable to walk due to spina bifida. Medical examination revealed that the 22-year-old possessed the ability to walk and did not have spina bifida.[18]

Avenues of normalized developmental childhood behavior and activities are often foreign to an FDP child victim. Windows of potential independence such as school are often thwarted by the presence of a nurse or other in-home medical staff. When the victim is elderly, in-home healthcare is also a factor. The presence of medical staff within the home may occur with the veiled insistence of the offender. Children who are ill and require in-home healthcare generally lack consistent school attendance with truancy justified as medical need. School absenteeism translates to a loss of education and social interaction for the victim. School attendance officers may routinely provide insight regarding educational deprivation for school-aged FDP victims and are a source of knowledge within the investigative process.

The display of opposite-spectrum emotions by school-age victims may be outward indicators of abuse. The probable inwardly normal child expressing confusion regarding his or her visibly abnormal medical and intra familial situation is likely. An FDP child victim may be missing school as an escape from the realities and struggles of peer pressure that all children experience. FDP seemingly ill child victims may acquiesce to the alleged safety that an FDP offender has so carefully led the child to believe exists within his or her custody. The child will probably show a gradual increase into the retreat of the family home/hospital and will eventually cease school activity altogether and drop out if the abuse cycle is not interrupted. A parent as an FDP offender seems to instill his or her own version of reality through actions involving a child victim and keeps a child victim dependent through a lack of coping ability skill. The child's abnormal situation is bolstered by what the offender portrays as normality. As FDP offenses continue and a child victim matures, like all children, controlling the child victim may become challenging; child independence thwarts parental control. So long as the FDP child victim remains dependent upon the FDP offender, control is seemingly assured.

The FDP victim learns that life is less difficult while hospitalized and waited upon. The struggle that is present in school, as evidenced by peer relationships and belief that the child victim is different and sick, enables the FDP victim to passively allow victimization in order to escape his or her own reality. It is likened to a child wanting to stay home from school and watch cartoons all day rather than deal with the struggles of structured learning. Normal mothers won't allow it—FDP mothers would probably welcome it and even encourage the practice if doing so would provide a pathway for FDP offender gain, generally seen as attention.

Caution is again advised and the reader is reminded that the presence of any one known FDP behavior or the collection of these behaviors does not necessarily indicate the presence of victimization with an FD/FDP factor and all alternative causation possibilities should be explored to reduce incorrect FD/FDP correlation when dissimilar motivations are present.

Two Combine to Make One

The relationship between the FDP victim and offender is usually viewed as intertwined and symbiotic. There is often an element of mutual anxiousness present as the offender becomes dependent upon the child to meet his or her needs.[19]

In many FDP child abuse cases, the victim displays separation anxiety when secluded from the offender.[20] This behavioral display is understood because victims often believe that the offender is an appropriately loving caretaker. The victim depends on the caretaker for emotional and physical needs. It really doesn't matter to the child that those needs have a fabricated origin. The needs are real and require specialized care that the victim may believe must come from the offender. FDP victims may initially display terror during separation from the offender; however, this behavior sometimes progresses to a passive helpless state as the child seeks to reunite with the offender whom he or she has become dependent on.

Case Study

Jennifer began treatment for unexplained recurrent ear infections when she was 4 months old and later became a poster child for the local hospital's pediatric home health-care program during her chronic hospitalizations. A picture of Jennifer receiving an injection, by a nurse, into her intravenous line was placed on a hospital brochure.

Hospital staff described Jennifer's mother (Jane) as overprotective and overcontrolling. Jane would not allow Jennifer to speak for herself and put prompted Jennifer's responses. While hospitalized, neither Jennifer nor Jane left the hospital room nor interacted with other patients.

When Jennifer was 6 years old, physicians found an unexplainable contaminant in Jennifer's blood and notified the police department that abuse was suspected. Pursuant to a multidisciplinary staffing, covert video surveillance was installed in Jennifer's hospital room. As Jennifer slept while under the cloak of a blanket, Jane could be seen manipulating Jennifer's IV line. Jane had visited the restroom prior to this exchange. Physicians opined that they believed this was a poisoning event.

Jane was arrested and interviewed by the police, viewed the videotape, and initially denied responsibility. A limited confession was followed by revelation that Jane had injected Jennifer's IV with dirt, fecal matter, and toilet water. Jane was charged with aggravated child abuse and custody was given to her father.

Recognizing a Victim's Testimony

Children who are nonverbal, either due to prematurity, other medical conditions, or as a conditioned response, may possess optional communicative ability. Nonverbal communication is sometimes expressed through behavioral response mannerisms that reflect internal justification for outward demeanor such as estrangement, apathy, or malice. Communication becomes a matter of the observer's ability to recognize behavioral clues set forth by the victim either through demonstrated or omitted behavior during interactional observations between a suspected offender and child victim. An outside observer's recognition of potential patterns of FDP abuse may provide the key necessary to unlock the seclusion barrier that generally encompasses the life of the FDP child victim. FDP child victims often lack both physical and cognitive developmental skill necessary to recognize the existence of abuse or even question the detailed actions of the offenders that are likely to have caused the injury.

Whether or not the children are actually aware of what the offender is doing to them through either fabricated or induced illness usually depends upon the child's physical and developmental age and the covert skill of the offender. Certainly, the longer the abuse continues and the older the child is, the more likely that the child may know what the offender is doing. Knowledge or suspicion of FDP abuse does not mean that disclosure will ever be revealed spontaneously. In some cases if the abuse is present throughout the life of the child, then the child may feel that whatever action is being done to make them sick or make them think that they are sick is normal. The child may not necessarily view the offender as anything less than ideal even if the abuse is blatant as the offender bestows attention upon the victim when observed by others. The child interprets whatever is happening as normal behavior.

If a child expresses concern to other family members by verbalizing or questioning the validity of illness or treatment, these concerns are often overlooked or rationalized by the family as normal and the opportunity for intercession in the cycle of abuse is lost. Disclosure of abuse by victim to independent sources usually is not seen because the child may feel that the behavior/action is normal, believe that the illness origin is genuine, or have been told that family problems (or illnesses) are to be kept within the confines of the family. Reinforcement of this rationalization often originates from a victim's failed attempts to gain help from within the family and the victim's daily repetitive conditioning through lifestyle management that reinforces belief that this child is ill. The reinforcement is external to all who come into contact with the child and internal to the child victim himself or herself.

Sex and Age of Primary FDP Victims

The FDP child victim's gender has been readily identified in both male and female categories. It does not appear that a victim's gender predicates a preferential victim status.

The target-object platform that FDP offenders appear to operate within may account for the apparent lack of gender discrimination.

A study conducted by Rosenberg of 117 FDP cases originally published in 1987 provided the following information:

Gender ratio: 46% male, 45% female, 9% unknown
Victim's age at diagnosis: 1–252 months
Onset of symptoms/signs to time of diagnosis: days to 240 months[21]

Victim Mortality

The mortality rate of FDP child abuse victims ranges from 9% to 31% according to various studies.[22],[23] The death of any victim is dependent upon many factors but a singular problem seems to reoccur in most FDP deaths that are known to this author: a factor of failure to thrive is present. Children fail to thrive in FDP cases because of chronic disease initiated by the offender. The root causes of the failure to thrive are the direct or indirect offender's actions. FDP child victims that die as a result of failure to thrive in this manner are child murder victims (see Chapter 11).

Common Traits Found in FDP Victims

- Dependent
- Display separation anxiety
- Immature
- May enter into a symbiotic relationship with the mother (offender)
- May collude with the offender
- May view the offending parent as an ideal parent
- May passively tolerate medical procedures (while in the offender's presence)
- Excessive school absence/inappropriate learning levels
- Not involved in normal social developmental programs/activities
- Failure to thrive may be present
- May be utilized as emotional leverage in court proceeding

Elder Victims of Abuse with an FDP Factor

Elder abuse is often underreported and is estimated to occur in 1%–2% of the elderly population.[24] An estimated 1 in 10 older adults experience abuse. Only 1 in an estimated 24 cases is reported.[25] The percentage of caregivers who are family members is 75%, and 70% of them are females who function with little assistance. Many of these female caregivers have unmet physical and emotional needs of their own.[26],[27]Elderly patients are vulnerable and subject to financial abuse, scams, isolation, falls, malnutrition, dehydration, trauma, neglect, physical abuse, dementia, depression, and others.[28] The number of older adults in the United States is estimated to be 90 million by 2050.[29]

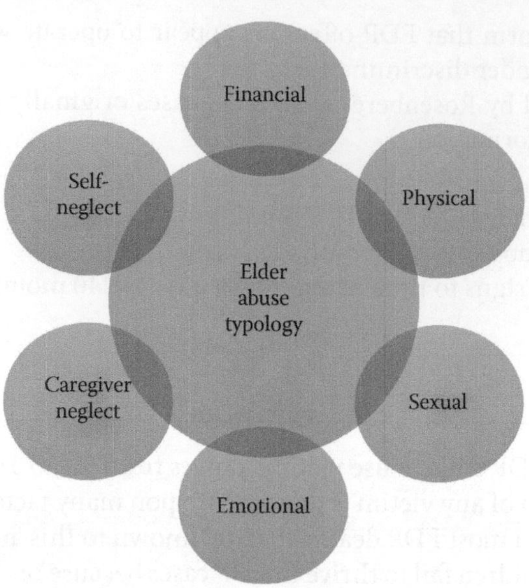

Figure 2.1 FDP elder abuse typology.

The vulnerability of the elderly combined with the significant likelihood that their caretaker is a female, in an often nonsupervised and isolated home setting, renders the elderly susceptible to FDP abuse. When an elderly person interfaces with a health-care provider, there is a window of opportunity to evaluate presenting medical conditions on the platform of FDP abuse when indicated.

Elder abuse with an FDP factor requires a high level of suspicion and knowledge to make a necessary potential link to adult proxy FDP abuse. Elder abuse warning signs include telltale signs of fear, silence, or the inability to interview the elderly patient alone. There are six major categories of elder abuse: financial, physical, sexual, emotional, caregiver neglect, and self-neglect[30],[31] (Figure 2.1).

These categories are contained with the 2010 Affordable Care Act within the Elder Justice Act (EJA). The EJA outlines penalties for failure to report elder abuse, penalties to long-term care facilities that punish an employee for reporting violations, adult protective services funding in all 50 states, training grants, and the establishment of forensic centers and support for development of forensic expertise.

Case Report

A 79-year-old woman with a multitude of legitimate medical ailments was being cared for by her son in a private home. The son controlled medication administration, insisted on knowing all details about clinical assessments and labs and daily meetings, and repeatedly requested psychiatric medication for his mother. FDP suspicion subsequent to a multidisciplinary staffing restricted the son's access to his mother and her condition improved. Medications were halted and within days the woman was admitted to a new hospital outside the area, followed by admission to other hospitals where no medical reason for admission could be found.

The son had a verified history of doctor visits (up to 40 per year for psychosomatic issues). When confronted, he denied that he had been manipulating his mother's health status.[32]

Notes

1. The American Heritage®, *Dictionary of the English Language* (5th ed.). Boston, MA: Houghton-Mifflin, Harcourt, 2011.
2. Geberth, V., *Practical Homicide Investigation* (3rd ed.). Boca Raton, FL: CRC Press, 1996, p. 710.
3. Ressler, R., Burgess, A., and Douglas, J., *Sexual Homicide: Patterns and Motives.* Lexington, MA: DC Heath and Co., 1988.
4. American Psychiatric Association, *Diagnostic and Statistical Manual of Mental Disorders* (5th ed.). Washington, DC: American Psychiatric Association, 2013, p. 325.
5. Rosenberg, D.A., Web of deceit: A literature review of Munchausen syndrome by proxy. *Child Abuse and Neglect*, 1987;11(4):547–563.
6. Rosenberg, D., From lying to homicide-the spectrum of Munchausen syndrome by proxy, in: *Munchausen Syndrome by Proxy*, Levin, A. and Sheridan, M. (Eds.). New York: Lexington Books, 1995, p. 19.
7. Hanon, K., Child abuse-Munchausen syndrome by Proxy. *FBI Law Enforcement Bulletin*, December 1991:8–11.
8. Weber, S., Munchausen syndrome by proxy. *Journal of Pediatric Nursing*, February 1987;2(1):52.
9. Ozturk, N., Erkek, N., and Sirinoglu, M., Think again: First do no harm a case of Munchausen syndrome by proxy. *Pediatric Emergency Care*, 2015:1–2.
10. Libow, J. and Schreier, H., Three forms of factitious illness in children: When is it Munchausen syndrome by proxy? *American Journal of Orthopsychiatry*, 1986;56:602, 604–609.
11. Yorker, B.C., Nurses accused of murder. *American Journal of Nursing*, October 1988;88(10):1327–1332.
12. Sigal, M., Altmark, D., and Carmel, I., Munchausen syndrome by adult proxy: A perpetrator abusing two adults. *Journal of Nervous and Mental Disease*, 1986;174:696–698.
13. See Note 5.
14. See Note 5.
15. Karlin, N.J., Munchausen syndrome by proxy, *Battleboro Retreat Psychiatry Review*, December 1995;4:3.
16. Sigal, M., Gelkoph, M., Meadow, R.S., Munchausen syndrome by proxy: The triad of abuse, self-abuse and deception. *Comprehensive Psychiatry*, 1989;30(6):527–533.
17. Waller, D., Obstacles to the treatment of Munchausen by proxy syndrome. *Journal of the American Academy of Child Psychiatry*, January 1983;22:30–85.
18. Meadow, R., Management of Munchausen syndrome by proxy. *Archives of Disease in Childhood*, 1985;60:385–393.
19. Rand, D.C., Munchausen syndrome by proxy: Integration of classic and contemporary types. *Issues in Child Abuse Accusations*, 1990;2(2):83–89.
20. Crouse, K.A., Munchausen syndrome by proxy: Recognizing the victim. *Pediatric Nursing*, 1992;18(3):249–252.
21. See Note 5.
22. See Note 5.
23. Alexander, R., Smith, W., and Stevenson, R., Serial Munchausen syndrome by proxy. *Pediatrics*, October 1990;86(4):581–585.
24. National Center on Elder Abuse, A response to the abuse of vulnerable adults: The 2000 survey of state adult protective services, in: Teaster, P.B. (Ed.). Washington, DC, 2003. http://www.elderabusecenter.org/pdf/research/apsreport030703.pdf. Accessed on November 1, 2013.

25. Acierno, R., Hernandez, M.A., Amstadter, A.B., Resnick, H.S., Muzzy, S., and Kilpatrick, D.G., Prevalence and correlates of emotional, physical, sexual, and financial abuse and potential neglect in the United States: The National Elder Mistreatment Study. *American Journal of Public Health*, 2010;100(2):292–297.
26. Conlin, M.M., Caranosos, G.J., and Davison, R.A., Reduction of caregiver stress by respite care: A pilot study. *The Southern Medical Journal*, 1992;85:1096–1100.
27. Zarit, S.H., Reever, K.E., and Bach-Peterson, J., Relatives of the impaired elderly: Correlates of feelings of burden. *Gerontologist*, 1980;20:649–655.
28. Powers, J., Common presentations of elder abuse in health care settings. *Clinics in Geriatric Medicine*, 2014;30:729–741.
29. U.S. Census Bureau, U.S. Census Bureau projections show a slower growing, older, more diverse nation a half century from now (press release), December 12, 2012. https://www.census/gov/newsroom/releases/archives/population/cb12-243. Accessed on November 1, 2013.
30. Lachs, M.S. and Pillemer, K., Abuse and neglect of elderly persons. *The New England Journal of Medicine*, 1995;332:437–443.
31. Kruger, R.M. and Moon, C.H., Can you spot the signs of elder mistreatment? *Postgraduate Medicine*, 1999;106:169–183.
32. Singh, A., Coppock, M., and Mukaetova-Ladinska, E., Munchausen by proxy in older adults: A case report. *Macedonian Journal of Medical Sciences*, June 15, 2013;6(2):178–181.

3

Understanding Factitious Disorder and Factitious Disorder by Proxy

Everything that we see is a shadow cast by that which we do not see.

Martin Luther King, Jr.

General Understanding of Abuse

The predisposition for a parent or caretaker to abuse a child has been linked, in many cases, to a family history of abuse and should be considered as a probability factor in the overall evaluation of abuse cases.[1] Intergenerational abuse is defined as possible negative consequences for abused or neglected child victims later in life.[2] Research has revealed that a childhood history of physical abuse often predisposes the survivor to violence in later years. Sometimes, a correlating factor is the influence of alcohol or chemical substances by the abuse; this may become relevant in cases of emotional and physical abuse.[3] It is illegal for one person to mistreat another, regardless of the relationship between the two. Anyone treating another person in an abusive manner (whether direct or indirect) is held accountable by standards set forth under national and international law.

In FDP abuse situations, the actual number of cases is unknown; estimates range from 1 in 1 million children to 2.8 in 100,000 children. It is estimated that 200 cases of factitious disorder by proxy (FDP) with child victims occur in the United States annually. The biological mothers of the children that are usually white, educated, and 20–30 years old are 90% of the perpetrators. In ~10% of cases, fathers collaborate; it is more rare for a victim to collaborate. FDP victims are usually white and under 7 years old with boys or girls being equally victimized. Mortality rate may be as high as 10%.[4]

FDP is an international problem. Feldman and Brown cited 59 articles from 24 countries where 122 FDP cases occurred in an atmosphere of 9 independent languages.[5]

When intervention of any form is initiated within a suspected abusive situation, environmental factors and an examination of family dynamics are important to consider. Looking for known stressors often present in abusive situations may help to identify catalysts linked toward inflicted abuse situations. Factors that may influence suspected abuser stress, precipitated abuse, or neglected patterns include:

1. Physical and social isolations (perceived or actual)—*Is the abuser cutoff from family?*
2. Poor impulse control
3. Unrealistic expectations (of the victim)
4. Difficult pregnancy, delivery, infant prematurity, or infant illness
5. Lack of parental knowledge regarding child development
6. Poverty (causes stress/marital strife)

7. Characteristics that the caretaker perceives as negative in the dependent (child/adult) such as physical, emotional, or psychological handicaps

"Target" or "special child syndrome" is generally described when repetitive child abuse occurs to handicapped children. These children may be victimized as a means of caregivers' coping mechanisms in response to stress or the devaluation of the child facilitating detachment thus allowing abuse to enter the dynamic. Identification of targeted children is often difficult because additional pressure caused by their special needs often isolates them or creates a world that is filled with medical intervention as a means of norm. Characteristics of an abuse victim may also be targeted and they may possess special needs as a generalized observational entity. Characteristics found within this victim grouping include

Children

- Presence of hyperactivity, aggression, and disobedience
- Clumsy, awkward, shy, or weak
- Sickly, unwanted, or unattractive
- Poor appetite or speech difficulty
- Excessive/constant crying (colic, illness, etc.)

Adults

- The presence or suspicion of Alzheimer or dementia
- An income source that facilitates caregiver intervention services
- Isolated living environments that do not encourage regulatory oversight
- Caregivers who are reluctant to allow visitation or rarely allow the subject outside contact
- A subject (victim) who has limited or no family interaction
- Family or caregiver(s) directly or indirectly financially dependent upon the subject

The presence of these characteristics does not necessarily mean an abusive situation exists; however, these and other factors seem to repeatedly be present in cases involving FDP abuse. These factors may mutate within the FDP cycle of abuse and the subject's position within that cycle may change from attribute to deficit for the abuser. If the subject is perceived as a handicap to the abuser, even if the subject's behavior is considered normal for a given situation, there is significant victim harm risk.

In most child abuse instances, a crisis will precede an abusive incident and is commonly referred to as a "trigger mechanism." The triggering mechanism appears to overwhelm the abuser (generally the parent or caretaker) and even little things can create an overreaction. The crisis or triggering mechanism could be a traumatic event such as the death of a family member, illness, or loss of a job. The greatest stressor that precipitates a triggering mechanism is often created by ordinary daily occurrences. When reviewing the lineage of events leading to an act of abuse, ordinary daily occurrences may not be recognized as items of concern—they are often overlooked.

Common/daily occurrences for children are often directly related to their developmental age (i.e., toilet training). Common/daily occurrences for dependent elderly adults could also relate to their developmental state of regression (i.e., toilet training). Toilet training as a trigger mechanism for abusive behavior toward abuse victims (children or dependent adults) places the caregiver in a role that requires patience and dedication and the absence of anger, violence, or rage. For children, toilet training is a repetitive learning process. Children abused in concert with toilet training are thought to be victims when a caretaker's expectations do not meet the child's reality or ability. For dependent adults, there is frequently no expectation that a situation will improve because the scale is developmentally on the decline. Caregivers may become frustrated and the person whom they are entrusted to care for may become victimized.

Victimization involving child abuse may take many forms. Normal daily activities associated with being a child such as soiled clothing, unwillingness to eat, talking back, or fighting with siblings may also act as triggering mechanisms for abuse. Caregivers straddle a line between disciplining a child and abuse. How situations are resolved seems to hinge on resolving issues reasonably in accordance with acceptable societal norms and maintaining control in the resolution process. Loss of control often equates to abuse. The intent of that abuse may dictate judgment depending upon the degree of victim injury. Not all instances of victim harm are intentional. Scalding a child with tap water in an effort to cleanse/purify the child's skin is the most frequently seen accidental cause of injury in children.[6]

Unique Sphere of FDP Behavior

Although many known abuse factors seen in straightforward child or elderly abuse situations may be present within the specialized delivery system of abuse with an FDP factor, there appears to be a peculiar essence in factitious disorder (FD)/FDP situations that transcend conventional abuse methodology. The sphere of understanding required in FDP abuse and FD false victimization investigations begins with knowledge of "normal."

How society determines what is considered normal is predicated upon many factors. The norm or base for a person's behavior is dependent upon how outside influences are internally processed. A group of people's ideas becomes the standardized acceptable behavioral level when they are similar. Accepted behavioral levels are gauged according to social, economic, environmental, and inner-personal approval. Conduct acceptance produces standards within communities.

The dictionary defines normal as functioning or occurring in a natural way—free from emotional or physical disorder.[7] Within the realm of FD/FDP as it pertains to criminal investigations, an understanding of societally defined norms within behavioral conduct is necessary. According to this definition, the actions of an FD/FDP offender are abnormal—even within the defined context of recognized abuse. An investigation (criminal or civil) involving an FD/FDP factor requires the investigator to deviate from normalized investigative procedures in terms of approach. Procedurally normal approaches are often insufficient to produce effective interventions when FD/FDP factors are present.

Attempted infiltration with the abnormal sphere of commonly misunderstood behavior found within criminal or civil cases involving an FD/FDP factor when approached from a conventional rationale method limits investigatory ability to see beyond traditional reasoning. In order to reveal actions that place a person's behavior within the realm of FD/FDP as a quantifier to criminal acts, one must step into that abnormal sphere of understanding while maintaining a firm grip upon societally dictated norms of acceptable behavior.

Understanding the FD/FDP methodology within the cycle of abuse allows exploration of potential pathways. Historical ingredients found within examination and recognition of environmental conditions, familial relationships, and the offender's conflict resolution patterns appear to provide potential avenues of inauguration into or continuation of FD/FDP behavior. Criminal acts or civil infractions that involve FD/FDP methodology have historically been undetected and highly effective for the abuser (regardless of targeted outcome). Offending within a sphere of FD/FDP criminality or civil wrongdoing has been facilitated due to a lack of outside understanding, recognition of the offender's thought process, and an unwillingness to consider that unconventional and highly covert motives exist within case investigations. The facilitation of FD/FDP as an abuse delivery system is now seen within highly skilled acts of covert abuse (FDP delivery systems) and falsified victimization or other reports to law enforcement or other nonmedical authority bases. It is seen because it is recognized through the education of those entrusted with victim protection on all professional levels.

Loneliness and fear of isolation appear to be prevalent factors for some FDP offenders. The FDP offender's goal may gravitate to a perceived intrinsically essential action as the offender migrates toward dependence upon self-worth verification based upon collective reactions. These reactions are in response to inflicted/falsified victim harm, allegations of victimization, or purported heroism. FDP offenders seem to have an ability to transpose themselves to what they perceive as society's defined role (generally a nurturing parent figure or appropriate adult caregiver) while concealing their authentic secret of deviant FDP thinking and action.

Offender's potential motivational factors seen within FDP as a delivery system in child abuse/homicide are as follows:

- Like a drug, the offender loves the *attention* gleaned from hospital staff, family members, doctors, etc.
- The offender creates a *niche* and becomes aggressively bolder.
- If a victim dies as a result of FDP abuse, the offender may *gravitate to another* child instituting victim replacement. The victim is utilized as a secondary object for the purpose of attaining attention.
- Outsmarting the doctors seems to provide *psychological gratification* to the offender. The offender knows what is wrong with the child and sees that the doctor cannot figure it out.
- Offenders may *fear* going home and being alone. They may find "normal life" *boring* in comparison to the activity level seen in the hospital setting.
- The presence of *a triggering mechanism* may precede an FDP occurrence. Triggering mechanisms may range from simple fear of being isolated to the threat of a victim's hospital release.
- *Revenge* on the doctor that "disappoints" the offender.
- Invoked as a method of *escaping domestic violence or marital neglect.*
- Established as a vehicle to *attain the attention, love, and nurturance of a spouse.*
- Developed as a means to *attain a break (vacation) from parental responsibilities.*
- *Praise as a hero* for "saving" a child may be repeatedly sought by an offender in attempts to *re-create euphoria* encompassing the events.

Offender's potential motivational factors seen within FDP as a delivery system in elder abuse/neglect/suspicious deaths are as follows:

- All potential motivational factors seen within child abuse/homicide cases.
- The continuation of *dependency*.
- An elder family member who requires a high level of care often surrenders all measures of control to the caregiver. There is *a continued transference of power* when this occurs.
- FDP as *a homicidal delivery system* through unsuspecting medical staff.

"Believe It or Not"

Within circles of law enforcement and other specified groups, there exists a very real belief that FD/FDP concepts are simply contrived notions formulated by researchers seeking self-promotion through expert witness status. This philosophy may easily become a detrimental factor in the due course of major case investigations when an FD/FDP factor is dismissed before it is adequately explored. There may be a number of reasons why an FD/FDP factor is overlooked within casework including the lack of education regarding its existence, inability to effectively gauge an investigative stature linking criminal activity to an FD/FDP delivery system, or choice to exclude the FD/FDP element because it confuses juries. It appears that in communities within the United States where large children's teaching hospitals coexist with progressive policing agencies, an understanding of the existence of FD/FDP is prevalent. The pervasive educational element that often exists through media coverage of FD/FDP abuse identification provides awareness on professional and nonprofessional levels. In rural areas of the United States where there may be a lack of an easily accessible, modern, and progressive hospital system coupled with old-fashioned policing philosophy, criminal detectives often encounter resistance. When a potential causation of abuse (FDP) or underlying factor in suspected falsified criminalization reporting (FD) is linked to the FD/FDP factor, the investigative complexity and complicated believability associated factors requires a multidisciplinary investigative approach.

Envisioning FDP and FD

Motivation origination for an individual's actions has been classified as 10% instinctual, 20% physiological, and 70% psychological in regard to human behavior.[8] Formulation for the division and confines of normalized behavior are believed to originate from the age of 0–6 when it is believed that people formulate the basis for who they are. This time is referred to as the formative years during a person's lifetime. To understand FD/FDP behavior, it may be helpful to look at the formative influences that the offender was exposed to during childhood. Examination of formative influences may provide justification for the hypothesis that FDP is a multigenerational condition whose seed of abnormal thinking begins during "formative years" then is later paralleled into the offensive behaviors associated with either FD/FDP. The manifestation of misdirected and reinforced factitious activities seen in adult offender traits may act as reinforcement for abnormal childhood ideals or maligned coping mechanisms. The offender's decision process associated with FD/FDP behavior appears to be a matter of choice to rational outside observers. Behavioral effect evaluation, however, differs with regard to accountability; FDP behavior as an abuse mechanism is considered criminal and prosecuted, while FD behavior as falsified victimization is generally considered a form of mental illness and not generally criminally prosecuted successfully.

The establishment of a link of abnormal origination during the formative years is not necessarily a defense or mandatory formative link to the abnormal thinking of an FD/FDP offender but is theorized to be present in the quest for an origination point for this diversion from behavioral norm. The need to establish an origination point is demonstrated within attempts to reprogram or rehabilitate persons actively participating in FD/FDP-related infliction. It is also relative as a potential intervention window in the cycle of abuse associated with intergenerational theories of FD/FDP. Most known confirmed FD/FDP offenders initially relay that they don't know why they have either harmed themselves (FD) or another (FDP). The validity of this denial is questionable and often debated and may be viewed as another mechanism to escape responsibility or avoid prosecution.

Within the interview scenario of FD/FDP offenders, an "in" or "window of opportunity" is needed to gain access to the offender's closed circle. Understanding origination may prove to be the key required to afford access with the functional circle of the offender's behavioral abnormality and serve as the doorway to previously unchartered understanding.

The actions of mentally ill persons are sometimes excused as involuntary responses to individually altered states of norm. The action or inaction of an FDP offender is not excusable in this manner for the following reason: The cunning use of a target, often seen as a child or elderly person, requires that offenders conscientiously choose to physically utilize that target for the purpose of attaining a goal or fantasy. The deliberate and self-initiated utilization of this target victim is an action that society holds the offender responsible for despite any justification or denial the offender may provide. Utilization of victims in this manner is criminal abuse.

An individual can present multiple roles during their lifetime. The human lifetime is a metamorphosis of the human being and follows a natural progression associated with a time element. A typical offender of FDP possesses the ability to flex between the role that society dictates as a loving, devoted mother and the role that the offender activates within FDP abuse upon their child. FDP offenders appear to be very goal-oriented, inwardly directed persons who wear "two hats" simultaneously and have the ability to repress the hat of choice at will. The attainment of the offender's goal indirectly achieved through the active infliction or inactive toleration of harm to the target child supersedes the presumed inherent knowledge that child abuse is wrong. It is a matter of choice.

What Does the Offender Gain through FDP Abuse?

The benefit gained by the offender from FD/FDP infliction is shown in Figure 3.1.

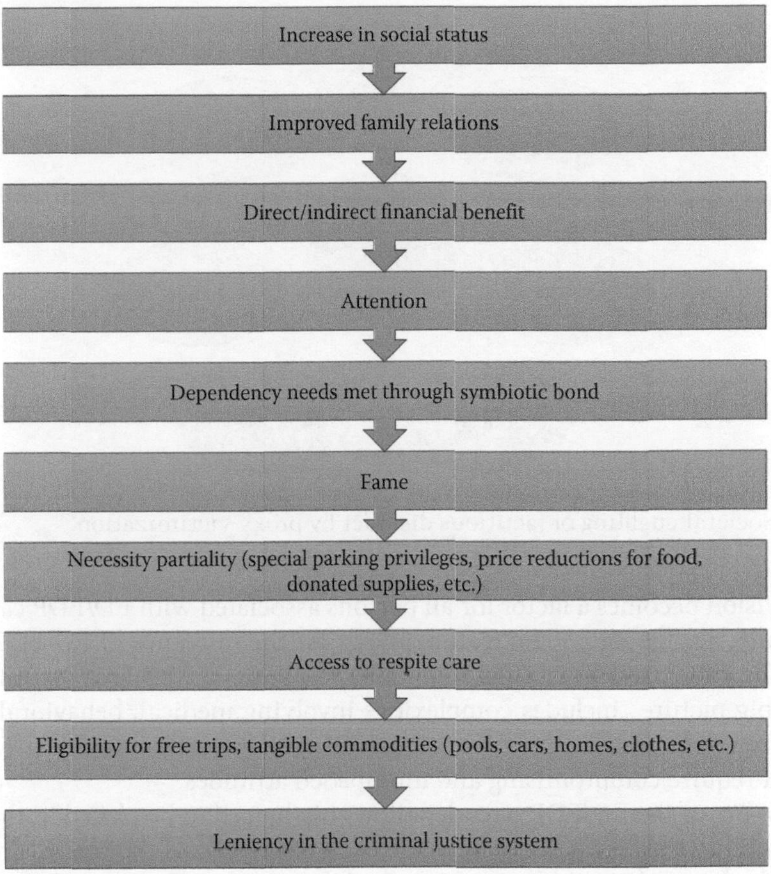

Figure 3.1 Factitious disorder/factitious disorder by proxy abuse: offender gain.

How Society Enables FDP Child Victimization

A diagram of the factors leading to child victimization—family, ignorance, tunnel, susceptibility, fallacy, defense, and placement (FITS FDP)—is depicted in Figure 3.2.

In *family* parenting responsibility, FDP offenders are allowed to assume the primary caretaker role for the victim. Limitless and often unchallenged authority over the victim provides opportunity for victimization access and pathways.

Ignorance of persons who are in close contact with the offender may enter into the enabling factor. People in positions to create significant and long-lasting change within the family infrastructure (criminal investigators and social intervention specialists) are often unable to see the patterns of FDP victimization. This inability is generated from ingrained investigative standardization techniques (often with law enforcement) or total enmeshment with the façade created by the FD/FDP offender (seen within medical circles and the victim's family). An unwillingness to expand criminal, civil, or medical investigations to the sophisticated degree required for FD/FDP may be an issue. Investigatory reluctance to link an abuse case to FD/FDP may occur because there are investigative monetary constraints or a belief that FD/FDP is not real because offender benefits and therefore motive are generally intangibles.

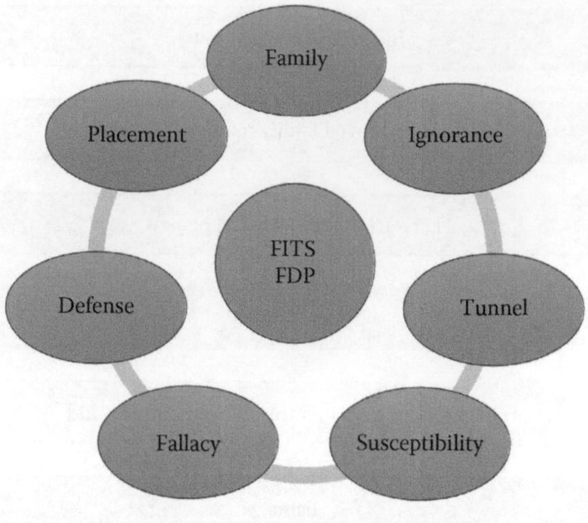

Figure 3.2 Societal enabling of factitious disorder by proxy victimization.

Tunnel vision becomes a factor for all persons associated with FD/FDP case investigation. Generally, no one individual feature allows for the inference of FD/FDP underlying behavior to be conclusively attached to an alleged abuse or factitious victimization situation. The "big picture" includes complexities involving medical, behavioral, and observational correlations. Individual professional disciplines involved within FD/FDP case management require compromising and unimpeded attitudes.

Susceptibility of the FD/FDP offender allows his/herself to be placed in the position of offender capability through a series of behavior or observations thought to create a devalued sense of self-worth or self-being. Susceptibility factors also provide environmental clues in FD/FDP typology identification.

Fallacy or misunderstanding regarding FD/FDP investigative dynamics may cause a deficient connection between alleged abuse (FDP) and falsified victimization reporting (FD). It is important to not associate an abuse or victimization case with FD/FDP when the more directed pathway of intentional injury is present without the intangible benefit seen within known factitious related issues. For example, a person who kills another for directed monetary gain absent any other extenuating factors or a person who alleges a rape to manipulate a divorce proceeding absent other extenuating factors has directed motive and is not necessarily receiving indirect benefit commonly viewed within an FD/FDP circumstance.

Defensive blind trust, coupled with group labeling, creates an aura of naiveté for FD/FDP identification regardless of an individual's ability to discern. Societal group labeling allows categories of people, in this case most notably mothers, to rise above normal suspicion indexes. The presentation of FDP offenders from their maternal role challenges an ordinary person's rationalization ability. The "cop" aura of suspicious intellect permeates within the evaluation of FD/FDP identification, and it crosses into medical and psychological professional realms. The identification of FD/FDP within medical/psychological entities asks doctors and psychiatrists to also be detectives.

Placement of value upon a victims' life by an FDP offender or upon their own life in FD cases absolutely occurs within each instance of FD/FDP infliction. In FDP abuse situations, the choice to utilize a victim for self-gain is a conscientious decision of the offender

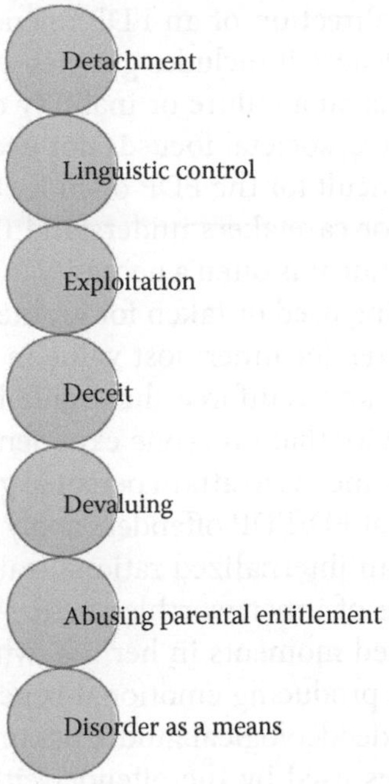

Figure 3.3 Factors present during factitious disorder by proxy victimization sequences.

circumscribed by the power to halt or possibly reverse the effects of the action or inaction created. This choice is ever-present. This says something profound about what value the FDP offender places upon the life of the victim despite what the offender may portray when his/her actions are eventually exposed. It is why abuse cases, even those that rise to the level of homicide, are criminally tried as straightforward abuse or murder. The delivery system is FDP, but the offender's opportunity to prevent death or halt abuse is clear. Why FDP offenders choose to abuse or to kill does not detract from victimization outcome.

During the initial assessment phase of FDP cases, consideration of F.I.T.S.F.D.P. should be evaluated. Factors present during the FD/FDP victimization sequence include detachment, linguistic control, exploitation, deceit, devaluing, abuse of parental entitlement, disorder as a means, and standard categorization (Figure 3.3).

Factors Present during the FDP Victimization Sequence

Victimization Pathways

The FDP offender's goal may gravitate to an intrinsically essential action as the offender comes to rely on collective results of the victimization for intimate self-worth verification. FDP offenders seem to have the ability to externally transpose themselves into what they perceive as society's dictation of the nurturing mother while concealing their authentic secret of deviant FDP thinking. The generally accepted developmental norm of forward direction in a person's life often takes the following route: infancy, childhood, teens (optional dating, engagement, marriage) parenting, and then grandparenting. This forward direction requires a diminishment of "taking and self" and elevation of "giving and selflessness." The forward direction of an FDP offender's life appears to differ from standardized developmental because it includes glitches within the standardized levels. It appears that these glitches focus on a failure or inability of the FD/FDP offender to cope with the reality that as people age, societal focus is not necessarily upon them—it is upon their children. It also seems difficult for the FDP offender to embrace the fact that societal culture demands that parents or caretakers understand that the focus of attention from adult onto a child or other dependent is often a necessity for survival. This focus shift could leave the FD/FDP offender feeling used or taken for granted.

People have a tendency to render innermost value in accordance with interreactionary response to circumstances and reinforce that value by memory recall of the event. Insignificant daily routine activity that everyone experiences is usually handled in stride by society and either viewed as a means to attain personal goals or accepted as part of life. It appears the critical thinking that FD/FDP offenders apply toward process perceived mundane activity patterns reflects an internalized rationalization equating mundane activity with neglect producing a sense of inner worthlessness. An FD/FDP offender's desire to recapture previous or anticipated moments in her life, which imparts inner value, seems to be strong. Significant events producing emotional benefits of contentment, usefulness, and distinction appear to provide ideological guidelines or pathways toward contentment. FD/FDP victimization pathways used by the offender either select by design or activate through opportunistic deployment—a measurable detection guideline. If FD/FDP behavior is recognized, then victimization pathways may open the evidence vault (see Figure 3.1).

The categorization of known FDP offenders skewed so heavily within the biological mother grouping creates a profile distinction emanating from experience and reason. Generally, for most women who bear children the time preceding childbirth, is retrospectively considered a period when love was optimal between her and her partner. It was a time when the expectant mother and medical staff interacted in a perfect world where she was taken care of and the center of attention. Belonging, security, contentment, and attention created a distinctive setting during pregnancy and for a while life was good. It would be easy to view this time with longing when faced with the harsh reality of parenthood. Most women, although they may briefly long for respite after children are born, do not act upon this desire because the child comes first.

Theoretically, FDP offenders may elect to set the personal desire to regain "attention" benefits into motion and formulate a plan to attain this goal through FDP infliction. The FDP offender may see herself caught in a circle of despair without escape and become susceptible to preconceived escape thoughts that are manifested in child abuse through an FDP delivery system. The willingness of an FDP offender to victimize a child or other dependent is a choice to escape his or her own perceived reality of worthlessness. It becomes a decision to go back rather than forward in the scale of directional norms. The results of such actions may be viewed as distinctive FD/FDP victimization incidents whose value is determined by the effect upon the offender's self-esteem.

FDP Reactionary Gap

The sincere rehabilitation of an FDP offender resulting in the transformation of critical thinking to acceptable behavior, as dictated by society, must incorporate a veritable change in moral and primal thinking. Determining whether an FDP offender is truly rehabilitated or merely portraying that which society deems as acceptable can only be measured through long-term verification of lifestyle management. The unfortunate factor in most FDP cases is that "custody" of a child victim is often returned to the offender prior to verification of proposed rehabilitation. The risk potential to the victim remains constant or escalated due to the greater ability, daring, or need of the offender if a victim is prematurely reunited with an abuser. Society tends to want reunification of families even when circumstances include prior instances of abuse or neglect. Dependency courts are often asked to render qualified decisions on this subject and understanding that the victimization risk factors are part of that consideration. Keeping a dependent away from an alleged or confirmed abuser is not necessarily predicated solely upon past behavior. In cases of abuse with an FD/FDP factor, it is important to remember that FD/FDP offenders are masters of disguise. It is how most are able to chronically offend without detection and it is a way of life with denial prominently configured within. Extreme caution is warranted regarding reunification between FD/FDP offenders and dependents.

Recognizing What You See

Believing that something is real or fabricated is often a matter of personal opinion predicated upon the evaluator's education and experience that is molded through environment. To consider theoretical belief as a viable answer for concealed behavior lacking common understanding, the recognition of direct or indirect proof is likely to be a determinant. Recognition of FDP requires an in-depth assessment of an alleged victim's medical history, physical condition, lab results, and family functioning.[9]

Theory does not convict criminals or authorize dismissal of a criminal complaint. Theory provides a technique or strategy to either reveal hidden truth through increased understanding or contemplate behavior through recognition of the offender's often unseen motivation, methodology, and benefit present in FD/FDP cases. The pursuit of theory justification may also provide a criminal exoneration formula by absolving suspicion of wrong doing or failing to clearly produce evidence to support probable cause that a crime has occurred. In FDP case analysis, elemental criminal charges of homicide or abuse may be so clear that the delivery mechanism of FDP becomes secondary within the prosecution phase of justice. It may also be considered nonrelevant by the prosecutor but highly significant as an attempted defense. What it will not be is nonexistent.

Sphere of Victimization

Sexual arousal is connected to certain fetishes within the realm of sexual deviancy and serves the purpose of fulfillment of those needs.[10] In FDP cases, it is theorized that the planting of the offender's fantasy begins at the moment of initial planning, which may be a brief or elongated time period. A forward enactment sequence occurs—seen through activation of a medium (victim) selectively utilized by the offender for specific purpose. It appears that the offender makes a conscientious decision, during enactment of infliction or simulation, to offend. In the aftermath of "planted fantasy" through victim exploitation lies fulfillment of the offender's desire or goal. FDP offender fulfillment is attained indirectly through attention and/or personalized interactive reactionary result(s) between the offender and his/her chosen agent(s). Personal merit gained by the FDP offender is gauged upon the degree and duration of attention gleaned from the chosen agent at the victim's expense.

- The enactment sequence, itself, displayed either by direct physical abuse of the victim (FDP production) or by effecting treatment for falsified illness through the deployment of silence or denial regarding why a victim may be ill or alleging symptoms (simulation) does not appear to fill the void theoretically present in the FDP offender. The void is fulfilled when the attention or other factors are met. The void is theoretically connected to the offender's lack of constitutionality outside the confines of the regimented world of the hospital coupled with an inability to cope with the selflessness that is required of motherhood.

FDP Offender Typology Categorization via Action

Offensive action of FD/FDP offenders may be categorized in accordance with the presumption that thought precedes action. Action severity, however, does not necessarily occur in logical or standardized order; therefore, the severity of offensive actions (simulation or infliction) may be integrated within one another and executed in random order. A universally present factor with the action typology is the offender's discontent (Figure 3.4).

FD/FDP Infliction as Punishment

Sex may be used as a punishment through either withholding or forcible infliction and it is centered upon control. In FD cases, self-abuse is often utilized to obtain the primary gain of attention/self-worth verification but also may be utilized as individually self-inflicted punishment for inner feelings of inadequacy. Behavior seen with situations involving FD

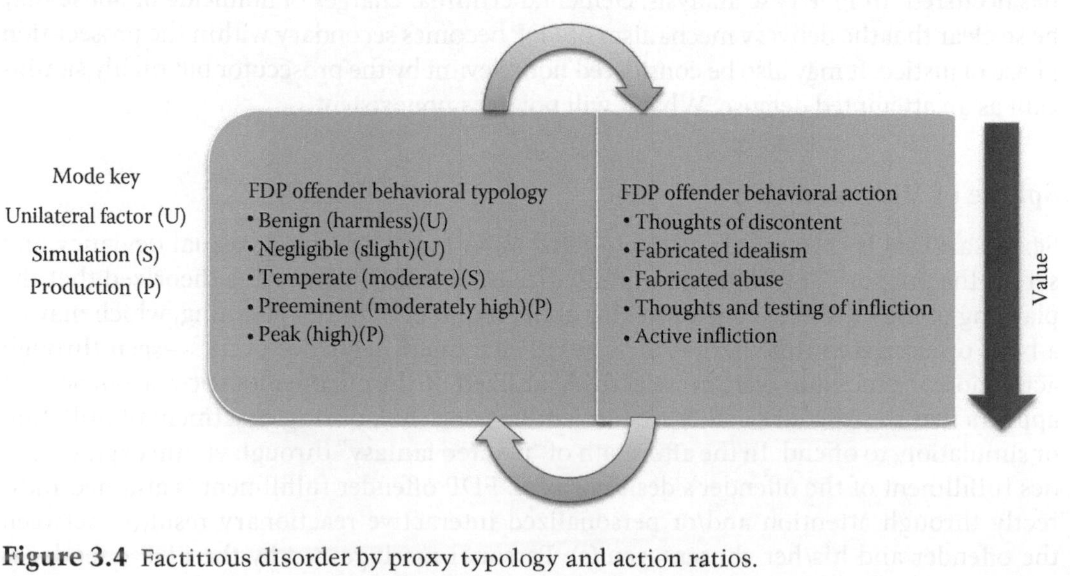

Figure 3.4 Factitious disorder by proxy typology and action ratios.

aligns itself to an FD offender controlling entities through deception or self-infliction by withholding the truth and/or inflicting self-harm. The FD offender controls the ability to resolve the situation yet allows it to manifest itself into perhaps larger issues. These issues may be seen as developmental actual illness within the offender (medical cases) or panic/concern/attention when an FD offender utilizes policing agencies in a falsified victimization status.

FDP infliction onto a victim echoes the primarily evident outward gain directive of attention/self-worth verification but may also represent directed punishment. Punishment may theoretically represent a misplaced assault by the offender related to the offender's level of self-esteem. The intensity of the assault is often determined according to the offender's need for reinforcement of worthiness, vindication of innocence, or the offender's specific level of presumed worthlessness during the time immediately preceding the attack. Consider the viciousness of FD infliction with immediately visual results, such as violent suffocation versus the more subtle, often delayed, effects of poisoning or the immediately benign effects of illness fabrication. Although each of these victimization tactics may ultimately mean the death of the victim, the range of inner offender rage viewed through victimization methodology is large. Whether the offender has control over his/her rage in the context of mental health parameters or these actions are beyond the offender's control rendering them temporarily mentally ill is an argumentative entity with many factors to consider. The conscious intentional actions of an FDP offender upon a target victim are considered intentional acts of abuse in whatever manner they are delivered directly or indirectly. FDP offenders are held accountable for their abuse to their victims, while self-inflicted harm demonstrated by an FD offender upon his/herself is generally considered involuntary and associated with mental illness.[11]

Eating Disorders

Some identified FDP offenders have also been found to have various eating disorders. Examining the dynamics present within each provides interesting correlations. One such case involved an infant that was subjected to induced vomiting by her mother. The child's medical status was failure to thrive caused by illicit doses of ipecac syrup as the offender sought to make the child conform to her ideal of thinness.[12]

Psychological effects seen within eating disorders and examination of known FDP cases have provided motivational similarities. Power and control coupled with concealment factors and denial and a fundamental need of belonging appear to be present in both situations. Offender profiles are also similar.

Clinical Definitions

The two most widely known eating disorders are anorexia and bulimia. Anorexia is described as a "refusal to maintain a minimally normal body weight.[13] Anorexia nervosa is also considered self-inflicted starvation. Anorexics use eating or not eating as a means of control over their bodies and lives; they often deny that they have a problem. Characteristically, anorexics have distorted body images; depression; preoccupation with food, calories, or eating; avoidance of food-related social activities; mood swings; excessive criticism of their bodies; and hunger denial. Anorexics often wear baggy or layered clothing in order to hide obvious physical ramifications of their problem.[14] Bulimia is a process of binging on food then purging it through various methods.[15] Binges are sessions of uncontrollable eating followed by purging the body of the food consumed. Binging and purging are usually conducted secretively. Bulimic activity may alternately occur with strict conventional dieting and/or excessive obsessive exercise.

Behaviors associated with anorexia and bulimia are individualized for each victim and may be viewed as control techniques or coping mechanisms for dealing with perceived difficult issues or situations. Eating disorders appear to have the ability to easily take over a victim's life and the lives of others around them. The physical appearance of the eating disorder victim may not accurately reflect victim endangerment. People who experience eating disorders risk death either from medical complications or from a prevalence of suicide and rarely respond quickly to therapy. It is believed that issues of poor self-image and feelings of inadequacy are commonly present within person with eating disorders. Punishment for unattained perfection of self and of others is sometimes a catalyst as a negative coping mechanism. Eating disorders make the victim feel in control and powerful. Deception and lying to hide reality appear prevalent for the person affected with an eating disorder. The premise may allow victims to maintain their feeling of being in control of themselves and their environments while effectively hiding reality by pretending that everything is all right.[16]

Similarities between Eating Disorders and FD/FDP

People who have eating disorders utilize food to deal with inwardly held problems in much the same manner that FD/FDP offenders are thought to utilize themselves or targeted victims as chosen resolution pathways to various inadequacies in their lives. In both eating disorders and FD/FDP cases, there is a consistency that "something" is lacking in the life of the offender, which promotes the potential for either to exist. Food (eating disorders) and designated victims (FDP) are both considered nonessential/inanimate objects while being utilized for specifically desired outcomes. Within the application of FDP victimization and eating disorders, either punishment or the need to maintain control over oneself or situation through manipulation appears to be possible motivation within a seemingly unending abuse cycle.

Victims of eating disorders reportedly feel isolated and alone in their struggle. During investigative interviews with FD/FDP suspects, the issue of perceived isolationism reoccurs as an important factor. Nonjudgmental listening is often considered the preferred method of extending help to persons with eating disorders as unconditional love provides strength to overcome. Effective interviewing of FD/FDP offenders mirrors this understanding from a different perspective. The bond that must exist between interviewers and offenders is a union bridging a gap of misunderstanding and skepticism. Keeping the lines of communication open is an important segment for both assistance and verification of responsibility within theoretical FD/FDP case evaluation. Whenever people deviate from what is viewed as normalized behavior (even normalized criminal behavior), it is likely that they will be afraid to ask for help and voraciously hide reality. One of the most effective phrases that any interviewer can deliver is "You are not alone." (see Chapter 6 for additional interview criteria.)

FDP Fact Sheet

- Seemingly loving mothers can produce illness in their children that eludes detection.
- FDP offenders may lack a history of overt criminally identified behavior.
- FDP offenders do offend upon their own children privately but then expose the battered child as sacrificial merchandise.
- Nonoffending parents may not be aware that abuse is transpiring.
- FDP is a specific behavior resulting in direct and intentional child abuse. The abuse may occur through an unaware third party (medical staff) or directly by the offenders hands-on actions.

Notes

1. *Black's Law Dictionary*, Revised 5th ed., p. 1398.
2. Widom, C., *Victims of Childhood Sexual Abuse-Later Criminal Consequences*. Washington, DC: National Institute of Justice Research in Brief, March 1995.
3. *Miranda v. Arizona*, 384 U.S. 436, 86 S. Ct. 1602, 16 L. Editions Second 694, 1966.
4. Pinto, S. and Walsh, K., *Quick Lesson about Munchausen Syndrome by Proxy*. Glendale, CA: Cinahl Information Systems/Ebsco Publishing, 2014.
5. Feldman, M.D. and Brown, R.M., Munchausen by proxy in an international context. *Child Abuse and Neglect*, 2002;26:509–524.
6. Krieger, J.J. and Robbins, R., The adolescent incest victim and the judicial system. *American Journal of Orthopsychiatry*, July 1985;55(3):419–425.
7. *The American Heritage Dictionary*, Second College Edition. Houghton Mifflin, Boston, MA, 1982.
8. Geberth, V.J., *Practical Homicide Investigation* (3rd ed.). Boca Raton, FL: CRC Press, 1996, p. 406.
9. Hochhauser, K. and Richardson, R., Munchausen syndrome by proxy: An exploratory study of pediatric nurses' knowledge and involvement. *Journal of Pediatric Nursing*, October 1994;9(5):313–320.
10. Schreier, H. and Libow, J., *Hurting for Love*. New York: Guilford Press, 1993, p. 81.
11. Update with dsm 5 and verify.
12. Feldman, K., Christopher, D., and Opheim, K., Munchausen syndrome/bulimia by proxy: Ipecac as a toxin in child abuse. *Child Abuse and Neglect*, 1989;13:257–261.
13. American Psychiatric Association, *Diagnostic and Statistical Manual of Mental Disorders* (*DSM-IV*) (4th ed.). Washington, DC: American Psychiatric Association, 1994.
14. Gross, J., *Understanding Eating Disorders*, http:www.ithaca.edu/orgs/wishes/wishes1/amy-sign.html. Accessed on November 1, 2013.
15. American Psychiatric Association, *Diagnostic and Statistical Manual of Mental Disorders* (*DSM-IV*) (5th ed.). Washington, DC: American Psychiatric Association, 2013.
16. See Note 12.

4 Assessing Potential Lethality of the FDP Abuse Offender

There are monsters, and it's okay to be afraid of them, but it's not okay to let them win, and it's not okay to be one.

Anonymous

The assessment of potential lethality or injury degree is a process that has many variables. Lethality assessment has many similarities to profiling, and it is not an exact science to absolutely prevent or foretell the future. Lethality assessment, like profiling, is a tool used to provide opportunistic intervention through heightened awareness of the known patterns of factitious disorder by proxy (FDP) victimization escalation. Recognition of FDP abuse patterns and anticipation of likely futuristic contingencies or events may afford a detective initial intuitive response. By anticipating reactions and actions, a reactive policing strategy easily adjusts to an anticipatory investigative criterion.

Lethality Links

The extent to which an FDP offender will progress in order to achieve the desired effect directly relates to the offender's perceived level of unfulfilled needs. The greater the individual need, the more risk posted to the victim because desperation easily clouds judgment. Diminishment of fear controlled by ignoring caution and confidence derived from skill and personal conviction create a potentially explosive risk situation for victims. Actions of the FD/FDP offender are likely to become bolder as offensive sequences repeat and escalate. The sequential offensive actions of the FD/FDP offender may be influenced by many factors; therefore, offense methodology mutation is possible. The mutation factor potential requires investigative flexibility.

An element of the unknown creates a sense of urgency for careful, yet expeditious, protocol in FDP abuse investigations because the life of the victim is at risk. No one has a device or innate sense to alleviate FDP victim risk altogether. The assessment of victim risk is predicated upon understanding common behavioral FD/FDP abuse patterns gleaned from known cases. The following victimization abuse cycle has been repetitively seen in FDP cases. The cycle itself has mutative capabilities and is not necessarily ordered in every case.

Intelligence Information

It is impossible to know a person's futuristic behavior with certainty because a person's actions are influenced by so many factors. The futuristic behavior of an FDP offender, however, is often a point of contention that guides case direction to accommodate primary concerns of victim safety and the potential of threatened harm to the victim's sibling(s). Threat assessment between people or within a person is formulated from a combination of demonstrated activity and verifiable responses to particular questions.

Evaluation of potential threatened harm within FD/FDP cases is ideally derived from the experience and license of trained professionals. Ideal situations in most criminal cases, however, seldom occur without exigent mitigating factors requiring immediate action. In these situations, determination of threatened harm and the action taken to address it may become the responsibility of a multidisciplinary team. The police detective's investigatory tools utilized for evidence gathering may simultaneously provide proof or contradiction of FDP criminal activity through a window of opportunity. Information gathered may also enlighten the potential for futuristic victim harm. In situations where an FDP offense is clearly identified, the following questions may illuminate the answer to an often continuing debate regarding threatened harm to surviving children within an FDP family and appropriate legal intervention. Analysis of the information gleaned from these questions may provide insight into the thinking process of the FDP criminal. Evaluators are cautioned to recall that the validity of statements rendered by FD/FDP offenders often contain the element of veiled deception, and truth is often a matter of the offender's interpretation of reality.

Intelligence/Interview Questioning

SIDS/Homicide

1. How many children has the defendant (Def.) given birth to?
2. How many of those children are currently living?
3. What were the circumstances of the children's death(s)?
   a. Locations
   b. Interfamilial relationships
   c. Economic status of the family

Paternal Factors

4. Has the Def. been or is the Def. currently married or involved in an exclusive relationship? If multiple marital relationships have occurred for the Def., why were these relationships dissolved?
5. How did the Def. feel about her significant other (husband) when their child was living or hospitalized? What was daily life like?
6. How did the interaction between the Def. and her significant other change when the victim was hospitalized?
7. How did the Def. view her significant other (absentee, supportive, loving, cold, etc.)?

Reality Perceptions

8. How did the Def. envision motherhood prior to giving birth?
9. How did the reality of motherhood differ from what was envisioned?
10. What outside influences have contributed to the alleged actions of this Def.?

Direct Actions/Escalation Sequences

11. How many times did the Def. interfere with the victim's health? How was the interference accomplished?
12. When was the first time the Def. *thought* about using the victim as a target, and what gain was expected?
13. What initial benefit did the Def. gain by either making the victim ill or telling someone that the victim was ill?
14. Did the results of the initial victim infliction justify the method? What amount of time transpired between initial victimization acts and subsequent events? During that time, what was happening in the family or social arena of the offender?
15. Did the Def. experience a sense of relief after FDP infliction? Was this feeling of relief tempered with feelings of guilt?
16. Did the Def. feel that he or she had the ability to stop the ongoing FDP infliction or did she proceed on impulse as a result of individual need?
17. How long did the Def. think about FDP infliction before action was taken? Where did the idea of FDP infliction originate?
18. During the time FDP infliction was considered but not yet acted upon, did the Def. "test the waters" by either self-infliction (FD) or preliminary victimization acts? If applicable, how was this accomplished?

Defendant Understanding

19. Once the Def. saw the victimization resulted in a desired outcome for him or her, how did he or she feel about their role as caretaker?
20. Did the Def. recognize that inner feelings of contentment or discontentment were directly linked to the FDP infliction?
21. Was the Def. attempting to either protect or help the victim from a detrimental situation or abusive partner by means of FDP infliction? *Some identified FDP offenders have attempted to justify abusive acts upon their children for the purpose of obtaining invasive medical procedures in the name of child welfare or to bolster evidence of a nonoffending parents' responsibility of wrong doing once they are accused of FDP abuse.*
22. If the intent of the Def. was *not* to kill the victim but only to have the victim temporarily stop breathing or be otherwise ill, why did the Def. purposefully continue chronic FDP infliction and escalate use of force within the abuse cycle?
23. Were the injuries present on the victim prior to death permanent or could they have appeared to be permanent to the Def.?
24. What did the Def. think the victim's future (and his or her own) would be like? With this in mind, did the Def. feel that the victim would be better off dead? Is there a religious inference associated with this thought pattern/where does the Def. feel the deceased victim is presently?
25. Does the Def. feel somewhat relieved that the victim is deceased? Does the Def. feel that the victim is now at peace? (*Lead-in to potential confession to correlate possible hidden intent*)
26. Has the Def. "found God" while in jail/prison? If so, how has this affected his or her belief system?

Coping Abilities

27. Did the Def. see parenthood (or the caretaker role) as overwhelming? *Consider the physical age, maturity level, economic status, isolation/support system, and amount of responsibility of the Def. at the time of the victimization.*
28. *What was the Def.'s childhood like? Check for potential evidence of intergenerational FDP or FD.*
29. Has the Def. ever idealized or attempted suicide? Why?
30. How did the medical staff's response and interaction with the Def. affect her ego?
31. When the Def. was away from the "medical scene," what was life like? How was time spent, and how was this time viewed by the Def.?
32. Who was responsible for primary care of the victim during the victim's hospitalizations or medical treatments?
33. Did the Def. have any hobbies/activities outside the home and role of caretaker? (*Lead-in to exploration of isolation factors*)
34. Is the Def. concerned about his or her families' reaction to the truth regarding victimization responsibility? What are these concerns? (*Obstacles to attaining a confession*)

Infliction/Outcome Relationships

35. Does the Def. have dreams or nightmares about what occurred to the victim? What is the context of these dreams/nightmares, and how does the Def. interpret their meaning?
36. Who does the Def. blame for the death of the victim?
37. Does the Def. understand what happened to the victim, why the victim died, and who is responsible for the victim's injuries?
38. Does the Def. view himself or herself as responsible for the victim's injury/death or is it attributed to the actions/inactions of others? (*Potential lead-in to shifting responsibility [reality perceptions] and a confession gateway*)
39. Do the events surrounding the life/death of the victim seem real or unreal to the Def.?
40. How has the Def. coped with the rigors of incarceration? What has been the single greatest adjustment (isolation)?
41. How do the other inmate's view/treat the Def.?
42. Throughout the victimization and prior/post to the victimization, what types of television programs or movies did the Def. watch? (*FD/FDP has been portrayed on various media outlets. Look for origination ideation here.*)
43. Does the Def. feel that he or she was a victim of domestic violence or child abuse?
44. If the Def. admits FD/FDP infliction, ask yourself why? *Admission is generally a unification requirement to regain access to a surviving victim of abuse.*

How Dangerous Is the Abuser Utilizing FDP as an Abuse Delivery System?

A perpetrator that maintains control over a victim for a prolonged time period while systematically inflicting pain appears to utilize the victim as an object. If the perpetrator allows or initiates victim death, the misery and suffering that life would prolong dies also. FDP offenders are not known to view their patterns of criminal victimization in this manner and are not usually known to "allow their victims to die" as directly seen in direct physical abuse homicide. The death of an abuse victim within an FDP methodology is most often attained through the inability of the child's body to cope with the offender's direct chronic infliction of foreign matter or harm.

FDP offenders do not show their victim's compassion or mercy as we have seen in even some of the sadistic killers. FDP offenders' actions are in many ways more wretched than a sadistic killer's because FDP offenders have an ever-present avenue to halt and potentially reverse a victim's anguish by stopping the deception and telling the truth. The vehicle to accomplish this is right in front of them all the time—the medical staff. Consider the number of hospitalizations, length of stay, and follow-up care associated with an FDP victim as missed opportunities to halt the abuse cycle. The inferred realization is that FDP abuse is deliberately sadistic.

Infliction of FDP is often a crime of family shame and it is hidden. A correlation between FDP infliction and incest highlights similar trends including lack of disclosure to anyone, including close family members because both types of offenses are deviant and offend social consciousness. Rationally, the offender may assume that no one has the capacity to understand motivations for such deviant abuse. It is theorized that within a sphere of standardized "norm," FDP offenders realize that their actions are improper but chose to place personal wants/needs above all others, even the lives of their children or parents. This understanding renders FDP offenders dangerously heinous.

Many of the dynamics of the FDP offender closely emulate psychopathic personality traits, which include

- Complete disregard for community behavioral standards
- Apparent absence of guilt regarding the victimization
- Failure to learn from punishment (recidivism)
- Desire for immediate satisfaction
- Can "go in" and "out" of feelings
- Undue dependence upon others[1]

The Victim as an Object

Figure 4.1 illustrates the victim as an object.

FDP Continuum

The likelihood of violence escalation is often determined by the "core behavior" of the offender. Within stages of core behavior, the examination of (1) verbiage, (2) amount of force, and (3) sequence of acts may facilitate the tenacity of plausible offender characteristic relating to the threatened victim injury. The stages of independent core behavior become elemental for consideration in abuse cases with an FDP delivery system when the core behavior is related as follows:

1. *Verbiage* is seen as inquisitive or supportive statements to medical staff.
2. *Force* viewed finds the context of allowable invasive procedures upon the victim and overt force exerted by the FDP offender in cases of directly inflicted harm (factors that influence are physical/mental stature of the offender and victim).
3. *Sequence* of acts, tracked via the amount of hospitalization, afforded the victim coupled with diagnostic procedures performed.

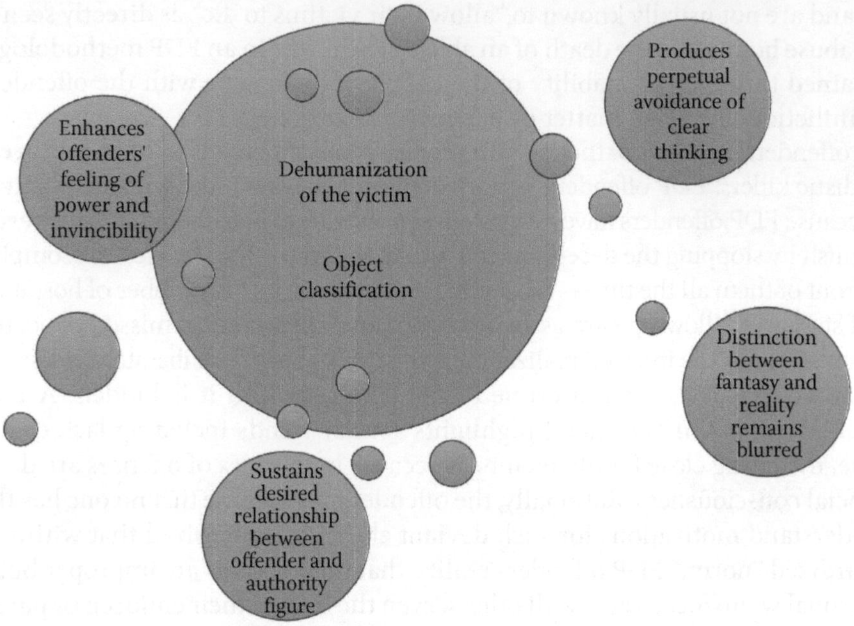

Figure 4.1 Victims as objects.

FDP Abuse Continuum (Figure 4.2)

Victim's Death Risk Assessment

To determine the likelihood that a target–abuse victim within an FDP infliction sequence will become a homicide casualty, examination of the offender's behavior relating to interaction with the target and medical staff may indicate the degree of injury the offender is willing to exert upon the victim in order to achieve his or her goal. Considering the series of events preceding criminal acts is important within the evaluation. How the victim is violated may indicate inner typology of the offender. The degree of the injurious act or allowable invasion by medical staff into the victim's body within a range including external diagnostics and internal examination (surgical procedures) indicates the inner ability

FDP continuum with probable cause escalation sequences		
Gratification scale		
Process		Offender actions
Escalation of infliction to meet desired needs for gratification	⇨	Restlessness Idealization of fantasy Thought of victimization Repression of victimization ideals
Demonstrated achieved gratification through increased infliction	⇨	Initial testing through fabrication Demonstrated fabrications Thoughts of infliction Active infliction
Secondary gratification achieved through the attention surrounding the victim's death	⇨	Death of the victim and/or appropriation of another victim
Downtime	⇨	Repeat of the cycle

Figure 4.2 FDP abuse continuum: probable cause escalation.

or level of willingness the FDP offender considers acceptable. It is the level of willingness the FDP offender assumes regarding victim injury in order to achieve the completion of a desired fantasy that reveals lethality potential.

When the potential willingness of the offender to permanently harm the victim becomes great, the life-threatening potential to the victim becomes equally great. The victim becomes an object to the offender and the object is disposable/replaceable. The victim is no longer a child or dependent who is the perceived object of the offender's love but the means by which the offender can attain a goal or fantasy. If the victim dies during the process, death is a by-product of the offender's pursuit of desired fantasy.

Unlike other circumstantial victims, EDP offenders do not arbitrarily select FDP abuse victims. Within the innermost thoughts of the FDP offender, could child victims have actually been produced for the purpose of object victimization? The victim may also have fallen into the role because the offender's reality of parenthood fell far short of the idealization so often present during pregnancy, especially for a "first" child.

The FDP offender expresses his or her opinion of the victim's life value with each directed offense or allowable diagnostic procedure performed upon the victim. With each needle poke, each day spent in hospital that should have been spent at work or play, and each normal developmental activity that is missed, the offender exhibits the degree of devaluation held for the victim and renders the life of the victim null and void. The value/infliction reaction is perceived as the offender's declaration that the life of the victim is insignificant and extraneous, and this understanding places a target victim in a position of severe danger on a continual basis.

Considerations

- The manner (how) a victim is violated.
- The degree of the injurious act or allowable invasion by medical staff into the child's body indicates the inner ability or level of willingness of the victimization the offender will undertake to achieve desired fantasy.
- The victim becomes a replaceable object to the FDP offender.
- An FDP victim's death is a by-product of the FDP offender's pursuit of his or her desired fantasy or goal.
- In devaluing the victim, the FDP offender is stating opinion regarding the value or worth of the victim's life with every act of abuse deployed.
- By allowing the victim to die, an offender may think this is a portrayal of mercy or it may be a situation where the FDP offender has just gone too far. The homicide of the FDP abuse victim may be intentional or unintentional.

Harsh Reality

Almost every expectant mother has a mental picture of herself and her child as "perfect." For most mothers, the reality of parenthood may be shocking but reality takes precedence over the illusion of perfection. Reality includes hard work with newborns equating to sleep deprivation, diaper duty, and allowing the center of attention to refocus from mother onto child. It appears that FDP mothers may not make this adjustment and often linger in the fantasy world of "perfect" child and "perfect" life. Although the demands of parenting thwart this idealization externally, what occurs to the mother inwardly is highly personal and generally not known to anyone (including a spouse).

FDP offenders often describe their children (whom they are abusing) as "miraculous." It is during this time that the idealization of victimization is likely to occur as the FDP offender methodically seeks methods for which her fantasy could replace reality. The desire to attain the fantasy of "perfection" may be guided according to relative individual need and becomes a test of the offender's ability within each instance of infliction. The FDP offender's ability is predicated upon practice through repetition. Acts of FDP victimization are not usually singular in number and are not necessarily confined to singular victims.

Some FDP offenders may view their child victims as personal possessions to justify abuse or even death. If a person is a possession, FDP offenders may think they have a right to offend or kill at will. The actual number of children who have died as a result of FDP infliction is unknown because the majority of FDP cases have historically evaded detection. Mortality estimates range from 10% to 22%.[2],[3] Mortality rates are considered low.

Intentional Torture

Consider infliction of pain due to medical procedures that are caused by the actions/inaction of the FDP offender. When an FDP offender controls the amount of pain a target victim endures and maintains the willingness to perpetrate, they become intentional torturers. The offender's actions seen through the withholding of knowledge, infliction, or fabrication of symptoms that must be medically treated or explored or the presentation of the target victim for medical procedures correlates the offender's intent. In FDP abuse cases, the added factor of indirectness must be included in the formulation analysis for intentional torture but the outcome remains constant.

It is theorized that an FDP abuser may "record" a sequence of FDP-related actions and surrounding events for later recall. The "recording" of the events may be secretively kept in a diary or more commonly stored within the offender's memory. Memories are recalled through dialogue concerning the victim's illness(es) or through objects derived from the scene of the FDP infliction and are often considered "trophies." Objects utilized to inflict FDP abuse or associative treatments may be kept as "souvenirs" for the purpose of recall stimulus and are often overlooked as potential sources of evidence. Offender's "downtime" may be spent in a circle of recall within the aurora of an FDP episode while the offender revels in the knowledge that deception has been completed without detection. These thoughts are believed to further the offender's desired fantasy.

Multiple Abuse Victims through an FDP Conduit

There is a question of threatened harm to siblings of FDP victims when FDP abuse is resolved within a specific child victim. Historically, the infliction of abuse by an FDP offender onto a victim has resolved in one of the following manners (Figure 4.3):

If an FDP victim becomes verbal, there is a risk that the actions of the FDP offender will be discovered. In cases where the child has either expired or becomes too "dangerous" for FDP infliction to continue without significant exposure risk, the offender will need to find a suitable victim substitute to continue FDP victimization pathways. It is very common for this substitute to be a younger sibling of the initial victim. In some instances, FDP abuse may be inflicted on children simultaneously, but it is more likely that the FDP offender will concentrate on one victim at a time. Keeping in mind that FDP offender gain

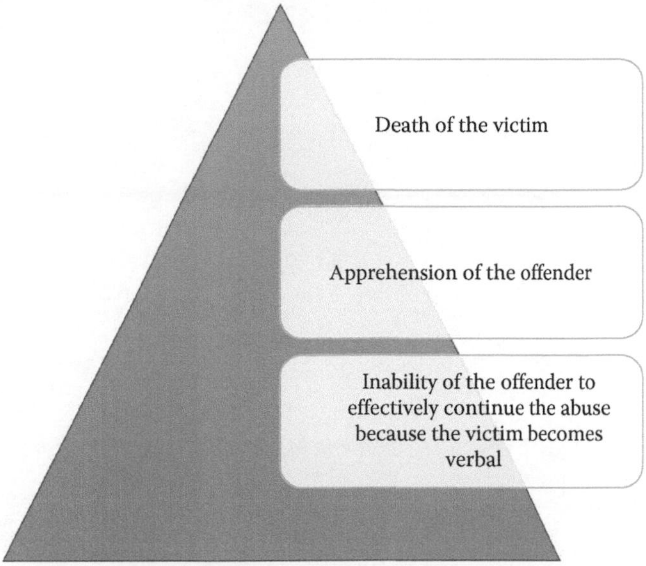

Figure 4.3 FDP victimization: final resolutions.

centers around attention, it is not rational to think that more than one victim would be needed to attain desired attention in a hospital setting.

It is unknown if FDP abuse is multigenerational and linked to the cycle of abuse in a domestic forum. Whether or not child victims actually know what the FDP offender is doing to them in the format of induced illness will depend upon the victim's physical age/maturity and covert skill of the offender. Certainly, the longer the abuse continues and the older the child victim becomes, the more likely the child may be aware of the offender's actions. In some situations, the offender's behavior may be present throughout the child's life rendering the actions "normal" for the victim. The victim may not view the offender as anything less than ideal, even if the abuse is blatant. Attention upon the victim, bestowed by the offender (when observed by others), and the victim's understanding of normal behavior create their own reality.

It is not likely that the FDP child abuse victim will have the capability to verbally assist within an abuse investigation, and it is necessary to consider traumatic consequences when an FDP child abuse victim is told the truth regarding his or her victimization. It would be wise to elicit the help of trained professionals when dealing with this aspect of the investigation to lessen the probability of further victim damage.

FDP elderly victims may also have verbalization constraints regarding what is happening to them because like their child victim counterparts, some lack the ability to discern or have lost the ability to speak due to various medical issues.

Notes

1. Coleman, J.C., Butcher, J.N., and Carson, R.C., *Abnormal Psychology and Modern Life* (7th ed.). Dallas, TX: Scott, Foresman and Co., 1984, pp. 247–250.
2. Meadow, R., Munchausen syndrome by proxy. *Archives of Disease in Children*, 1982;57:92–98.
3. Kaufman, K.L., Coury, D., Pickrel, B., and McCleery, J., Munchausen syndrome by proxy: A survey of professionals' knowledge. *Child Abuse & Neglect*, 1989;13(1):141–148.

False Reports and Serial Victimization

5

Injustice anywhere is a threat to justice everywhere.

Martin Luther King, Jr.

Review and Expansion of Factitious Disorder/Factitious Disorder by Proxy Understanding

Investigators should be aware that the actions of repetitive alleged crime victims might fit into known parameters found within factitious disorder (FD) methodologies or measurable abuse seen within abuse cases with an Factitious Disorder by Proxy (FDP) delivery system. In cases where the criminal actions of an alleged offender spark a voluminous question of believability due to alleged acts and certain factors are present in the offender's character, FD/FDP linkage should be explored as victimization validity is considered. Cases that are connected to monetary gain (insurance fraud or civil suits) or direct actions (identifiable homicides or abuse situations without indirect delivery) are probably not FD/FDP connected.

The methodology of the FD/FDP offender has been identified through an avenue of sought-out medical care either for the offender himself or herself (FD) or the offender's target victim (FDP) who is often a child or other dependent. Investigators rely on the intuitiveness and observatory skill of medical personnel to be alerted when FD offenders self-inflict harm or FDP offenders inflicted abuse. When FD/FDP offenders choose a nonmedical setting to attain their sought reward, seen within law enforcement and firefighter realms or in the civil arena, recognition of the proxy role must come from within the profession targeted. At times, this recognition is either difficult to access or nonexistent and the cycle of abuse is unimpeded.

In FD and FDP cases, the most apparent common denominator is *attention* afforded the offender. This attention is often seen directly through the favorable physical and emotional response of medical staff and family toward the offender and appears to appease the offender's incessant need of *self-worth verification*. Even the more indirect actions of peripheral personnel, such as police and social service agencies, add to the attention glow. The FD/FDP offender enjoys the notoriety and he or she plays the role of the victim (FD situations) or role of the doting caretaker (FDP situations). The actions or inactions of the offender feed the spiral web of deception created by the offender to attain personal satisfaction.

FD/FDP offenders who choose medical venues to attain their goals seem to have a commonality of various degrees of medical knowledge. This medical knowledge aids the offender providing the skill necessary to offend while minimizing the threat of getting caught in the deception. Medical personnel forge ahead in the treatment of either the offender or the offender's proxy with the best of intentions and often become perplexed due to illness they typically have never seen before. Medical personnel often experience repetitive contact with an offender or offender's proxy, and this contact pattern may have multiple etiologies. Changing symptoms within apparent multiple forms of illness creates medical perplexity leading to increased offender attention either directly (FD) or indirectly via proxy (FDP). The attentiveness of medical staff feeds the FD/FDP offenders desire for belonging and verification of self-worth found within a world where reality is what the offender creates.

Through education, medical personnel have become more astute regarding their own secondary victimization as a means of inflicting harm upon an FDP abuse victim through the delivery system of FDP. Within a diagnostic venue, medical staff has also become more knowledgeable regarding patients who have seemingly undiagnosable illnesses. Cases that baffle medical staff and seem unbelievable according to known diagnostic standards now include the diagnostic potential of FD or FDP—even when the diagnostic potential begins as a theory.

FD within Criminal Victimizations

Within law enforcement, the presence of the phenomenon of FD-related acts has extended the standardized protocol seen within FDP abuse-related situations within the medical realm. These ulterior cases involve child custody, homicide, kidnapping, robbery, sexual battery, domestic violence, elder abuse, and animal cruelty. Virtually, every aspect of criminal and civil investigation now has the potential for inclusion of the FD or FDP factitious factor. Common elements seen within these cases include the following.[1]

Common Elements within FD/FDP Cases

The common elements within FD/FDP cases are shown in Figure 5.1.

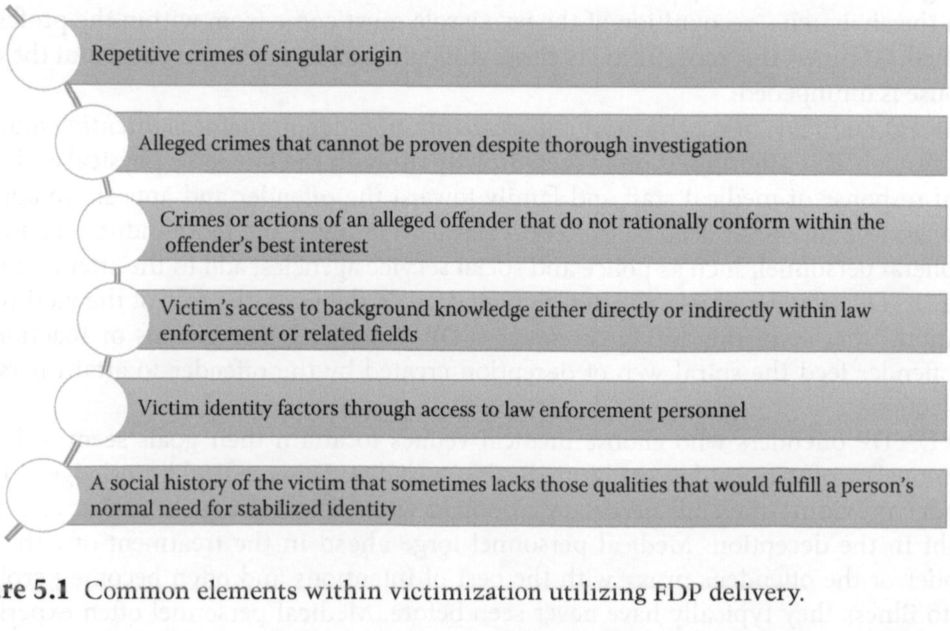
Repetitive crimes of singular origin
Alleged crimes that cannot be proven despite thorough investigation
Crimes or actions of an alleged offender that do not rationally conform within the offender's best interest
Victim's access to background knowledge either directly or indirectly within law enforcement or related fields
Victim identity factors through access to law enforcement personnel
A social history of the victim that sometimes lacks those qualities that would fulfill a person's normal need for stabilized identity

Figure 5.1 Common elements within victimization utilizing FDP delivery.

FD/FDP Transference: The Police Connection

A gravitation for people, especially females, to become enamored with uniformed professionals in the law enforcement, fire, or medical fields has long been identified with the term "crush" or "groupie." Although motivations of persons drawn to these professionals are varied, the fact that certain persons choose to identify themselves through a designated professional opens the door for possibility of forced association in the form of alleged victimization. For these people, the attention and perceived personal caring of the professional is optimal when they are victims or the caretaker of victims. The helplessness of these victims is swept away through the professional's actions as the victim or caretaker of the victim is perceived as the most important person at that given time. The very qualities that make any professional great (empathy, dedication, drive, caring, nurturance) become attention vehicles for the FD/FDP offender and provide a sense of belonging within a world that may otherwise be unattainable.

The factor regarding a relationship between a professional and FD/FDP offender is that professionals who tend to excel in their positions project genuine caring to those they serve (in this case an FD/FDP offender). In doing their job, professionals attend to victims on a professional basis but for an FD/FDP offender, the attention may be perceived on a personal basis. The reality of the relationship may be strictly professional but for FD/FDP offenders, the connection is very personal. Alleged victimization investigations center on many forms of extended attention to an alleged victim. For a person who lacks other significant avenues of self-identification normally achieved through work, family, hobbies, social activities, etc., the role of victimization or the connection that it has for the FDP offender (as a proxy is utilized in the victimization role) provides belonging. Victimization produces the optimum feeling of importance, belonging, and nurturance for as long as the professional bestows their attention upon the FD/FDP offender. Identifying with this feeling may be addictive if you consider the alternative of boredom and discontent thought to be present in the FD/FDP offender's real world.

In many cases, once the attainment of the "police connection" is made and associated with inner personal satisfaction of identity due to heightened attention afforded the FD/FDP offender, it often may become a difficult adjustment for the FD/FDP offender to return to their nonheightened state of norm. FD/FDP offenders may find that they prefer, ponder, and even fantasize about that "exciting" time in their lives when they alone were the center of everyone's attention as a victim. In some cases, if the "norm" does not adequately meet the mental and emotional needs of the FD/FDP offender, then a conscientious choice to return to the "victim" role in a weak or injured status may be considered or enacted. The FD/FDP offender may create a factitious scenario to adjust the attention deficit by placing themselves or their proxies directly back into the limelight as repeated victimization emerges.

Whether a suspected FD/FDP offender was legitimately victimized initially may be irrelevant if repetitive cases of grandiose alleged victimization are subsequently presented. Theoretically, in situations involving repeated false victimization offenses, some form of legitimate victimization, heroic action, or significant interaction with professionals may have occurred at some point during the FD/FDP offender's lifetime. The direct interaction with the professional and the indirect interaction associated with whatever event occurred may have provided the ideal or experience of attention for the FD/FDP offender, however brief. The situation may have been negative and of high profile due to alleged criminal severity—a crime that outrages the public's sense of accepted norm. It may also have been a situation in which the FD/FDP offender was publicly recognized in a positive or hero mode—of highest esteem. From one end of the spectrum to the other, the attention afforded to the FD/FDP offender would be paramount and all the emotions connected with the event including verification of self-worth, attention, notoriety, belonging, personal gain, and happiness provide indelible personal knowledge of what may be lacking within the FD/FDP offender's real world.

Involvement of Police Personnel in the FD/FDP Snare

Neither FD nor FDP behavior is confined to any specific race, group, sex, or occupation. Law enforcement offices, therefore, are not exempted from becoming potential victims or offenders. Case studies of FD/FDP offenders have identified a crossover between FD and FDP via medical venues and other professions, especially law enforcement. Similarity between law enforcement professionals and their medical professional counterparts is staggering when you consider core behavior and other profile factors.

Accessibility to law enforcement by the FD/FDP-related offender either on an interpersonal or professional level is elemental when law enforcement staff is utilized in an FD/FDP status. Accessibility tenure between the FD/FDP offender and police officer affords the offender familiarization of peculiarities that exist within this relationship and varied degrees of interpersonal knowledge. Most people are quite aware that police personnel generally and collectively have a unique culture validated through character. This character is often directly or indirectly projected onto those whom officers encounter. FD/FDP offenders appear to view the relationship between themselves and the officers as intimate regardless of actuality. Perceived value of the FD/FDP offender's life may become intertwined with how they view their interpersonal interaction with the law enforcement professional.

When an FD/FDP offender is a caretaker and has adopted the rationalization that personal validation rests within interaction with law enforcement professional, the FDP victim may be utilized directly as an expendable target object. Creation of external situations (false victimization reports) or internally produced situations (simulated or induced medical ailments within self or the proxy) creates threatened harm potential or criminal victimization allegation. Both victimization pathways may naturally create increased attention and concern within the officer, and this is easily projected to the FD/FDP offender either through personal or professional interaction. The FD/FDP offender may interpret the officer's active interest on a personal level regardless of intent. This interpretation is thought to become the basis for the FD/FDP offender's fantastical basis of altered reality in direct application to law enforcement enmeshment.

In some situations, officers are actually involved in interpersonal relationships with the FD/FDP offender and for various reasons seek to terminate the relationship. These reasons may or may not be the realization of the FD/FDP status. The threat or actuality of a discontinued relationship between the FD/FDP offender and a law enforcement officer may generate a justification or catalyst for the FD/FDP offender to victimize self or a proxy. Whatever actions/injuries or deviant acts befall the proxy victim or the FD offender himself or herself become the officer's fault (in the FD/FDP offender's mind). When an FDP/FD offender's true abusive behavior is either proven or suspected, blame and denial are almost always presented prevalent factors.

In situations whereby law enforcement officers have assumed the role traditionally held by physicians, in FD/FDP situations, as a vehicle to obtain the FD/FDP offender's intangible goals of attention, verification of self-worth, belonging, or others and that role becomes threatened with extinction, there is great danger to the vehicle and the FDP proxy victim. Extrication of the officer (vehicle to goal attainment) by various means including homicide, relocation, formal complaint, or reputational damage is likely. The foundation or basis of potential complaint by the FD/FDP offender should be reviewed with the totality of the domestic situation and understanding or application of known FD/FDP dynamics. Detectives should question the circumstances of the relationship demise between the FD/FDP offender and the law enforcement officer and any other influential factors such as satanic involvement, stalking, or domestic maneuvering (civil litigation) or other issues present.

In some cases, the FD/FDP offender will relocate before a formal misconduct complaint is initiated within law enforcement. Such complaints will require investigative probes to determine who ended the relationship and why. Generally, marital relationships that end in divorce or separation produce some amount of animosity between the participants. One or both participants may find themselves alone, isolated, or depressed. People in these situations may either cope with their situations and go on, seek revenge, or attempt to manipulate the partner back into the relationship through coercion, guilt, fear, pity, or genuine remorse. If participants desire reunification and these measures fail to attain a reconciliation blame may become a suitable replacement for the demise of the relationship. Some FD/FDP offenders may become so distraught regarding estrangement from the partner who is a (professional) police officer that absent reunification, drastic infirmity may appear to be the only answer. The intensity level of infirmity (illness or victimization status) ranges from simple falsification to directed homicide in FDP cases. The range within FD-only situations may be seen as an upsurge in self-victimization up to and including suicide or increased reports of criminal victimization status.

If the time frame between the ending of an interpersonal relationship involving an FD/FDP offender and significant injury to an FDP abuse victim or the FD offender themselves yields a gap, this delay may fit into the realm of relative thinking that allows the FD/FDP offender preparation time. Preparation time is considered a nonoffending FD/FDP time designation for the offender to digest the scope of futuristic implications that being without the spouse or significant other will produce. Potential FD/FDP offender's conscientious decision to offend in hopes that such actions will rekindle a lost interpersonal relationship is reasonable—at least in the offender's view. Conscientious decisions to harm oneself or another (victim) may occur by either direct or indirect harm infliction.

Playing the role of a crime victim for FD offensive modalities may become a consideration for the FD/FDP offender. Direct self-infliction of harm or applied abuse without an FD/FDP factor is generally viewed as physical abuse, while indirect infliction of self or via a proxy is seen through omission or setting the opportunity for injury to occur (i.e., providing a child with a key and showing them how to place it into an electrical socket or failure to ensure safety for young children near windows they may fall out of). These types of victim harm are different from those related to FD/FDP within examination of intent. FD/

FDP infliction is generally an indirect process of harm or instituted behavior formulated to elicit additional reactionary processes from those brought into the offensive abuse action unknowingly. The participation of these unwilling abuse participants creates a secondary victimization within the group. It is a by-proxy use of professionals as an instrument of the FD/FDP offender's will.

The entrenched coping method that all FD/FDP offenders appear to embrace by either direct denial or reality transference will most likely elicit a negative response through direct questioning. The psychological aspects of an interviewer's theory of criminalization in FD/FDP criminal case evaluation require a delicate delivery process applied after a careful and thorough analysis of the FD/FDP circumstantial totality. How a person thought to be inflicting FD/FDP reacts to the allegation has many possibilities including complete shutdown with vehement denial or flight.

Gravitation

Not all FD/FDP offenders immediately gravitate to an optimum allegation of crime victimization. Events or alleged victimization may be a building process that ebbs and flows within a learning experiential curve. FD/FDP offenders may become described as "professional victims" due to repetitive incidents of alleged victimization events that have a marked increase in injury severity or heightened victimization degree. The correlation between FD/FDP offenders within the medical realms and those suspected within the police realm have striking pattern resemblances that indicate a testing of accepted crime patterns and methodologies.

For FD/FDP offenders, the longer the masquerade of self-victimization or proxy abuse continues, the more skilled the offender may become. Concurrently associated with this relationship is the task factor of involved personnel to determine confirmed, fictitious, or self-induced criminal complaint origins. The task factor seen through investigatory time commitment with attention to detail may give the FD/FDP offender added accessibility to the law enforcement process and personnel, and this prolongs the frenzy of attention sought by the FD/FDP offender.

Most law enforcement professionals have some knowledge of criminal cases that were unresolvable or highly suspected of a falsified origin. These situations have historically been "high profile" both internally within law enforcement agencies and publicly either due to the staunch attitude of the alleged victim or criminal actions alleged. Many case detectives assigned to these alleged victimization cases show many of the same associative behaviors as their medical counterparts. The frustration factor, believability factor, repetitive nature of the alleged crime, and extraordinary measures undertaken to resolve the allegation (clear the case complaint) emulate the commonalities and measurable patterns established by the FD/FDP offender in medical-related or law enforcement–related scenarios. Professional response to scenarios presented by the FD/FDP offender generates a means to feed the offender's need for attention and identity. A law enforcement officer may see alleged repetitive victimization as a personal challenge to resolve and exhibit tenacity commensurate with the desire for successful case resolution. The officer may arrive at an end point in an unresolvable victimization case investigation that factitious origination may be plausible. It is important to understand why such factitious origin may have produced a false allegation of criminal victimization, and this can be quite complicated. Questioning a suspected FD/FDP offender is likely to produce withdrawal of the criminal complaint, uncooperativeness, or offender and his/her family to relocate.

Identification Indicators

Clues that may alert investigators to the presence of false victimizations are identified as

1. Discrepancies between victimization history and clinical investigative findings
2. The absence of physical evidence that normally would be found in cases of alleged physical abuse
3. Details of alleged abuse that cannot be environmentally verified
4. Abuse allegations that are bizarre or highly improbable
5. History of abuse that changed elementally and/or takes on new details as it is repeated
6. Distorted facts that cannot be checked
7. Victims who do not recover from their abuse
8. Victims who are eager to tell of their victimization and recite their allegations as a routine manner
9. Victims less interested in building a case (catching the perpetrator) than in the attention surrounding the allegation
10. Victims who excessively doctor shop or cop shop searching for answers they seem to be looking for and in doing so welcome multiple physical exams, treatments, or extended interviews
11. Adult victims who infer that their children are involved or are becoming assimilated into repeated alleged criminal victimizations

Importance of Attention

The relationship between an alleged event and presence of an FD/FDP offender producing circumstances that result in a temporary environment of heightened attention provides potential motive for all forms of victimization fabrication. Alleged events portrayed by the FD/FDP offender may be a combination of real and fabrication. Checking victimization detail history may provide an avenue to case resolution or criminal complaint withdrawal. The identification of measureable benefit to the FD/FDP offender who concocts stories of criminal victimization that are verbally falsified or falsified through evidence creation (illness or injury) is elemental to understand victimization motive. Understanding motive is a gateway to uncovering the truth regarding FD/FDP sequencing through medical or other professional victimization modalities. The investigative interview process is complicated in FD/FDP inference cases.

FD/FDP-related factors now present an answer to "why" historically presented within repetitive case investigations of abuse or other criminal acts that remain unresolved. These factors are also relative in situations where theoretical false reporting was a factor.

Why people choose to leave the realm of reality and take up residence in a fantasy world shaped through fabricated victimization is a difficult concept for most stabilized people to rationalize. By understanding underlying factors and warning signs associated with FD/FDP, the solution index to formerly unresolved criminal or civil cases affords the investigator a wider resolution spectrum.

It is important to consider that not all cases of unproven criminal or civil victimizations are necessarily fabricated. The ability to differentiate between valid (founded) alleged victimizations and those that are contrived or fabricated often rests within the interviewers' ability and the examination of physical evidence (when it exists). Of those cases deemed fictitious, the phenomenon of FD/FDP should be considered. Looking into the alleged victim's social, residential, and intrafamilial history is a valid means to enhance investigative suspicion that may later validate theory or suspicion of FD/FDP when alleged case facts cannot be proven or cases remain unresolved—especially those occurring in "serial nature." Investigators are reminded that viewable reality is often separate from actual reality in FD/FDP-related cases, and the FD/FDP offender's view of reality may be contorted.

Law Enforcement Personnel as FD/FDP Offenders

An apparently consistent component in FD/FDP activity is a reactionary response of directed blame when the behavior of the suspected FD/FDP offender is either confronted or confirmed. Accusation of blame emulating from the FD/FDP offender is often directed toward alleged actions of medical personnel and occasionally directed toward law enforcement officers (as previously discussed). Blame has been cast upon law enforcement officers in situations where evidence did not validate reported victimizations.

Cases of false victimization in which police officers are reporters appear to be extremely rare. Research suggests the rarity of their existence is due to minimization when identified and reluctant to obtain confirmation from departmental origination sources. Traits and behavior associated with FD/FDP is generally not something families acknowledge or openly speak of, ever, even if the behavior is appalling. In many ways, law enforcement is a family. Police agencies promote camaraderie among employees. The severe nature of the law enforcement profession with the overhanging reality that death is possible each and every workday and one officer's life is dependent upon another officer's action(s) promotes cohesiveness. An agency's reputation is directly related to an employee's actions, and when those actions become an embarrassment, the behavior is not exactly hidden, but it is not necessarily readily available or broadcast. Public records requests regarding these alleged fabricated situations have been known to become "lost" or files "incomplete." Officers who are involved in fabrication of violent situations, self-inflicted injuries, or other crimes either are generally allowed to resign or are fired.

Falsified victimization or falsified victimization response (based upon contrived situations by a law enforcement officer) is known by those in direct contact with the event. These are internal witnesses usually bound by the unwritten, undocumented family code of loyalty and understand the reality that repercussions may follow disclosure. There is a reluctance to reveal or comment upon people or situations when in an informal manner, the repercussion could equate to your own well-being.

FD behavior by police officers has been described as two distinctive types:

1. The officer is involved in an incident that places him or her into a victim or hero status. It is theorized that the origination of this FD mode is related to a failure to cope with various stressors.
2. The officer who creates or invents a situation to achieve peer acceptance. It is theorized that origination of this FD mode is connected to a desire to achieve credibility.[2]

FD activity within law enforcement circles is also explained by understanding that the retelling of experiences (war stories) by police officers strengthens camaraderie and solidifies acceptance within the closed circles of a particular group or subculture. This well-known protocol of police and other professions may be lined to FD if the initial experiences or alleged incidents were fabricated.[3]

There appears to be a significant difference between war stories of factual basis that become embellished over the years and war stories of fallacious basis that are representative of an inflated imagination or deviant act. If an action or situation with a falsified base is embellished over time, it produces the same affect of attention or belonging that factual-based stories elicit. The difference is that embellishing and repeating falsified-based stories make them all the more real to the storyteller. It makes them part of their identity that is based upon a lie. This is a link to understand why FD was known for so many years as Munchausen syndrome.[4]

The law enforcement officer who utilizes the technique of "tale-telling" to achieve acceptance within the profession presents the question of stability. One must consider the following: If fantasy is an acceptable basis for personal foundation of reality, then how is it possible that the person (police officer) can effectively deal with the job requirement of mediating the true reality of life? In dealing with critical situations, which ebb and flow, within the life of all police officers, the only advantage that officer may ultimately have is his or her powers of observation. Reality plays an intrical part in an officer's ability to recognize negative situations or forces that may bring harm to his or her self or peers. The value of honesty may be considered the most important aspect of police work not only for integrity and the command of respect but also for the very real aspect of survivability in the real world.

Conclusion

FD/FDP factors were once considered conduct directed only within the medical profession, but this view has expanded. The applied behavior of FDP abusers and FD offenders has been recognized within the criminal justice perspective. This recognition has provided latitude to potential causation of previously unresolvable alleged victimizations outside the realm of the medical community. It has also opened the door to unreported abuse situations through a professional and public education knowledge base.

Victimizations, alleged situations, unbelievable heroism, or criminal acts that had no previous rational substantiation for being now have a probable rational truth factor when FD/FDP behavior is proven within them. A means of enhanced policing capability that has projected from within the scope of FD/FDP has been understood and continues to change criminal and civil investigative methods through clever application of reason.

As a means to further the pursuit of justice for substantiated victims and to uncover the deception of falsified victimization reports, FD/FDP understanding has added a new layer to investigative protocol. There is still much to be discovered regarding the ever-changing modes of FD/FDP application within a host of situations, but knowing that the behavior associated with FD/FDP activity is real and studied is encouraging.

Notes

1. Artingstall, K. and Brubaker, L., Munchausen syndrome related offenses, *Law and Order Magazine*, October 1995, pp. 83–90.
2. Divasto, P. and Saxton, G., Munchausen's syndrome in law enforcement. *FBI Law Enforcement Bulletin*, April 1992, pp. 11–14.
3. Puglielli, M. and Burke, T., Munchausen syndrome in law enforcement. *Law and Order Magazine*, April 1992, pp. 81–83.
4. Dryden-Edwards, R., Munchausen syndrome. www.medicinenet.com/munchausen_syndrome/article.htm. Accessed on 10 May, 2016.

Interviewing the Factitious Disorder/Factitious Disorder by Proxy Offender

6

Education is the most powerful weapon which you can use to change the world.

Nelson Mandela

Interviews

When a person is the perpetrator of illness or crime and when they alone have that knowledge, then wellness or case resolution is easy for that person to predict; there is calm. The foreknowledge of illness or crime origination provides a sense of control to the offender. This control may equate to the ability to sustain life, encourage or produce death, or institute resolution to a seemingly unsolvable problem. The dynamic of factitious disorder (FD)/factitious disorder by proxy (FDP) behavior makes an offender powerful through resolution pathway control over primary victims and all aspects of secondary victimization!

FD/FDP offenders know that they hold secrets that are believed to be unrecognized, and most adapt to whatever threat of discovery presents by varying their delivery mode or ceasing the behavior until the threat of discovery is diminished. FD/FDP offenders play a game of chance with the threat of detection being the greatest loss factor. It is the pathway alongside victimization for FDP abuse situations or the alleged criminal case victimizations in FD application that produces attention and belonging craved by the FD/FDP offender. Reality is what the offender defines, and the portrayal of factitious anything as real is quite convincing. Offenders project that they believe what they are stating as truth—so you will believe it too. The pattern of lying is absolute and entrenches itself within the FD/FDP offender in ways that circumscribe a way of life. Finding truth within this world is challenging.

FD and FDP are separate entities that may share common behavioral and motivational origins but are not mutually exclusive. Criminal or civil cases, which possess the shadowy hint of either an FD or FDP behavioral link, require an understanding of fundamental substantive law violations that supersedes recognized identification of behavioral patterns related to FDP in terms of charging accountability. To effectively investigate criminal or civil law violations, which also include an FD, FDP, or combination sequence, understanding the psychology that may be present in the offender's mind is a window of opportunity. Awareness of the "factitious disorder arena" may not be enough to facilitate effective case resolution. People who utilize FDP/FD behavioral methods are usually astute, intelligent, and skilled; their actions are generally of covert serial nature. They are not intimidated by the notion of criminal investigation, prosecution, or the judicial system. It has been my experience that most FDP offenders are sophisticated criminals who delight in testing a detective's abilities in incomprehensible ways. If a detective (intervener) has prominent knowledge and investigative skill regarding FD/FDP, then the control factor required to bridge the gap between the world of reality and that of the FD/FDP illusion is possible.

There is a remarkable difference between detectives who understand the behavior of FDP/FD and those who do not. Understanding FD/FDP concepts followed by intervention into potential case sequences means hope for a victim. Lack of FDP/FD understanding or knowledge in many types of cases limits the effectiveness of the intervener on dimensional levels. Understanding the complexity of FDP/FD is an investigative tool in the belt of any investigator, prosecutor, or police officer.

The first step in interviewing an FD/FDP offender is determining who will conduct the interview/interrogation. FDP cases involving child or elderly victims generally interact with child protection or social protective personnel because they are criminal investigations with dependent individuals. Some policing agencies advocate that non–law enforcement staff conduct dependant victim interviews. If this is customary, then shared interview results are sometimes possible. More often, however, criminal interviews of suspects are conducted under custodial or perceived custodial circumstances with proper notice of Miranda rights. FD/FDP offenders are generally not dissuaded by application of Miranda.

The appearance of promissory or coercive questioning is not permitted within the investigatory interview. In criminal child abuse cases of any type, detectives are to avoid any promise or threat connected to either child custody or future reunification between the suspected offender and child victim as related to the offender's disclosures. Undue influence exerted upon an interviewee by an interrogator can occur when the internally created agency pressure to resolve a case is prevalent and the interrogator allows this pressure to direct his or her own behavior in the interview process. Law enforcement detectives/interrogators are minded that they must work within the confines of the law and that information obtained outside that scope will likely be suppressed but more importantly may enable further victimization menace. The means do not necessarily justify the end result if the process to collect information is unlawful. In some situations, the dire actions of an FD/FDP offender may have resulted in horrific abuse or victim death that when viewed tests the composure of anyone—perhaps anyone other than the FD/FDP offender. The FD/FDP offender will be looking for the interrogator's reaction and loss of control within the interview process, and composure is required to be effective.

Persons known or suspected of measurable child abuse seen within the many facets of FD/FDP may have varied reactions to a multitude of investigative questioning techniques used for the purpose of truth determination. There are many factors, known and unknown, that influence the manner in which a person accused of perpetrating abuse with an FD/FDP factor may react. Although individual reactions to various direct and indirect questioning cannot be cemented into specifically formatted protocol for FD/FDP offender interviews, commonalities found within many of these interviews and empirical research provide a suggested guideline. This guideline must remain flexible as the interviewer attempts to enter the imaginary realm created by the FD/FDP offender. Through the understanding and anticipation of the most common accusatory reactions in FD/FDP abuse investigations, a necessary level of investigatory preparation is attained by the interviewer. Preparation is needed to effectively approach the topic of

FD/FDP abuse sequencing because FD/FDP offenders have highly polished lying skill, and rationalization seen through diversion, denial, or orchestrated emotional outburst. This skill set is to be expected.

Preparation

Preparedness for interviewing an FD/FDP offender should begin at the moment a case comes to the attention of the interviewer. It is necessary to prepare for the interview by documenting all aspects of the investigation, reviewing the case file, and obtaining background information of the interview subject. The interviewer must also prepare himself or herself mentally and logistically. Mental readiness for an FD/FDP interview is attained through self-confidence derived from understanding the complicated aspects of FD/FDP investigations, patience, and predeveloped contingency plans. In other words, do your homework. Interviewers should be mentally prepared to control their attitudes, prejudices, moral beliefs, and emotions when conducting investigative interviews.

Interviewers should not allow the interview to be rushed or themselves to yield to external pressure and be rushed. There is no timetable or time constraint during which an interview must be concluded. Take all the time that is necessary and/or allowable. It is important to obtain elements of the crime either on tape or in writing whenever possible as a product of the investigative interview during the initial investigative sequence. If something is forgotten, you may not be able to go back and obtain it later. Tape-recorded or video-recorded (with sound) statements are preferable to handwritten statements due to clarity, verification of authenticity, content/meaning accuracy, and emotional affect conveyed by the person being interviewed.

The interview subject should be guided within the interview process but not coerced. If open, nonspecific questions are utilized, the subject many not know or be willing to begin at a specific point. If subjects are willing to talk about the situation in narrative form, let them. It is preferable to allow the subject to tell his or her story initially without interruption. When the subject's initial statement is concluded, specific questions to clarify and expand a sequence are indicated.

Application of *Miranda*

Application and delivery of *Miranda* in case investigations involving an FD/FDP factor should be gauged in accordance with the custody status of the suspected offender at the time of interview. If the offender is free to leave (not in any form of actual or perceived custody), then *Miranda* generally need not be extended. The investigator's intent to arrest is seemingly irrelevant. The question that is posed is the issue of custodial interrogation. Defendants need not be physically restrained in order to construe that they are in custody. The location where the interrogation takes place often becomes a pivotal point in later argument that the defendant was in fact not free to leave and therefore entitled to *Miranda* application prior to interrogation. If the interview takes place in a police facility, there is a general presumption that the defendant is not able to leave and *Miranda* should be extended prior to interviewing the subject.

Many law enforcement interrogators have found that application of *Miranda* has a chilling effect upon their potential communication with the suspect/defendant. The manner of *Miranda* delivery appears to play a significant role in the communicative relationship between interviewer and interviewee. All points of established *Miranda* rights must be conveyed to a suspect when appropriate or to a defendant in custody, but these points can be softened to include a realistic approach of affording the interview subject the opportunity to present his or her position and justification or explanation for alleged behavior. The understanding of an interviewer's need to weigh both sides of any situation and the nonuniqueness of FD/FDP-related investigations often bridges the icy waters enveloping *Miranda* rights application and delivery in FD/FDP-related investigations. Investigators should not be frightened or apprehensive by the requirement to extend *Miranda* to defendants or suspects (within the range of circumstantial requirements). Gracefully delivering *Miranda* to the interviewee enhances the likelihood that any information or confession obtained will withstand later suppression attempts within the courts. It is a delicate dance between ensuring the structure of a criminal case and gracefully providing an atmosphere that will allow an interviewee the atmospheric comfort required to produce truthful statements regarding a most disturbing criminal behavior. The world of the FD/FDP offender is ever so close to crashing when the FD/FDP offender is in the company of an interviewer skilled in the knowledge of FD/FDP behavior. Knowledge tips the scale of control from the FD/FDP offender to the interviewer.

Challenge of the FD/FDP Interview

Historically, suspect interviews with known or suspected FD/FDP linkage have been unsuccessful and the admission of guilt illusive. Theoretically, an alleged offender may be so immersed in the sequence of lies during the interview that they see these lies as reality. The offenders may also believe their deceptions are true or genuine in origin and/or simply choose not to reveal the truth due to the magnitude of the offense or personal impact that disclosure would elicit. Subsequently, interviewers have been tasked with the responsibility of attempting to point out reality to an offender whose reality base may have been altered to accommodate and protect the deception. Interviewers also sometimes find that FD/FDP suspects are staunch liars who refuse to admit responsibility and convey truth regarding their behavior because that would put an end to the deception and all that is entailed within it. It does not seem to matter that truth disclosure could end the pain, suffering, and torture of the victim, even when a child is the proxy, and it does not appear that probable victim death is enough to motivate honesty.

During investigative interviews, FD/FDP offenders have exhibited intense emotions such as crying, anger, or rage that might be expected of a person accused of abuse with an FD/FDP factor. These emotional exhibitions, while appearing genuine, upon closer examination appear to be calculated mechanisms to escape the attempted exposure to reality that the interviewer is attempting to implore upon the accused FD/FDP offender. This evasive technique has been observed to flow as if regulated by a faucet switch being turned off as quickly as it is turned on. Within interview facilities, it would be common for an FD/FDP offender to display very intense emotion or behavior in the interviewer's presence and then immediately calm when the interviewer leaves the room unless the FD/FDP offender knows or believes he or she is being observed while alone.

Necessary skills for an FD/FDP offender to further deceptive acts are generally well rehearsed. If the offender has not previously been in the position of being accused or questioned regarding the possible existence of FD/FDP behavior, offender's ability to retort during the interview is lessened. Most cases, however, do not fit into this category, and it is probable that the offender will have had significant time to prepare statements aimed at creating doubt in the mind of the interrogator. FD/FDP offenders are generally planners who are so effective at their deceptions that they may not fear accusation or discussion regarding the allegations. This confidence provides seemingly limitless opportunity to offend, but it also provides interviewers opportunity to catch the FD/FDP offender in their lies. It is as if the investigative interview is a stage for the FD/FDP offender and the interviewer/interrogator is insignificant.

It is not uncommon for FD/FDP offenders to answer questions with questions and offer alternative reasoning for alleged acts. Interviewers should anticipate that the FD/FDP offender would be well versed in knowledge surrounding FD/FDP; the offender may make open-ended statements that cannot be proven or disproven. They may verbalize to the interviewer that they know that what they are saying, in their opinion, is not tantamount to the admission of guilt and may have had previous interaction with the criminal justice system.

The manipulative skill that FD/FDP offenders normally direct toward medical professionals they encounter seems easily redirected toward the interviewer. The abilities of the FD/FDP offender to maintain deception displayed in the interview forum is similar to the deception level seen within the medical abuse sequences. It is important that the interviewer understand that in FD/FDP cases knowledge and patterns possessed by the offender are systematic on the medical level and applied as an extension of skill within the interview itself. FD/FDP offenders are generally knowledgeable regarding hospital procedures, routines, schedules, and illness as it pertains to themselves or their victims and it is seen within the confidence levels they possess during offensive actions.

Offenders gain skill with each offense or interaction they encounter, and it is likely that they think about how they would respond to obstacles within their victimization process. One of those obstacles is getting caught and finding themselves sitting in an interview room with an interrogator. People who commit crimes do this all the time and rehearse in their minds (mentally prepare) how they might react because it is likely their life or their death. Police officers, who also face life/death situations, in a different modality, mentally prepare in anticipation of the dreaded deadly force situation. The analogy is that when the stakes are high, contingency planning is necessary and highly polished skill sometimes allow for error due to over confidence. It is logical to believe FD/FDP offenders prepare with their own contingencies that may be deployed if their criminal actions are discovered.

FD/FDP Offender Reactions

The repetitiveness of FD/FDP-related actions might provide an avenue for the offender to *detach* himself or herself from the actual abusive action inflicted upon the victim and hide the reality of the self-imposed role of *abuser* (FDP) or *victim* (FD) internally within their minds.[1] This mechanism of outward denial may be engaged to allow for the offender's self-preservation. For example, the horror and shame caused by deliberate infliction of harm onto a child would be a difficult reality to openly recognize and still maintain a "normal" lifestyle above the suspicion of family members or outside observers (professional or other). FDP abusers utilizing children or dependent adults have been deemed "great pretenders." Such offenders may lie to themselves regarding parental or custodial worthiness and subconsciously believe they are not responsible for infliction of harm upon the victim. This responsibility detachment fosters the ability to hide from the reality of what actually occurs during each instance of FD/FDP infliction, thus perpetuating created fantasy goals. If a person is permitted to acknowledge their abusive actions during the infliction of harm, they may then see how those actions have affected their victims in horrible and usually painful ways. For some people, this makes FD/FDP offending difficult because the victim is not an object—he or she is a person and reality collides with fantasy.

Determination regarding the existence of conscious detachment between the FD/FDP offender and victimization or an offender's conscientious choice to not disclose the clearly recalled event of FD/FDP abuse may be unknown within the investigative interview process. For either hypothetical situation, if conscious acceptance of the FD/FDP offender's role is not attained during the interview/interrogation process, obtaining a confession or admission of abuse responsibility may not be possible.

When an FD/FDP offender is confronted, the interviewer should recognize the dynamics of denial likely to be prevalent in the offender's mind. The initial reaction of an accused FD/FDP offender is often shock, surprise, and an expression of outward disbelief. This reaction is likely to be followed by attempts to thwart responsibility by offering alternative explanations for an FDP victim's illness causation or alleged criminal victimization in FD situations. Alternative causation explanations offered by the FD/FDP offender often change over time to accommodate either changing physical symptoms within the victim or alleged victimization sequencing. Alternative causation brought forth by the FD/FDP offender also creates an accuser confusion factor that helps tip interview control in favor of the offender by creating doubt. The key to obtaining an admission of guilt when interviewing an FD/FDP offender is providing the pathway to allow an offender the ability to acknowledge the reality of what he or she has done to a victim in the form of direct or indirect harm (FDP) or false victimization reported to law enforcement (FD).

When presented with overwhelming evidence of victim abuse (FDP) or falsification of reported criminal acts (FD), the offender is not likely to readily accept responsibility or acknowledge their part within the victimization scheme. The presentation of incontrovertible evidence to the FD/FDP offender such as video surveillance, victim/offender separation test data, and expert testimony is not likely to produce a responsibility reaction within the offender. Reality may not be enough to persuade the FD/FDP offender to tell the truth regarding their role in victimization or falsification. Lying is a way of life for the FD/FDP offender, and it is unrealistic to expect explicitly truthful statements to readily flow without incentive.

Confrontation of the FD/FDP offender may also elicit a reactionary response of suicide, especially if the interviewer/interrogator is successful in obtaining a confession. In the interview process with an FD/FDP suspect, a confession is often the product of a collision with reality. FD/FDP offenders fluctuate between the world of fantasy and their created world of reality omitting their part in the abuse involving infliction. Coming to terms with the truth is a matter of surrendering to actual circumstance—actual reality—not one that is contrived. Individual offender response to that admission seems to be predicated upon how the FD/FDP offender's family or support circle reacts to disclosure, the consequential severity of victim harm, and the offender's internal capability to assume responsibility. Confession time is a dangerous time for the FD/FDP offender in custody and a potentially deadly time for both offender and abuse victim if the offender is not confined.

Vernon Geberth's observations that suicide is often considered a viable solution to a severe physical or psychological dilemma may be directly relevant to the confrontation process that occurs in cases involving an FD/FDP factor. The psychology of suicide is ranted in depression. Depression is a mood disturbance characterized by feelings of sadness, despair, and discouragement. These feelings become exaggerated and out of proportion to reality. Depressed people perceive themselves negatively. Futures are viewed with despair.[2]

When an FD/FDP offender confession occurs, admission of responsibility for associated victimization may appear to shock everyone, including the offender. Engrained denial within the FD/FDP offender's mind appears to be significant. At the point that an FD/FDP offender faces the reality of his or her behavior and acknowledges their role in victimization, suicidal tendencies may be prevalent once shock subsides. Interviewers should be aware of this tendency and take necessary measures to protect the confessed FD/FDP offender from harming himself or herself.

When an FD/FDP offender is confronted and realizes that he or she has been exposed, extreme elements of fear and shame may be present. These combined elements may serve to seal the offender's ability to "come clean," but unless an "out" is presented, truthfulness regarding the offender's responsibility for criminal acts of abuse or falsified crime reporting is unlikely. The stance taken by the interviewer/interrogator is critical in attaining a successful interview outcome producing an admittance of responsibility. If the interviewer is nonjudgmental and appears genuinely apathetic to the FD/FDP offender, the avenue for dialogue should remain open. Getting the FDP offender to see an FDP abuse child victim as vulnerable and human is necessary.

An effective interview tool is the FDP offender's love for the child victim. Most offenders will not be readily able to explain why they committed acts of abuse upon a child—especially if the child is their own. These types of FDP offenders will initially profess genuine love for their child and staunchly deny victimization responsibility. Subtle suggestion that parental love for a child means doing the right thing and protecting the child whenever possible is a gateway. The FDP offender has an opportunity to help a victim and quite possibly reverse permanent physical damage to the (surviving) victim by disclosing exactly what was done to either make the victim ill or make it seem that they were ill. Telling the truth is the FD/FDP offenders' chance to redeem themselves in the eyes of everyone, and in doing so, right a wrong. Only the FD/FDP offender may know the manner in which alleged victimization occurred or how a proxy victim was assaulted. Disclosing the methodology of abuse allows medical staff to correctly treat symptoms created by the FDP offender. Without this knowledge, the likelihood of victim demise is large and irreversible damage is likely. How a surviving FDP victim will view his or her abuser in the future may very well be determined by the willingness of the offender to help the victim by disclosing truthful facts to the interviewer. The window of opportunity to provide life-changing relationship preserving disclosure is immediate and not likely to ever resurface again. If the FDP offenders (likely) professed love for the FDP child abuse victim is genuine and strong enough, then the offender may theoretically find the strength to place the child victim before himself or herself. This is what any "good" parent would do for their child.

In cases of self-inflicted injury commonly seen in FD situational contexts, accessing the angle of love within the family is an effective gateway toward attaining truth. Who or whatever the FD offender loves may be used as reality points. There is a theoretical link that FD/FDP behavior may be multigenerational. When children are present in either scenario, their potential abuse victimization should be assessed but for the FD offender who has not extended their own self-victimization (in any form) to their child, the potential opportunity to halt the cycle of abuse or prevent potential future child harm is at hand. Pointing out to the FD offender that telling the truth is a proactive means to prevent harm may assist in obtaining truthful statements.

If a point is reached within the interview when the offender comes close to admitting the reality of the situation, and thereby the false allegation or abusive act, the interviewer should expect the offender to attempt a retreat. This retreat may manifest itself in the direct refusal of the offender to answer any further questions or the offender threatening to end the interview if the current line of questioning does not stop. Although this manipulative technique may test the interviewer's patience, it is best to momentarily retreat from the current line of questioning and revisit the issue(s) in another form later during the interview. This process may repeat itself a number of times during the interview process because arriving at a point of truth disclosure is a process.

Revisiting a sensitive topic or area within the interview is an action that allows FD/FDP offenders to feel that they are in control when in reality they are being manipulated by the interviewer. This is role reversal for the FD/FDP offender, as the interviewer possesses the ability to reproach issues in an alternative manner during a chosen time. By controlling perceptions within the interview process, an interviewer of FD/FDP offenders directs the pathway toward the FD/FDP offenders' attainment of reality on a real level. It is a route that may be time consuming and filled with twists and turns. Patience is required. If the FD/FDP knows that the interviewer does not believe him or her, the interviewer may be viewed as an enemy and prevent the necessary bond between offender and interviewer required to traverse the plain between fantasy and reality. Disclosure of doubt regarding the FD/FDP offender's denial of responsibility is a delicate process that must be met with support and care to facilitate continued dialogue and produce truthfulness. This complicated investigative interview process requires skill because just as the FD/FDP offender pretends, so does the interviewer as personal feelings regarding the (often) heinous actions of the FD/FDP offender are repressed. It is usually quite difficult for an interviewer/interrogator to harness personal feelings when child victimization, child death, or severe elderly abuse is a factor within the FD/FDP victimization methodology. Nevertheless, control of these emotions is required.

When FDP offenders utilize their own child as a target proxy and within the scope of FDP infliction outwardly express their love for the child, the question of sincerity presents. Most people would interpret demonstrated or purported love between parent and child as a natural situation but in cases of FDP child abuse the bond appears to also have a symbiotic component because the child is the vehicle used by the offender to attain a desired status or entity. FDP offenders have a fear of losing their victims. A parent who is an FDP offender, in this situation, has a fear of losing the child as a parent but perhaps a greater fear of losing a way of life.

The FD/FDP offender's fear of losing the child should be addressed during the interview because it appears to be one of the primary blocks to obtaining a confession of responsibility. The interviewer may choose to address the FDP offender's need to admit wrongdoing before treatment could begin that would ultimately lead to a normalized futuristic relationship between the FDP offender and his or her victim. Care should be exercised to omit promissory statements of reunification since the likelihood that a child victim will be placed into protective custody or the offender otherwise restricted from access is high when FDP cases are substantiated. The almost certain separation between an FDP offender and child proxy should be minimized during the interview. If the offender chooses to make admissions regarding FD/FDP, realization of loss of child, proxy, personal freedom, personal standing within the family, and shame may flood the offender's thought process overwhelming real or contrived offender rationality.

It appears that the biological family network of the FD/FDP offender plays an intricate supportive role in the ability of FD/FDP offenders to promote victim infliction or patterned victimization fabrication. FD/FDP offenders often describe their spouses as non-supportive when describing the circumstances surrounding victim illness or other circumstances because by design primary responsibility for victim care rests with the FD/FDP offender. At times, physical absence of the non-offending FDP parent for many reasons including work deployment or choice may be seen as a catalyst to inflict abuse or facilitative excuse to offend. It appears that the FD/FDP offenders' deception often includes their spouse, who may outwardly defend and/or support an accused FD/FDP offender through their attempted thwarted responsibility allegations or claims of innocence. It is generally unknown if the FD/FDP offender's spouse routinely has personal doubts or suspicions regarding FD/FDP offender behavior leading to abuse or other falsification avenues.

Spouses of FD/FDP offenders should be interviewed in seclusion from the offender. Presenting evidence to spouses of FD/FDP offenders in support of theoretical FD/FDP behavior alluding to guilt with rationalization of probable reality of criminal responsibility may not be enough to convince them that FD/FDP is a reality. Interviewers should remember that FD/FDP offenders' spouses have likely been afforded the greatest personal offender access and therefore are likely the most significantly entrenched within the offenders' twists of reality. When allegations of FD/FDP behavior are revealed, non-offending spouses are likely to be in a heightened state of denial and defense followed by significant anger.

FD/FDP offenders appear to highly value the personal benefit of bestowed attention and other intangible rewards attained through FD/FDP behavior that the pathway of victimization or falsification outweighs as allowable and justified. The choice to victimize or lie is vetted as correct because it gives the FD/FDP what they want. What has been described as natural instinct for caretakers to protect their dependents is either pushed aside or buried to allow the FD/FDP offender the ability to abuse. After the abusive act (inflicted or verbalized lie), the FDP offender then reinstates the masquerade of a doting parent whose life centers on a chronically ill child that apparently no one can heal. This likely occurs with each and every instance of FDP infliction upon a child by an FDP parental (custodial) offender.

FD offenders seem to possess the chameleon ability to shift between self-abuser and alleged victim then continue an often times long portrayal series of false victimization. For FD offenders, it appears that the ability to grasp the focused attention of crime victims outweighs inconvenience or personal injury associated with the deception. How the allegation of criminal victimization affects the FD offender's family in terms of publicity, internal strife, or consequential interpersonal discord does not seem to matter. The effects of FD alleged victimization in terms of how it may negatively impact others does not outweigh the outcome value to the FD offender: It's all about them.

Confrontation of the FD/FDP offender may ignite responses ranging from vehement denial to attempted suicide. The attention factor upon an accused FD/FDP offender is significant and theorized to fit neatly into the offender's desires—just in a way that they may not have initially envisioned. Within the offender response range to detection, the following responses are noted: psychiatric deterioration, parental removal of a child victim from a medical facility against medical advice, disruption of rapport between medical staff and the alleged FD/FDP offender, and upscale abuse upon the FDP victim to the point of death. FD/FDP offender accusation or the threat of discovery can be dangerous to all involved, and safeguards are necessary.

When a victim's medical condition or series of reported criminal victimizations become tentatively aligned to FD/FDP, suspected offenders have been known to commence a harassment campaign against the accusers (medical staff, law enforcement officials, social worker [child protection] staff, or family members). Harassment is viewed as means to thwart responsibility or cast doubt/blame away from the accused. Recruiting other patients to complain upon the competency of physicians is especially prevalent. Written, oral complaint or instigating unusual events at the physician's workplace and/or home have been noted. The FD/FDP offender may also threaten to litigate but fail to take action[3] (Figure 6.1).

Case reports of FDP victimizations verify the belief that FDP attacks are premeditated and carefully executed covert acts of victim abuse performed with professional precision. Production or simulation of FDP events are rarely identified firsthand by medical professionals or law enforcement officials without the aid of carefully devised

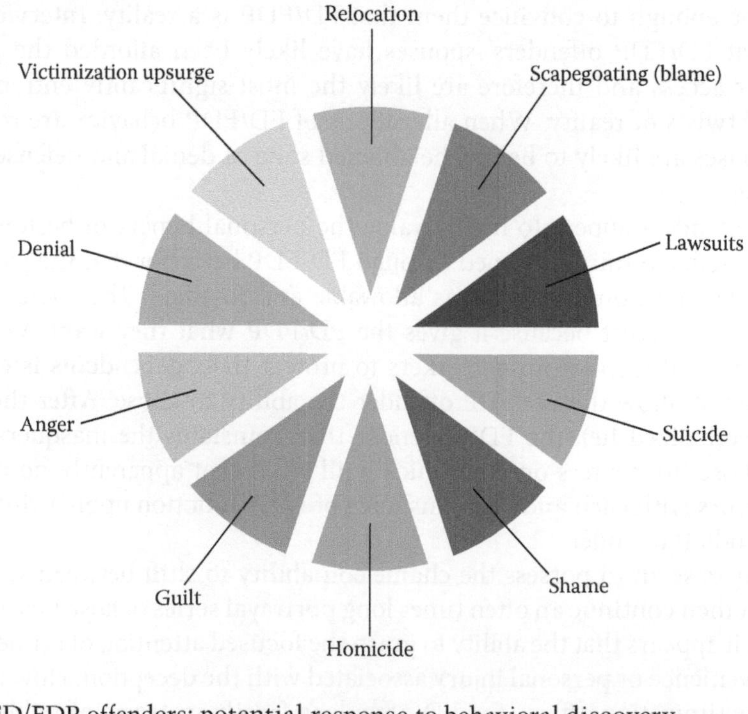

Figure 6.1 FD/FDP offenders: potential response to behavioral discovery.

strategic planning. The most common method of FD/FDP presence verification within abuse case investigations is video surveillance and suspect/victim separation documentation. Attaining video surveillance data within a hospital setting generally requires investigative search warrant application through a multidisciplinary team forum. Evaluation of FDP victim health status in conjunction with alleged FD/FDP offender access removal generally produces vast health improvement within the victim. Data collected from the victim/offender separation is quantitative but generally requires legal inference through restraining orders or forced separation if the offender is incarcerated (see Chapter 7—Evidence).

FD/FDP factors found within abuse/homicide investigations or falsified victimization reporting are difficult to understand within examination of injury and circumstance. Unlike directed physical or sexual abuse upon children or the elderly, the delivery method of the abuse is cloaked and the fact the victim is being injured is an indirect process not easily identified. FDP victim injury is perpetrated through actions of persons historically held above suspicion (mothers). Medical professionals who act in good faith in the treatment of apparently sick individuals become unwilling instruments of medical abuse because of the direct actions of the FDP offender. Engrained medical staff convictions to search out the origin of a person's illness and relieve the problem become the vehicle used by the FDP offender to maximize the desired effect of attention and verification of self-worth. FDP and FD offenders exploit the qualities of conviction and tenacity found within the professional worlds they invade. They use people (victims) that professionals are sworn to assist as vehicles of self-gain and in the process expand their victimization from the directed victim onto the professional caught in the FD/FDP snare. It is not acceptable on any level, and it is criminal.

FD/FDP offenders who utilize professions other than those found within the medical field (law enforcement or firefighters) do so as very convincing crime victims. Tact and skill and education are required to identify the potentiality of FD/FDP presence within all professions, and there is a believability factor due to the bizarre nature of these acts. Professionals generally want to believe that victims or reported victimizations are truthful regarding statements/allegations, and they train within the supportive role. Medical staff does not generally train within the criminal detective role. To uncover FD/FDP within a medical setting, medical staff is required to somewhat cross into the realm of forensic case analysis. When law enforcement is called into a medical case of FD/FDP, they enter from a perspective of criminal abuse investigation and the entire case dynamic changes. It takes a multidisciplinary grasp to enter the world of FD/FDP and emerge with the identification of reality.

When an interviewer is confronted with the possibility of an FD/FDP factor, the interviewer must search deeper and perhaps more diligently than is normally deployed within a case investigative series to find the hidden abusive causes present. Root causes of abuse or the reasons why an FD offender falsifies victimization reports are often masked within the world of hospitalization and medicine. The interviewer's introspective thought process regarding the expectation of how the FD/FDP offender will react to questioning must be open-minded enough to allow the premise that things are not always as they appear and no one is above suspicion. In most FD/FDP cases, there is a marked absence of other abuse forms such as sexual abuse or direct physical abusive injury.

Victims are not routinely brought to the attention of police departments in the bold manner of other abuse victims—they are referred by medical staff or citizens/family members who have directly or indirectly been educated regarding FD/FDP parameters as a form of abuse. In some instances, the reporter may have a higher understanding of FD/FDP concepts than the agency that it is reported to. People who report FD/FDP abuse may become frustrated when the agency or professional does not act quickly to resolve the complaint. This perceived inaction might be actual and based upon the receiving agency or professional's lack of FD/FDP understanding, investigative skill, or demonstrated lack of evidence. FD/FDP has become a baseline rule-out entity in cases of unresolved crimes. It has also become investigative protocol for medical professionals challenged with an inability to resolve apparently complex medical ailments in their patients. The multitude of FD/FDP cases found within medical literature provides an educational basis of understanding FD/FDP within the clinical setting. Social understanding of right vs. wrong and laws governing criminal behavior demand that law enforcement be educated regarding FD/FDP existence as a factor in abuse cases and patterns of unresolved victimization. Ignorance of FD/FDP is not acceptable—ever-increasing numbers of FD/FDP-related cases in both medical and law enforcement realms demands law enforcement awareness.

FD offenders as serial victims of crime or FD-related behavior seen within situations of heroic or exemplary behavior illustrate how knowledge of FD/FDP collides within application. Understanding the reasons why FD/FDP behavior occurs provides alternative understanding or reasoning why a person falsifies criminal reports of victimization; it also reveals why individuals lie about their roles in the resolution of crime. Singular and serial cases of alleged criminal victimization that cannot or have not been resolved may provide parallel case status with unresolved repetitive illnesses through the FD/FDP link. Knowledge of FD/FDP continues to grow within the medical field as evidenced by large amounts of medical literature/publications. FD/FDP research and practical application of knowledge as a crossover into law enforcement realms remains scarce, and if recognition does occur, information is often downplayed. In cases involving FD/FDP, the ability of an interviewer to successfully navigate the internal and external deception field created by the offender to arrive at a place that facilitates truthful response(s) is complicated. The interviewer is influenced by educational parameters of knowledge, field experience, and interrogation skill as the FD/FDP offender's ability is predicated upon practice, knowledge, and offending ability. The match is formidable.

Offender Response

Most identified FD/FDP offenders are associated with average to high intellectual skill levels, but it is assumed that those with lower intellectual skill levels exist. The level of intellectual skill possessed by FD/FDP offenders appears to facilitate the range of deviancy seen within cases. Skill ability is also a factor in potential challenges within the interview process.

FD/FDP offenders possessing high intellectual levels appear to almost enjoy the process surrounding detection especially when detection involves the expansion of professional response. When police become involved in abuse or other case types that have potential inference of FD/FDP, the involvement opens a new or additional door of offender attention. The attention emulates from a source (police) that may have previously been untapped, and it is challenging/stimulating on a likely heightened basis from the levels previously attained from medical staff. Theoretically, FD/FDP offenders see everything like a wager and the risk of their actual behavior being caught/exposed is negated by attained reward. In most cases, by the time law enforcement is associated with an FD/FDP case, polished offender skill is evident and for chronic FD/FDP offenders the challenge to inflict harm or perpetuate the charade of victimization has been dulled because the offensive behavior has been prolonged without detection. The desired effect of unimpeded and prolonged fantasy attainment may not necessarily be attained unless the situation is grand.

Law enforcement appearance within chronic abuse or falsified victimization schemes found to exist in FD/FDP series methodology often creates a new dimension and challenge within the fantastical world of the FD/FDP offender. A heightened awareness of offender's "self" and refocus of attention directly onto the FD/FDP offender is heightened attention attained in a new forum (the police detective). The fact that FD/FDP offenders are generally adept intellectually and physically regarding covert abuse infliction added to the challenge presented when they come under suspicion of FD/FDP behavior by professionals perpetuates the likelihood of increased victim infliction and escalation translating to increased offender attention. Victimization escalation is likely tempered with exposure fear that FD/FDP offenders may realize means loss of target victim control, the end of a prolonged self-victimization, and exposure of reality effectively ending their self-created fantasy world. Fear of these loses could temporarily temper the FD/FDP offender's actions as law enforcement presence means that a very real possibility of detection exists. Law enforcement being called into a situation where FD/FDP behavior may exist is a high stakes game of detection within FD/FDP victimization sequences. Risks are high, but attention and interaction with a new set of "professional" secondary victims are equally high so the games continue.

The profile of an FD/FDP offender will predicate the methodical investigative stature utilized within the investigative interview process. If the intellectual offender level is great, the offender's displayed trapping ability likely to be utilized within the interview process is significantly strengthened. Knowledge regarding an FDP victim's illness or FD offender's intricate details surrounding reported (self) criminalization status is likely to be prevalent. Low intellectual capabilities within the FD/FDP offender could be attributed to isolation, lack of inherent ability to offend, or lack of victimization practice. FD/FDP offenders with low intellectual capabilities increase the likelihood of a successful interview resulting in truth disclosure because the opportunity window is opened wider when the FD/FDP offender has less offensive skill. For offenders confronted early within their victimization pathways, early intervention may find that less time to prepare response contingencies tips the investigative scale in favor of the interrogator.

It is hoped that some FD/FDP offenders may want their self-abuse or abusive actions upon others to stop and may have underlying feeling regarding this. It is difficult to assess the reality of this hope when FD/FDP is nonreality-based, and FD/FDP offenders are master liars. However, assuming that there are some FD/FDP offenders who genuinely long for self-behavioral modification, law enforcement brought into the realm of an FD/FDP case could be viewed as a desired entity—a way for the FD/FDP offender to stop their behavior and victimization. This is a pathway that should be explored during the investigative interview process. Investigators are reminded that the reality base of an FD/FDP offender is not normal and a truly remorseful FD/FDP offender may lack the ability or desire to expose their true feelings regarding their role in victimization. The nature of

FD/FDP actions centers upon living life through lies, and this makes the determination of validity difficult in FD/FDP interrogation efforts: how can FD/FDP offender response be evaluated as genuine? The answer is cautiously and carefully.

Shell of Protection

Exposure of FD/FDP behavior within investigations has interactive family dynamic concerns that act as potential roadblocks within the investigative process. FD/FDP offenders have reasons why they fail to disclose their abusive or falsification tendencies and there has been debate regarding the ability or inability of an FD/FDP offender to provide truthful statements when confronted. Truthful disclosure regarding offense responsibility will mean a lifestyle change for the FD/FDP offender due to permanent or temporary loss of the object utilized to attain fantasy fulfillment (usually a child in FDP situations) or the loss of the response vehicle used for that same fulfillment (professional response groups within medical–law enforcement or fire department response in FD situations). FD/FDP offenders may fear family reprisal due to the abuse magnitude or associated family shame. Most insignificantly, FD/FDP offenders may fear incarceration—not due to the logistics involved, but rather the associated isolation and anonymity that incarceration bestows from within.

The breakdown of the shell of protection FD/FDP offenders attain from within the family (note family within hospital vs. biological family) is formidable for the FD/FDP offender. Secondary victims found within FD/FDP cases provide the existence of a fantastical reality that entails offensive behavior so rehearsed and repetitive that the dynamic becomes a chosen way of life to the offender. The prospect of losing the protective barrier attained through anonymity and nondetection allowing the offender to dwell within the world of the professionals and garner attention and sense of being is not something that FD/FDP offenders want. It is not due to fear of punishment that the FD/FDP offender may become a difficult interview subject. The difficulty rests within offender fear that the reality and way of life the offender has so carefully orchestrated is now threatened by exposure and collapse.

Judgment of intrafamilial contacts and zero support of personnel may be of high concern. Innate FD/FDP offender desires to be loved and accepted by medical or other professional personnel seen as *family* and that potential loss is probably frightening. Breakdown of this fantastical world may be of primary concern to the FD/FDP offender at the time of exposure. Child victim's (FDP) welfare is likely to remain secondary even though FD/FDP offenders portray otherwise. Apparent parental concern toward child victims may be a continuation of the deception according to review of known cases. There is, however, an apparent tipping point regarding truth disclosure that is derived from showing an FD/FDP offender that disclosure is at hand and providing a reason and pathway for probative redemption through truthful disclosure of abusive acts.

Publication and media attention surrounding FD/FDP case scenarios educates all viewers, including FD/FDP offenders. Progressive evidentiary cover-up is a concern. The behavioral patterns of FD/FDP offenders portray a sophistication in prethought victimization methodologies that extends into all realms of professional inclusion into the FD/FDP snare. It is likely that FD/FDP offenders formulate contingency plans and response protocols should they encounter law enforcement or other regulatory agencies and find themselves in suspect roles. The assumption that pivotal contingency plans have been devised by the FD/FDP offender to address the interjection of law enforcement should be uniform for each suspected FD/FDP abuse or false allegation case encountered. The interviewing technique associated within these types of cases should be adjusted accordingly. In many instances, the interview scenario between FD/FDP offender and the interrogator can become a professional game of cat and mouse with control of the interview passing from player to player.

Portrayed Multiple Personality Concerns

FD/FDP offenders have responded to questioning regarding their role in abuse or falsified reporting of crime in terms of "other self." Episodes of recalled actions that are emotionally significant or particularly intense seem to be viewed by FD/FDP offenders in two distinct categories: inside and outside of oneself. The response an FD/FDP offender has to allegations of abuse in terms of "other" seems to be a mechanism to escape direct responsibility when confronted. Interviewers of FD/FDP offenders may find that speaking to them in the realm of "other self" is a pathway toward facilitating dialogue by allowing for responsibility escape while establishing effective pathways within investigative interrogation.

FD/FDP offenders may portray themselves in an authoritarian manner during the investigative interview process as they defer responsibility by indicating that they cannot control their *other self*. They may seemingly truly believe this. The technique of placing responsibility for one's actions onto another has been identified in interrogations as attempted manipulation and to establish a futuristic defense platform. When an FD/FDP offender expresses that they truly believe they are more than one person, the interviewer should ask when the *other* person appeared in such a significant manner that the *whole person became aware of the part*. If the FD/FDP offender truly feels different while offending, then how does the alternative person, or *other*, consider the nonoffending part? Is the establishment of a multiple personality a convenient explanation when detection becomes a reality?

The *reality* of living with the stigma of an FD/FDP offender status is intense public scrutiny that affects the offender's self-view and coping mechanism regarding self-responsibility for offensive actions. Conventional interviewing methods may be ineffective when confronting an FD/FDP offender. The reality base of an FD/FDP offender infliction is thwarted through deceptive acts and the *other self* may emerge within the interview process. Allowing an FD/FDP offender to embrace and divulge this belief as a receptive listener facilitates supportive structure during discussions. Ask how the person being interviewed views the person who committed abuse or falsified victimization. Allowing the FD/FDP offender to express thoughts regarding how FD/FDP offenses have changed his or her life is powerful venting that may facilitate acknowledgement of the *other person* within the interview. There is great fear associated with disclosure for all FD/FDP offenders because the *whole* offender may be fully aware of their *lesser self* who only surfaces during times of dire circumstance. The *whole* offender may only feel in control of the *lesser self* when kept hidden and blamed or responsibility may be seen as belonging to the *lesser self.* As a means of self-preservation, the *whole* FD/FDP offender may create someone to blame regardless of reality. Admissions of responsibility require accessing the FD/FDP offender's *lesser self.*

Recalling that FD/FDP offenders seem to create a factitious vacuum in which they reside helps outsiders to understand that an FD/FDP offender's reality is not what is dealt to them according to fate. Reality is what offenders choose to recall and elaborately create to make their individual worlds temporarily *perfect* or at least acceptable.

FD/FDP offender behavioral observations are often subtle entities as the demarcation line between perfection and reality is crossed. An interviewer attempting to bridge this threshold does so through short interjections of specific non-offensive reality into the inner circle of perfectionism in which the FD/FDP offender dwells. Look at who surrounds the offender; it is normally immediate family who strongly vocalize the accused FD/FDP offender's innocence or adoptive family found within professional communities who are often shocked regarding abuse allegations. Strength is drawn from them. Perhaps the greatest fear an interviewer of FD/FDP offenders must overcome is the fear of the withdrawal of family support and associated personal judgment. The disclosure of FD/FDP reality and admission of abuse is contrary to what a family wants to believe. There are so many reasons why this is accurate including self-admission that *they should have recognized the problem* especially prevalent if a proxy victim dies. The ability to persuade the FD/FDP offender that reality is preferable to fantasy is a difficult task but recognizing this may allow the interviewer to understand why an FD/FDP offender chooses to linger in fantasy when provable reality is present. This understanding may help to bridge the gap that prevents FD/FDP offenders from being truthful with themselves and with you.

Fantasy versus Reality

Personal desire is sometimes viewed as reality for the FD/FDP offender, and when confronted about discrepancy, defensive posture emerges through denial of the statement or other intended meaning. FD/FDP offenders sometimes reveal that former or estranged spouses or other family members are dead. Death is a relative state the offender may convey in either a physical or emotional status. Dismissal of a spouse/family member emotionally may be viewed as a technique of disassociation if the spouse/family member is directly related to an FDP child abuse victim. Specific association of the child victim as direct connection to a spouse is often seen through the traits/characteristics attributed to one parent or the other. If the offender feels that the child is not connected to him or her and verbalizes issues such as anatomy or traits as likened to their spouse (or significant other), this disassociation may help facilitate the death of the child victim. The child becomes a symbol of the relationship or person viewed as dead.

A fine line between love and hate may have validity here in the potential transfer between a family member and a child victim. Allegations of domestic violence between FD/FDP offenders and their spouses often surface with intense emotions. FD/FDP offenders have stated that they were greatly wronged by their spouses either in actuality (physical abuse), intangibility (emotional abuse) or through a fabricated series of victimizations. An FD/FDP offender's verbalization of events associated with spouses or significant others may be viewed as a means to justify committed action or abuse and spoken as a need to convey to the listener. FD/FDP offenders often see their role in existing interpersonal relationships as that of a victim. They may view themselves as clean and holy. People tend to recall their victimization and relive it through verbal testimony to others in attempt to reaffirm innocence and justify action or inaction. By telling the story of one's victimization and gaining approval of the listener, a character vindication occurs along with some amount of sympathy. The process and result produces attention for the storyteller.

Suggested FD/FDP Interview Dialogue

When FD/FDP offenders realize they are not alone in their behavioral choices, they may be somewhat comforted. If the interviewer behaviorally understands the experience of self- or applied abuse or reported victimization and this understanding is effectively conveyed to the FD/FDP offender, open communication becomes possible. The eloquent observation that change is always a possibility in one's life serves to further bridge the communicative gap surrounding an FD/FDP offender. Allowing an interview subject to exit an interrogative sequence with dignity provides further enhancement of communicative possibilities.

For FDP abuse cases that rise to homicide, issues of the FD/FDP offender's self-blame for the victim's death may be prevalent. The interviewer may see this manifested in staunch denial and vehement accusations toward others or a more introverted response of uncertainty and trepidation. Reassurance conveyed to the suspected FD/FDP offender that blame is pointless for things that cannot be changed might ease tensions. The following is an example of FD/FDP interview predicate utilized during the interview of a suspected FDP homicide suspect.

> Something had to make you do these things. I think that he made this happen. I sit here today with you and I can understand how this could have occurred. I can understand why this happened. I can see that this is not only your responsibility. I can see that the responsibility also belongs to someone else. You must have had an idea of what being married to _____was going to be like, didn't you? What you thought your life was going to be wasn't what it turned out to be, was it?
>
> I'm not here to judge you. I'm not here to prove anything. I am here to better understand why your situation progressed to this point so that something good can come out of this whole mess. You see, you're not alone in your feelings and your motivations for why certain things happened in your life are not unique. You are not alone in your fears about allowing yourself to admit what happened. Everyone has fears—things that they are afraid of. Fear is a funny thing, though, once you understand what causes fear, it becomes a less controlling force in your life. We understand that you are concerned about what other people are going to think because you are not the only person that has found herself in this position.
>
> I want you to understand that you're not alone anymore. I can only imagine just how alone you must have felt all this time. I understand what happened to you. I know how this happened and I know why you haven't been able to tell us directly. I've studied all of the events that occurred in your life and I want you to know that I know! There's no reason for you to hide anymore or to pretend. It's OK for you to be scared. It's OK for you to let yourself feel anger and sorrow at the same time. It's OK for you to tell me. I understand.
>
> There isn't anything that we can do that will bring your child(ren) back, but there is something that we can do today, right here and now, that will make their lives more meaningful.

> I'm sure that if they're looking down upon us today and were able to speak, they'd want their mommy to tell the truth and to get better. You know that those children loved you unconditionally. Your children, like all children, would want their mommy to be well. Your children would want their other brothers and sister—your living children—to be safe, happy, and able to love their mother. Do you really think you can continue your life without dealing with your past? Healing can't begin until fear and hurt are gone—really gone, not just pretend. The only way to get rid of the hurt and fear is to confront it by telling the truth. You may never have this opportunity to do the right thing again.

Hidden Admissions

When the FD/FDP offender rationalizes a victim's condition by offering injury or death explanations such as a child gave himself or herself an overdose by misreading dosage or a child was infected through dirty medication then needed, inner knowledge of FD/FDP infliction mode may be revealed. Allegations by the FD/FDP offender that an abuse victim is responsible for a medical condition may also indicate FDP offender–victim collusion. This may not necessarily indicate conscious acts of wrongdoing by the abuse victim who may be exhibiting learned behavior from the offender as a state of norm. The delivery manner of these types of offender statements may be clues to the offender's inner feelings. For example, excitement may indicate patterned fulfillment, and downtrodden/bashful demeanor may indicate sadness at the realization that the offender now has to substantiate her deviancy due to threatened exposure. Exhibitions of contrasting personalities with outward actions/reactions to various types of questions are sometimes viewed as an FD/FDP offender's manipulative behavioral ability.

If the FD/FDP offender is in actuality not the mother of a child proxy abuse victim but another relative, statement(s) made by that relative concerning the lack of a suspected FD/FDP offenders ability (generally the biological mother of the victim) to offend may become direct testimonial linkage regarding abuse infliction knowledge. In some cases, when the FDP offender (not the victim's biological parent) is a relative of a child abuse victim, interviewers may find themselves interviewing a biological mother as an FD/FDP suspect when in reality they are interviewing a witness. This witness may possess innate knowledge of FD/FDP tendencies and refuse to disclose it. Refusal of a relative to disclose known involvement of abuse may emanate from a history of intrafamilial abuse or self-abuse. There may be threats of punishment associated with disclosure or family shame. Identification of an FD/FDP offender is not always direct and in accordance with standardized investigative assumptive procedures. What seems real may not be and those who seem to be a suspect may be revealed otherwise. Adaptation during the interview of any circumstances connected to FD/FDP is required along with the very real need to remain open-minded to allow the pathway to truth to reveal itself.

Investigative Observations

Medical maladies that are not medically substantiated are sometimes indexed as potential indulgences of FD/FDP offenders. The FD/FDP offender commonly interprets fabrication as true belief. Use of computer-voice stress analysis devices or polygraphs within the investigative process may or may not illuminate as deception. If you truly believe you are telling the truth, can you fool these machines? Most FD/FDP offenders are confident that they can.

In some FD/FDP cases, superstition or religious belief plays a prominent role in the care of an ill child or other dependent. Ideals are commonly passed down from generation to generation unless they are culturally specific. Belief may be indicative of further misconceptions commonly associated with superstitions. An in-depth check into the cultural heritage of the suspected FD/FDP offender to determine if actions are cumulative cultural diversity or family specific is warranted. The use of this example of abnormal/misconceived thinking within the interview process as a reference point to perceived normality is useful. If an FD/FDP offender is perpetuating a mutigenerational cycle of abuse/infliction, it will be necessary to establish a reference point of the offenders own victimization to anchor the notion of acceptable versus unacceptable behavior and right versus wrong. The interviewer should not assume that these concepts are innate in the FD/FDP offender when a multigenerational abuse link is suspected.

An FDP child abuser's statement of residential relocation, although sometimes veiled, may indicate the presence of prethought within the offender's mind. Flight factor seems predicated upon threat exposure seen by questioning the validity of a child's illness. This questioning may originate from any professionals involved within the FD/FDP deception or it may originate from other sources. Perceived exposure by the FD/FDP offender may be of slight circumstance such as a passing remark or it may be grandiose such as a criminal arrest. The tolerance level to exposure possessed by FD/FDP offenders seem directly linked to their longevity as an offender directly supporting their offending skill capability and associated confidence levels. These observations fit directly within known FD/FDP offender profile standards.

A focal point or catalyst of FD/FDP origination may stem within a community event such as a fundraising effort for an FDP child abuse victim (seen as a chronically ill child). The ability to recognize motive in cases involving FD or FDP equates to an ability to link direct or indirect associated gain to an offender. Accessing individuals who are knowledgeable about the family before public attention was invoked coupled with review of family dynamic changes with the advent of a victim's chronic illness or an FD/FDP offender's status as the chronic crime victim provides a range basis of measurable change. Associated gain is indirect deduction of intangible assets such as attention or belonging. The intangible gains attained from FD/FDP infliction may be mingled with tangible benefit but not as a primary motivator. Long-term FD/FDP abuse methodologies have financial and relative components to them despite the factitious world encircling. How is a family financially supported during the chronic hospitalization of a child? How does an FD offender provide living essentials if always playing the role of victim? Employment is generally limited or nonexistent for the FD/FDP offender so creativity to ensure adequate financial coverage to exist is required. The choices at hand involve secondary victimization and fabrication to extremes.

FD/FDP offenders accessing the medical professions may have legitimate initial doctor visits or may result as an over anxious response to a normal condition. Patterns of hospitalization for children take on a different air when fabrication or suspected fabrication is introduced. Fabrication levels may show an escalation in intensity, frequency, and alleged severity that often correlate within known characteristics of an FD/FDP offender.

When authorities begin to suspect FD/FDP as a causative agent for a victim's illness or a person's unresolvable reported status as a crime victim, how and how much of this suspicion is initially shared with the suspected FD/FDP offender may have bearing on immediate futuristic behavior. It is not uncommon for FD/FDP offenders to become *experts* in the field of FD/FDP investigation and disclose this during the interview process—especially at the point when they become aware they are suspected of FD/FDP behavior.

During the investigative process, it is important to remember that FD/FDP offenders have capabilities of deception far beyond the norm seen within society. The FD/FDP offender's manipulative skill has historically been so entrenched within their character it becomes rather natural. Intermeshing of factitious circumstances within the world of reality and bending reality through fabrication or idealization aides the FD/FDP offender to believe fantasy is reality. This premise is often seen during the investigative interview.

When an FD/FDP offender has progressed to the point of active infliction, it is rational to believe this offending status has emerged from a prolonged period of *practice*. Within the FD/FDP probable connection, a practical link of self-abuse or crime victimization reporting placing the FD/FDP offender within the role of victim is possible. FD offenders who are intertwined within the hospitalization/medical realm or those who fit into the category of self-inflicted crime victim should be looked at closely when they possess access to dependent children or the elderly or when immediate dependents (familial or other) have died while in the custody of the suspected FD/FDP offender. FD/FDP offenders may have a history of self-hospitalization and signs or symptoms of illness that mirror their dependants.

When illness is falsified within an FD format upon oneself then unresolvable illness appears within the dependant (child or elderly) of the same FD offender, consideration of projected abuse methodology is warranted. It is likely that FD offenders who gravitate to FDP infliction have had significant *practice* regarding every aspect of abuse infliction. Reviewing the initial sequence of an FDP abuse victim's hospitalizations may reveal that the FDP offender was searching for medical causes to explain real or fabricated abuse victim behavior that may have been considered *less than perfect*.

Seeking blame for lack of child parenting skill rather than considering the cause of a child's undesired behavior as a consequence of parenting responsibility may prompt respite within the world of FDP abuse infliction. A *medical parenting partnership* is the resulting link when FDP offenders use the medical profession through victim abuse to tell themselves they are good parents. FD/FDP offenders garner medical staff support physically, emotionally, intellectually, and interpersonally when dependants or themselves are hospitalized. The same warped interaction is interpreted when FD/FDP offenders utilize other professions—especially law enforcement.

As FDP child abuse victims mature, associative upbringing challenges test the parenting skill just like any other child would. When an FDP mother sets the reliance predicate for coping or addressing parental issues upon medical or other professions, a grave concern regarding long-term victim morbidity exists. An overwhelmed parent who chooses to transfer parental responsibility to others through shared parenting found within FDP abuse methodology presents a high degree of instability. Such a parent may not be willing to recognize his or her own parental failure and when confronted with abuse suspicion, may escalate infliction abuse upon the child to reinforce attention required for him or her to believe through external/internal validation that he or she is not only good, but also an exemplary parent. It does not seem to matter that the FDP offender knows that parental worthiness is directly opposite what is portrayed, acknowledged, or projected. FDP offenders have summarized this concept by stating: "I am consumed by being a parent."

The reality of FD/FDP as an entity in abuse cases or self-reported factitious crime victimizations is that it does exist. FDP is a known factor in child abuse and is generally seen as a rule in or out entity when unresolved illness is present in a child. FD has long been recognized within medical circles, but it now is a factor when repetitive crime victimization with singular victims cannot be resolved. The dynamics of FDP differ from traditionally known child abuse formats, and countermeasures are predicated upon initial theoretical links generally within the medical realm. Bringing law enforcement into these theoretical abuse situations early helps to establish criminality of the cases, but more importantly, it aids the victim through a medical–law enforcement partnership.

For many professionals on all platforms, acceptance and recognition of FD/FDP remain difficult due to *believability issues* that dance with their scientific counterparts. Thorough investigative procedures are critical to provide provability for initial *suspicion* or theory of FD/FDP existence. FD/FDP recognition is predicated by professional intuitiveness and education. The relationship between law enforcement, medical personnel, social services, and the judiciary creates components for interdisciplinary team assembly required in FD-/FDP-linked cases toward efforts of identification and case solvability.

The complicated potential status of FD/FDP offenders with alternative coexisting issues illustrates the wide-ranging aspects of an FD/FDP case investigation. An alleged multiple personality issue, presented either as defense modes or perhaps in actuality, is an example regarding knowing the limits of interviewer capability. Criminal case detectives are generally not doctors; therefore, during the interrogation process, care should be taken to not address potential medical or psychological offender needs. Criminal interviewers cannot render or suggest medical/psychological treatment and should refrain from addressing these issues. If a true multiple personality situation exists within the FD/FDP offender, detectives may find that by diagramming the offender's behavior on opposite spectrums, clarification of presence may emerge. Clarification of claimed multiple personality or multiple situational levels may provide offender characterization understanding and establish a multiple-level basis for investigative stance within the interview process.

FD/FDP Offender Confrontation/Interview Techniques

Procedural Summation

- Statement of the situation (clear and simple).
- Supportive versus accusatory: "We know other mothers that have done similar things; you are not alone in your feelings right now."
- Diversion/offender's aggressive referrals to thwart suspicion.
- Stress health of the victim; emphasis should be placed upon the importance of knowing what is medically wrong with the victim. Lack of understanding the exact nature of infliction or fabrication is a medical emergency.

- Love of the offender for the victim-bonding as an investigative tool.
- Unknowns in the victim's medical future catalyst. The opportunity to either reverse or halt further victim damage rests in the hands of the FD/FDP offender through avenues of honest disclosure. This opportunity may never reappear and present choices have long-term effects on physical, emotional, and relationship levels.
- Be prepared to protect an FDP victim immediately through court-mandated protective measures at the time an FD/FDP offender is confronted or accused. FDP abuse is a crime of shame similar to incest, and there is a natural tendency to tell no one. There is also a legitimate concern of *evidence disposal.* The FDP victim is considered the most significant *evidence* within a criminal case prosecution. Offenders who realize this may move toward directed homicide followed by cremation. Means required to protect *evidence* in suspected cases of FDP that rise to the level of victim death involve court orders and medical examiner holds on deceased victims—especially when cases are in the suspicion index and not yet linked to provability.

FD/FDP Criminal Abuse Investigative Interview Tips

1. If the FD/FDP offender is aware of the suspicion link, he or she may have an attorney on retainer. Be prepared for statements such as: "I have nothing to say" and being handed a phone with an attorney on the other end.
2. Be prepared for the FD/FDP offender to advise his or her children: "they are taking me (your mommy or daddy) away." Law enforcement may have to restrain family members when removing an FD/FDP offender from their presence. This offender statement elicits sympathy and support from family immediately present and establishes a unification base of support.
3. Be ready for feigned illness as an escape mechanism utilized by the FD/FDP offender at the time of custodial arrest or when threat of custodial arrest is likely.
4. Do not expect FD/FDP offenders to be ignorant regarding FD/FDP research. FD/FDP offenders will have been actively engaged in all aspects of infliction much longer than agency staff or professionals who engage them. The exceptional deceptive ability of FD/FDP offenders should be recognized by the interviewer and the offender's knowledge of FD/FDP explored.
5. Be honest with yourself regarding how you feel about people who victimize children and the elderly. Deal with your emotions on this subject before you attempt to understand and interview the offender.
6. Interviewers are human and being perfect is not part of being human—everyone makes mistakes. When professionals enter the world created by FD/FDP offenders, not all cases end favorably for victims. Professionals doing their best is what is required to survive those cases that end in victim death. Be kind to yourself and get educated.
7. Parental reaction to the loss of a child and a child's reaction to the loss of a parent or other family member are wide-ranging. There are no right or wrong outward responses absolutely indicative of foul play during an interview. Keeping an open mind as FD/FDP offenders are interviewed provides investigative options and enhances the possibility of uncovering the truth.

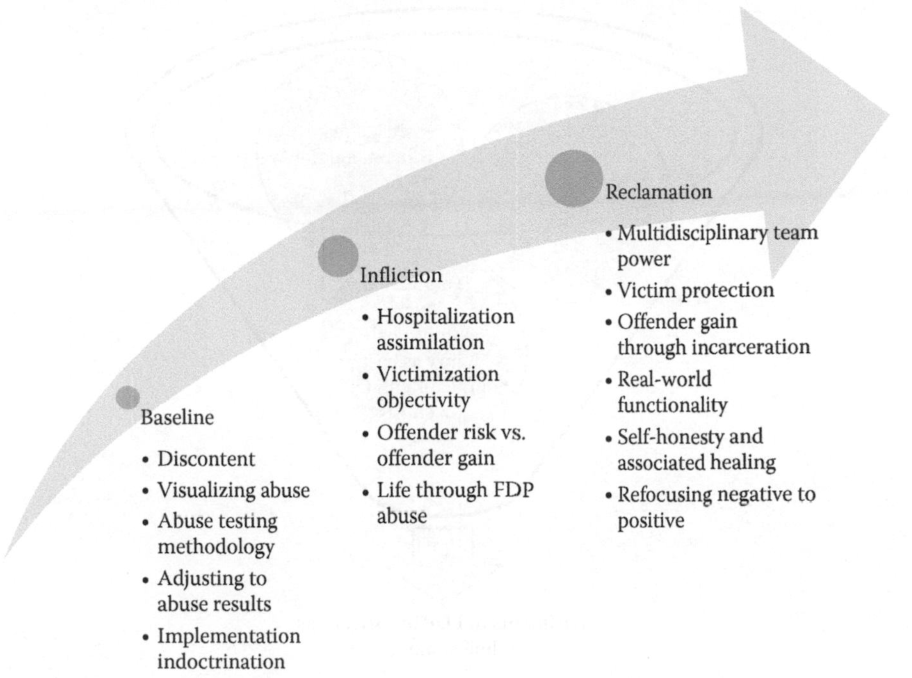

Figure 6.2 FDP victimization sequencing.

8. It is not the interviewer's obligation to believe witnesses; it is their job to be objective fact finders.
9. Consider all possibilities and listen to all witnesses before attaining a conclusion.
10. Do not be influenced by political pressure in your case evaluation (Figure 6.2).

Clinical Interaction/Interviews with Suspected FDP Offenders

Although the physicians' role is medical–patient safety and therefore forensics are part of the interview mantra. Using open-ended questions, structured interviews, and active listening is helpful. Questions should be gauged to the developmental ability of children or their parents being questioned. Consideration of maltreatment of a victim, especially a child as part of the differential diagnosis, is difficult to bridge for many physicians. Controlling prejudice and preconceptions is required and required self-awareness.[4] Obtaining clear, accurate history is vital to a physician when evaluating a situation for abuse, but this is invariably difficult if not seemingly impossible when an the object of the interview is a person whose behavior is likened to FD/FDP behavior.

When clinicians suspect that patients (FD) or the parents of patients (FDP) are exaggerating symptoms or fabricating or inducing illness, the basis of doctor–patient relationship predicated upon trust and confidentiality changes. This change often places the clinician into an uncomfortable and unfamiliar position.[5]

Clinicians view the interview of a person suspected of FD or FPD behavior from a medical diagnostic viewpoint. The main objective for a medically based interview is to

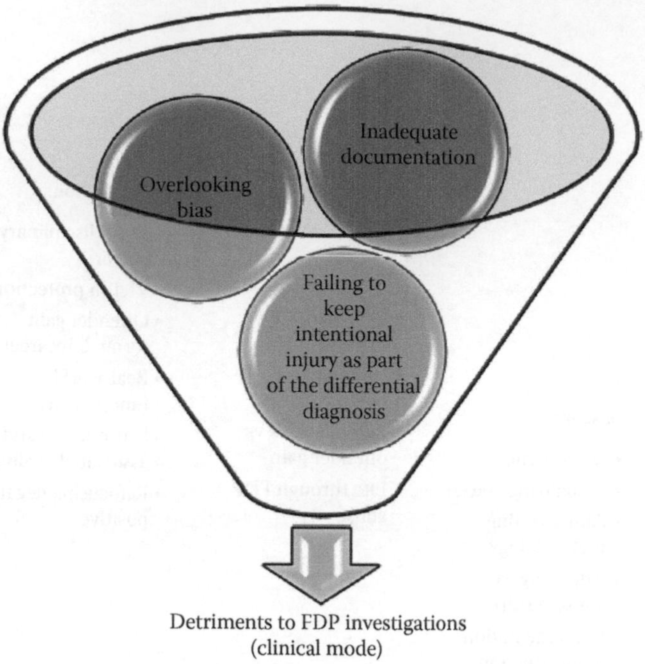

Figure 6.3 FD/FDP case investigations: interview obstacles.

assess the health status of a patient and plan a treatment pathway. Delving deeply into questions pertaining to the establishment of a crime, within FDP victimization, requires detailed interview processes commensurate with a criminal investigation. Evidence gathering from a child protective service or law enforcement platform produces a detailed level of fact-finding that may be absent when clinical staff alone conducts suspect interviews.[6]

Within an FDP interview sequence, the interviewer should be aware that three items may be detrimental to the interview process, and therefore, awareness is critical to enhance the likelihood of success[7] (Figure 6.3).

Notes

1. Geberth, V.J., Suicide. *Law and Order Magazine*, October 1996, pp. 163–166.
2. See Note 1.
3. Rosenberg, D., From lying to homicide, in: *Munchausen Syndrome by Proxy*, Levin, A. and Sheridan, M. (Eds.). New York: Lexington Books, 1995, p. 24.
4. Stirling, J., The conversation—Interacting with parents when child abuse is suspected. *Pediatric Clinics of North America*, 2014;61:979–995.
5. Commentary. WWW.thelancet.com, Vol. 383, April 19, 2014.
6. American Professional Society on the Abuse of Children, *Practice Guidelines: Investigative Interviewing in Cases of Suspected Child Abuse*. Chicago, IL: American Professional Society on the Abuse of Children, 2002.
7. See Note 4.

Crime Scene and Evidentiary Procedures

7

Trust but verify.

Ronald Reagan

Evidence by Definition

Evidence is the fundamental element upon which all criminal cases are built. It is also the data that determines the conclusion of every criminal case. Evidence is of paramount importance in the evaluation of FDP. The value of evidence within this evaluation is attributed to how the court views the evidence, evidence strength and (type), and the court's reaction to it. Courts must determine that a crime took place and that the suspect (defendant) was responsible for the crime. There are seven basic types of evidence: toxicology, pathology, statistics (repeated instances), inconsistencies, confession, eyewitness, and evidence of attendance (access)[1] (Figure 7.1).

Within FDP investigations, evidence has a twofold purpose: it provides verification for a medical diagnosis and proof for legal proceedings. In FD situations seen as chronic victimization reports, evidence either substantiates a victimization claim or supports the establishment of a falsified report. Evidence gathering in FD- and FDP-linked casework is complicated by disguise and deception making evidence recognition problematic. An associative factor of misinterpretation when potential FD/FDP evidence is collected and linked to medical or legal investigative work may impede the investigative process if probable evidence is evaluated on the sole basis of face value. Detectives are often reminded in the course of FD/FDP investigations that acceptance of anything at face value without specific verification and intuitive linking is a mistake. Evidence can either be direct or circumstantial.

In FDP abuse or homicide situations, what happened is determined by fact and proven by evidence to support the fact; it is not determined by psychiatric expertise when facts are disputed and no diagnosis determines behavior.[2]

An intangible line exists between the recognition of behavior as mental illness and accountability. Medical entities are capable of identifying behavior, recognizing consequences, and placing an appropriate label (diagnosis); they are not empowered with the determination of accountability. Accountability rests within the criminal justice system and such determination is often predicated upon the examination of modus operandi (MO), intent, and measurable gain.

In various cases involving a factitious element, the evaluation or recognition of measurable gain isn't usually directly evident; it is indirectly obtained. Direct benefit is usually something easily defined because it cannot be denied. Direct benefit may affect its benefactor monetarily or through other tangible assets and has a value to anyone receiving it.

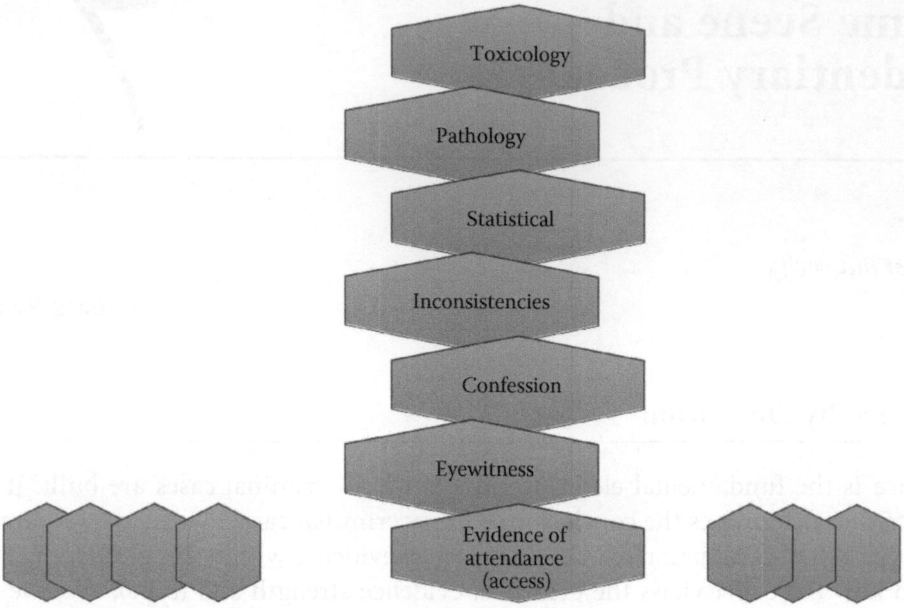

Figure 7.1 Evidence typology.

Indirect benefit is measurable gain cloaked in a shroud of secrecy and difficult to recognize. The benefactor usually receives intangible gain(s) whose value is specific, extraordinary, and odd in terms of normalized behavior. Even if the intangible gain is blatantly displayed, it may not be recognized by anyone other than the specifically direct benefactor. Recognition of the hidden indirect value to an offender radiating from the victimization of another through illness, deception, or death of the victim is often difficult to measure without a confession.

MO in criminal or civil cases involving a factitious disorder factor provides behavioral clues regarding methodology of victimization. Gathering evidence is painstakingly detailed and calls for investigative inferences and multidimensional collaboration often within the medical or psychological field.

FD/FDP Crime Scene

In generally accepted crime scene scenarios, the crime scene will "talk" to the detective if the detective knows how to listen to the crime scene. In FD/FDP investigations, the opposite is true; the detective must often rely on a medical professional's investigative ability to recognize the presence that a crime has been committed and the crime scene is obscured. Recognition factors are predicated upon education and experience and unfortunately, in many communities, notification may take years. Medical staff may be reluctant to notify law enforcement when all they have are suspicions or theory. When probable recognition of FD/FDP does occur, medical staff is generally a vehicle of victim abuse attainment, and there may be fear of victimization accountability and a reluctance to report when this is realized.

The gathering of "proof" in FD/FDP suspected situations often produces direct confrontation with suspects. Suspect response to this confrontation or accusation is often effectuated escape through relocation. Residential relocation to a new community facilitates an undetected repetitive abuse cycle to continue as concept isolation generally prevails. Relocation also allows an FD/FDP offender to begin a new victimization cycle with unsuspecting secondary victims and simulate ignorance when confronted with suspicion or questions.

An FD/FDP crime scene has qualities of progression, transformation, and instability—all obscured in deception. A time element or constraint is a qualitative/investigative motivator in FD/FDP crime scene analysis that ignites concern regarding victim safety. This concern often limits the investigator's ability to "sluggishly" examine the spoils of a possible criminal act. When FD/FDP offenders are alerted that they are under suspicion of wrongdoing, victims whom are placed in a higher risk of jeopardy and threatened harm may gravitate to a demonstrated victimization enhancement. Investigative expediency to address a likely upsurge in victim harm must be tempered with an entire family's flight/reality and victimization recidivism concerns. If suspicion/theory of FD/FDP cannot be validated, chronic victimization escalation is likely. It may occur in a different location and may extend to victims other than presently connected, but it is likely to repeat (Figure 7.2).

Flexible criminal investigative protocol establishment before an FD/FDP case is disclosed to a suspected FD/FDP offender is crucial for effective case management. The life of the FDP victim often dangles within the balance of criminal conduct theory versus provability. Provability of FDP as a factor in suspected abuse cases is conditional upon proper evidence collection and recognition that the evidence collected (which predicates the initial or enhanced mobilization of suspicion) has value.

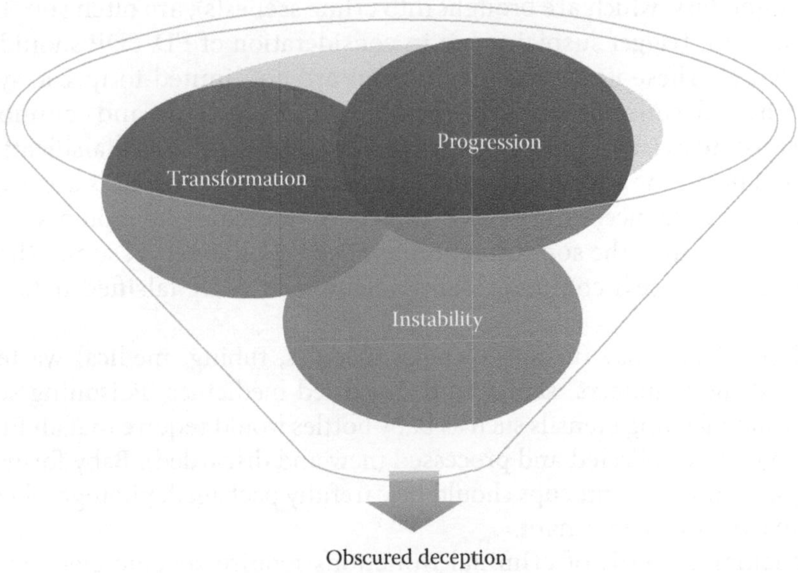

Figure 7.2 Crime scene qualities with factitious factors.

Rapists may bring along a "rape kit" when they perpetrate. The FDP offender utilizing abuse methodology may also bring along items elemental to a "FDP kit," but more often than not, FDP kit items are appropriated at or near the crime scene. For example, pillows and the offender's body are frequently utilized in the smothering of young FDP child victims; hypodermic needles may be "lifted" from hospital carts for poisoning by injection; poisons injected are frequently appropriated from bacteria found in hospital toilets and dirt on the floors; the falsification of medical charts requires only a pen in the hand of an FD/FDP offender and opportunity to write on a medical chart. Falsification of symptoms without infliction needs nothing at all other than the offender's body and mind, and the presence of blood in a child's diaper can be initiated through the FDP offender expressing his or her own blood and placing it into a diaper (blood attained by the offender biting his or her own tongue or by other means).

Consequently, the definition of a crime scene at the site of an FD/FDP investigation may be vast and may incorporate ordinary items that normally would be overlooked due to acceptable presence. Items of evidentiary value are often hiding in plain sight. Specific items that detectives should search for and account within a search warrant should be formulated from a combination of known factors and theories concerning the proposed origination of a victim's illness. The greatest evidence in an FDP case, however, often remains locked within the mind of the FDP offender, and accessing this evidence requires directed interview skill.

Tangible Evidence

Tangible evidence is anything capable of being treated as fact, real, and concrete.[3] Within the realm of FD/FDP victimization, the frequently utilized hospital setting presents specific collection, identification, and recognition needs. Items frequently utilized by FD/FDP offenders, which are brought into crime scenes(s), are often simplistic things that alone may not trigger suspicion but in consideration of FD/FDP should be seen as potentially lethal. These items may include but are not limited to ipecac syrup, cellophane wrap, hypodermic needles, over-the-counter medications, and common ordinary household substances (salt). For FDP cases involving medical chart falsification, writing utensils accessible to the offender should be collected, and if hospitals are utilizing electronic data, in accordance with patient protection measures, computers must remain locked when not in use. The sophistication of FD/FDP offenders assumes that they may have the ability to access computer data systems and enter falsified data if provided access.

Tangible evidence may include syringes, needles, tubing, medical waste, blankets/towels, cups, drug containers, sheets, and discarded medicines. Poisoning suspected to originate through feeding utensils such as baby bottles would require that all FDP offender accessible utensils be collected and processed (new and discarded). Baby formula, mixing utensils, baggies, nipples, and cups should be carefully packaged, photographed, and submitted for analysis of contaminant.

All particular patterns of criminal inflictions require specific evidence gathering techniques that are adapted to the peculiarity of individual crime methodologies. There is one universal rule in all crime scene processing applications: photograph the scene and evidence. Photographs provide clear documentation of known and unknown evidence and provide prosecutors with a visual way to describe and present evidence during trial. Photography memorializes place and items at a particular date and time and this documentation cannot be refuted. In FD/FDP case investigations, a photograph or video provides analysis potential of identified and unidentified evidence that may later be linked.

Persons involved within an FD/FDP case investigation (witnesses, suspects, arrestees, professionals) should also be photographed during the course of the investigation. Photographing the victim at the time of offender detention is also recommended. FDP victim photographs or video generally produces visual accuracy of illness or injury that is likely to later be absent when viewed by a jury (if the victim survives the abuse). It is important for jury members to visualize the degree of illness or injury sustained by an FDP victim. Victims who survive generally recover and age by the time an FDP abuse case reaches judicial levels within the criminal justice system. Child victims or elderly infirm adults will have been segregated from their abusers and are not likely to recall or aid in prosecution efforts. Memorializing the effects of abuse upon a victim through the visual aid of photography/video becomes an invaluable resource to prosecutors, child protection advocates, and others. Additional victim abuse photography during recovery processes provides contrast views during healing and shows viewers the contrast and pathway between an ill victim and their present state. Within criminal prosecutorial venues, victim photographs tell part of the abuse story.

Intangible Evidence

Some evidence that may be present in FD/FDP applications as it pertains to criminal activity is generally not clearly evident and is considered intangible. Relativity of intangible evidence is generally presented through expert witnesses. Intangible evidence includes behavioral warning indicators, FDP warning signs, statements of the victim seen through behavioral observation, intangible gain or benefit derived from FDP victimization, verbal (only) falsification of a victim's signs/symptoms of illness, confusion generated through mountains of lies perpetuated by an FD/FDP offender, and others—see Chapter 1 for a listing of FDP behavioral indicators and warning signs.

Common Evidence Found in the Hospital

When unsure of the abuse vehicle utilized during FDP abuse, almost anything may be considered potential evidence. From the review of documented FDP abuse cases, evidence diversity potential is understood. FDP abuse evidence found within dirty laundry containing vomitus, soiled diapers, discarded sharps within the general sharps collection wall container, the general trash, existing medications being administered to the FDP victim, and the toilet are just some evidentiary sources.

Levels in prescription bottles should be documented and assessed according to prescription, date, dosage, and amount remaining. These medicines should be photographed, collected, and analyzed for content. Levels in oxygen or other tanks, if present, should be photographed, observed, and analyzed. All medical equipment located in the abuse victim's hospital room should be photographed then either collected or certified to be in good working order by an independent evaluator. Lab specimens should be collected in the following manner: samples of contaminated specimens and samples of noncontaminated specimens for comparative purposes.

Poisoning Cases

FDP infliction through the mode of poisoning is a fundamental method of achieving FDP benefit through both direct and indirect victim abuse. Direct victim abuse by an FDP offender has been viewed as the direct consequence of an oral or intravenous introduction of a foreign substance into a victim's body. Indirect victim abuse through poisoning occurs when the victim's body reacts to the poison, creating signs or symptoms of illness, and the medical staff takes measures to counteract the conditions created by the FDP offender's actions. Countermeasures sometimes increase the FDP victim's signs/symptoms (viewed as illness), or attempted treatment is ineffective because medical staff do not have knowledge of the origin of what is making the victim ill. In some situations, the poison provided to the abuse victim by the FDP offender overtakes the victim's ability to survive its lethality, or the treatment is not tolerated. The FDP abuse victim then becomes a homicide victim.

Poisons utilized in FDP abuse cases may be appropriated illegally or legally from within or outside the hospital. Items only become poison vehicles in FDP abuse cases when the substance is administered improperly through dosage deviation or delivery. Items such as ipecac, prescribed or over-the-counter medications, are routinely obtained through store purchase. Care should be taken during evidence collection in suspected FDP poisoning cases to ensure that store receipts are collected if located and investigative parameters extend to credit card purchase review. Witnesses should also be interviewed to determine if they purchased suspected poisons and if so, what they did with these products.

Common Poisons

The availability of "common" poisons found within the hospital setting is vast. Common liquid poisons utilized in FDP abuse infliction occurring within the hospital setting include toilet bowl water, human feces and urine, liquid soap, common dirt, laundry soap, cleansing liquids, and others. Liquids used as poisons require specific collection criteria including systematic measuring of liquid levels during the investigation and at case conclusion. Photographing liquid levels of suspected poisoning agents during the investigation is recommended. Unused liquids suspected of poisoning utilization should be collected for comparative analysis. If toilet water or dirt is suspected as a poisoning agent, then samples of toilet water and dirt (dust, floor residue, urine bowl remains, etc.) should also be collected. If the suspected poison origination area is completely wiped clean and housekeeping services are not responsible, this should be noted in the investigative report.

Detectives should keep in mind that in general changing forms of infection might equate to changing infliction vehicles or contamination sources. Victim infections of multiple origins do not usually occur naturally. It appears that one of the repetitive ports of poisoning in FDP abuse cases is a victim's site of bloodstream access (intravenous lines, ports, catheters, etc.). These areas are generally well maintained medically because the risk of any foreign body into a human creates infection, bacterial growth, and clot risks, making people sick or causing death. Documentation of medical precautions to prevent contamination at bloodstream access points should be carefully noted. Documentation of these precautions may later assist prosecutorial efforts if an FDP abuse methodology via poisoning is established. If a patient (FDP victim's) infection is caused by sloppy medical procedure(s), then more than one patient may be affected simultaneously because medical staff errors due to negligence may not be a singular issue. In many abuse cases that involve FDP poisoning, initial diagnostics may include immunodeficiency. Detectives should ask whether the absence or presence of immunodeficiency could account for multiple sources of infection. Consideration of migrating or changing infection signs/symptoms is also relevant as types and delivery systems of FDP abuse by poisoning have transformed pursuant to detection threat.

Salt Poisoning

Poisoning by the administration of salt has occurred historically and continues to dominate media coverage in modern times. A lethal dose of ordinary table salt may be as little as half a teaspoon in a small baby.[4]

Symptoms of Salt Poisoning[5]

See Figure 7.3.

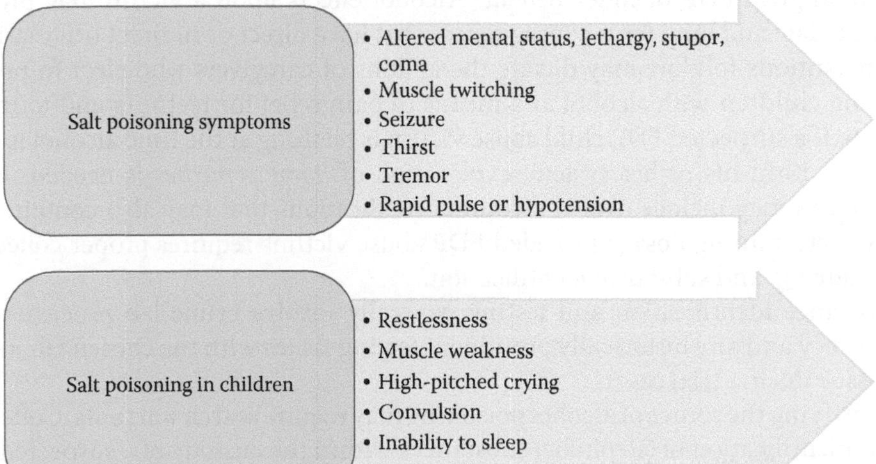

Salt poisoning symptoms
• Altered mental status, lethargy, stupor, coma
• Muscle twitching
• Seizure
• Thirst
• Tremor
• Rapid pulse or hypotension
Salt poisoning in children
• Restlessness
• Muscle weakness
• High-pitched crying
• Convulsion
• Inability to sleep

Figure 7.3 Physical symptoms of human salt poisoning.

Case Report After repeated hospitalizations in multiple U.S. states, a 5-year-old child died. The child's mother administered fatal doses of salt through the child's feeding tube when the child was in the bathroom where there were no surveillance cameras. Attention and a sense of belonging were attained by the mother through the avenue of social media as ~43,000 pages on Facebook depicted the child's demise. The mother was charged with first-degree manslaughter and second-degree murder and convicted of second-degree murder. She was sentenced to 20 years to life in prison. The presiding judge bestowed leniency in the sentencing because "although the crime was unfathomable in cruelty and brought her son five years of torment and pain," it appeared to the judge that the mother "suffered from Munchausen by proxy" and the judge likened it to a mental illness.[6],[7]

Alcohol Poisoning

In some FDP abuse cases, alcohol or other foreign substances are detected within the victim's blood. It is important to determine if the foreign substance identified is a by-product of substances produced naturally in a body or as a result of foreign matter introduced from an outside source.

- Suspected FDP abusers should be evaluated for the presence of alcoholism. The potential link between introduced alcohol and a triggering event associated with alcoholism is often relevant. If deliberate alcohol poisoning has occurred to a victim, examination of the presence of measurable secondary offender gain garnered through repetitive attention gathering mechanisms is pertinent. If secondary offender gain is direct, this may indicate that the abusive situation is not linked to an FDP format. Direct gain is generally indicative of simplistic abuse methodology absent the complication of indirect FDP infliction. Direct versus indirect secondary gains are not mutually exclusive.
- Determining what effect the ingestion of alcohol produces within a suspected FDP victim helps to outline the predicate for the likely presence of identifiable tangible or intangible FDP offender benefit. Alcohol effects upon a victim may produce immediate and long-term consequences that have direct or indirect origination.
- Superstitious folklore may dictate the actions of caregivers who elect to provide young children with alcohol as a means of pain relief for teething and to induce sleep. If a suspected FDP child abuse victim is teething at the time alcohol is identified within his or her system, exploration of *home remedies* is needed. Home remedies may include over-the-counter medications that may also contain alcohol. Determining dosage provided FDP abuse victims requires proper collection, measuring, and substance identification.
- Substance identification and testing generally involve crime lab processes. Lab accuracy and any historically prominent testing issues with the chosen lab may be at issue during trial cases.
- Identifying the source of alcohol poisoning may require search warrants. Collection and identification of (alcoholic) substances within the custody of a suspected FDP offender entail searches of home, business, and conveyance. Matching suspected alcohol sources to foreign substances found within an FDP victim is a scientific process.

- Exploration of alternative illness causation in a suspected FDP abuse victim establishes criminal defenses but is also part of prosecutorial criminal case preparation. Seeking alternative illness causation in suspected FDP abuse victims is part of the medical mantra utilized by FDP offenders within the FDP abuse cycle. We see the investigative pursuit of medical illness causation as a means of abuse victimization through unsuspecting secondary sources (medical staff). Looking for alternative illness causation changes to defensive posture or elemental criminal investigative process when FDP abuse methodology is suspected.

Temperature-Taking Discrepancy

FDP abuse cases may contain discrepancy regarding an abuse victim's bodily temperature fluctuations. FDP offenders have reported the presence of fever in victims that cannot be verified. Temperature discrepancy testimony should include the following procedural verifications when considering the validity of reported fever:

- How was the victim's temperature obtained (orally, rectally, scanning, ear wand, or others)?
- Who obtained the victim's temperature and was the taking of the temperature witnessed?
- Was the victim heavily clothed or wrapped prior to obtaining a temperature reading?
- Had the victim eaten/been fed immediately prior to or during the time the temperature was obtained? If so, was the item ingested cold or hot?
- Were weather conditions at the time the victim's temperature was obtained conducive to environmental location warming trends?
- How many times was the temperature of the victim taken? At what intervals?

Suffocation and Asphyxiation

One of the most commonly recognized forms of FDP abuse infliction is suffocation. Suffocation may leave no evidence or occasionally the presence of petechiae, indicative of asphyxiation. If an unstable FDP offender is confronted with a colicky or otherwise legitimately ill child, the FDP offender may react from a platform of frustration or emotion and become forcefully injurious in an effort to "stop" caretaker pressure demands. This scenario is especially prevalent when FDP victims are infants. The demands presented by infants are actually needs but may not be viewed in this manner by an FDP offender. A longing for transference of parental responsibility by the FDP offender is theoretically likely, and for the FDP offender, the most immediate pathway to transfer parental responsibility to another is to place the victim back into the care of a medical professional. The emergence of a fresh episode of FDP infliction or fabrication may occur or directed harm to a victim seen through suffocation may emerge. The FDP offender takes control of a situation they view as "out of control" and directs the circumscribing behavioral pathway to a more controlled atmosphere in the hospital setting. The hospital setting is viewed as a safe place where the fear and associated pressure of parenting is erased because the burden of responsibility is placed on someone else. If suffocation is suspected as the mode of FDP abuse infliction, the following questions should be explored:

1. Could a victim's suffocation represent directed FDP offender frustration due to an inability to cope with parenting demands?
2. Was the relationship between a suspected FDP offender and his or her spouse or other family members unstable during the time preceding the discovery of victim suffocation?
3. How could suffocation have occurred? Personal enmeshment between the FDP offender and victim seen through FDP offender hand or upper body contact with the victim's airway is one method. Another method involves the use of apparatus including cellophane, blankets, clothing, diapers, pillow, or ligature.
4. Was the FDP victim prescribed an apnea monitor prior to the theoretical suffocation event? Did the apnea monitor have recording capability? If an apnea monitor was present but not in use during an FDP victim's alleged cessation of breathing, why was it not in use?
5. For elderly victims of suffocation with an FDP factor, exploration of external rewards may not reveal motive in cases of homicide. Elderly victims of FDP abuse provide the same intangible rewards to FDP offenders that child victims do. Case factors regarding FDP offender gain do not seem to differ between victim's ages.

When suffocation is utilized as a method in FDP abuse of children, it may come to the attention of professionals in the form of apnea with an unknown cause. In many situations, an apnea monitor will have been either prescribed to the FDP victim or demanded by the FDP offender. Detectives should understand that the presence or absence of an apnea monitor does not guarantee the life or death of the assigned patient. If an apnea monitor is available to a suspected FDP abuse victim but is deliberately not utilized or utilized incorrectly, even a deliberate action of apnea monitor omission is not prima facie evidence of a crime. FDP offenders of child abuse victims who fail to correctly utilize apnea monitors create highly suspicious victim injury or death circumstances, and these actions may later be woven into a prosecutorial position of demonstrated neglect. Apnea monitor use omission alone does not cause injury or death.

Suffocation as a prevalent means of FDP infliction presents in a number of ways: actual infliction or presentation through fabrication. When FDP child victims are portrayed as afflicted with apnea (cessation of breathing), no medical cause can be determined, and nobody other than the suspected FDP offender ever views associated symptoms, then verbal fabrication (only) of breathing cessation is possible. FDP offenders "tell stories" or "fabricate" an illness within the child victim without directly inflicting harm onto the FDP victim within this method. Enhanced story telling may occur without directly inflicting victim harm and has been detected in situations where various types of equipment (apnea monitors) are tampered with. FDP falsified/simulated apnea has also been identified when FDP offenders remove apnea lead wires from FDP victims, places the lead wires upon the FDP offender's chest as he or she holds his or her breath, and then reattaches the apnea leads to the child victim producing a simulated breathing irregularity on the apnea monitor. The rouse is accompanied by FDP offender lies producing secondary situational harm pathways as medical testing is initiated to determine the origin of alleged breathing cessation in the FDP child abuse victim.

If a suspected FDP child abuse or other victim is alleged to have apnea and is actually observed with distress or the telltale signs of apnea whose origin cannot be explained, it is likely that apnea may originate from an external manipulative action by another person. Apnea that is directly produced by external intentional means should always be considered a directed homicide attempt. Infliction of apnea is intentionally produced when an FDP abuse victim's air intake is restricted and suffocation occurs. Suffocation can be accomplished by improper placement of external objects such as blankets, towels, clothing, plastic bags, toys, hands, and body parts or by the improper placement of a victim's head onto various services (mattress, seats, chest of the FDP offender, etc.), thereby preventing air intake. Suffocation may occur undetected in situations of isolation with an FDP offender or in full view of witnesses. One FDP child abuser appeared to have successfully suffocated her child in the car, on the way to the hospital, while holding the child against her breast as the unsuspecting driver raced toward the emergency room totally unaware.

Suffocation is a nearly perfect crime. Suffocation is often not detected because it leaves so little evidence behind. If suffocation is suspected as the mode of FDP abuse infliction (fabricated or induced), scientifically proving that suffocation-induced apnea or death by suffocation has occurred may be difficult. Medical testing is generally inconclusive when suffocation is a direct result of intentional FDP physical abuse, and indirect factitious claims regarding suffocation cannot generally be proven medically.

Covert Video Surveillance Evidence

In many situations, the most useful tool for diagnosing FDP abuse is covert video surveillance.[8]

Videotaping-suspected FDP offender behavior within hospital settings might provide significant evidence to support theoretical victim suffocation, but collection of this evidence places a victim in harm's way. Within the realm of FDP abuse case investigation, theory alone is generally insufficient to substantiate permanent victim/offender separation, but it may be enough to substantiate a protection order to allow data collection within a victim/offender seclusion test platform. A comparative analysis of seclusion testing, medical record review coupled with catalyst identification through socialization pattern analysis, and combination of expert/local opinion is needed to link theory to practical reality on an evidentiary basis. FDP child abuse situations have historically been linked to undetected homicides that are discovered after a homicide victim's subsequent sibling(s) die or are identified as suspected FDP child abuse victims.

Video surveillance may be utilized within the hospital setting as a method of obtaining positive proof that FDP victim abuse is occurring. Videotaped evidence does not provide a magical solution regarding FDP provability and should be considered only one tool in the complicated process of gathering evidence to either prove or disprove the presence of FDP abuse. Video surveillance as a sole method of FDP provability is not recommended because there is an associated danger factor for suspected FDP abuse victims. It is questionable which danger is greater when FDP abuse is suspected: allowing a suspected FDP offender–victim access while in the confines of a hospital setting or being unable to prove the presence of FDP abuse as a causative agent for a suspected FDP victim's illness. When links between suspected FDP abuse and victim illness cannot be established, the opportunity to intervene within the cycle of abuse is lost; abuse is likely to continue and the risk of continued victim abuse resounds. Invasive medical testing or increased lethality concerns along with probable relocation issues may become by-products of ineffective intervention efforts as FDP suspects become aware of threatened exposure.

Using video surveillance to help determine the presence of FDP abuse when located within a hospital setting creates liability questions and debate centering on the following issues:

- Child protective intervention versus lack of proactive intervention efforts
- Victim safety versus allowable abuse
- Consequences related to the reluctance to initiate video surveillance
- Expectations of privacy in a hospital setting
- The Health Insurance Portability and Accountability Act (HIPAA), a federal law that requires health providers to take certain steps to protect the privacy and security of patient health information[9]

Covert video surveillance may serve several purposes including either proving or disproving the theory of FDP abuse. A potential victim of FDP abuse may be rescued from abuse, or video may prevent a victim's demise. The gathering of evidence is not entirely without risk to a victim, but the alternative may be unrestricted suspected FDP offender access without accountability when legal authorities lack the tools (proof) to effectively chronically and acutely intervene.

Covert video surveillance in FDP cases is considered a method of assessment to determine a diagnosis that is linked to a criminal act (abuse through an FDP methodology) when the cause of a victim's illness cannot be proven by other means and the cause is theoretically linked to an FDP methodology. Covert surveillance is not always implemented in suspected abuse cases involving an FDP factor because whenever there is enough evidence to support the victim's removal from the offender's access, a victim should be shielded through protective custody means. Video evidence in FDP cases may also be accessed through social media or public media measures. (See Chapter 12 for further details.)

An analysis of U.S. Fourth Amendment violations regarding the videotaping of persons in hospital rooms is generally considered irrelevant since there is "no reasonable expectation of privacy in a hospital room." U.S. Supreme Court case *Katz v. United States*, 389 U.S. 347 (1967),[10] provided a privacy expectation reasonableness standard for U.S. citizens. The ruling stated that where a person reasonably expects that his or her conversations or actions would not be overheard or observed, a search warrant is necessary in order to listen or look in. "Listening" without first obtaining a warrant in locations of expected privacy (in this case the location was a telephone booth with the door closed) was deemed unlawful.

In FDP abuse investigations occurring in hospitals, the interdisciplinary response to case investigation is likely to encompass professionals representing legal, law enforcement, and medical and social services/child protection. Hospital legal entities may be concerned regarding the placement of video surveillance within a hospital room citing patient privacy concerns, liability, and victim protection. Hospitals are places where patients are assessed, observed, and monitored through viewing by nurses, doctors, and other health-care personnel. Patients know this because it is the core of hospital functioning and therefore, the expectation of privacy in a hospital room is limited.[11]

The United States v. White, 401 U.S. 745, 745 (1971)[12] is a Supreme Court case that clarified the expectation of privacy by the use of electronic surveillance evidence with the establishment of one-party consent. Medical staff can provide this consent.

The Fourth Amendment protects citizens against unreasonable search and seizure and requires the issuance of warrants to be based upon probable cause supported by oath or affirmation. Affirmation must describe the place to be searched and the person/things to be seized.[13] People have a right to be secure in their persons, houses, papers, and effects, against unreasonable searches and seizures.[14] The definition of "state action" means that actions are taken for some state purpose. Any crime described in a state or federal statute is considered a crime against the state or federal government.

Understanding how law applications interact within the scope of video surveillance placement within a hospital setting when FDP abuse situations are theorized provides clarity. During the interdisciplinary process that circumscribes FDP abuse investigations, police apply for a search warrant to videotape (only) the activities within a specific hospital room location. A warrant application must specifically name the child (victim), the mother, the hospital, and all items to be seized as evidence. Evidence may include body fluids, diapers, clothing, vomitus, blood secretions coming from the victim, and devices and instruments that may have been used to inflict bodily injury on a potential suspect or abuse victim. Evidence may also include potable water or false injury evidence such as fake blood or animal blood and other items.[15] The warrant must be dated and signed under penalties of perjury and reviewed/authorized by the court.

In the United States, laws are complicated and interwoven as one affects the other, but taken in totality, obtaining a warrant for video surveillance in a child's hospital room may be permissible for specific reasons:

- Protection of the child patient
- Constant monitoring/assistance in diagnoses and treatment
- Protection of the facility and employees from allegations of negligence (Figure 7.4)

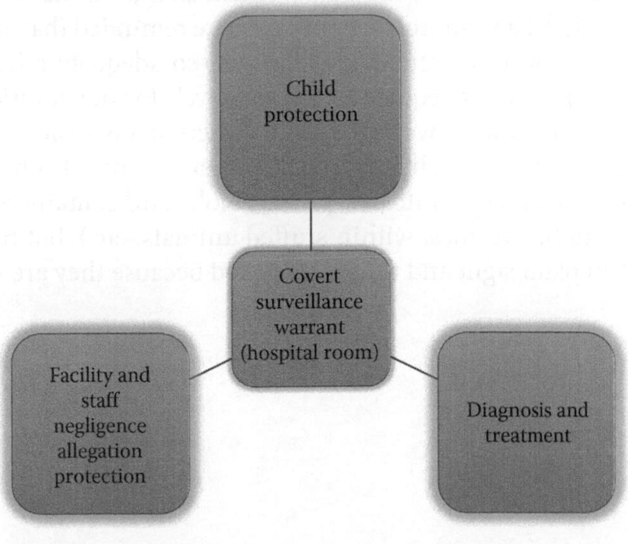

Figure 7.4 Hospital-based video surveillance justifications.

Within a criminal procedural contact, there are exceptions to the rule of obtaining a warrant for evidence collection that include consent, plain view, and open fields or exigent circumstances. Exigent or emergency situations require prompt action to prevent imminent danger to life or serious property damage or are situations required to forestall imminent escape of a suspect or destruction of evidence. Establishment of exigent circumstances is evaluated on an individual case basis based upon the facts known to officials.[16] Probable cause that a crime has been committed is required to make a warrantless search constitutional. The existence of exigent circumstances is a combination of law and fact.[17] Factors of urgency, destruction of evidence, site danger, and a suspect's knowledge that police are actively investigating their suspected behavior are considered when determining urgency.[18]

Warrantless evidence seizures are permitted when exigent circumstances are present. In FDP cases, exigent circumstances tend to include imminent danger to human life.[19] Detail required to substantiate the exigency of evidence seizure absent a signed warrant creates confusion and debate. Whenever possible, taking the time to obtain a warrant to substantiate the placement of video surveillance as a means of evidence collection is advised.

Exigency may be determined by degree of urgency involved, amount of time needed to get a search warrant, whether evidence is about to be removed or destroyed, danger at the site, knowledge of the suspect that police are on the trail, and/or ready destructibility of the evidence.[20] Exigent circumstances as they pertain to the legality of hidden video cameras in hospital rooms are found reasonable as related to U.S. Supreme Court recognized exceptions to the exclusionary rule for a search warrant.

Search Warrant Affidavits (Video Surveillance)

The following search warrant format example may be reproduced to obtain a court order for covert video surveillance in FD/FDP abuse cases. Investigators are reminded that video surveillance should be monitored by law enforcement so that immediate victim intervention is available if needed. Law enforcement officials are reminded that anything is possible within the duration of video surveillance placement so adequate relief is mandatory of involved observers to maintain adequate awareness levels for the duration of surveillance. During the execution of a search warrant, places where items related to FDP abuse may be hidden should be targeted search locations. These areas include obvious hiding places (trash cans, drawers, diaper bags, suitcases, purses, biohazard containers, toilets, under the edges of molding or in bed frames, within stuffed animals, etc.), but be aware that items may also be hiding in plain sight and thus overlooked because they are not concealed.

Application and Affidavit FDP Related Search Warrant Exemplar

APPLICATION AND AFFIDAVIT

IN THE CIRCUIT COURT OF THE NINTH JUDICIAL CIRCUIT IN AND FOR ____________COUNTY, ___________(State)

____COUNTY CASE NUMBER____

APPLICATION AND AFFIDAVIT FOR FDP-RELATED SEARCH WARRANT

STATE OF ___________________

COUNTY OF _______________

Personally comes the affiant, **Deputy** ___________________, a sworn law enforcement officer, to-wit: **a Deputy for the Sheriff of** _________ **County,** __________**(State),** before **The Honorable** _____________________________, **Judge, in and for** _________**County,** ____________**(State),** __________**Judicial Circuit**, who makes this application and states under oath that affiant has probable cause to believe that certain laws have been and are being violated in and on certain premises and the curtilage thereof in ____________ County, __________(State).

These premises are described as follows:

_____*(Name of Hospital)* , *(Full Hospital Address)* . *(City, County, State)* ______a ________story building, Room Number _____, located on the ______floor, or such other room as the below mentioned victim may be located. The room number is located on the wall outside the hospital room door. The room has a bathroom. Located in the room is a ___*(list contents found within the room- for example: hospital crib, a chair that may be converted into a bed, various storage cabinets, dresser...)* __.

This premises occupied by: *Patient/Victim (Victim's Name, r/s, D.O.B), Suspect (Suspect's Name, r/s, D.O.B.)* and under the control of *(Name of Hospital)* and that there is now being administered on said premises and curtilage certain direct or circumstantial evidence of inflicted or fabricated illness or injury to *(Victim's Name)* *to wit:* *(List Items Sought)* such tangible evidence including, but not limited to: bedding, clothing or other similar items which purportedly depict evidence of bodily fluids (such as blood, vomitus or other secretions), coming from the victim; instruments and/or devices that might tend to inflict bodily harm or injury upon another such as sharp instruments that may be utilized by the suspect perpetrator to cause injury to him/herself in an effort to use the results of any such injury as false evidence of injury or illness to the victim; any substance(s) that might be used as false evidence of injury or illness to the victim such as animal blood or fake "blood" or any other substances that may be utilized to falsely represent illness or injury to the victim. Any behavioral manifestations by the suspect consistent with the infliction of injury upon the victim to induce symptoms of illness or injury and any behavioral manifestations by the suspect, which depict the suspect fabricating evidence of, purported illness or injury should be noted.

Insert the crime committed and the State violated this is in violation of: State Statute____________________. *Describe substantive statutory violation*. The facts tending to establish grounds for this application and the probable cause of your affiant believing that such facts exist are as follows:

Your affiant, Deputy ________________________, is and has been since month and year of your employment, a duly sworn Deputy Sheriff for the Sheriff of __________ County, *(State)*.

In your affiant's duties as a ___________detective with (Agency), your affiant had the occasion to be assigned this case concerning abuse with a FD/FDP factor. FDP is a form of abuse most perpetrated upon a child or other dependent person and occurs when an offender fabricates a victim's illness. The offender is typically the caretaker of the victim and is typically identified as the victim's mother. The responsible parent constantly seeks medical treatment for acute illnesses in the victim that may be present but caused by the falsification or induction of illness symptomology. Introduction of falsified or induced illness by the FD/FDP abuse Suspect occurs through various means including: *(List Specific Suspected Case Methodology)*. Experts believe that one motivation behind FDP abuse is to focus attention upon the responsible abuse suspect.

NOTARY PUBLIC

<Name>
Commission # 12345
<Jurisdiction County
My Comm. Expires Jan 1, 2025

Witnessed by: <Name>   Notary Public

Development of Probable Cause

On ___*(Date)*___, *the (Name of Police Agency)* was contacted by the ___(Name of Physician)___ of the Child Protection Team concerning this matter. According to Dr. ________, a ___(age of victim, race and sex)___ child *(full name of the child); (date of birth),* was admitted to the *(Name of the hospital and location)* and there were medical suspicions of factitious illness. The mother reported illnesses that included the child *(list specific symptomology)*. Medical tests and procedures were performed on the child and no cause for these illnesses could be found. The symptoms were witnessed only by the mother and by no medical personnel.

On *(date),* your affiant met with Dr. __________, who stated that the child was admitted to ___*(Full name of the hospital, location and room #)*___ on *(date)* for a history of ____________. Dr. ____________, upon consulting several physicians, became concerned the ___*(describe symptomology testing results)*___ were fictitious.

According to Dr.__________, the child had been admitted to the hospital ___times and had seen a doctor_____ times. Early stage complaint(s) included: *describe the medical ailments, signs, symptoms [for example- apnea, vomiting, fever....]* Medical complaints evolving within hospitalizations or in subsequent hospitalizations included: *describe the medical ailments, signs, symptoms [for example-vomiting and hematemesis (vomiting blood)* . None of the vomiting or apnea episodes were witnessed by anyone other that the mother of the child. There was never any vomiting or apnea that occurred within the hospital that could be verified as originating from the child.

Victim/Offender Separation Data

On one occasion the mother was told the child would be released but that she should bring the child back to the hospital, especially if the child vomited blood that was clotted. ____ hours after the child was released from the hospital, the mother brought the child back to the hospital and with her she brought a blanket. The mother claimed that the child had vomited clotted blood and the blood was present upon the blanket. The blanket was turned over to the hospital.

Catalyst Placement Results

Dr. ________visited the mother while she and the child were admitted to the hospital on one occasion and told the mother that the child was fine and could be released. Dr. _______ left the room and came back a very short time later. The mother presented him another blanket at that time and stated the child had just vomited upon it. A small splash of what appeared to be blood was found on the blanket but there were no other signs upon the child indicating recent blood vomiting. Upon the mother's presentation of this apparently blood tainted blanket, her demeanor did not reflect any sense or urgency.

Expert Medical Opinion

The expert medical opinion of Dr.(s)_________________________ is that the mother is presenting either her own blood, fake blood or blood from another source in order to manipulate the hospital staff and hospital physicians to perform testing including intrusive procedures upon the child. Tests that have been performed on the child thus far include: ___________*(list all testing, procedures and the results)*___________.

Dr.(s)_________________expressed concerns relating to _________________________.

Dr.(s) _______________believe that if the child was vomiting blood, there should also be blood in the child's stool. No blood has been found or claimed to have been found in the child's stool that further lends support to the physician's suppositions that the blood is being introduced from a source other than the child. Based upon the aforementioned facts concerning this case, Dr. ___________ feels the working diagnosis for this child's alleged illness(s) is Factitious Disorder by Proxy (FDP).

------PLACE THE PHYSICIANS CREDENTIALS HERE-include relevancy to FDP casework. A growing number of communities have "local experts" who have dealt with previous cases concerning abuse with a FD/FDP factor. If your community lacks such a person you may wish to contact a large teaching hospital for a medical staff referral.

You affiant requests a court order to enter said premises to install video surveillance equipment, monitor and videotape persons within room number______ or such other room as the child may be located in at the ____*(Name of the hospital address, city, county, state)*_____for any actions that would indicate how the purported signs of illness and/or injury to said child are manifesting themselves, whether by induced injury or illness or by the introduction of false evidence of illness or injury.

Due to the secretive nature of the actions of perpetrators in cases of abuse with an element of Factitious Disorder by Proxy, there is usually little or no physical evidence available to link the perpetrator to the instances of abuse against the victim or to the creation of symptoms in said victims. Often, the perpetrators of such abuse, where the symptoms are fiction created by the perpetrator, introduce signs of illness through artificial means, whether by inducing injury to the victim or by creating physical evidence in a false manner. These fictitious signs of illness are usually created in secret. Traditional investigative methods such as interviewing, undercover surveillance, informants and witnesses are often ineffective and inadequate for the detection of such evidence, or are so time-consuming as to create an unnecessary delay and potential further injury and/or death to the victim.

Based on the foregoing and your affiant's knowledge, training and experience, your affiant has probable cause to believe that the evidence being sought may be evidentiary in nature.

Your affiant has diligently interviewed experienced medical personnel who are knowledgeable about the child's medical history and believes that there are no other reasonable means to further isolate the cause of the child's medical condition.

WHEREFORE, your affiant makes this affidavit and prays for the issuance of a Search Warrant in due form of law for the installation of a video surveillance camera to be placed in the above described premises for said property heretofore described, and for the recording and subsequent seizure and safekeeping thereof of a period not to exceed _______hours from installation. Subject to the Order of a Court having jurisdiction thereof, by the duly constituted officers of the law affiant further prays for authority to search the above described premises and any persons thereon reasonably believed to be connected with the said illegal activity for the property described in this warrant and of the same of any part thereof be present to siege said items.

The Return portion of this warrant will reflect the actual seizure of the evidence retrieved (Video tape or other items). Your affiant understands that the Return portion of this Warrant Application must be returned and filed with the_______ County Clerk of Courts within (___) days of its execution and that I have (___) days to execute the search warrant.

____

Deputy, Affiant

SWORN TO and SUBSCRIBED before me this _____day of ______, 2015

____

JUDGE

_________ **County, (State)**___________

___________________ **Judicial Circuit**

<Name>
Commission # 12345
<Jurisdiction County
My Comm. Expires Jan 1, 2025

NOTARY PUBLIC

______________________ ______________________

Witnessed by: <Name> **Notary Public**

FDP-RELATED SEARCH WARRANT

IN THE __________JUDICIAL CIRCUIT, IN AND FOR ________________COUNTY, (STATE), IN THE NAME OF THE STATE OF ____________________________

TO:____________________________, SHERIFF OF _____________________COUNTY, (STATE) AND/OR ANY OF HIS DEPUTY SHERIFFS OR AGENTS THEREOF, AND _________________, CHIEF OF THE ______________________POLICE DEPARTMENT AND/OR ANY OF HIS POLICE OFFICERS OR AGENTS THEREOF

WHEREAS, complaint on oath and in writing, supported by affidavit, having been made this day before the undersigned,

WHEREAS, said facts made known to me have caused me to certify and find that there is probable cause to believe that certain laws have been and are being violated in and on certain premises and the curtilage thereof in ________________County, (State). These premises are described as follows:

(Name of Hospital) , *(Full Hospital Address)* . *(City, County, State)* a _________story building, Room Number _____, located on the ______floor, or such other room as the below mentioned victim may be located. The room number is located on the wall outside the hospital room door. The room has a bathroom. Located in the room is a *(list contents found within the room-for example: hospital crib, a chair that may be converted into a bed, various storage cabinets, dresser...)* .

This premises occupied by: *Patient/Victim (Victim's Name, r/s, D.O.B), Suspect (Suspect's Name, r/s, D.O.B.)* and under the control of *(Name of Hospital)* and that there is now being administered on said premises and curtilage certain direct or circumstantial evidence of inflicted or fabricated illness or injury to *(Victim's Name)* *to wit:* *(List Items Sought)* such tangible evidence including, but not limited to: bedding, clothing or other similar items which purportedly depict evidence of bodily fluids (such as blood, vomitus or other secretions), coming from the victim; instruments and/or devices that might tend to inflict bodily harm or injury upon another such as sharp instruments that may be utilized by the suspect perpetrator to cause injury to him/herself in an effort to use the results of any such injury as false evidence of injury or illness to the victim; any substance(s) that might be used as false evidence of injury or illness to the victim such as animal blood or fake "blood" or any other substances that may be utilized to falsely represent illness or injury to the victim. Also, any behavioral manifestations by the suspect consistent with the infliction of injury upon the victim to induce symptoms of illness or injury. Also, any behavioral manifestations by the suspect that depict the suspect fabricating evidence of purported illness or injury. This is in violation of:

State Statute: ____________*Describe substantive statutory violation(s).*

AND WHEREAS, The facts tending to establish grounds for this application being set-forth in the affidavit of Deputy __________ a member of the __________County Sheriff's Office.

NOW, THEREFORE, you and either of you, with such lawful assistance as may be necessary, are herby commanded, in the daytime, nighttime or on Sunday as the exigencies of the situation may require, to enter the aforesaid premises together with the yard and curtilage thereof, any and all outbuildings and vehicles thereon, and any persons thereon reasonably believed to be connected with the said illegal activity, for the property described in this warrant, and if the same of any part thereof be found, you are herby authorized to seize and secure same, giving proper receipt therefor and delivering a complete copy of this warrant to the person in charge of the premises, or in the absence of any such person, leaving a completed copy where the property is found, and making a return of your doings under this warrant within the(10) days of the date hereof, and you are further directed to bring said property so found and also the bodies of the person or person s in possession thereof before the Court having jurisdiction of this offense to be disposed of according to the law.

FURTHERMORE, you or either of you, with such lawful assistance as ay be necessary, are authorized to install a video surveillance camera to be placed in the above-described premises for the recording and subsequent seizure of images only.

WITNESS my hand and seal this _______day of ____________, 20____

____

JUDGE

NOTARY PUBLIC

<Name>
Commission # 12345
<Jurisdiction County
My Comm. Expires Jan 1, 2025

______________________ ______________________

Witnessed by: <Name> Notary Public

INVENTORY AND RECEIPT

LIST AND DESCRIBE SPECIFIC ITEMS THAT ARE SEIZED

DATED this ________day of ____________________, 20___.

____

Deputy Sheriff

____

RETURN

STATE OF ____________________

COUNTY OF __________________

Received this Search Warrant on the ____day of ________, 20___, and executed the same in __________County, (State), on the _______day of ____________, 20__, by searching the premises described therein and by taking into my custody the property described in the above Inventory and Receipt and by having read and delivered a copy of this Search Warrant and Inventory Receipt to: (*Name of Suspect and Location where the receipt was presented)*

____

Deputy Sheriff

I, ______________________, the Deputy Sheriff by whom the Search Warrant was executed, do swear that the above Inventory and Receipt contains a true and detailed account of all of the property taken by me on said Warrant.

____

Deputy Sheriff

SWORN TO AND SUBSCRIBED before me this ________day of ___________, 20___.

____

Notary Public or Deputy Court Clerk

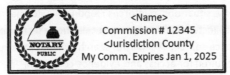

NOTARY PUBLIC
<Name>
Commission # 12345
<Jurisdiction County
My Comm. Expires Jan 1, 2025

_______________________ _______________________

Witnessed by: <Name> Notary Public

Cell Phones and Computer Evidence

Photographs or videos of an FD/FDP victim hospitalized or otherwise medically compromised tell the FD/FDP offender that the victim was truly ill and in some situations reinforces responsibility denial portrayed belief. Photographs or videos can easily be collected by the use of present cell phone technology, and a cell phone may easily be overlooked as an evidence source. A separate search warrant for cell phones may be necessary to provide the legal basis required for access and evidence collection. In general terms, when cell phones are listed upon generalized search warrants, the phones are collected as part of the wide range of evidence gathering. Writing a search warrant for cell phone usually occurs when the device is already in custody and has specified requirements within the search warrant format. Warrant language utilized within the specialized cell phone application includes the following:

Cell Phones and Computer Evidence

Photographs or video of a FD/FDP victim hospitalized or otherwise medically compromised tell the FD/FDP offender that the victim was truly ill and in some situations, reinforces responsibility denial portrayed belief. Photographs or video can easily be collected by use of present cell-phone technology and a cell phone may easily be overlooked as an evidence source. A separate search warrant for a cell phones may be necessary to provide the legal basis required for access and evidence collection. In general terms, when cell phones are listed upon generalized search warrants, the phones are collected as part of the wide range of evidence gathering. Writing a search warrant for cell phone usually occurs when the device is already in custody and has specified requirements within the search warrant format. Warrant language utilized within the specialized cell-phone application includes the following:

Search Warrant Application-Cell Phones

1) (Describe the Phone device here.)

2) The aforementioned evidence being sought is in the form of contact/phone lists, call logs, SMS (Simple Message Service, a/k/a text) messages and / or graphic or video files and/or any other data that may be relevant to this investigation which are stored within the phone device. Said evidence is currently being kept under the control of the __________County Sheriff's Office Evidence Warehouse and which property has the unique address of ____________Street, City, State and is particularly described and can be located as follows:

3) *DIRECTIONS:* You may include written directions and a map to the location where the cell phone is being housed.

4) Credentials: Your affiant, Deputy ________________________, is and has been since month and year of your employment, a duly sworn Deputy Sheriff for the Sheriff of ________ County, (State). *Training and Experience should also be included here.*

- Your affiant is familiar that computer systems and cellular devices can be used as instruments in a criminal act or the fruit of a crime. Computers and cell phones can store information in internal or peripheral storage devices, including but not limited to fixed disks, external hard disks, floppy diskettes, tape drives, optical storage devices, and numerous other storage devices of data.

- Also, based on your affiants' personal use of computer systems and cell phones, your affiant knows that users of cell phone technology often save information or created files to storage devices/media.

- Your affiant requests the authorization to analyze for any electronic data processing and/or storage devices, computers and computer systems which also includes central processing units, internal and peripheral storage devices such as fixed discs, internal/external hard drives, or other storage devices, together with system documentation, operating logs and documentation, appropriate cables and connecters, memory storage devices or media such as optical disks, programmable instruments such as telephones, "electronic address books", portable data assistants, or any other storage media where data can be stored, together with indicia of use, ownership, possession, or control of such records. Other property of relevance to this incident includes video cameras (digital, analog or any other format), still-photo cameras (digital, analog, or any other format), paper printouts from the printers (e-mails, chat logs, written passwords/login names), and Internet access documents. The actual analysis of any seized digital evidence will be conducted at a later time due to the protracted time a computer forensics investigation takes.

5) Probable Cause: As a result of your affiant's training and experience as set forth above, your affiant has probable cause to believe the following:

(Insert your narrative here. This is where you describe your Probable Cause.)

Based on the foregoing and your affiant's knowledge, training and experience, your affiant has probable cause to believe that the evidence being sought may be evidentiary in nature. **WHEREFORE,** your affiant makes this affidavit and requests the issuance of a Search Warrant in due form of law authorizing a search of the above-described property by officers of the law for evidence heretofore described and for the seizure and safekeeping of said evidence, subject to the order of a Court having jurisdiction thereof.

____

DEPUTY ____________________, Affiant

SWORN TO and SUBSCRIBED before me this ___ day of __________, 20__.

Judge

_______________**County, (State)**

________________________**Judicial Circuit**

NOTARY PUBLIC

<Name>
Commission # 12345
<Jurisdiction County
My Comm. Expires Jan 1, 2025

____________________ ____________________
Witnessed by: <Name> Notary Public

The "return" portion of this warrant will reflect the actual seizure of articles. The examination may exceed ten days or more based on the high volume of data to be processed and examined, but all results will be submitted as evidence at a later date.

The return portion of this warrant will reflect the actual seizure of the evidence retrieved (the iPhone). Your affiant understands that the return portion of this warrant application must be returned and filed with the Orange County Clerk of Courts within (10) days of its execution and that I have (7) days to execute the search warrant.

Your affiant or his designee has taken custody of the *cell phone* and the articles needed for analysis are properly logged. The exhibits will be physically examined, documented and later examined for evidence of these crimes. The results of the examination will be presented by your affiant or designee and later forwarded to the Office of the State Attorney.

Search Warrant Affidavit/Premises

Suggested Order of Inclusion

1. List items to be sought within the search warrant.
2. Describe the law violation/statue numbers that apply to your case.
3. Provide a legal description of the premises to be searched and include location directions.
4. Search warrants that have multiple affiants or coaffiants should contain multiple credentialing criteria.
5. Specifically list probable cause for the issuance of the search warrant and include multidisciplinary resources.
6. The use of a specialized "expert" search warrant application may be necessary for FDP abuse situations. Credentialing details of any "experts" utilized in the formulation of probable cause are required within the body of the warrant application.

Covert Video Surveillance Installation Equipment: FDP Investigations

Covert Installation Logistics

The logistics for placement of covert video surveillance within a hospital may initially require extensive preparation. Preplanning what equipment will be necessary for installation is a recommended time-saving procedure in FDP case application. The following is a suggested equipment list for installation of covert video surveillance in a hospital setting:

Single-Camera Installation

- Mini surveillance camera with auto iris pinhole lens
- Portable AC/DC time-lapse VCR (with date/time generation)
- BNC cable runs (various lengths)
- Video monitor
- Camera-mounting brackets
- Hole-boring tools
- Tie wraps, clippers, and gaff tape
- Power adapters for camera, VCR, and monitor
- Stinger/s
- Ladders
- Timer

Multicamera Installation

Additional units of single-camera installation equipment and a switcher, multiplexer, or quad split will be needed.

Options

- Two-way glass that may be installed as a bathroom mirror
- Motion sensors

Camera Placement Positions

- Within a closed receptacle (such as a television) aimed at the hospital bed on an elongated angle
- Directly over (perpendicular to) a hospital bed, mounted within the ceiling
- Within the bathroom vanity mirror
- With a wide-angle lens from any corner of the room

Determining When a Video Surveillance Warrant Is Needed

Video surveillance may be considered not necessary when an effective FDP victim intervention is provable or justified without it. Implementation of covert video surveillance should not supersede victim safety concerns. If an FDP victim is in immediate danger, the victim should be protected and removed from that environment.

The decision to include an audio component within covert video surveillance may present. Consideration regarding an additional component of audio is generally guided beneath wiretapping laws. Most laws pertaining to wiretaps that allow interception of oral communication do not cover abuse situations. U.S. federal law regarding wiretapping is found in Title 18, Chapter 119, and Section 2500. Individual policing agencies should reference state law when determining if sound should be off or on during video surveillance recording. In most instances, sound/audio should remain deactivated.

When records or evidence is stored on magnetic media such as tape, diskette, and hard drive, it is common to find that specific records authorized to be seized are inextricably mixed and without technical difficulty or extremely time-consuming procedures are inseparable from other records, programs, or files (e.g., similar to a bound-volume book containing financial records, addresses, diary, and notes). Current technology also allows the storage of sounds, images, and video "movies" as digital files on a diskette or chip in a recording device, as well as on different formats of magnetic tape. The storage medium containing records or evidence relating to the crime under investigation will be seized for analysis, but only those items authorized to be seized by the warrant will be printed out, disclosed, stored on an evidence disk, or otherwise copied for evidence purposes. Any other items that can be separated out from such evidence will be returned upon completion of the forensic analysis.

Video Surveillance: Child Protection Application

Criminal and dependency FDP cases are predicated upon identification and collection of evidence to justify individual burden of proof degrees. The difficulty in gathering evidence in FD/FDP cases rests within the issue of victim endangerment as irrefutable substantiation of evidence is sought. In all FDP cases, whenever justification for victim access removal from a suspected FD/FDP offender is obtained, regardless of the exigent concerns presented within the FD/FDP abuse methodology, a victim should be taken into protective custody. The variable that exists in custody determination is recognizing when justification is attained. In suspected FDP abuse situations, the execution of protective intervention measures during viewable inflicted abuse falls beneath the umbrella of covert video surveillance within a hospital setting. As law enforcement personnel observe the actions of suspected FDP offenders on a nearby monitor, how long should an apparent or suspected act of abuse be allowed to take place before intervention occurs? For purposes of establishing evidence predicate suitable for later prosecution and criminal conviction, there is no specific guideline delineated within the United States. Other countries have established various time allotment requirements to fulfill a required burden of proof; however, a specific time element requirement is not always without significant risk to the victim.

The foremost directive of victim protection in an abuse case investigation should guide detectives monitoring video surveillance that reveals "viewable abuse." A general palatable guideline to help determine the length of time needed to expose a potential victim to a suspected FDP abuser's actions is the amount of time necessary for a law enforcement officer to justify probable cause needed for an arrest. If law enforcement can articulate, either by what is actually seen or through what a medical expert can interpret, that child abuse (in any form, including a direct action attributed to an FDP sequence) is occurring, the point of intervention has arrived. Intervention sequencing by law enforcement when

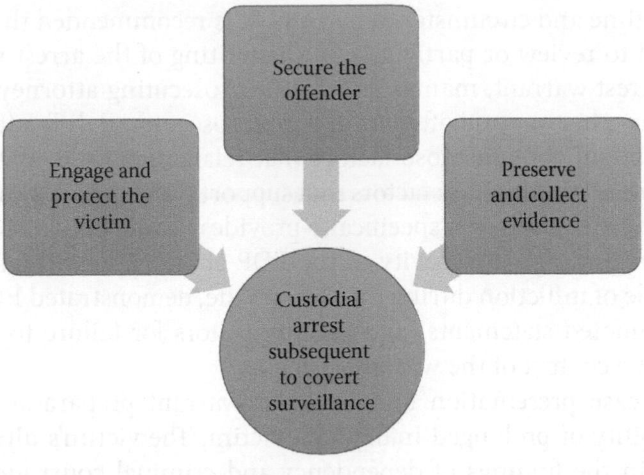

Figure 7.5 FDP offender arrest procedures.

affecting the custodial arrest of an FDP offender subsequent to surveillance monitoring is as follows:

1. Engage and protect the victim from further harm while rendering first aid.
2. Secure the FDP offender.
3. Secure and collect evidence along with witness statements (Figure 7.5).

Fruits of an Evidentiary Search Warrant

It may become necessary to search the personal belongings (purse, drawers, bags) of the FDP abuse offender. Searching items that belong to the offender will require a search warrant. Evidence yielded from this warrant will generally be of circumstantial nature but often helpful in the criminal case building process.

Within the course of evidence gathering in an FDP abuse investigation, it is likely that search and/or arrest warrant(s) will be utilized. Both documents allow the display of evidence as justification for issuance. The writers of these documents should keep in mind that these warrants are considered public records and media will have access to them. Information pertinent to the investigation that cannot be commented upon by prosecutors and/or police agencies during an investigation will generally be available to all after an arrest is achieved. Disclosure of the facts to media through the right of public records access may work favorably for the prosecution. Disclosure will generally preclude an FD/FDP offender from using the media for personal gain when the reporting of fact tends to deflate the establishment of a factitiously based defense and may set groundwork for public opinion regarding the FDP offender's actions if criminally convicted.

Expert Arrest Warrant

When sufficient evidence has been collected to establish that probable cause exists for the arrest of a suspected FDP offender, obtaining an expert arrest warrant is often preferred to directed arrest if time and circumstance permits. It is recommended that the prosecuting attorney be asked to review or participate in the writing of the arrest warrant. Utilizing an expert FDP arrest warrant, mantra affords the prosecuting attorney initial input into case preparation in a big way and often minimizes prosecutorial difficulties at trial. Expert arrest warrants should contain those factors that relate directly to FD/FDP research by incorporating specific existing case factors that support these theories and proven research entities. The expert arrest warrant specifically provides the educational element necessary for judicial understanding. The gravity of the FDP abuse case, with emphasis on flight, recidivism, upscale of infliction during the victim's life, demonstrated FDP offender instability (including quoted statements) and liability factors for failure to intervene may be explored within the context of the warrant.

Protocol for case presentation and/or arrest warrant preparation is important to lessen the probability of prolonged injury to a victim. The victim's ultimate fate may be intertwined within the findings of dependency and criminal court judgment. A shared judiciary view of FDP acceptance and understanding as an authentic element in abuse or homicide cases often rests with how a case is worked and evidence collected. The following is a suggested protocol for case presentation in a courtroom setting and arrest warrant inclusion order in preparation of criminal violations of law (abuse or homicide) involving the inference of FD/FDP.

Expert Arrest Warrant Application: Sequential Order

Charges and Warrant Justification Method

Probable Cause Introduction

1. Affiant's biographical information
2. Report initiation and involved agencies education
3. FD/FDP definitional parameters
4. Typical behaviors associated with FD/FDP
5. FD/FDP and physicians (relationship)
6. Doctor shopping/help seekers/doctor addicts
7. FDP characteristics and warning signs (historical information)
8. FD/FDP abuse case investigations (historical relevance/same type crime)
9. Medical history of the victim/witness testimony
10. Medical expert opinions and relevant facts
    a. Physicians' credentials
    b. Physicians' opinions
    c. Expert physicians' credentials
    d. Expert physicians' opinions
    e. Nurses' credentials
    f. Nurses' observations as case evidence
11. False and distorted medical history of the victim and/or offender
    a. Diagnosis
    b. Defendant's reaction to medical care plans
    c. Defendant's participation in the illness

12. Medical neglect and abuse
    a. Illnesses and their etiologies
    b. Defendant's accessibility to the victim; instrumentation failures
    c. Lab correlations
    d. Temperature falsifications
    e. Drug or poisoning infliction
13. Victim/offender seclusion data
    a. Within the hospital
    b. Measurement when accusation/suspicion of FDP infliction is made known
14. Rejected offers to help the victim
    a. Social services intervention resistance
    b. Specialized physician attachment refusal by the defendant
15. Psychological/behavioral characteristic
    a. Media attention
    b. Media attention versus the well-being of the victim
    c. Deliberate manipulation of the media by the FD/FDP offender
    d. The victim's role within the media; publication falsification; prepping the victim for exposure; dressing the part; normalized childhood activities distorted (media coverage); profile criteria/evidentiary
    e. Unnatural calmness
    f. Victim's behavior when exposed or isolated from the defendant
    g. Defendant's occupational education as an infliction means
    h. Nonoffending parent's role
    i. Defendant's rapport with medical staff
16. Appropriation of money/financial gain and the ability to manipulate
    a. Lawsuits
    b. Abuse of private and governmental programs
    c. Embezzlement and lack of prosecution due to victim's illness(s)
    d. Gifts, trips, and services
    e. Charitable fund raiser benefiting the FDP victim and his or her family
    f. Solicitation (purported need or want) for expensive items
    g. Defendant spending demonstrated application of fraudulently obtained proceeds
17. Organized fraud
    a. Medical services—payment through insurance companies or Medicare
    b. Charitable organizations utilized as monetary sourcing

Potential criminal charges attached to FD/FDP activities include aggravated child abuse, willful and wanton torture, attempted murder, murder, extortion, organized fraud, child endangerment, child neglect, crimes against the elderly, elder abuse, medical fraud, and others.

Definitions (Arrest Warrant Application)

- Affiant(s)—the law enforcement official requesting the warrant.
- Defendant—the alleged suspect to be incarcerated.

- Arrest affidavit—detailed portion of the arrest package, retained by the courts.
- Arrest warrant—portion of the package that is read to the defendant at the time of arrest.
- Complaint number—the number assigned to the case by the clerk of the court.
- Plaintiff—state of ________________.
- Judge—the person who must evaluate your justification/evidence for granting a warrant.
- Bail—amount of money the defendant must pay in order to be released from jail prior to trial. Sometimes, depending upon the egregiousness of the offense, there is no bond.

Evidencing Opinion

Expert opinion is often considered strong significant evidence in FD/FDP cases. Expert opinion derived solely from recognition of FD/FDP profile criteria may be effectively challenged as prosecutorial evidence of criminal conduct; therefore, the scope of expert opinion must contain evidentiary elements (corroborative evidence) whenever possible. When criminal convictions with an FD/FDP factor are based solely upon the attachment of an FD/FDP criminal offender profile and there is a lack of corroborative evidence, criminal convictions may become problematic or otherwise challenged. The utilization of "experts" within courtroom testimony or warrant configuration should be tempered with an assessment of their ability to link theoretic and established FD/FDP profile criteria directly to specific case evidence such as victim/offender seclusion testing, covert surveillance product, or measurable secondary gain for the FD/FDP offender.

Paper Trail: History, Interviews, Directed Intervention, and Evidence

Part of the evidence associated with FDP cases is medical documentation that is often vast and verifies that the cause(s) of an FDP victim's illness(s) cannot be determined, baffle the medical professionals, or typically have "never been seen before." Law enforcement officials tasked with criminal investigations involving an FD/FDP factor should be aware that the likelihood of multiple jurisdictions being involved in the investigative process is high. FD/FDP victimization often encompasses multiple medical facilities that are geographically separated. Tracking a suspected FD/FDP offender's movement via residential, employment, or family links will produce a list of probable medical or criminal justice alternative location infliction sites. Medical or victimization records in these identified locations should be extended accordingly utilizing known and alias suspect identification data. The older the FDP victim is, the more comprehensive the medical documentation will likely be.

Many issues that must be addressed in the development of a homicide or abuse case containing an FDP factor appear to be standard and derived from the review of a multitude of identified criminal case investigations containing an element of FD/FDP. Routinely dividing FD/FDP case investigations into areas of history, interviews, directed intervention, and evidence (HIDE) organizes investigative workload.

FD/FDP Investigative Organization

When organizing FD/FDP criminal case investigations, remember the acronym HIDE and recall that within FD/FDP factors as they relate to abuse or homicide investigations, evidence is often hiding in plain sight (Figure 7.6).

History may include a summation of geographical residential history of the FD/FDP offender. This information may be formulated into graph format to show the relativity of multiple jurisdictions that are often present. History should also include a separate summation of utilized hospitals (emergency room and hospital admission), emergency services (fire department, emergency medical services [EMS], or private ambulance services), and publicly accessible records of police service calls or reported situations within the FDP offender's residence.

Domestic profile history pertaining to the FD/FDP offender's family including social, legal, and welfare venues should be reviewed. Domestic events correlated with FDP victim illness upsurge(s) may provide powerful insight into theoretical FDP abuse triggering mechanisms and victimization sequences. A review of 911 call logs may be useful in FDP criminal case development. Listing significant events that are either directly or indirectly linked to an FD/FDP such as births, deaths, and divorce may illuminate a connection between the event and FD/FDP illness exhibition. Analysis of time measurement between FDP victim hospitalizations and FDP offender demeanor/lifestyle pattern changes may reveal FDP victimization patterns.

Relevancy of familial history in FDP investigations is found within the contextual victimization plurality found in many FDP abuse cases. FDP victim multiplicity has been linked to undetected homicides; therefore, all FDP case investigations should include medical examiner and death record searches for child decedents connected to the suspected FDP offender. In some cases, FDP child homicide victims have not been the FDP abuser's dependants, but the FDP offender had victim access as a temporary custodian such as a babysitter or other types of caretaker. Searching public records through media outlets and the Internet may illuminate an FDP offender's undetected role in the death or harm of an FDP victim, and this role may be masked within the form of a "hero."

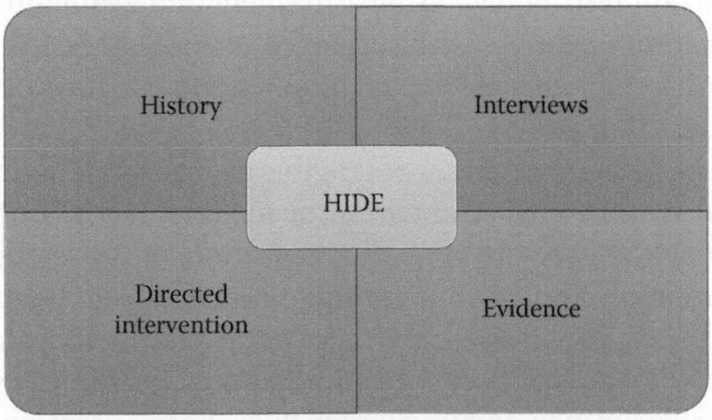

Figure 7.6 FD/FDP criminal case file organization index—history, interviews, directed intervention, and evidence.

FDP case investigations that uncover a link to decedents that an FDP offender had access to should include medical examiner/autopsy report review if available. Within review of these records, the potentiality for death causation review may become possible as previously ruled death causations come under review.

Home health-care/visiting nurse service records are often kept separately from other medical records and should be explored within the FD/FDP case analysis. Professionals attached to these records may become witnesses requiring debriefing. Education provided by visiting nurse service staff to FD/FDP offenders within the course of victim medical treatment pathways may provide technical expertise and offending know-how to the FDP offender. Health insurance investigatory reports are also a good source of information.

Interviews comprise a larger portion of an FDP investigation portfolio. The importance of effective witness interviewing cannot be understated. Witnesses include FDP offenders. Information pertaining to solidification of FDP theory supporting probable cause within a statutory criminal violation may be either lost or gained through witness interviewing. Medical personnel attending FDP victims (physicians, nurses, patient admission staff, ambulance drivers, EMS, emergency room clinical staff, home health-care workers, specialists, psychologists, pediatricians), siblings, other relatives, neighbors, family friends, teachers, clergy, persons with victim access during and preceding victim health changes, caretakers of the victim, and, in some situations, the victim should be screened for information and statements relative to the FD/FDP case. Witnesses should be interviewed separately and their testimony locked into official sworn statement format.

Directed intervention is a significant step in the FD/FDP investigative process and clear documentation is required. Directed intervention occurs at the point that FD via falsified reporting/self-infliction or abuse of another with an FDP methodology factor is suspected. Initial suspicion does not necessarily mean that concerns are immediately conveyed to a suspected offender or his or her family members. Directed intervention is often a result of a multidisciplinary case staffing and may measure the cause versus effect theory of catalyst placement when FD/FDP abuse theory is not yet provable. Initial intervention has ranges and may be direct (removal of a suspected FDP victim from a suspected FDP abuser) or indirect (heightened awareness of the medical staff). Directed intervention may provide irrefutable unspoken FDP child victim testimony through the evaluation of victim/offender seclusion testing data as measurement and evaluation of an FDP victim's health are measured commensurate with suspected offender access limitations. Unspoken FDP victim testimony found within directed intervention efforts is often a key component within criminal prosecution efforts.

Evidence may include a combination of tangible or intangible sources and expert opinion. Analysis, categorization, and summation of medical records pertaining to an FDP abuse victim or FD self-abuser are generally a portion of the evidence package. These records are often immense and include multiple medical establishments from multiple jurisdictional locations. The analysis of medical records may include the following: hospital charts, medical notes, home health-care documentation, personal health records kept by the FD/FDP offender, insurance documentation/files, hospitalization/medical staff documentation of specific medical events, and internal risk management files. Hospital-related diagnostic testing including victim/offender separation data analysis provides evidentiary categorization clarity.

Organization of the FD/FDP Criminal Case File

FD/FDP criminal case file organization should include relevant factors pertaining to criminal acts supported from medical documentation and investigative analysis/work product. The following items may provide investigative clarity through case submission and should be included in a criminal case submission package:

- A chart linking significant interpersonal relationships and the connective link that exists between professionals and the FD/FDP offender
- Flowchart of significant events
- Medical access/visit summary chart for the FDP abuse victim and FD/FDP offender (if applicable)
- Documented events placed in chronological order according to date
- Witness statements and conflicting statement summary
- An education section where events are sorted by document number and referenced by supporting evidence then linked to an educational element based upon case law or theoretical research
- Expert medical opinions
- Physical evidence (includes video-related or audio-related [911] evidence)
- Intangible gains as evidence
- Victim/offender separation testing data
- Glossary of terms

Internet

The Internet is a modern element found within society that a large number of people utilize. Items that people elect to post upon social networking sites reflect many things about them to the point that within a forensic evaluation of a person, psychiatrists may look at a person's Internet presence to help confirm, corroborate, refute, or elaborate their general impression of that individual. What a person places on the Internet is digital evidence used by psychiatry within the assessment of impairment, credibility, dangerousness, and risk. Identity exploration is facilitated through the Internet, but problematic Internet use including Internet addiction or dependence is possible.[21]

A person's "profile" on social networking sites projects a picture of them. When the profile is an honest one, the picture is accurate, but when it is not honest, whether intentionally placed or surreptitiously posted (by another), the view is projected and interpreted by those who view it as a reflection of accuracy. Arrest records and court cases also contribute to the individual's "Internet presence or digital footprint."[22]

Social support online regarding the illness of a child or self and victimizations is a regular occurrence for those who frequent social networking sites. Some seemingly place all aspects of care or experiences on the site, awaiting response in the form of socialized support. From that support, the leap to a well-intended or vicariously placed financial support services found within collective charity donation sites also occurs. Conducting an FD/FDP offender background check should include a wide ranging Internet search that includes social media sites, go-fund-me sites, and traditional computer site search realms.

Within a criminal context, evaluating the content of an FDP offender's Internet postings is a potential evaluation of digital evidence. Postings have been linked within the context of furtherance of FDP attention seeking behavior and as a chronology of abuse events within the context of the continuum of FDP victimization.

Mothers utilizing the Internet as an attention gathering mechanism are not uncommon for parents of chronically ill children. Vivid description of a child's illness escalation, medical treatment, wish organizations, contact with palliative care teams, and sought-after online donations for a child's health needs occur. When FDP is a consideration as the cause for a victim's illness(s), querying the Internet for blogs and accessing research sites pertaining to FDP infliction (accessed by the suspect) are recommended.[23]

Medical staff may be invited to view blogs by FDP parents. When fundraising activity on blogs is found and suspicion of FDP abuse is present, alerting law enforcement is recommended. Fundraising for FDP victims is tantamount to fraud and potential grand theft.

Case Reports

Three children presented with complex medical conditions and that were ultimately found to originate from illness fabricated by their caregivers. In each case, the mother kept a blog of her child's illness and hospitalizations. A physician was initially invited to view victim #1's blog and alerted the child protection team. Blogs were found on various websites and located by entering a search on the Internet with the child's first and last name. The mother's blogs were public and nonrestrictive. In two of the cases, the mothers had public and private blogs in addition to Facebook pages.

Examination of the blogs revealed criminal evidentiary value including distortion of fact, escalation and attention patterns, exposure of the children to public viewing, attitudes toward medical providers, and fundraising and charity[24] (Figure 7.7).

Other Evidence Resources

- In cases involving over-the-counter medicines or controlled prescribed substances, witness statements may include local pharmacist's testimony regarding drug dissemination type and number. A pharmacist's opinion is generally considered an expert testimony.
- Community contacts found within the FD/FDP investigative expanse may provide FD/FDP behavioral clues that further support profile entities within the case evaluation. The educators, Sunday school teachers, clergy, neighbors, and parents of children associated with child FDP victims are sources of information that may provide helpful insight when inquiries are made.
- When the FDP suspect is a caretaker of a suspected victim, there is a probable lineage that generally occurs in the developmental aspect of FDP abuse infliction. To understand how FDP abuse may occur to a child, information attained from the answers to the following questions portrays a picture of the FDP child victim and FDP offenders interactive life and helps illuminate behavioral measures that may link to victimology.
  - What is believed to have caused the victim's illness(s)?
  - Who had access to the victim before and during apparent illness upsurges? (*Illness upsurges in FDP abuse cases are either fabricated or induced injury.*)

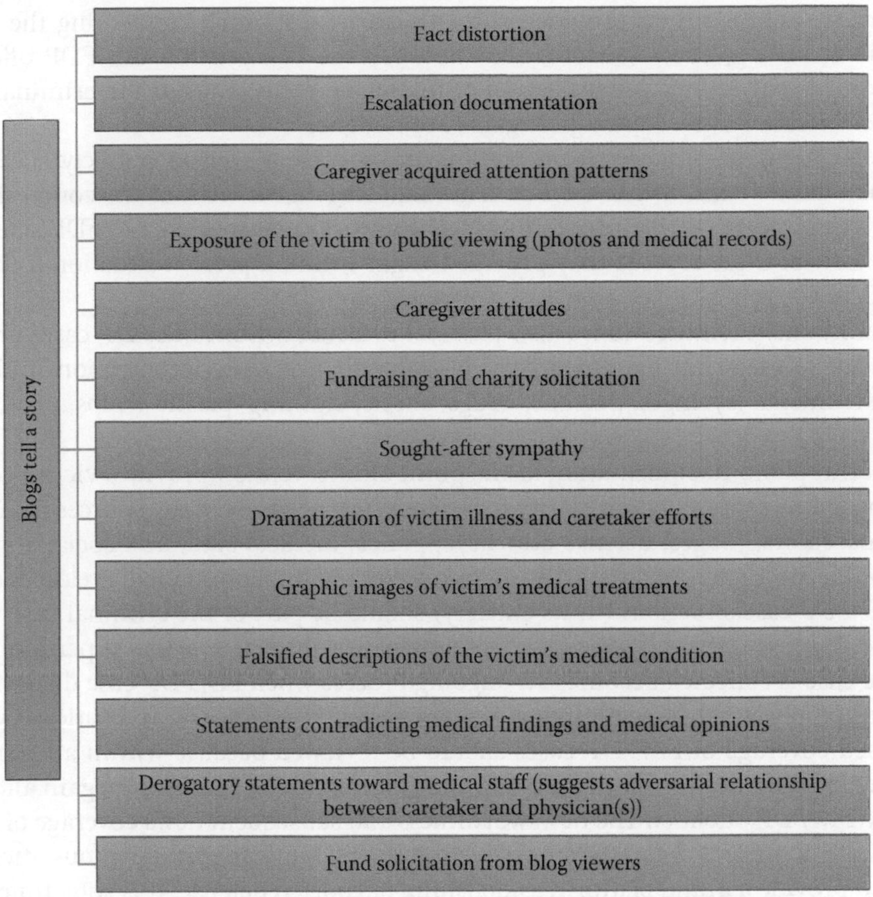

Figure 7.7 Criminal evidentiary value of blogs.

- How did the FDP victim's illness(s) develop?
- What has the FDP victim's health history been since birth? What was the suspected FDP offender's health history prior to the victim's birth and how has that changed?
- Which caretaker normally disciplines the FDP child victim?
- What is the health history of other children within a suspected or proven FDP child abuse situation?
- What is the identity of all physicians involved in the case?
- What is the FDP victim's current developmental level (*child victims*) or cognitive level (*adult victims*)?
- Does the FDP child victim attend school or daycare?
- Is there a history of abusive or neglectful contact toward an FDP abuse victim?
- Has the caretaker been formally or informally educated in any aspects of medical care?
- Does the caretaker have a history of seeking repetitive medical treatment for his- or herself or the child? If so, is the origin of this treatment known or identified?

- External observations provided through expert testimony concerning the cause (victimization)/effect (benefit) seen between the FDP victim and FDP offender require analysis and identification of intangible gains. Within the criminal case inclusion of FD/FDP intangible gains are evidence.
- Depositions or other legal proceeding transcripts as well as publicly accessible documents found within civil or criminal files (via the clerk of the court) should be reviewed when the proceedings are linked to a suspected FD/FDP offender. Review of these records may provide insight within a present situation linked to FD/FDP.
- Commonly identified sources of physical evidence within FD/FDP cases are not always present but may include video surveillance and victimization infliction instruments (syringes, poisons, drugs, sheets, clothing, plastic wraps, pens, pencils, etc.)
- Victim photo documentation at the point of intervention provides victim condition status representation clarity for later review needs by many sources including prosecutors, judges, defense attorneys, police, medical staff, and social services. Media coverage contained within video feeds and publicized media releases of the FD/FDP case situations (in its entirety) should be part of the criminal case package. Ensuring that all media (video, newspaper, magazine articles) pertaining to the case is collected becomes an ongoing process when FD/FDP case dispositions are complicated by litigation that may last for years. Newscasts and nationally televised coverage of FD/FDP cases should be reviewed because within all forms of media, there may be hidden witnesses or illumination of secondary gain afforded the FD/FDP offender. The newsworthiness and subsequent news coverage of these events, in and of themselves, provide the FD/FDP offender momentous attention and provide a grand platform establishing purported defense. It is sometimes difficult to conceptualize that the media also becomes a tool for the FD/FDP offender; however, by providing attention (whether solicited or unsolicited) through the media, the FD/FDP offender is thrust into the coveted center role of importance if only for a given moment in time.
- 911 emergency dispatch call logs and audio may accompany FD/FDP situations as offenders reach out to policing or fire department professionals within the scope of FD repeated self-victimizations or FDP abuse victimizations. Whenever an FD/FDP case investigation is connected to an emergency call process such as those contained within U.S. 911 service procedures, legally securing this communication (via search warrant) as soon as possible is warranted to prevent automatic erasure. Collection of this evidence via warrant also protects the evidentiary chain of custody and validates the source of the recording in the process.

Souvenirs and Trophies

It is theorized that FDP offenders may "record" a sequence of FDP-related abuse actions and surroundings for later recall. The "recording" of the events may be secretively kept in diary form or more commonly stored within the FDP offender's memory. Memory recall through external dialogue concerning an FDP victim's illness(s) makes it possible for an FD/FDP offender to relive experiences, and by extending recall to others, attention is refocused onto the FD/FDP offender. Objects derived from the scene of FDP inflictions, seen as "trophies," may also provide memory recall stimulus to the FD/FDP offender.

The visual depiction of victimization found within photography or video may serve as recall stimulus to an FDP abuser. This media is often an overlooked potential evidence source in abuse or homicide cases that have an FD/FDP factor. The FDP offender's "downtime" may be spend in a circle of recall within an aurora of FDP infliction while reveling in the knowledge that completed deception with detection has occurred within an offending methodology. This thought pattern is believed to further the offender's desired fantasy and empowers further victimization by establishing ever-increasing offense confidence levels.

FD/FDP Offender Exposure Effects

Considering the question regarding potential for FDP methodology (MO) changes within an FDP abuse continuum, external conditions within the offense window should be considered. Generally, in any type of criminal activity, offender MO has change ability and may occur to produce a more favorable offending methodology, to thwart detection or as a matter of growth within an offender's ability to victimize. FDP offenders mirror any other criminal behavior in this respect.

For example, the types of poisons utilized within an FDP abuse infliction may change due to source availability or because the contagion has been medically identified and resolved. The rouse attached to a particular poison is only valuable to the FDP offender when medical staff is struggling to identify the source of an FDP victim's illness and successfully treat the associated signs/symptoms. The heightened sense of urgency in the medical quest to identify significant victim illness places the FDP victim (and thus the FDP offender) into the limelight where attention is foremost and focused. When attention, focus, and treatment are successful, medical staff moves on to the next customer, and the FDP offender becomes less significant and therefore may feel neglected. Changing poison sourcing or delivery recreates an illness threshold in the FDP victim that recalls medical staff to an urgency level producing the desired FDP offender secondarily attained gain of attention.

FDP abuse is generally a chronic series of events occurring over prolonged periods of time. The ability of an FDP offender to obscure abusive acts and to effectively produce illness through specific offensive methodologies increases with practice. FDP offenders may "test" criminal act offenses until one is found that produces desired effect and is presumed to be optimal. The FDP offender may elect to stay with a particular offense delivery system forever or may choose to modify/change the delivery because the results are inadequate or they fear discovery. Resolution of an FDP abuse victim's ailment(s) may be a catalyst for increased levels of abuse or a total change or mutation in abuse methodology. A new illness or newly identified symptoms occurring at the medical resolution of a suspected FDP victim's chronic illness could mean that an FDP offender has changed to a new, different form or source of infliction.

An FDP abuse victim's actions may precipitate FDP offender changes within the regularly delivered MO or signature of the offensive act. In FDP abuse situations, this change may be activated by a child victim's developing maturity and associated ability to speak and act out when awareness of abuse infliction is occurring. Within elderly victims, external sources or service agencies may recognize potential abuse and an exposure threat occurs. It appears that an FDP offender's gratification or reward system is directly related to the consequences of offensive abuse action upon a victim. Probable cause injury escalation appears to be cyclic but is not always absolute and may be affected by external causes.

FDP abuse offenders are known for their patience and meticulous planning capabilities required to have the ability to chronically offend without detection. If apparent signs of physical abuse are observed on suspected FDP abuse victims, something has precipitated that discovery. It is possible that bruising, cuts, or other notable marks upon an FDP victim are a result of medical treatment or testing and this possibility should be thoroughly investigated. It is also possible, however, that the FDP offender has overstepped the infliction methodology and caused a directed injury to the FDP victim or lost the patience to withstand long-term chronic infliction without realizing an immediate result. Visual markings upon an FDP victim may indicate that the FDP offender's control level was somehow compromised producing careless abuse infliction delivery. Obvious evidence of physical abuse upon an FDP victim suggests that an attempt to control or quiet the victim through conventional abusive control measures or a directed attempt of homicide possibly occurred. Evaluation of obvious victim injury will predicate the possibilities to be considered.

Infliction Triggering Mechanisms

A careful review of events immediately preceding FDP victims' hospitalizations may yield clues regarding triggering mechanisms for infliction. Triggering mechanisms may be subtle events or circumstances or they may be blatant, evaluating the statements of victim/offender family members and close family friends. In FDP cases, an FDP offender being left alone with the FDP victim may be enough to trigger infliction that occurs either as opportunistic victimization in furtherance of FDP offender gain attachment or in retaliation (seen as punishment). Retaliation may be viewed as punishment by the FDP offender to whoever placed him or her in the position of caretaker over the FDP victim viewed as desertion. The FDP offender may view "desertion" as a form of neglect. Jealousy or anger regarding whatever circumstance isolated the FDP offender with the FDP victim may become misplaced punishment found within directed FDP victim abuse or continued FDP infliction of harm.

For example,

> A wife is repeatedly left at home with her child while the husband works, spends time with friends, or engages in recreational activities. The wife may view this repetitive behavioral pattern with disdain and connects the child to the situation as an anchor and causative agent. The wife may become angry with the husband and displace that anger onto the child and offend. If the wife has previously experienced hospital life, she will know that placing the child back into the medical setting with some form of ailment will cause the husband's attention to refocus upon the child and upon her. The child has now become a vehicle for the needs of the FDP offender. The level of infliction upon the child victim may progress as the needs of the FDP offender increase or the FDP offender's desire to punish the husband becomes more prevalent.

Multiple Suspects and Victims within FDP Abuse Situations

In abuse cases with an FDP factor where more than one FDP suspect exists, determining whom had direct victim access preceding or during a suspected abuse sequence becomes an important aspect of suspect elimination. In FDP cases, pinpointing and recognizing that a potential abusive act has occurred becomes intricately connected to medical observatory skill. When multiple FDP suspects have shared victim access and equal opportunity for isolated presence, it may be impossible to initially eliminate either as suspects based solely upon access. Considering the application of attained indirect benefit via FDP abuse pathways while evaluating potential FDP offender gain may illuminate motive and initiate correct focus onto the person responsible for FDP falsified illness. Usually, only one suspect will truly benefit from the illness or death of an FDP victim. FDP warning indicators are usually present within the abuse cycle on an acute and chronic evaluation scale but will likely be hidden.

Thus far, presentation of FDP abuse has been focused upon a singular victim chronically abused. In some situations, these victims become inappropriate target victims either due to significant FDP offender detection risks or because the victim has died as an undetected victim of homicide. In some situations, victim death does not equate to FDP abuse cessation and another victim (usually within the family) is chosen; these cases are considered serial FDP abuse situations. In apparent serial (more than one victim) FDP abuse situations, investigators should consider common factors present within individual cases, and each victim represents case individuality. Common factors may include the following:

- Identify witnesses who had opportunity and motive to offend upon the victims *who had access.*
- Determine common locations of victimizations.
- Rule out causation.
    - Elimination of environmental or hazardous substances at the locations common to multiple victims. *Search for contaminants such as lead, carbon monoxide, radiation, or other substances.*
    - Determine if the victims were tested for the presence of any suspected or known toxins.
    - Determine if a toxin could have been present and if it likely would have produced illness or symptoms similar to the victim's. *Expert testimony will be required to make such a determination.*
    - Establish that laboratory tests been evaluated for accuracy.
    - Establish that the lab performing testing has been certified.
    - If a suspected victim contaminant is determined, list and investigate all potential sources. Ask if the identified contaminant could have occurred as a result of a hereditary or preexisting condition within the victim or as a result of a drug reaction.
- Abuse allegations as leverage in a divorce situations.
- Directed motive (usually monetary) that may evolve within an FDP abuse situation. Monetary motivation for victim injury may be identified as abuse or homicide but may lack the FDP factor.

- Determine the immediate- and long-term benefit that was gained by the FDP suspect through individual victim illness or death. Recall that FDP offender gains may be tangible and intangible.
- Look for common denominators found within all cases. *Common denominators in FDP abuse cases may include illness types, infliction methods, interpersonal situations, and the age(s) of victims.*
- Determine if FDP victimizations may be linked on a graduated infliction abuse scale, noting severity increase between cases.
- Conduct body exhumations according to court order as needed for cases involving multiple deaths, especially when death causation was undetermined, attributed to SIDS (infant cases), or otherwise odd.

Unexplained Blood Loss

Found within several suspected FDP abuse victimizations, child victims have required blood transfusions due to medically unexplained blood loss. The blood loss could be due to a medical condition that is unrecognized or it could be intentional. One explanation for blood loss is intentional extraction of victim blood via syringe by the FDP offender. There could be several reasons why this type of FDP offender activity occurs, and the reasons are not always linked to commonly understood FDP methodology. Religious or superstitious beliefs held by the suspected FDP offender or medical misinformation or misunderstanding might prompt an FDP offender to remove a victim's blood in this manner. Blood removal seen as a victim cleansing ritual by a suspected FDP offender attempting to cure an apparently ill victim may be linked to alternative faith entities. Personal belief within faiths not commonly practiced within the United States does not justify victim illness or death. A question of directed homicide should always be explored. When the cause of a victim's medical condition (blood loss) is unclear, the following should be addressed:

- Who had access to syringes and to the victim?
- Was the victim's body carefully examined for evidence of puncture?
- When family members (other than the FDP suspect) are present immediately after or perhaps during a suspected FDP abuse infliction, could these family members be suspects or catalysts to abuse?
- What are the religious beliefs of the FDP suspect and his or her family?

Repetitive Ailments/Recidivism Issues

- Pneumonia is frequently and repetitively found listed within FDP victim medical records review when FDP abuse cases are identified. Root causes for diagnosed pneumonia or any other repetitive ailment should be explored. FDP offender neglect of an FDP victim found with demonstrated lack of appropriate care is sometimes present and identified as the cause or as a contributory factor.
- Identified FDP abuse case review may show that an FDP victim suffered recurrent and unexplained episodes of apnea (cessation of breathing). When the theoretical development of FDP is proven within a suspected abuse case, each apneic episode or event may be considered an intentional act of attempted homicide. Linking apneic episodes to criminal behavior may theoretically be achieved by citing

catalyst events found within the social life of the suspected FDP offender, viewing these events as triggering mechanisms, and then linking a downward spiral seen within an FDP victim's health status. Repetitive ailments or recurrent crisis (attacks) found within FDP abuse methodology are individual acts of intentional torture, whether directly or indirectly formulated.

Extended Evidence Collection

FDP victimization is characteristically long term and repetitive. During an investigation, information should be collected regarding the FDP victim's prior injuries, medical visits, hospitalizations, and (if applicable) school attendance records. The admissibility of this information within criminal case applications will be determined by the prosecutor but is generally considered corroborative evidence in proving intentional abuse or homicide with an FD/FDP factor. Historical information helps to provide common links in serialized FDP case analysis and clarity in singular FDP victimizations. An overview of historical case evaluations is especially helpful for FDP victimizations involving purported multiple offenders and multiple victims and to sort out accidental versus intentional victimization issues.

Anonymous Correspondence

Anonymous notes or letter may be encountered during an active FD/FDP abuse investigation. These items may be found within search warrant delivery or they may be sent to professionals involved within the case. Received letter or note origination should be sought within established criminal investigative procedural methods to determine authenticity and evaluate content.

Within FD/FDP investigations, however, odd materials are sometimes utilized as a means of letter/note configuration, and the meaning of letter/note content can be veiled. A particular letter received by the lead investigator conducting an inquiry into a suspected FDP child abuse situation was constructed of small stickers theorized to have originated in a childhood "first calendar." Personnel at local stores carrying this type of calendar were accessed to determine their recall for recent sales of this type calendar. If odd types of communication are received during an active FD/FDP investigation, researching origin is important, especially if such communication is directly or indirectly threatening to the person addressed. Odd materials such as calendar stickers can be acquired as gifts, and FDP cases involving infants or young children may necessitate tracking potential sources connected to prenatal baby showers or other FDP victim celebrations such as birthdays. Accessing gift lists from these types of special events may be helpful.

Victim/Offender Seclusion Data

In FDP case investigations, the most common method of securing evidence is through the suspect/victim seclusion test. Simply stated, the suspected FDP offender is secluded from the sole (unmonitored) presence of the suspected FDP victim for a specified time period. Evaluation of the victim's medical status during the time of separation from the suspected FDP offender should be carefully documented noting changes in the victim's symptoms (lessening or cessation). If the FDP suspect is then reunited with the victim and provided sole access, measurement of the victim's condition should also be documented noting any change. Reuniting a suspected FDP offender and victim is often an unavoidable situation when victim/offender seclusion data are inconclusive and a theoretical FDP abuse situation has not evolved to the point of criminal charging probable cause. At the point where child protective measures are justified, child victims are generally removed from the custody of the FDP offender and placed into a temporary foster care environment.

Within the hospital setting, nurses may correlate the victim/offender seclusion accessibility factor needed to establish predicate for implied offender responsibility as victim/offender seclusion data are collected.

Within the scope of FDP investigation, child protection venues are generally activated, especially when the victim is a child. It is likely that foster care services will be employed as a measure of child protection and foster parents should be asked to monitor an FDP victim's health situation as a means of victim/offender separation data collection. The following is a generalized log form that temporary guardians (foster care) may use to log observations when an FDP victim is within their domain. See Chapter 9 for further details.

DAILY OBSERVATION REPORT

Name of the Child:

____

Foster Care Parent:

____

Date of Placement: ____________________ Placement Time: ____________________

Condition of the Child on Placement Date:

____

Date	Time of Observation	Medical Status	Medical/Behavioral Problems Noted	Eating Habits	Other Observations

Notary Seal

____

Foster Care Parent

____of ____

<Name>
Commission # 12345
<Jurisdiction County
My Comm. Expires Jan 1, 2025

______________________ ______________________

Witnessed by: <Name> Notary Public

Victim Neglect Evidence within FDP Abuse Investigations

One of the components of FDP child victimization is the unseen force of child neglect. Child neglect is perhaps even more masked than child abuse offenses within FDP methodology. FDP child neglect factors not caused by poverty are a perversion of known neglect patterns and appear as an enhancement of victim control within the FDP infliction scale as follows:

Neglect Not Caused by Poverty	FDP-Related Child Neglect
Absence of, or poor, attachment	Over-attachment and control of the child
Failure to adequately feed the child	Failure to properly feed the child; certain foods withheld due to alleged medical abnormality
Lack of appropriate and consistent behavioral or environmental limit setting	Excessive elemental limits placed upon the child
Failure to ensure the child receives proper/ adequate medical care	Insistence that the child receive excessive medical care (later identified as unnecessary)
Failure to ensure the child attends school (truancy)	Failure to allow the child to attend school producing isolationism, seclusion and dependency
Lack of developmental stimulation[25]	Lack of developmental stimulation away from the FDP offender's presence

Distinguishing between neglect with an FDP element and simple neglect due to other causes can be found within the examination of attainment methodology, and the measurement of personal gain afforded the FDP offender as a result of neglectful behavior upon the FDP victim. A mother who neglects her child in concert with a drug dependency yet gains nothing more than time and perhaps increased monetary resources (money that would have been spent on a victim's needs) for self-indulgence of drugs would not generally be linked to FDP neglect offender status. If that same mother, however, repeatedly neglected to provide essentials to her child and that action caused the child to be hospitalized or the mother insisted that the child be hospitalized and secondary gain found within identified FDP victimization (attention, verification of self worth) form was achieved by the mother within that process, FDP may be applicable as neglect mutates to medical condition. Neglect can be seen within this scenario as fulfilling an FDP offender's want or personal need by utilizing another through neglect or abuse, directly or indirectly.

Evidence Collection Tips in FD/FDP Case Investigations

1. When a potential FD/FDP case is identified, research police and fire brigade dispatch logs to establish service call records to the victim/suspects residence or elsewhere.
2. Interview paramedic/police/EMT professionals regarding call response to situations found within tip #1. These professionals may be first outcry witnesses or provide collective summations pertaining to their observations regarding family dynamics.
3. Ensure that suspicions regarding FD/FDP are not placed into hospital records that suspected FD/FDP offenders have access to during active investigations unless you

want the suspected FDP offender to know. FD/FDP offenders commonly attempt or achieve access to medical records within the hospital despite countermeasures to protect access.

4. Look for "hero" status in FD/FDP offenders. The "saved" person may be the first victim.
5. Do not take anything at face value in FD/FDP case investigations. Verification procedures should be unilaterally applied in all aspects of the investigation.
6. Obtain a court order for a video surveillance, evidence seizure, and arrest warrant whenever possible. Court orders (warrants) protect the admissibility of evidence collected and arrest warrants allow prosecutorial input in a large way.
7. Maintain a proper chain of custody on all evidence collected. If specimens are collected by medical personnel and sent to laboratories for testing, ensure that the custody chain is maintained to and from the lab.
8. Utilize modern policing aids as evidence gathering tools within the case investigation. Resources such as Infotrak; the Internet; publicly accessible financial, property, and vital statistics records; computer voice stress analysis; polygraph; handwriting analysis; lab testing; national resource data banks; and expert testimony resources.
9. Do not attempt to build a criminal abuse or homicide case solely upon expert witness testimony. Evidence collection and recognition is very important to successful prosecution.
10. If you don't know, or you aren't sure, ask someone for assistance.
11. When in doubt, collect and secure potential evidence or isolate it in place and obtain a warrant if not in plain view. It is better to have the ability to discard unneeded items than later need them but not have them available.

Conclusion

The many facets of evidence gathering possible in FD/FDP investigations create a tendency to assemble such a complicated wealth of information that it is overwhelming to those who must review it and collect it. Jurors often seem to dismiss the seriousness of an FDP case noting a sense of astonishment regarding the abusive act of an FDP offender and attempt to explain it. When police prepare criminal FDP cases for prosecution then prosecutors enhance that preparation for courtroom presentation, care should be taken to strive for simplification when possible. Simplification may provide an avenue for jurors to achieve uniform understanding of the very complicated FD/FDP methodology. Detectives and prosecutors should be aware that their exposure to the many aspects of FD/FDP almost always produces an educational understanding far greater than a juror or a judge may possess. This associative knowledge gap facilitates a data tolerance gap that must be bridged through an understandable education platform to provide judge and jury with the tools necessary to render proper opinion based upon evidence. The simplest process for attaining consensus is for the preparer of the case to master his or her own understanding of FD/FDP so that it may be properly explained, understood, and effectively resolved. Understanding/educational subject mastery is fundamental to place the difficult concept of FD/FDP infliction into realistic terms of abuse or homicide.

Notes

1. Lucy, D. and Aitken, C., A review of the role of roster data and evidence of attendance in cases of suspected excess deaths in a medical context. *Law, Probability and Risk (Oxford University Press)*, 2002;1:141–160.
2. Ibid.
3. *The American Heritage Dictionary*. Houghton-Mifflin Company, 1985, p. 1242.
4. Davis, P., Deliberate poisoning in the context of induced illness in children. *Pediatrics and Child Health*, 2013;23(9):385–390.
5. http://www.tandurust.com/health-faq-5/salt-poisoning-symptoms.html.
6. http://www.nytimes.com.
7. https://en.wikipedia.org/wiki/Murder_of_Garnett_Spears.
8. Meehan, E.W.P., Merschman, K.M., and Chiang, V.W., An 18 month old girl with apneic spells. *Pediatric Emergency Care*, 2008;24:546–549.
9. http://www.medicinenet.com/script/main/art.asp?articlekey=31785.
10. *Katz v. United States*, 389 U.S. 347 (1967).
11. Robinson, E., Munchausen syndrome by proxy and covert video surveillance: Exploring legal problems and solutions for hospitals. *Medical Trial Technique Quarterly*, 1997;44:159–187.
12. *United States v. White*, 401 U.S. 745,745, 1971.
13. http://legal-dictionary.thefree dictionary.com/Fourth+Amendment.
14. Williams, J.S., *Constitutional Analysis*. St. Paul, MN: West Publishing Company, 1982.
15. Artingstall, K., *Practical Aspects of Munchausen by Proxy and Munchausen Syndrome Investigation*. Boca Raton, FL: CRC Press, 1999.
16. Flannery, M., Munchausen syndrome by proxy: Broadening the scope of child abuse. *University of Richmond Law Review*, 1994;28:1175.
17. Brady, M., Munchausen syndrome by proxy: How should we weigh our options? *Law and Psychology Review*, 1994;18:361.
18. https://en.wikipedia.org/wiki/Exigent_circumstance.
19. Yorker, B., Covert video surveillance of Munchausen syndrome by proxy: The exigent circumstances exception. *Health Matrix: Journal of Law-Medicine*, Summer 1995;5(2):325–346.
20. http://legal-dictionary. The free dictionary.com/Fourth+Amendment.
21. Recupero, P.R., The mental status examination in the age of the internet. *Journal of the American Academy of Psychiatry and the Law*, 2010;38:15–26.
22. Madden, M., Fox, S., Smith, A. et al., Digital footprints: Online identity management and search in the age of transparency. Pew Internet and American Life Project, December 16, 2007. Available at http://pewinternet.org/~/media//Files/Reports/2007/PIP_Digital_Footprints.pdf.pdf.
23. Brown, A., Gonzalez, G., Wiester, R., Kelley, M., and Feldman, K., Care taker blogs in caregiver fabricated illness in a child: A window on the caretaker's thinking? *Child Abuse and Neglect*, 2014;38:488–497.
24. Ibid.
25. Office of Juvenile Justice and Delinquency Prevention (OJJDP), *Child Neglect and Munchausen Syndrome by Proxy*. OJJDP, Washington, DC, September 1996, p. 4.

The Multidisciplinary Approach to FDP Abuse/Homicide Case Management

8

Do not go where the path may lead, go instead where there is no path and leave a trail.

Ralph Waldo Emerson

Organizational Diversity

Police personnel and prosecutors who are tasked with the investigation and prosecution of suspected abuse within the context of law violations face a unique challenge when any form of abuse (including homicide) involves an element of factitious disorder (FD)/factitious disorder by proxy (FDP). FDP methodology, complexity and offender skill within abuse patterns may quickly become an overwhelming identification task creating panic. This challenge is especially relevant to the law enforcement officer or prosecutor having the dubious responsibility of being the first to investigate or prosecute an abuse or homicide case in a particular geographic location—especially when the location is rural.

Although it is not optimal, law enforcement officers, prosecutors, defense attorneys, medical staff, and others connected within an interdisciplinary mode to a suspected FDP casc acquire their knowledge and associated professional skill through active cases. Relevancy linked to time constraints and likelihood of knowledge application may not occur until the need is presented. Therefore, professionals attached to an abuse or death case involving an FD/FDP factor often find themselves in investigatory and research positions simultaneously. Case protocol is written during the learning process of case evaluation. It is apparent that heightened awareness of FD/FDP as an element within abuse or homicide criminal casework is time sensitive, and the general foundation of professional education on this topic is linked to point of use. Since FD/FDP situations or at least the recognition of them remains relatively scarce, common knowledge regarding the existence of FD/FDP is uncommon. The second edition of this text was authored because the general professional knowledge base became obscure and this is a disservice to victims.

Diversity within any criminal investigation is significant, but generalized protocol coupled with investigative understanding (especially when complex victimizations such as those found within FD-/FDP-related events) is required to effectively intervene in a victimization abuse cycle. Sometimes, there is no time to get up to speed on complex criminology topics because the life of the victim may hang in the balance between knowledge and intervention. Knowledge prevents panic and provides the basis for sound investigative policy and procedures.

When a potential abuse/homicide case involving an FDP factor is discovered, there are three areas that must be addressed: medical resolution, criminal disposition, and victim protection. These areas of responsibility overlap one another and are not mutually exclusive.

The agencies/personnel who attach to an abuse or homicide case may easily negatively affect one another's resolution efforts. Within that impact probability, further harm may come to abuse victims when individual agencies act without regard for how decisions may impact their interdisciplinary partners' efforts as the total victimization picture becomes blurred. The best and recommended approach for handling a suspected abuse or homicide case with an FD/FDP factor is through the multidisciplinary approach to case management.

The complexity of all abuse/homicide cases with an FDP factor is accentuated by the gravity of the criminal act coupled with aggregate investigative participants involved in case analysis and disposition. In other words, one can easily feel overwhelmed. The nature of FD/FDP as an element within criminal case evaluations dictates that individual professions must work with one another from their perspective case roles with a common goal of child protection. The understanding and collaboration that investigative team participants possess, maintain, or acquire within the duration of an FDP case investigation are paramount to final outcome for an FDP victim. The conceptualization of individual professions motivated and directed by a search for the truth and resolution in favor of victim protection becomes the binding vehicle to achieve case resolution success through a spirit of cooperation.

Organizational diversity required for effective FDP intervention through case management is not always easily attained because different professional disciplines have culturally specific attitudes and platforms. Cultural destructiveness is a force often found within the union of multidisciplinary team participants and commonly referred to as "my way or the highway." Potential FDP multidisciplinary team members are usually professionally adept and have the ability to strongly convey opinions. These attributes are desirable for FDP multidisciplinary team members, but case resolution demands additional elements of flexibility (to accommodate change) and impartiality (to assure correctness). Impartiality is often successfully defended as a method of precluding alteration of evidence that may be presented during litigation.

A respectful understanding of skill and authority between the team members is often reflected through attitudes that intricately affect the team's practical ability to function. Understanding and respect among team members provide an investigative edge or advantage by relieving concern that individual (agency) action will impede the overall investigation. Incapacity will occur if a case or problem is identified, but no resolution plan can be initiated at the time or recognition due to opinion impasse among team members. Such incapacity could be lethal to the well-being of a victim since there usually is little time to arbitrate the debate during an actual FDP victimization sequence.

FDP offenders have been known to successfully apply universal deception to thwart detection. A primary factor toward attaining pervasive understanding among FDP multidisciplinary team members is that just about anyone can be fooled, for a time.

Thus, no one (including team members) is infallible. Building an effective multidisciplinary team response to FDP victimization is in many ways like scuba diving—good divers do not dive alone or blindly; diving is not entirely without risk, but risk can be managed through careful and accurate preparation.

Defining the Multidisciplinary Team

The concept objective of the multidisciplinary team is to establish a forum of multidisciplinary professionals to plan, implement, and evaluate interventions to promote victim

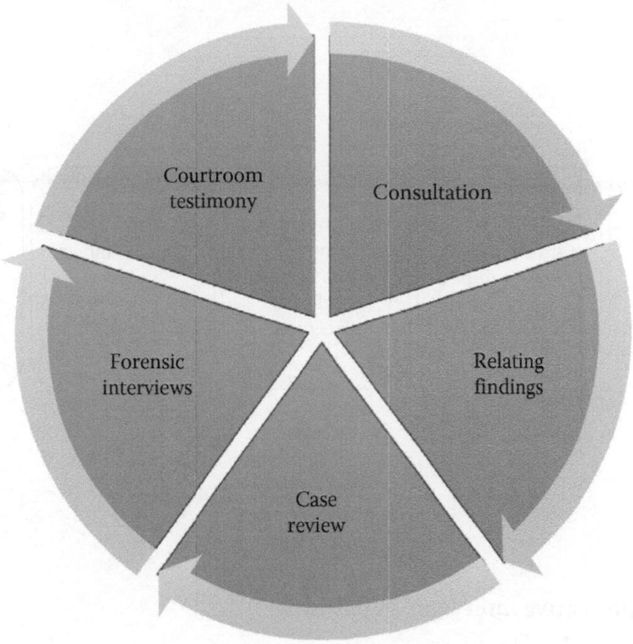

Figure 8.1 Multidisciplinary team functions.

safety through the implementation of best practice.[1] The multidisciplinary team is a forum of professionals from various disciplines whose goal is effective and enduring victim protection. In a sense, the multidisciplinary team ensures that best practice safety is maintained for the victim during the difficult process of FDP abuse identification. The structure of the team should provide clear procedures and protocols while managing the FDP abuse investigation and serve as liaison to supporting agencies. Five important tasks multidisciplinary team members perform include consultation, communication of findings with appropriate agencies, case review, forensic interviews and courtroom testimony.[1] Multidisciplinary teams provide clear procedures and protocols for case management, mentor other professionals, serve as liaison with CPT and law enforcement, initiate and implement quality assurance, track and report cases, and consult with other hospitals/physicians (Figure 8.1).[2]

Multidisciplinary Team Function

It is important to evaluate a suspected FDP abuse situation on a multidisciplinary level by including medical, psychosocial, child protective services, and legal services and law enforcement professionals because of case complexity. FDP abuse is a criminal action that is often interlaced within a medical diagnostic forum, and in approximately 30% of the cases, this behavior coincides with an authenticated underlying illness in the victim.[3]

Potential abuse reports made to state child protection agencies occur to determine if a child's health or welfare has been harmed. Intervention may occur in conditional stages (investigation to determine harm risk); indicators of significant harm risk promote child custody and care placement (foster system) and rehabilitative help for the parents; final case disposition is child and parent reunification/adoption/termination of parental rights (Figure 8.2).[4]

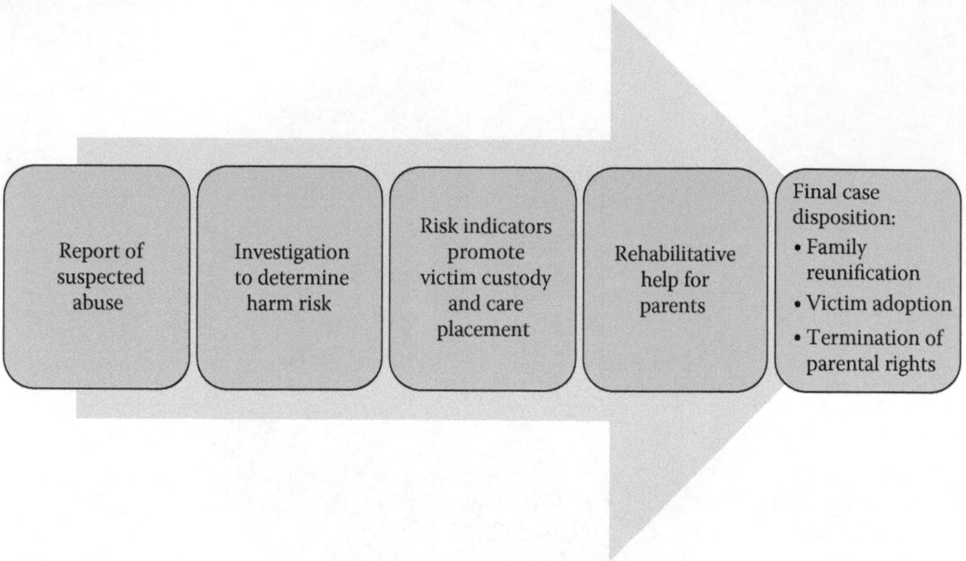

Figure 8.2 Child protective intervention pathways.

Recommended Team Members

When a potential FDP-related abuse or homicide case is uncovered, the case pathway is often initially uncertain. Variable factors that exist for professional service personnel and the FDP offender may create organizational confusion. This confusion may be manifested within a situation of developmental case transformation facilitating inefficiency within applied intervention efforts. To alleviate FDP organizational casework confusion, the cohesiveness of multidisciplinary team members is required. Team members are required to have a knowledge base that extends beyond the case at hand to project needed flexibility and intuitive interactive intervention possibility. FDP multidisciplinary team members must have the capability and desire to share their knowledge, supposition, and observations with others on the team for individual team members to function as a singular entity.

The first task in the formation of an FDP multidisciplinary team is the determination of positional team members. The FDP intervention team lineup shown in Figure 8.3 is recommended.

General Team Data

FDP multidisciplinary core team members/participants/alternates should be identified before convening a case staffing (initial investigative meeting assembly). Initial staffing should occur as quickly as possible once a potential FDP abuse/homicide case has been theoretically or otherwise uncovered. Team members should be knowledgeable regarding FD/FDP methodology fundamentals and aware of one another's specific job-related requirements and constrictions so that precious time within the actual staffing is not allocated to educating team member participants. There is usually not sufficient time for non-educated FD/FDP multidisciplinary team members to obtain a functional understanding

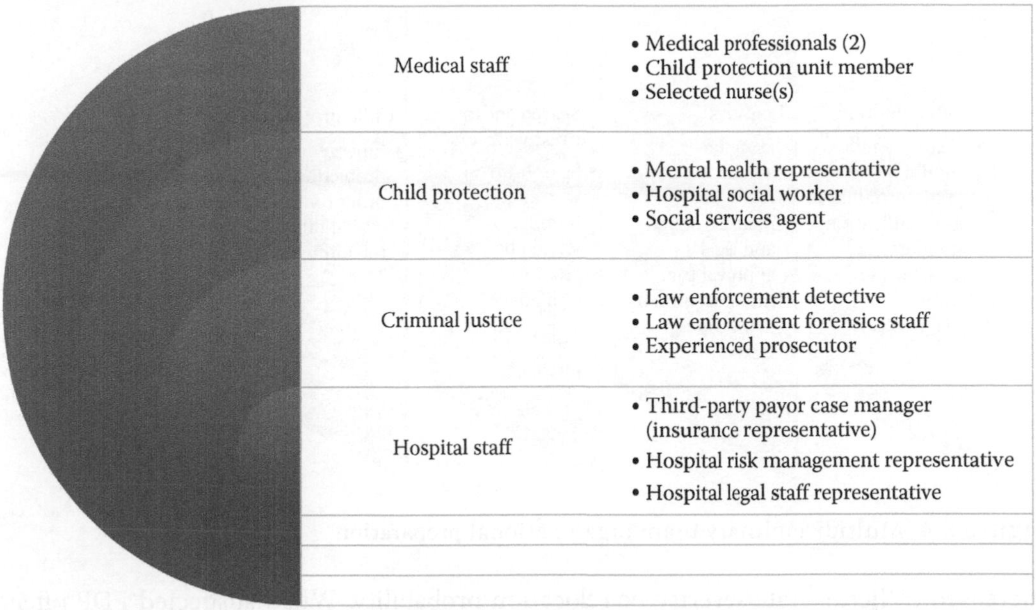
Medical staff
• Medical professionals (2)
• Child protection unit member
• Selected nurse(s)
Child protection
• Mental health representative
• Hospital social worker
• Social services agent
Criminal justice
• Law enforcement detective
• Law enforcement forensics staff
• Experienced prosecutor
Hospital staff
• Third-party payor case manager (insurance representative)
• Hospital risk management representative
• Hospital legal staff representative

Figure 8.3 Multidisciplinary team defined.

of FD/FDP while efficiently expediting the need to guard against victim endangerment and flight risk concern through action.

Team members who are new to their respective disciplines may bring a disadvantage to the team because they may lack *practical education* within their field. During the case staffing review and intervention planning process, inexperienced team members may be led by other team members as they attempt to *catch up* on issues that are often complex. Participation in a multidisciplinary FDP team staffing should not be viewed as an allowable training ground for new employees. Experienced staff should carefully supervise assimilation of newly qualified team members introduced into the multidisciplinary FDP team. Acute and chronic significance of an FDP multidisciplinary teams expeditious intervention plan and decisions regarding that plan must be understood by all team members as issues of victim/offender relocation, recidivism, and upscale victim infliction become the forefront of concern.

Multidisciplinary Team Organizational Preparation

Medical Staff

Diagnosing FDP is an immense clinical challenge that usually involves a multidisciplinary team approach (Figure 8.4).[5] Medical and mental health clinicians are generally not trained to approach their cases from an investigative mode of criminal suspicion of wrongdoing. This stance accommodates the methodology of a typical FDP offender skilled in deception who outwardly portrays appropriate behavior. When suspicions of FDP abuse are present, health-care personnel often *tip their hands* prematurely and make the suspected FDP offender aware that their behavior/actions are being observed. This awareness may inadvertently place an increased risk of harm upon the FDP victim through an

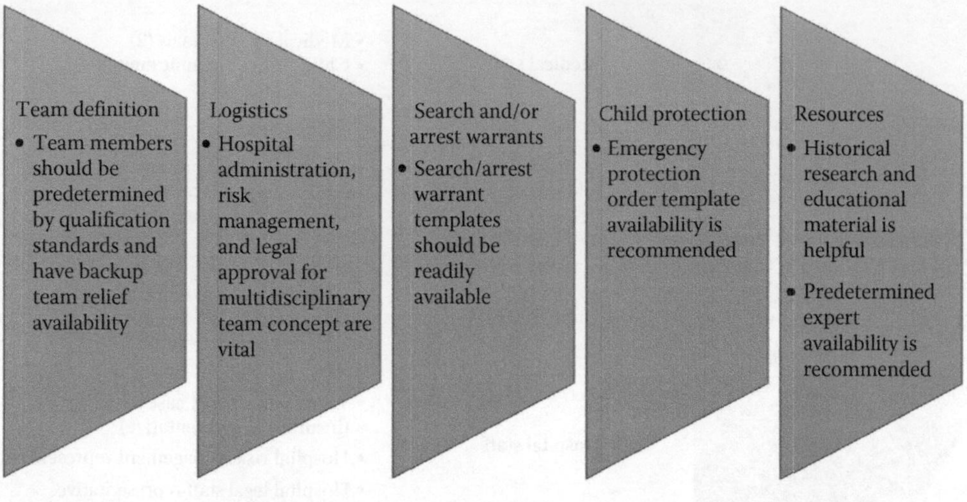

Figure 8.4 Multidisciplinary team organizational preparation.

increased infliction rate/severity or relocation probability. When suspected FDP offenders realize they are under investigation, the stage is set for the suspected offender to simply terminate contact with a particular hospital or health-care professional, relocate to another location, and continue the cycle of abuse with a new unsuspecting hospital and staff. Despite the development of protocol at many major teaching hospitals, many health professionals remain unfamiliar with FD/FDP dynamics. Laws pertaining to the protection of dependents (child, elderly, or impaired) require designated professionals, including medical staff, to report known or suspected abuse to law enforcement/social service protective staff officials.

Nurses who are the most likely to observe interaction between a potential FDP offender and victim may have the most firm grasp on the *total patient package* that includes the coordination of multitudes of specialty doctors. Nurses who work with potential FDP victims may be able to assess and facilitate an early diagnosis of FDP if they recognize potential presence.[6] Nurses may find themselves in precarious positions within the world of the FDP offender—either completely convinced of a suspected FDP offender's innocence or suspicious but reluctant to step forward and vocalize these suspicions. There are situations where nurses vocalize suspicions but concerns are promptly dismissed.

The Primary Care Physician

General physicians, who are responsible for overall patient care coordination, may fail to see emerging patterns of potential FD/FDP abuse as specialists are consulted on victim symptomology specificity in the quest for medical identification of a person's illness(s). FD/FDP offenders are skilled at the use of multiple specialists within abusc cycles and know that specialists do not necessarily talk to one another. Recognizing that a medical case may be linked to an FD/FDP methodology requires an overall evaluation of a person's medical history, and this is usually the responsibility of a primary care physician. It is normal business within the field of medicine to believe obvious sincerity of people—especially when a parent of an ill child relies on parental observations to aid in diagnostic protocol.

FDP case direction is derived from the consensus of team members and provides an across-the-board consistency for personnel directly involved with FDP victims, offenders, and family members. Due to the nature of abuse or homicide with an FDP methodology, medical personnel associated with the case may find themselves in multiple roles that include caregiver, witness, and (previous) unknowing participatory vehicle (instrument) of abuse. Unique simultaneous roles stretch the expanse between voluntary and involuntary and require a prearranged understanding of the contributory position assumed by taking a position on the FDP multidisciplinary team. Multidisciplinary FDP intervention teams generally find that the "involved physician(s)" or nurse(s) may be ineffective as neutral team participants because they are often defending their well-intentioned actions and have demonstrated a failure to recognize their role in the potential encompassing FDP spiral. If they do recognize that role, most staff becomes quite angry that they have been placed into an involuntary and unknowing role as an instrument of abuse and objectivity is not always possible. It is important for members of the FDP multidisciplinary team to understand the overarching role the primary care physician holds within an FDP case review but recognize that an "involved" physician may be better utilized as a resource rather than a team member.

Case impact exerted by a primary care physician should be considered. Some physicians are not willing to consider FDP abuse as an alternative diagnosis for unresolved patient illness until all other avenues have been explored. Others are relatively *quick* to make a theoretical link to FDP abuse without significant explorations of other medical alternative causations for a person's illness(s). The two extremes represent a quandary for physicians, and there are no steadfast rules to guide them on this particular point.

Obtaining and reviewing medical records accurately and thoroughly then verifying the history found within the records from sources other than the suspected FD/FDP offender are needed services when considering a potential link between illness and possible FDP abuse. This review is time-consuming. Primary care physicians should be qualified to render an opinion, determined to uncover the truth and willing to work with other agencies within that process. The physician must also be willing to testify in court if necessary (and it usually is necessary).

Interagency Collaborative Staffing

Interagency blindness due to a lack of understanding team participatory roles, responsibilities, and authority can create confusion rather than foster clarity within a process known as "case staffing." FDP case staffing is an interdisciplinary team meeting process elemental to effective FDP case management and is likely to be repetitive within the duration of FD/FDP case evaluation. Staffing is a meeting of key authoritative personnel called together as an interactive "think tank" for the purpose of addressing immediate victim safety concern and to formulate an action plan. This action plan incorporates logistics and investigative parameters while scrutinizing identified behavior(s), established fact(s), and theoretical analysis of the case from individual professional angles. Staffing a case allows multidisciplinary team members to share and clarify known information, strategize and implement recommendations, and clarify involved agency/organizational roles, procedures, and expectations. Case staffing sets into motion a formidable weapon against FD/FDP through a collective response.

A staffing plan may formulate case direction that includes use of video surveillance, arrest/search warrants, and contingencies to address the removal of the suspected FDP victim by a suspected FDP offender prior to the establishment of enough evidence to change theoretical illness causation via FDP into probable cause of abuse. If search and arrest warrants are simultaneously obtained, they should be simultaneously executed by two teams of law enforcement officials. When an FDP offender is placed into custodial arrest, care should be exercised to preclude potential evidence destruction if the FDP abuser is allowed location access. Issues of offender privacy should not supersede evidentiary protection needs. Protection of an FDP victim should be paramount during the time of FDP offender custodial arrest to prevent directed upscale infliction of harm. An FDP abuser may realize that the victim is the most valuable piece of evidence within a criminal case and elect direct elimination of that evidence through homicidal measures.

At initial case staffing, the protocol format shown in Figure 8.5 may be followed.

The general reporting sequence of FDP abuse involves physician suspicion conveyed to child protective services and hospital administration, notification of this suspicion to law enforcement and social services, a scheduled initial staffing to formulate an intervention plan, execution of the plan and any needed modifications and follow-up contact (including psychological victim/family aide; Figure 8.6).

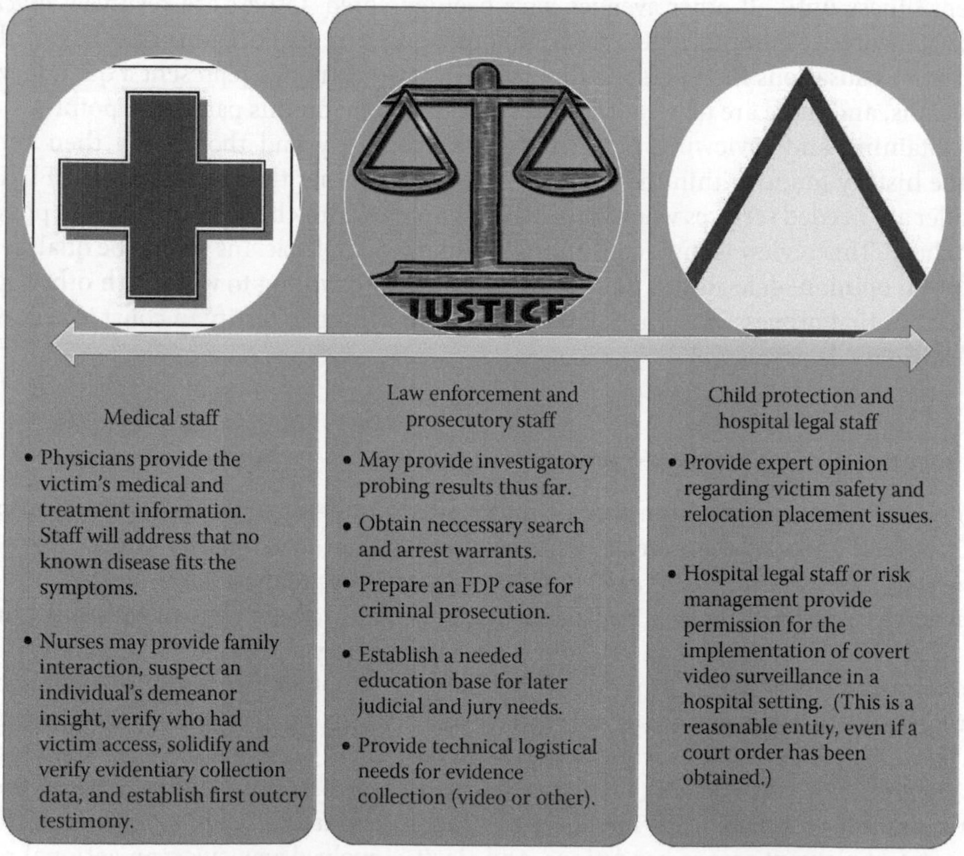

Medical staff
• Physicians provide the victim's medical and treatment information. Staff will address that no known disease fits the symptoms.
• Nurses may provide family interaction, suspect an individual's demeanor insight, verify who had victim access, solidify and verify evidentiary collection data, and establish first outcry testimony.
Law enforcement and prosecutory staff
• May provide investigatory probing results thus far.
• Obtain neccessary search and arrest warrants.
• Prepare an FDP case for criminal prosecution.
• Establish a needed education base for later judicial and jury needs.
• Provide technical logistical needs for evidence collection (video or other).
Child protection and hospital legal staff
• Provide expert opinion regarding victim safety and relocation placement issues.
• Hospital legal staff or risk management provide permission for the implementation of covert video surveillance in a hospital setting. (This is a reasonable entity, even if a court order has been obtained.)

Figure 8.5 Multidisciplinary staffing protocol.

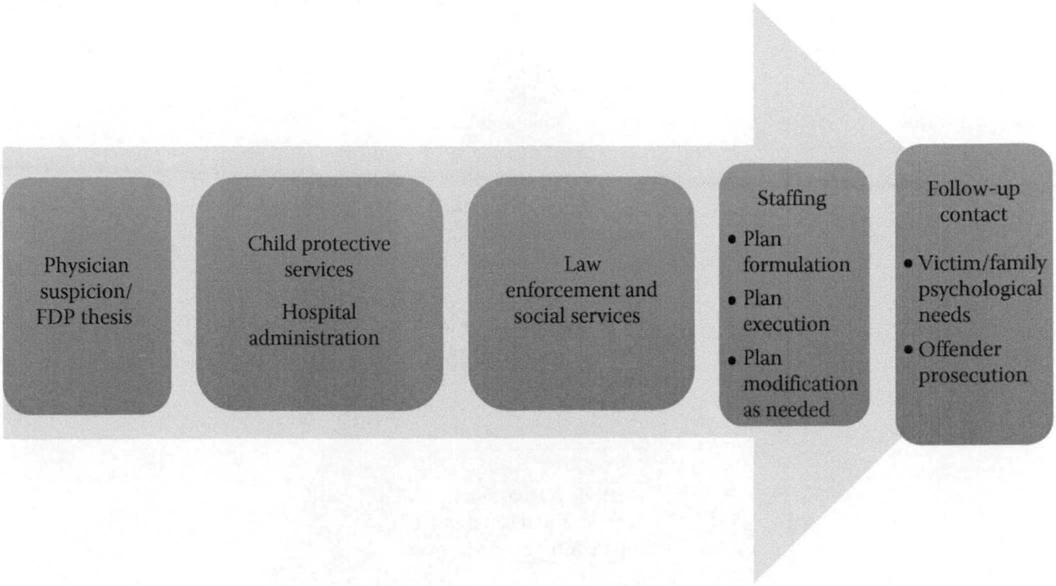

Figure 8.6 Factitious disorder by proxyabuse identification pathway.

Multidisciplinary team member competency is tested when a formulated plan is activated and results are analyzed. Team proficiency is measured within environmental change for the victim reflected in the victim's immediate and long-term health status. Members of an FDP investigative (assessment and intervention) multidisciplinary team should posses an ability to diplomatically and interactively project individual professional position/skill within the focus of child protection tempered by the confines of the law. Adaptation to unsuccessful implementation of team case management recommendations will require reconvening the team to further assess the case situation and adapt to those changes. Problematic issues such as denied court intervention requested in the form of warrants or custody orders will necessitate action plan review and modification to compliment judicial needs while maintaining victim safety concerns.

FDP Multidisciplinary Team Leadership Considerations

Active FDP multidisciplinary teams find that individual team member's time constraints and abilities may weaken team efficiency by lowering group focus levels. Group balance and functioning within the team concept are facilitated when a leader is chosen to facilitate positive proactive direction. A leader may quickly emerge or be preselected but should assume the leadership role based upon ability—not solely upon reputation or ranking. Any FDP multidisciplinary team leader should possess general knowledge of success and failure. As a leader, by knowing the ways to fail, alertness to pitfalls is generated and increases the likelihood of success. Effective leaders often have the attributes shown in Figure 8.7.

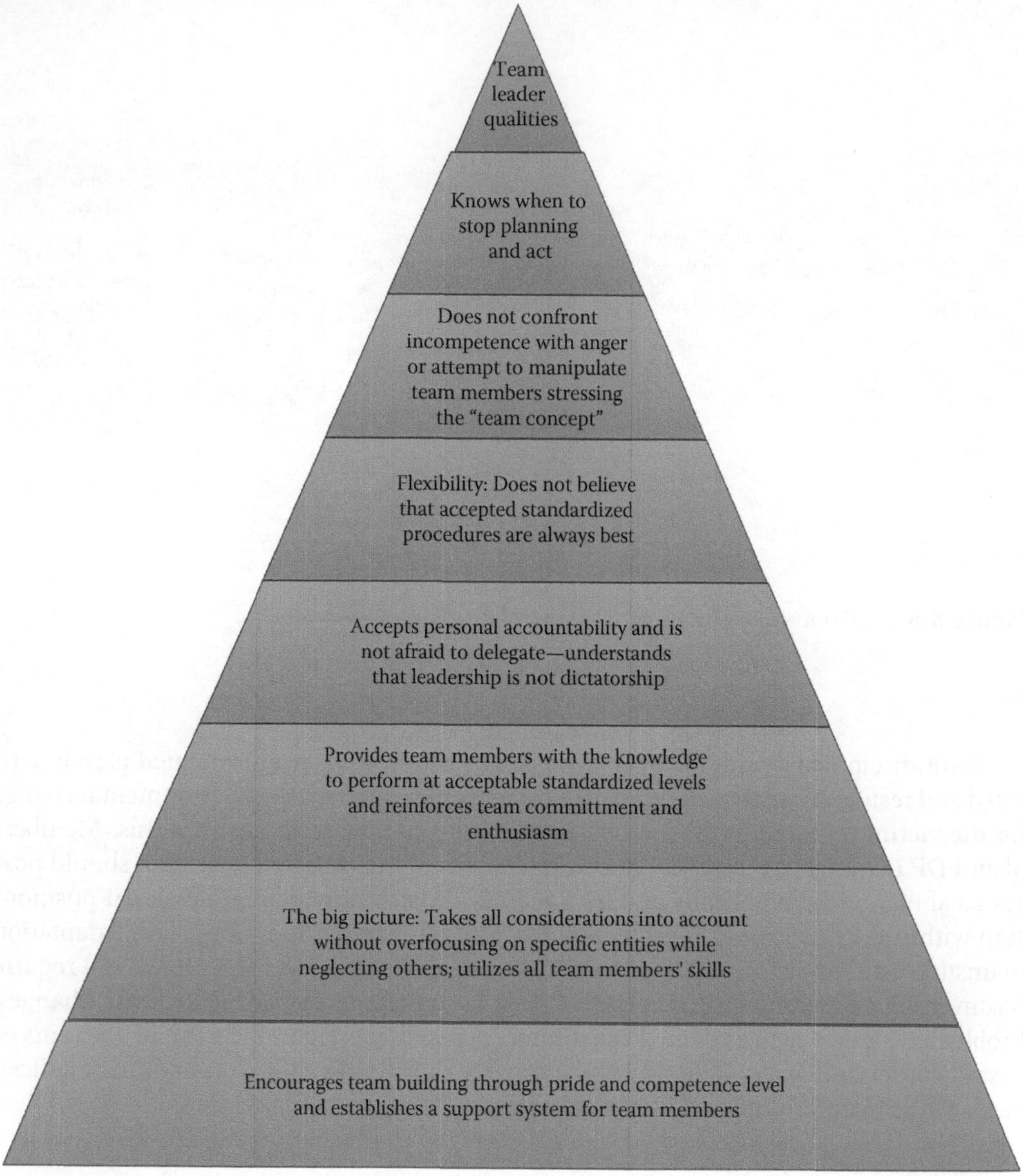

Figure 8.7 Multidisciplinary leadership qualities.

Why Is Multidisciplinary Team Protocol Necessary?

The development of FDP case protocol should occur before an FDP case is reported and the need for a staffing is presented. Protocol development is a process that requires inter-agency cooperation and unilateral understanding to allow timely free exchange of information, universal understanding, and recognition. Consistency of approach often lessens the opportunity for FDP offenders to continue victimization by controlling victim access while collecting clues to substantiate the theory of FDP victimization pathways. FDP case evidence is generally not easily recognized and usually not blatantly seen, which aligns with a prolonged investigative time period and multitude of witness testimony. Protocol is necessary for effective case management to ensure that every reasonable effort is afforded toward victim protection while endeavors occur to either prove or disprove relativity of the FDP theory.

Protocol also serves to bridge understanding within the distinctly individualized pathway each FDP abuse case travels. This interactional pathway differs from other criminal case protocol formats. Within other forms of major case management (direct homicide, property crimes, economic crimes, etc.), a law enforcement officer's conclusion is not necessarily dependent upon interagency collective agreement. Police agencies generally do not look to other agencies for case resolution, opinion, or evidence; case disposition is usually attained after all information is gathered and processed by a police detective who formulates a rational conclusion based upon the substantiation of clear and convincing evidence. Criminal cases with an FD/FDP factor differ from standardized case management protocol because case disposition requires interaction between collaborating professionals and no one discipline singularly holds the key to effective case resolution. Professional conclusions are collectively determined through an interactive case management platform as police work with medical staff to establish medical evidence that is also criminal evidence as the theory of FDP abuse methodology is either proven or disproven. Both police and medical representatives are also interactive with victim protection authorities that are challenged with the knowledge that premature victim custody removal may have dire consequences. Workings within an interdisciplinary case staffing fall beneath the watchful eyes of legal representatives on all participatory angles. The peculiarities of evidence gathering in FD/FDP cases, infliction spectrum, and unique criminalistics properties require unprecedented interagency cooperation to avoid error and/or the loss of potential evidence.

The standards of proof remain constant in any type of criminal investigation. FDP cases, however, tend to require escalated investigative sophistication for successful conclusion. The difference between abuse or homicide cases and those that contain an element of FD/FDP is the level of potential harm caused directly by the actions or inactions of the multidisciplinary team. Complicated aspects of overall FD/FDP knowledge required to obtain an effective intervention that will endure the rigors of the legal system remain challenging.

Unique FDP Victimization and Investigative Protocol

Understanding victimization sequences that commonly occur within an abuse or a homicide case that involves an FDP factor helps formulate a basis for intervention possibilities through the actions of a multidisciplinary team. All team members should be aware of the following issues that are likely to present within the framework of FDP victimization methodology. These parameters are helpful within the investigative and prosecution phases of case management:

- FDP victims cannot call for help—they must be found.
- FDP victims cannot escape the abuser without intervention.
- FDP offenders have the latitude of skill attained through endurance that often results in bold, brazen victim abuse.
- In FDP cases, threatened intervention or the FDP offender's knowledge of outside suspicion may cause an upsurge of victimization frequency/intensity or precipitate assaultive actions to temporarily cease.

- There is no absolutely accurate method of predicting intervention outcome in an abuse case with an FDP factor.
- Effective intervention in FDP abuse cases that have not risen to the level of homicide is either accomplished through the removal of the FDP victim from the offender's custody and/or the FDP offender's custodial arrest. Either action immediately halts the opportunity for additional abuse. *Caution should be exercised because removal of a victim from a suspected FDP offender's custody without sufficient evidence only provides a temporary solution or 'quick fix' to an abuse problem that will likely intensify in place or at another location upon reunification between the FDP offender and victim* (see Chapter 7).
- FDP recidivism may be lessened when public acknowledgement of FDP offender responsibility through media coverage occurs coupled with court-mandated victim protection measures. Identification and arrest of an FDP-related abuser alone appear to be insufficient to halt recidivism.
- FDP abuse offenders who publicly acknowledge criminal offense responsibility may shift from issues of *attention* to those of *attention through notoriety* established through the media. Public display of FDP abuse responsibility for notoriety purposes is thought to be an alternative form of indirect FDP justification and reward. FDP offenders may continue to see themselves as victims of forces beyond their control and use the media as a belief reinforcement vehicle.
- When FDP abuse patterns are identified within a suspected abuse case or homicide investigation and diagnosed by medical staff as an entity, protective services must render that abuse is *founded* and proceed in accordance with established agency dependency protocol.
- Not every suspected case of abuse or victim death (homicide) is confirmed. Alternative causation for apparent behavior associated with FDP may include the following:
  - Physical victim injury without an FDP correlation as accidental or directed abuse
  - Hereditary disease process
  - False allegations of FDP abuse to further a private personal agenda (divorce, inheritance, child custody)
  - False allegation of FDP abuse as a means of a criminal alternative defense for a person convicted of a crime (i.e., murder, sexual battery, white-collar crimes)
- Abuse with an FDP factor is abuse implemented by an offender to attain secondary gain and may occur in a variety of ways.
- FDP is a medical diagnosis and is not to be diagnosed by nonmedical personnel. Diagnosis of FDP within the context of a criminal investigation is allocated to licensed medical professionals only. *Use of a forensic pediatrician is recommended when the FDP abuse victim is a child because they are child abuse specialists. Originating medical suspicion of FDP abuse is likely to begin with a pediatrician, family physician, or nurse.*
- Within criminal investigations, suspicion of FDP methodology presence within abuse or homicide cases is proven by exposing the existence of statutory violations of criminal conduct (child abuse, elder abuse, homicide, battery, sexual abuse, etc.).

Effects of Community Involvement

Initial identification of FDP cases within individual communities usually formulates landmark case law for particular geographical regions and determines the identification of *local experts*. Criminal case management and prosecutorial outcome of local FDP cases may set the predicate for public opinion in future cases within the same particular geographic area. A poorly managed or executed case plan may have disastrous consequences for the immediate victim by also far-reaching and potentially unjust effects for outcome or intervention processes for potential future criminal cases possessing an FD/FDP factor. Poor management of an abuse or homicide case with an FD/FDP factor may occur at any level, within any participatory agency, and is not confined to simply one investigational aspect. A team effort is required not only for initial case intervention on a multidisciplinary basis but also for resolution of individual points within the final case resolution sequence.

Within an FDP case investigation, if the chain of evidence custody is not maintained by law enforcement officials, evidence may be suppressed leading to case dismissal. If a district attorney/prosecutor does not make appropriate criminal charging decisions, then the case may not be prosecuted adequately. Improper or lack of victim placement by protective service agencies may compromise the health and safety of an FDP victim beyond repair. If all multidisciplinary team participants fulfill their obligations yet the team fails to ensure that judiciary is educated regarding the many facets of FDP investigations, a criminal conviction of an FDP offender's behavior could mean little more than a warning and a greater ability to covertly offend upon a future victim.

When FDP abuse victims are theoretically identified and those victims are not adequately protected and die, issues of improper, inadequate, or ineffective intervention may arise. Intense public scrutiny, often on a multidisciplinary platform, may fuel an active civil litigation process. A combination of a civil litigation result and the effect of civil lawsuit process may inadvertently affect the behavior of professionals involved in an FDP-related case investigation. Professionals may *err* on the side of caution and *quick fixes* become replacement alternatives to long-term resolutions found within traditional and often time-consuming case protocol.

There is an intangible, yet real, economic factor associated with the measurable results of an FD-/FDP-related investigation within many public services agencies predicated upon time and resource allocation. Most public service agencies within the law enforcement corridor have experienced that convictions of criminal abuse or homicide or other crimes labeled with an FD/FDP factor are not easily attained and investigatory processes are likely to have astronomical funding allotments attached. The tendency for the FDP offender's vehement denial in the face of irrefutable evidence, low conviction rate, and high cost may formulate unwritten prosecutorial internal policy directing the FDP cases by resolved by plea bargain negotiation. The consequence of that practice is often revealed within a leniency toward the FDP offender resulting in premature reunification between the FDP offender and the victim. The victim may be returned to a place of risk and further abuse.

More relevant, however, is practice found within prosecutorial understanding that abuse or homicide cases with FDP methodology are just what they appear to be: abuse or homicide. FDP is a qualifier within a specific criminal behavior; it is not a cause or excuse for the criminal act. The actions of abuse found within an abuse cycle involving FDP are considered intentional willful acts of victim torture, and if a choice is made to include the angle of FDP within a criminal prosecution, then this understanding is generally displayed.

The degree of media involvement and subsequent public FDP case exposure also contribute to community standard establishment that may affect the prosecution of an abuse or homicide case beyond conduct code parameters established within the written law. If a case has no associated media coverage, then potential witnesses are often not aware that an incident has occurred and do not step forward with potential information. This nonmedia case may later quietly be disposed of by judicial process without the inference of established community input standards. It is important to remember that cases of abuse or homicide with an FDP factor are shocking to public conscience. This shock seems attributed to deviancy level and common FDP victim/offender roles (parent/child). Established community standards seen through vocalized public opinion regarding the methodology of FDP abuse/homicide and the heart-wrenching pathway child victims endure within the scope of abuse is formidable. Public opinion may serve as a watchdog between those who offend and those empowered within the process of justice to ensure that fairness and accountability for choice are uniformly applied.

FDP Case Management Protocol Development

Education

The first step in FDP case management protocol development is establishing the key educational component. To appropriately and expeditiously recognize FD/FDP behavior within a criminal context, basic understanding of the FD/FDP pyramid is required. Knowledge provides the ability necessary to intervene within the abuse cycle and enables the ability to address potential bureaucratic roadblocks that may arise during case investigation. Roadblocks or obstacles that may appear inevitably follow inaccurate conceptions, prejudice, or misinterpretation of data and are generally precipitated by an overall lack of subject matter educational knowledge. This deficit may apply to all disciplines involved in FD/FDP case-related situations.

Preparation

Readiness is a mandatory element in FDP intervention practices. Issues central to potential case direction may be varied and directly relate to victim safety or multidisciplinary team functioning. The following are potential actions/reactions that the multidisciplinary team should anticipate and develop associative contingency plans (during multidisciplinary staffing) to address:

- An upsurge in victim abuse that moves to immediate lethality (directed homicide)
- Direct or indirect increase in victim harm infliction
- FDP suspect/victim relocation. *Flight factors should have associated contingency planning*
- Movement of the FDP victim to an *underground* or sheltered environment thereby establishing the FDP suspect as solely controlling victim access
- Veiled attempts by the suspected FDP offender to commit suicide
- False reports of alternative victimization (sexual abuse, abuse or other). *These types of reports have been called into protective service agencies anonymously*
- The naming of alternative suspects (to thwart suspicion away from a suspected FDP offender)

Contingency plans to establish communication with team members who are absent from multidisciplinary staffing (usually due to unforeseen emergencies) should be planned for. If selected multidisciplinary team members should become unable to fulfill their participatory responsibilities for any reason, there will be a need to replace them. The ability to provide an adequate replacement is predicated upon educational preparation so that a replacement only needs case familiarization to be an effective team member. Time is elemental within the scope of FDP case intervention for the victim and the multidisciplinary team convened to address victimization. The readiness level each profession exhibits commensurate with the ability to interchange professionals within the specialized FD/FDP multidisciplinary team is reflected within preparatory means, and this includes pre-establishing staff with the required educational base, background, and competence level. Alternative sites for team meetings should also be predetermined and communicated to all team members.

An emergency or standardized kit, containing necessary paperwork required to implement FDP case-related procedures, is a time-saving measure that should be considered. Time is relevant in FDP case intervention because it represents victim risk and the potential loss of evidence. Some emergency-ready items are given in Figure 8.8.

Examples of protective orders, emergency shelter plans for FDP victims and their siblings, and a current listing of available foster care resources are helpful. Foster care parents utilized within the placement of an FDP child victim and siblings are a specialized category of caregivers. These volunteers should be knowledgeable regarding FD/FDP to better care for their charges in a protective mode and to have the ability to recognize potential evidence that may support either the FDP diagnostic link or associated criminal charging. Other items including participatory agencies (found within the multidisciplinary team), policies pertaining to investigation, expert arrest warrants template, video

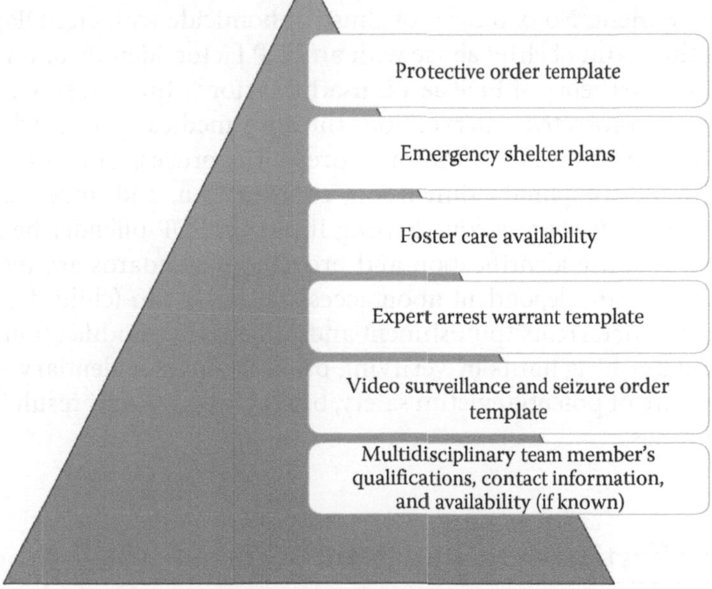

Figure 8.8 Emergency FDP victim protection resources.

surveillance, and evidence seizure template should be included. Generic forms of these documents that are developed under a computer macro format will allow for articulate deployment as needed.

The development or arrangement of an FDP multidisciplinary team is a form of interagency collaboration not unlike those found within other emergency management situations. The use of a memorandum of understanding (MOU) is strongly advised and should be contained within the FDP kit documents. An MOU allows all team participants' agencies to clearly understand roles and expectations during the activation of the team. Understanding includes the ability to verify legalities and questions regarding a process that is often present during individualized situational deployment. The time to address legal, moral and general procedural issues is before the need for an FDP multidisciplinary response to suspected abuse occurrences. Taking the time or mitigating response intervention during a suspected active FDP abuse situations may negatively impact a victim.

Cases That Do Not Meet FDP Criteria

Suspected FDP cases that fail to meet necessary criteria or probable cause for justification of criminal statutory charging may prevent authorities from immediately removing a suspected FDP victim from a suspected FDP offender's access. Lack of legal predicate to establish grounds for criminal charging of a defendant coupled with suspicion of ongoing child abuse often leave law enforcement agencies with liability concerns linked to intervention or lack of intervention. This concern extends to child protective/social services regarding victim custody removal, and since legal predicate is inextricably linked to founded medical evidence (supporting FDP diagnostic criteria), this concern is shared with medical staff and legal representatives for all agencies involved in the multidisciplinary team.

In any case investigation, on any level, there will be factors present to facilitate change or process improvement. No two cases of abuse or homicide with an FDP factor will ever be identical. In the realm of child abuse with an FDP factor, identification of the problem and provability of the theory of FDP as a causative factor within abuse are the foundation for the initiation of protective intervention. Intuitive medical personnel normally initiate initial suspicion and the identification process. The process of theory provability is a group effort of multidisciplinary dimension, coordination, and understanding. *It takes a village to save an FDP abuse victim.* Setting limits on FDP offender behavior can only be accomplished if abuse identification and provability standards are met. FDP offender's behavioral limits are dependent upon access to the victim (child dependency issues and placement) and deterrents (punishment and/or behavior modification through social intervention). Establishing limits by verifying proof through evidentiary means provides the greatest measure of potential victim safety, but this process may result in a situation of inconclusive findings.

Obstacles to Effective Case Management

There is a general idea in many communities that FDP is a contrived manifestation of someone's imagination: *FDP isn't real.* Argument often centers on a belief that FD/FDP is a grossly exaggerated problem that is inaccurately connected to abuse, homicide, or other situational cases. FDP has been referred to as a *designer diagnosis* and embellished in much the same manner as its namesake—Munchausen.

Understanding the notion that FD/FDP did not merely emanate out of thin air may provide clarification. Recognized standards in FDP abuse cases appear to have originated from the analytical study of identified cases. These cases involved medical staff that envisioned theoretical FDP possibilities linking unresolved and unidentified patient illness long enough to consider FDP an illness cause. This situation occurred repeatedly within multiple medical subsets and in multiple unconnected locations among unrelated families. Linking FDP behavior to abuse provided a mind-set conducive to provability through evidentiary means and stabilizing FD/FDP as a bona fide entity in real-world terms.

General knowledge of FDP has been available since 1951. It is relevant to recall that just because an idea may seem new to you does not necessarily mean that the idea has not been there all along and just not recognized. Knowledge base for FD/FDP has risen through education and reporting practices in much the same manner as domestic violence situations. Awareness, education, media attention and the consciousness of society, and community standards impacted reporting tendencies. Perhaps this change reflects accuracy in a societal trend dubbing FDP involving child victims as *domestic violence—at its worst*. The number of FD/FDP reported cases within medical literature are astounding.

Many fail to understand the complexity or sophistication of criminal conduct that involves an FD/FDP factor and fall under the influence of the often-present enormously deceptive FD/FDP offender ability. The difficult task of initial (first) FD/FDP recognition may be facilitated by a responder's deficit that may extend throughout the criminal justice process. Realization of how these factors may affect a professionals' interaction within the FD/FDP intervention process serves to guide the multidisciplinary response. The identified problematic professional response factors include the ones shown in Figure 8.9.

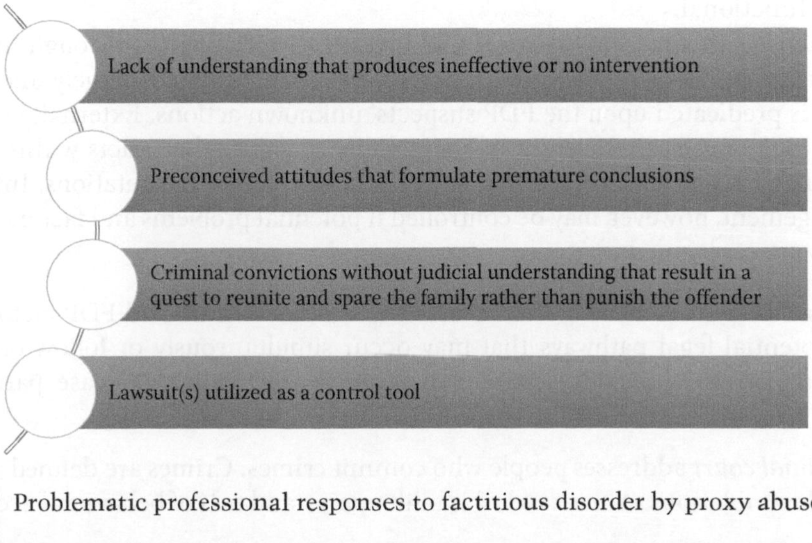

Figure 8.9 Problematic professional responses to factitious disorder by proxy abuse.

Problematic Professional Response

Obstacles have been identified in criminal case investigations involving an FD/FDP factor. These obstacles appear to originate from public and private understanding of FD/FDP as it relates to criminal investigations. These obstacles have been both prosecutorial hindrances and defense strategy resources.

Prosecutorial Obstacles

Standardized Problem-Solving Chronology To resolve obstacles that are present within an FD/FDP case investigation, identification of the problem, multidisciplinary role responsibilities, and a clearly defined action plan (protocol) may provide guidance. Case investigations that have a potential FD/FDP factor demand that intervention agencies maintain adaptability factors. Contingency plans to address prevalent issues are needed. Suspected FD/FDP offenders have been known to embrace ongoing informal self-education and use the media for attainment of goal. Media coverage of events often reveals infliction details that FD/FDP offenders adapt as their own. Although no two cases will be identical, various forms of methodology mutate. An FDP offender's knowledge pertaining to intervention efforts and intervention tactics makes the role of multidisciplinary team members challenging and may create professional apprehension. Multidisciplinary team members may merely work a case, or they may work smartly by carefully facilitating information exchange within the team. There is no absolute protocol or method of FDP interdisciplinary case management that fits every community or situational case. Adaptability is key (Figure 8.10).

Problem Definition Professional cultures inherently possess a narrowness of view (tunnel vision). Each profession within a multidisciplinary staffing model provides unique perspective that is commonly kept within a closed professional grouping. Elements of a peculiar language, prioritized dedication, accessibility, and chosen social circles may facilitate limited understanding, communication, and patience among interdisciplinary team members. A uniqueness of perspective generated from job requirements, regulations, philosophical ethics, and educational opportunity often serve to wider the functional cohesive gap among team members. The multidisciplinary team must overcome issues to become singularly functional.

FDP abuse cases present logistical and investigative challenges through internal and external case management pressures. External case management is largely uncontrollable because it is predicated upon the FDP suspects' unknown actions. Externally managing a suspected FDP abuse case involves an adaptability sequence that reacts within victimization that may have no discernable pattern or invoke changes or mutations. Internal FDP case management, however, may be controlled if potential problems and factors facilitating challenges are envisioned.

Directional Responsibilities Abuse cases that involve a child and FDP factor have two distinct potential legal pathways that may occur simultaneously or follow one another. These legal pathways include separate dispositions for individual case parameters as follows:

1. *Criminal court* addresses people who commit crimes. Crimes are defined as statutory law violations. American law is built upon standards of behavioral acceptance

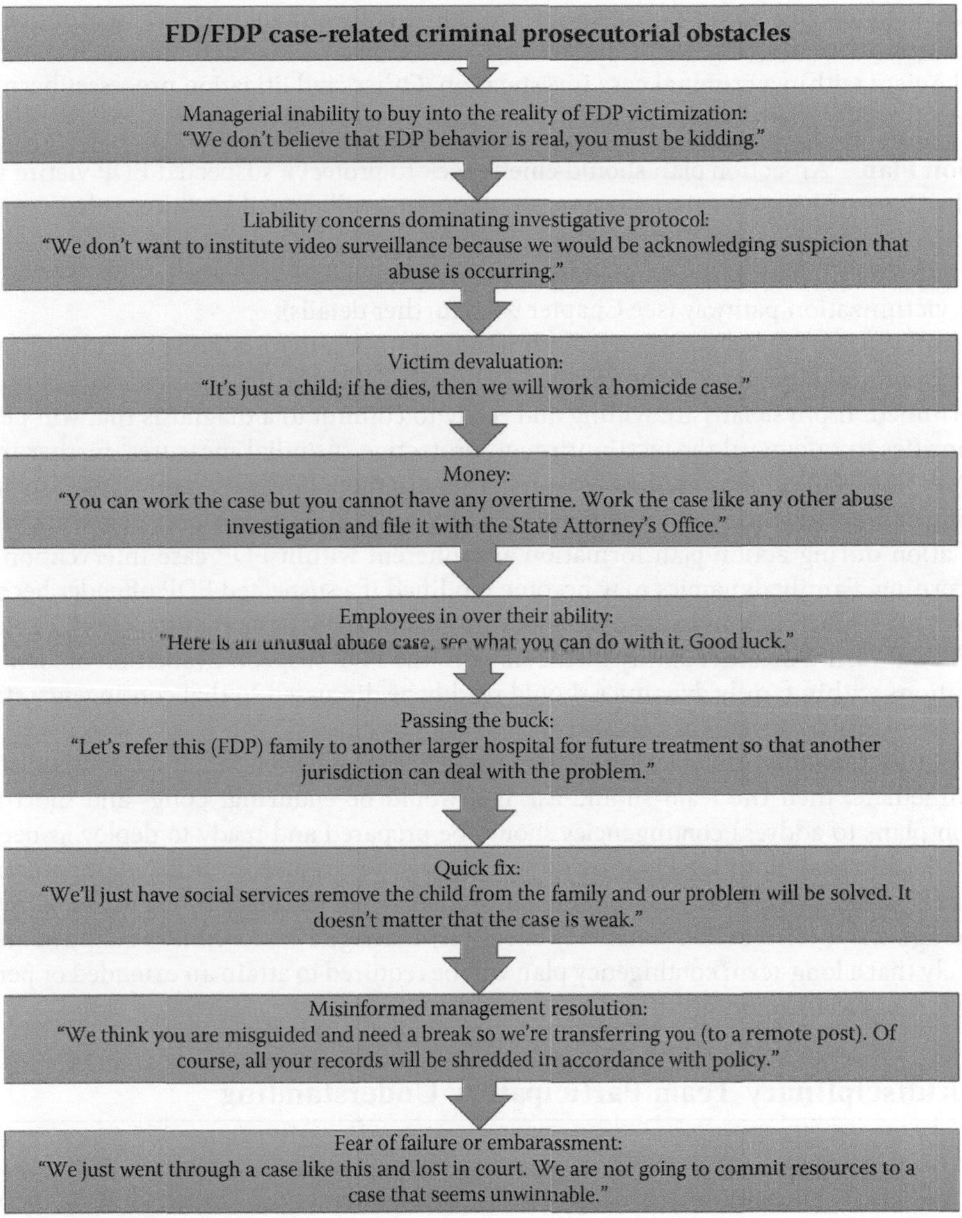

Figure 8.10 Prosecutorial challenges in factitious disorder/factitious disorder by proxy-related criminal case preparation.

and intolerable behavior set forth by society. Sworn law enforcement officials may arrest or detain anyone believed to have committed a felonious crime and, in certain situations, misdemeanor crimes.

2. *Dependency court* addresses the rights to caretakers to retain custody of minors or otherwise dependent persons. Taking away a person's right of custody is complicated and is guided by a fundamental need of dependent persons (child or the elderly) to be protected from harm.

Abuse with an FDP factor may contain additional pathways interrelated to criminal and dependency case routing. Medical pathways of case resolution often become the steering mechanism within a criminal case investigation. Other civil litigation processes become a by-product of the intervention effort.

Action Plan An action plan should chiefly seek to protect a suspected FDP victim from further harm. This protection, however, is often not legally possible without also attaining criminal case resolution. Victim safety planning should include lethality assessments to minimize victim risk factors and anticipate a suspected FDP offender's choices within an FDP victimization pathway (see Chapter 9 for further details).

Intervention is a key component within the interdisciplinary action plan. Identification of who will take primary responsibility for the direction of the investigation should be determined. If physicians are willing and ready to commit to a diagnosis that will permit authorities to safeguard the victim through protective custodial measures, further investigative intervention may not be necessary. This situation, however, rarely exists, so issues of continuing evidence gathering must be addressed. Flight factor prevalence and abuse escalation during action plan formation are inherent within FDP case intervention and concerning. Family dynamics may become modified if a suspected FDP offender becomes aware that his/her actions have come under suspicion. These dynamics may be detrimental to an FDP victim or other family members or to the FDP suspect. Evaluation of identified deviations within family dynamics should readily be discussed so that contingency strategies may easily be applied as necessary.

Within the structure of multidisciplinary FDP case intervention, if intervening action is immediate, then the team should ask if it would be enduring. Long- and short-term action plans to address contingencies should be prepared and ready to deploy as needed. Short-term action plans tend to provide specific answers to specific problems or situations, but FDP abuse is generally a complex chronic series of multiple problems or ailments. Although short-term action plans may effectively manage a case within a confined area, it is likely that a long-term contingency plan will be required to attain an extended or permanent remedy to the case situation.

Multidisciplinary Team Participatory Understanding

A paradigm (model) of practice in interdisciplinary FDP case analysis includes team member self-examination regarding team member interaction. Understanding the roles and responsibilities of multidisciplinary team members may require an ability to *step into another's shoes* figuratively. Positional understanding within the team creates an advantage linked to effective case compilation that the FDP offender is not usually prepared to deal with.

When medical staff becomes suspicious of FDP activity, child protective/child welfare agencies may be contacted initially. Most child protective agencies require staff to establish direct contact with a suspect expeditiously. Within the United States, law enforcement agencies are not always informed of a potential abuse case by child protective services, although predicated. In FDP abuse cases, delayed referrals to law enforcement complicate evidence gathering, and relocation concerns and foster the suspect's ability to develop an educationally based alternative defense.

In FDP abuse cases that law enforcement first realizes through the investigation of abuse or homicide, linking abuse to a potential FD/FDP element may originate from within the law enforcement window. There may be a tendency in these situations to not involve child protection agencies until absolutely necessary to preserve evidence, prevent relocation, and protect the integrity of the investigation by limiting suspect knowledge. Late entry of child protective agencies places a burden upon child protective staff expected to obtain custody or judicial orders for protection within a specialized victim abuse context. Delay would likely leave no time to formulate a multidisciplinary plan nor select qualified team participants, which may jeopardize victim safety.

The development of an FDP action team multidisciplinary checklist may ensure that team participant expectations are met and provide guidance. The development of law enforcement's roles and responsibilities within the FDP multidisciplinary approach should include evidence gathering and suspect arrest protocol. Team member responsibilities may overlap, and if this occurs, responsibility for a particular task should be assigned. Assigning responsibility will guard against team member dissention and be allocated to the team member most competent and professionally assigned (i.e., physicians should not be asked to perform investigative interviews; police should not be asked to provide medical diagnosis; social service workers should not be tasked with evidence gathering…).

FDP Investigative Checklist

- Who had access to the victim immediately prior to illness discovery or report of the (fabricated) illness?
- How many hospitalizations has the victim been subjected to?
- How many emergency room visits has the victim experienced?
- How many times has the local fire department rescue squad been summoned to the victim's residence?
- Has medical staff successfully identified the cause of the victim's illness? *Has the illness changed upon staff identification?*
- What is the residential history of the victim/family?
- Have medical treatment records been obtained from previous residential general locations (search within a grid)?
- Does the victim have any siblings who have died as a result of SIDS, undetermined causes or causes closely related to the victim's present condition? (*List causes, details and death dates.*)
    - Is there an apparent familial member illness pattern?
- Has the suspected FDP offender's behavior historically been linked to known FD typology?
- Do the victim's medical symptoms or ailments subside when the suspected FDP offender is restricted from sole unmonitored access?
- How does the offender view or envision the victim?
- Does the victim have a legitimate illness(s) coupled with unexplained complications or symptomology?
- What is the suspected offender's reaction to the victim's medical treatments and/or upscale in symptomology?

- What types or methods of formal/informal educational background does the suspected FDP offender possess?
  - What medical or educational resources are accessible to the suspected FDP offender and what has been accessed (*evidentiary platform*)?
    - Internet
    - Medical library
    - Public library
    - Medical personnel/acquaintances
    - Friends
    - Home health-care workers
    - Health-care supply company representatives
    - Physicians
    - Nurses
    - Nurses' aides and other clinical support staff
- Can an upsurge in an FDP victim's symptoms be linked to an external motivational factor for the suspected FDP offender?
- Who does the FDP offender identify with most closely within the hospital setting?
- What is the non-offending FDP parent's reaction to a child victim's hospitalizations?
- Is there a child custody or divorce dispute occurring during probable infliction or during the allegation phase found within the FDP cycle?
  - Are there allegations of sexual abuse in addition to FDP abuse? Who is making the allegations, and what external gains could be attained through accusatory validation of impropriety?
- Has the medical staff been eliminated as potential suspects within the FDP case investigation?
- How was the alleged FDP abuse/homicide case reported to authorities?
- What direct/indirect benefits does the FDP offender as a result of the victim's illness or treatment acquire?
- Has the suspected FDP offender received victim care education (child or adult)?
- (For FDP child victimizations) Was the suspected FDP offender a child when she became a mother?
- Are the suspected FDP offender's family dynamics consistent with a domestic violence scenario?
- Is the FDP offender afflicted with an eating disorder?
- Have physicians ruled out common FDP medical defenses?
  - Somatoform disorder
  - Cycle vomiting syndrome
  - Neglect due to economic constraint or personal gain
  - Other forms of physical illness or mental illness
- Has the media been utilized as a substitution agent for attention sought by the FDP offender? *Measurement of secondary gain is evidence.*
  - Has the suspected FDP offender made public statements through the media?
  - Has the suspected FDP offender utilized the media as a source for fundraising?
  - Has public deception fostered through media coverage surrounding the case progressed to organized fraud?
- Does the health status of the suspected FDP victim provide family income?
- What is the jurisdictional boundary of the case?

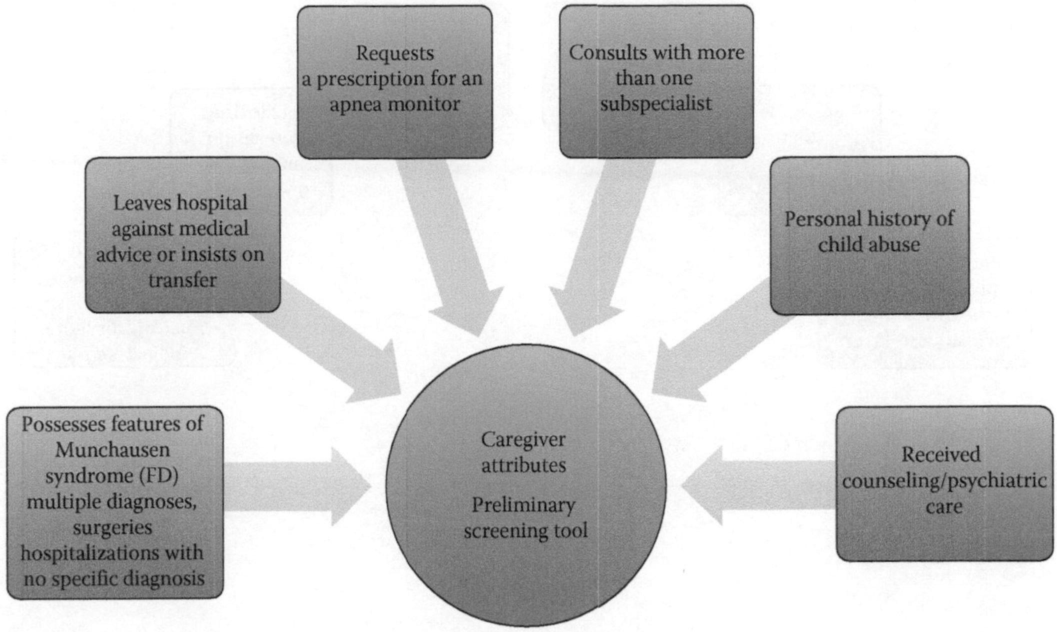

Figure 8.11 Preliminary screening tool—factitious disorder by proxy offender attributes.

- Multiple jurisdictional offense locations within a singular state equate to state jurisdiction regarding prosecution.
- Multiple state jurisdictional locations within an FDP case progression equate to the need for federal jurisdictional coordination.
- International jurisdictional locations require international coordination to establish primary locational jurisdiction and prosecution.

Preliminary Screening Tools

A preliminary screening tool for early detection of FDP (medical child abuse) has been developed. Screening items include the ones shown in Figures 8.11 and 8.12.[7]

Conclusion

Effective management when faced with an abuse or a homicide case that may have an FD/FDP factor includes formulating a team whose members have the ability to *step into other roles* momentarily to foster understanding. Understanding instills team cohesiveness by establishing role respect. Effective multidisciplinary team management provides an edge or investigative advantage when team members open their minds to new ideal potential and apply this understanding collectively in furtherance of victim protection.

FDP offenders have an uncanny ability to convince people of their innocence and unilaterally apply this behavior. Professionals, family members, the media, and judiciary may all become the targets of this ability. Provability of abuse or homicide is predicated upon

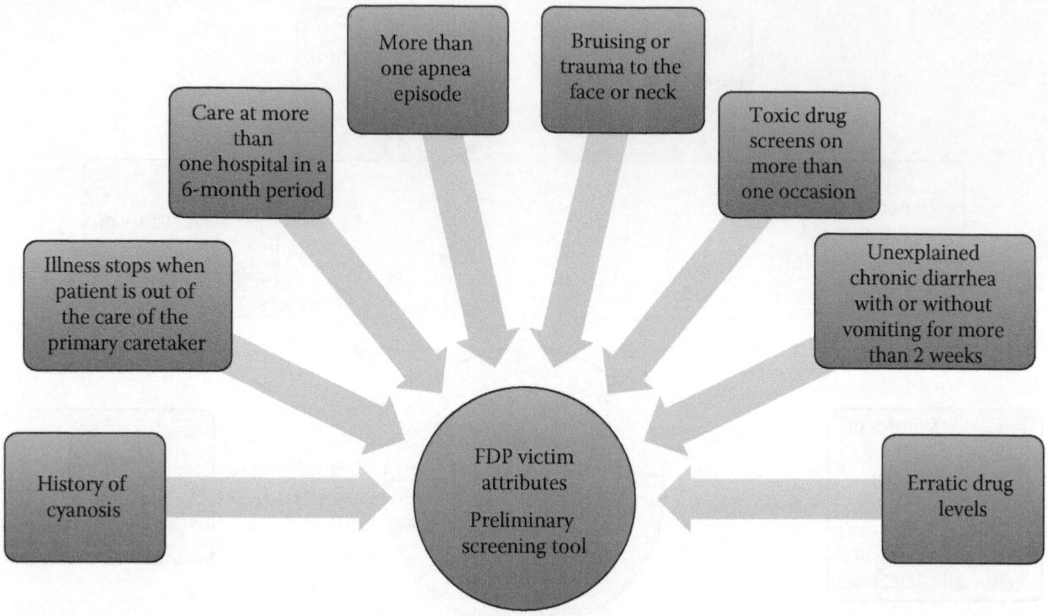

Figure 8.12 Preliminary screening tool—factitious disorder by proxy victim attributes.

evidence, and establishing this evidence when an FD/FDP factor is present is complicated. Evidence exists in many forms and access requires an interviewer's ability to cross a gap existing between standardized abuse/homicide investigations and those that are impacted by the factitious world of the FD/FDP offender. Intervention opportunity is, in many cases, the only hope that an FDP abuse victim may have. FDP multidisciplinary team members express attitude through team interaction and how that relationship is applied affects victim longevity—life or death.

Notes

1. Kisten, C., Tien, I., Bauchner, H., Parker, V., and Leventhal J., Factors that influence the effectiveness of child protection teams. *Pediatrics*, 2010;126:94–100.
2. Harr, C., Fairchild, S., and Souza, L., International models of hospital interdisciplinary teams for the identification, assessment, and treatment of child abuse. *Social Work in Healthcare*, 2008;46:1–16.
3. Rosenberg, D.A., Web of deceit: A literature review of Munchausen syndrome by proxy. *Child Abuse & Neglect*, 1987;11(4):547–563.
4. American Psychological Association, Guidelines for psychological evaluations in child protection matters. *American Psychologist*, 2013;68:20–31.
5. Bass, C. and Halligan, P., Factitious disorders and malingering: Challenges for clinical assessment and management. *Lancet*, 2014;383(9926):1422–1432.
6. Senner, A.L. and Ott, M., Munchausen syndrome by proxy. *Issues in Comprehensive Pediatric Nursing*, 1989;12:345–357.
7. Greiner, M., Palusci, V., Keeshin, B., Kearns, S., and Sinal, S., A preliminary screening instrument for early detection of medical child abuse. *Hospital Pediatrics*, 2013;3:39–44.

Factitious Disorder by Proxy (FDP) Abuse Victim Protection

9

Change will not come if we wait for some other person or some other time. We are the ones we've been waiting for. We are the change that we seek.

Barack Obama

Child Protection

There is a legal, ethical, and moral responsibility to report and identify the known or suspected maltreatment of children.[1] Professionals charged with this hefty responsibility are only able to achieve child protection through mandated reporting when they have the knowledge and skill to recognize the subtle form of child abuse found within FDP. Barriers regarding the ability to report suspicions of abuse include inadequate knowledge, lack of confidence, reluctance to initiate law enforcement involvement, family loyalty, and concern regarding victim impact.[2]

When a child's caregiver regularly presents a physician with false information and the physician fails to file a mandated report for suspected abuse, the physician has been civilly sued for medical negligence and failure to report suspected (child) abuse.[3] In some states, criminal punishment also attaches for failing to report known or suspected abuse.

The greatest deterrent to child protection in FDP child abuse cases is delayed recognition or the inability to recognize the abusive act. Effective FDP criminal child abuse investigations include evidence collection, intervention, and interagency collaboration dependent upon awareness. Effective resolution for FDP victims is initially contingent upon intuitive, informed, and vocal medical personnel at a time when definitive child abuse evidence may be lacking. The burden of evidence gathering to establish proof of abuse or death occurring as a result of FDP infliction processes normally encompasses an interdisciplinary team approach effort. This effort realistically translates into either a substantiated or a disavowed medical diagnosis of FDP and simultaneous establishment of evidence to support criminal case compilation as well as victim dependency relocation justification.

Interaction in FDP cases involves associated agencies with specific roles: law enforcement (criminal), social service (custody), medical (healthcare), psychosocial services (victim, offender, and family treatment), judicial and guardian services (court system), state attorney's office (prosecutorial), public defender (generally offender defense support), corrections (probation or jail staff), and other. Each agency responds to victim abuse or homicide FDP-related events from an individual perspective but within the commonality of victim protection. There are overlaps within this gathering of multidisciplinary professionals, and conflict may appear. The question regarding family unification when FDP abuse is identified complicates the role of social workers and judiciary. A formative understanding of FDP dynamics is needed as reunification is considered within immediate fallout of an unproven FDP situation or later, following criminal justice fulfillment of punishment (incarceration of the offender). FDP abuse is generally long term prior to detection. The point where an FDP victim is removed from the FDP offender's custody is connected to the provability of FDP allegation (suspicion) and concern that a child wrongfully removed from a suspected FDP offender's custody will be further damaged. It is often not until criminal investigation is initiated against an FDP offender that social service agencies are willing to intervene, in a custody manner, to separate a child victim from a suspected FDP offender.

Role of the Child Protective Caseworker

The majority (95%)[4] of FDP child abuse cases involve a minor child as either an identified or suspected abuse victim. State child welfare agencies may receive reports of known or suspected abuse, but such reports are categorized as allegation until validation of abuse occurs based upon presenting evidence. Unlike criminal investigations, child welfare (protection) staff members are not authorized to place criminal charges upon abusers but are empowered to remove a child or an elderly victim from an abusive environment or caretaker in most cases.

Within the course of a child protective investigation, some states allow child protective workers to obtain medical records without first obtaining a subpoena or court order. Child protection agencies may also request various investigatory subpoenas within dependency (juvenile) courts and share this information with law enforcement agencies. A close alliance between law enforcement and child protective caseworkers may ease the burden of verity upon both if investigatory efforts are combined within specified parameters.

Child protection staff usually formulates informed custody recommendations and a victim's custodial placement by direct observation of a suspected FDP victim and offender. In most states, a child protection worker is empowered to enact an emergency custody removal action when evidence exists supporting child abuse. Evidence (direct, testimonial, and circumstantial) may be collected from resources that include criminal case investigations, medical scrutiny, court proceedings, and the child protective investigation. Evidence to support a custody order is generally detailed. Testimonial evidence includes expert opinion, general witness observations, and educational resources.

Victim custody case management may include termination of parental rights or family reunification efforts navigated by child welfare workers whose primary task is assuring immediate and long-term child safety. While obtaining immediate custody of a suspected FDP child abuse victim appears a natural course of action, this reactionary response may have longer-term consequences of child endangerment. Premature removal of FDP victim custody is not always permanent, and permanency seems linked to evidentiary means. Child protective workers should not make custodial decisions in a vacuum; the use of the interdisciplinary team opens the door to alternatives enabling case veracity thereby enhancing long-term victim safety. Custodial decisions that occur outside the scope of the FDP multidisciplinary team risk retraction and possibly effective litigation response. When the decision to assume child victim custody is agreed upon through a multidisciplinary team review, validation of protective services workers' decision to move a potential FDP victim from parental custody to protected custody occurs. Judicial affirmation based upon evidence evaluation in accordance with burden of proof in dependency cases is realized on a broader scope within this team concept. It is a checks-and-balances application that affords both the FDP victim and suspected offender protection while maintaining the integrity of the multidisciplinary child protective effort.

Assessment of Victim Risk

Risk is like a wager. Although risk cannot be assessed with absolute certainty, there is a significant difference between those who make educated guesses and those who arbitrarily gamble. The outcome for each speculator may be identical, but the resolution method is unique and likely to profoundly affect results.

General principles that formulate conventional risk assessment guidelines do not always accurately reflect threatened harm potential in FDP cases. For generalized abuse or homicide cases, risk assessment indicators are measured within the context of (family) interaction and environmental evaluation. A commonly accepted predicate of this evaluation is that observations are true behavioral indicators. In FD/FDP cases, true indicators of behavior are often masked, hidden, contorted, and contrary. External indicators infrequently reflect actual home environmental circumstance and the often present concealed yet contorted way of life actually present. Evaluating the home life of a family engaged in an FD/FDP abuse situation may outwardly appear normal in accordance with care of a chronically ill child, but conducting an extended evaluation may yield a different reality. It is difficult to look beyond the appearance of normality to see the actuality of treachery. Home evaluation in an authenticated FDP abuse case can be like standing on a beach viewing a perfectly calm ocean—never suspecting that a volcano lurks beneath the serene water. It is not until one dives into the water that actualization of true danger occurs in conjunction with a sense of disbelief. The diver often remarks: "There was no way to see it until it was too late."

Another complication found within protective assessment of FDP victims is a commonly accepted trust of collective witness testimony as truthful validation of behavioral or environmental conditions. The FD/FDP offender's ability to manipulate perceived reality through elaborate methodological deception is formidable. Witness testimony by family members, acquaintances, and professional associates should be carefully evaluated because they too may have been caught in the offender's deception and what seems real may be inaccurate. The certainty of a suspected FDP offender's innocence often emulates from witnesses close to the situation. It is easy for anyone, including professional caregivers, to look at people or situations that outwardly project reassurance, formulate a "gut feeling" of innocence, and extend trust yet be fooled in the process. Deceptive abilities of the majority of known FD/FDP offenders' provide realization that potential abuse victimization scope and sophistication level should not be underestimated.

Unique FDP Intervention Risk Factors

When an FDP situation falls beneath the umbrella of suspicion case, intervention methodologies may create a situation of victim risk. How an FDP suspect and FDP abuse situation is approached sets the stage for potential relocation and upscale victimization. Inadequate monitoring during investigatory evidentiary collection could allow continued victimization and liability attaches.

Enabled Relocation

Enabled relocation occurs through opportunity. Minimal intervention and/or FDP suspect awareness that behavior has become suspect requires a victim protection plan to prevent the opportunity to offend. Lack of victim protective oversight facilitates supervision loss allowing further uncontrolled FDP offender choices. Relocation enhances difficulty in detecting an ongoing FDP victimization because "newly acquired" medical personnel often begin their medical investigative journey anew. Historical medical records, residential history, and identification of a victim's illnesses are often difficult to verify, and suspicion of FDP behavior is generally nonexistent. A pervasive relocation issue is that fluctuating community FDP awareness renders FDP abuse recognition sporadic. Relocation illuminates FDP victim lethality concerns bolstered by FDP recognition inconsistency, highly deceptive behavioral presentation by the FDP suspect, and potentially lethal abuse methodologies.

Upscale FDP Abuse Tendencies

FDP offenders who feel threatened by exposure may demonstrate a determination to "prove" the legitimacy of a victim's illness resulting in a surge in victimization sequences and intensified victim injury. Threatened exposure may facilitate an atmosphere of heightened caution within the FDP offender's offensive actions elevating abuse intricacy and concealment or spur a total change in the abuse delivery pattern. A heightened status of FDP abuse offense is directly related to heightened detection difficulty. Potential FDP abuse victims should not be considered safe from harm merely because they are hospitalized. In many FDP abuse cases, child abuse in the form of active infliction or continued indirect illness falsification occurs while the victim is hospitalized.[5]

Inadequate Monitoring

Practical inability of child protective services and dependency courts to adequately provide long-term family monitoring and child protection through prolonged family member separation also occurs in FDP abuse cases. Courts may consider family-based monitoring a viable alternative to the severance of custody between an FDP offender and victim. Monitoring difficulties may occur when staff involved within the monitoring process fail to understand FDP abuse dynamics. Monitoring is further complicated on a financial basis related to staff deployment (time) and staff attrition. Protective service staff typically have high attrition rates, and as staff replacement occurs, a fluctuating level of professional ability generally follows. FDP offenders effectively manage inherent human trust factors to their advantage, living up to their reputation as masters of deception. This ability, coupled with a social service staff pool that does not necessarily retain specialized skill levels within FD/FDP investigatory practices, eases the pathway for potential victimization. When the projected direct and observable FDP offender behavior is enacted and accepted as a true representation of character, an inaccurate assessment of reality and victim safety may result.

Allowing an FDP offender–victim access creates a significant victim risk situation and should not be considered without stringent safeguards. Judges who consider monitoring provisions in lieu of custody severance and should ask themselves if they are willing to assume the risk of further victim harm should the FDP offender reoffend.

Inherent Risk Factors Found in Abuse Cases with an FDP Factor

Inherent risk factor in FDP victimization directly relates to the actions of the FDP offender. Physical and psychological victim risk within a window of threatened harm may be affected

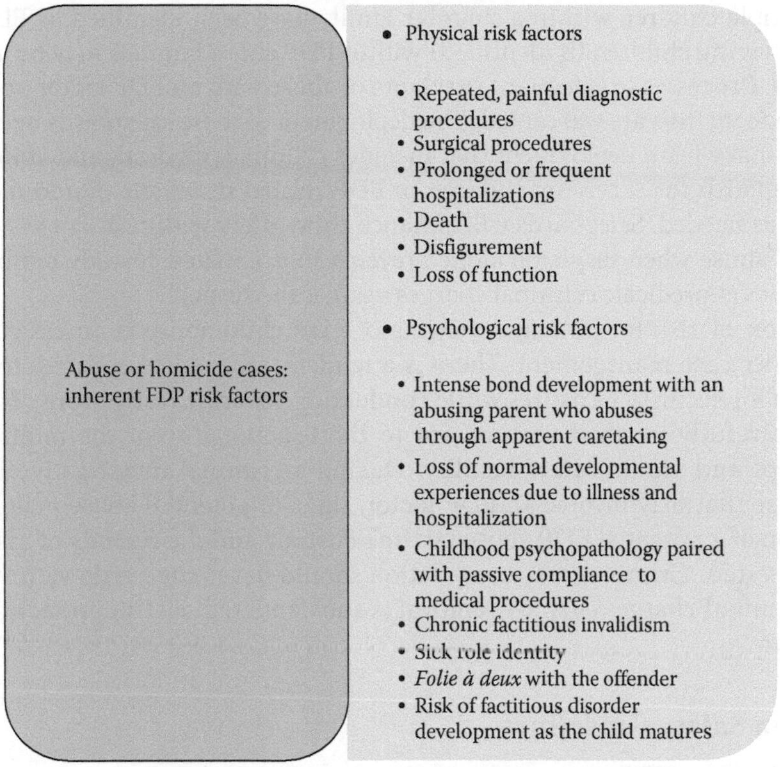

Figure 9.1 Physical and psychological abuse risk factors in FD/FDP scenarios.

by FDP offender's actions not contingent upon investigation methodologies. These are actions that occur within FDP victimization as a matter of FDP abuse methodology and may be affected by external forces exerted within the investigative intervention process. Referred to as a portrait of threatened victim harm, we see the gravity and range of often unseen and unrecognized factor present in many cases involving the FD/FDP factor. This portrait may set the predicate for understanding why it is important to establish swift and significant dependency and criminal court rulings in abuse or homicide cases with an FDP factor.

Long-term outcomes for FDP child abuse victims depend upon successfully separating the child victim from the abuse source, protecting the child victim from further harm, and alleviating harm previously inflicted (Figure 9.1).[6–10]

Victim Safety Planning in Abuse Cases with an FDP Factor

Safety planning is critical in the formulation of FDP case protocol. The quality of the FDP victim safety plan affects potential victim survivability and eminently impacts criminal case prosecution and victim protection efforts. Applied violence within FDP abuse cases is dependent upon many factors and cannot necessarily be predicted. Intervention plans may include contingency factors, but it is impossible to account for all possible FDP suspect responses within intervention deployment.

The identification of a possible FDP abuse situation/suspect is not always revealed within initial victimization cases. The skill of FDP offenders may allow for serial victimization ability. Multiple children within a singular family have been identified as FDP homicide victims. Surviving children (if identified) within FDP abuse families may be at significant risk of harm. Processes to safeguard survivors of abuse with an FDP factor and siblings of FDP homicide victims are warranted. The deployment of these safeguards occurs within a multidisciplinary team deployment that includes criminal, medical, and child protection efforts. Safeguards for surviving children in FDP-related situations should include covert monitoring as needed. Safeguards will enhance child safety within situations of suspected FDP-related abuse when suspicion alone prevents substantiated custody removal and evidence cannot yet predicate criminal charges against the suspect.

Reduction of risk for potential victims of FDP child abuse is an essential component of proper case management. There is a tendency for police agencies to internalize information for security measures while conducting covert investigations. This tendency should be carefully weighed with regard to the functionality of the multidisciplinary team concept and victim safety liability. During a criminal investigative inquiry into an abuse case that may involve an FDP factor, signs of potential abuse may be revealed. Reevaluation of a potential FDP abuse victim's custody and the custody of associated siblings is suggested. Criminal case compilation should never supersede victim safety. The moment criminal charges/custody removal is substantiated, victim protection measures should occur.

FDP Victim Safety Guidelines

Figure 9.2 illustrates FDP victim safety and protective guidelines.

Investigative FDP Victim Survival Strategies

FDP case investigations generally occur in hospital settings. Long-term victim placement considerations should be addressed before actual FDP suspect confrontation within this setting. Common guidelines found within an FDP abuse intervention plan help to prevent potential casualties caused, in part, from investigative blunder. The following are suggested protocols for reduction (not elimination) of potential FDP victim harm as investigative processes occur through a multidisciplinary intervention plan. Suggested strategies contain practical elemental issues while affording investigative latitude necessary for effective and meaningful case resolution (Figure 9.3).

- Do not make direct accusatory statements to the FDP offender without first securing the FDP victim. *The FDP offender's reaction will invariably be denial that is usually followed by portrayed anger. This anger may be directed upon the victim through a surge in FDP infliction.*
- Do not telephone the offender or discuss any aspect of the case over the telephone, text, or e-mail. *Communicating by phone, text, or e-mail cannot assure who is receiving or providing information. Information attained in this manner is generally inadmissible as evidence unless sourcing is confirmed. Ease of deceptive statements may be enhanced when attained remotely.*
- If it is necessary to remotely contact the offender during initial phases of the investigation, utilize caller ID block. *Blocking identification of an investigator's phone origination by dialing *67 or its equivalent prevents caller ID potential.*

Police and fire department dispatch

Notify the lead detective of all service calls involving the FDP suspect regardless of location.

School administration

Notify the lead detective if a suspected FDP victim or his or her siblings are absent from school.

Medical treatment facilities

Viable potential victims associated with FDP situations who are present at medical facilities (hospitals, clinics, emergent care, etc.) and exhibit an illness that cannot readily be identified should cause a multidisciplinary staffing to occur with immediate dependency/custody petition application whenever justified.

FDP family relocation attempt

Measures to prevent relocation or to remove custody of remaining children within the home are necessary when an FDP abuse victim is confirmed.

Planned temporary location changes

Planned vacations or trips that take a suspected FDP family away from a jurisdictional area should be controlled. Temporary relocations easily become permanent, limit victim/sibling access, and provide an opportunity for directed victim homicide as a means of evidence disposal.

Probable cause and what that means

When probable cause is established to substantiate that a victim is being abused, victims and their siblings (child cases) should be removed from FDP suspect access.

Figure 9.2 Victim safety guidelines when FDP abuse is suspected.

- The location of FDP child victims should be kept confidential once the victim is removed from the offender's custody. *FDP offenders may feel that the death of the victim would "make everything alright." This may be especially true if the victim is verbal and considered a witness to the abuse. FDP abuse victims are evidence in FDP criminal cases. Destruction of evidence is possible in any criminal case.*
- Develop a referral list. *A referral list is helpful in multidisciplinary case staffing. Contact numbers or website locations for local shelters, domestic violence programs, batterers intervention, child protection agencies, local and national FD/FDP expert referral listings, American Prosecutors Research Institute, Regional Information Sharing System, National Domestic Violence Hotline, National Victims Resource Center, and others may provide assistance in FD/FDP cases.*

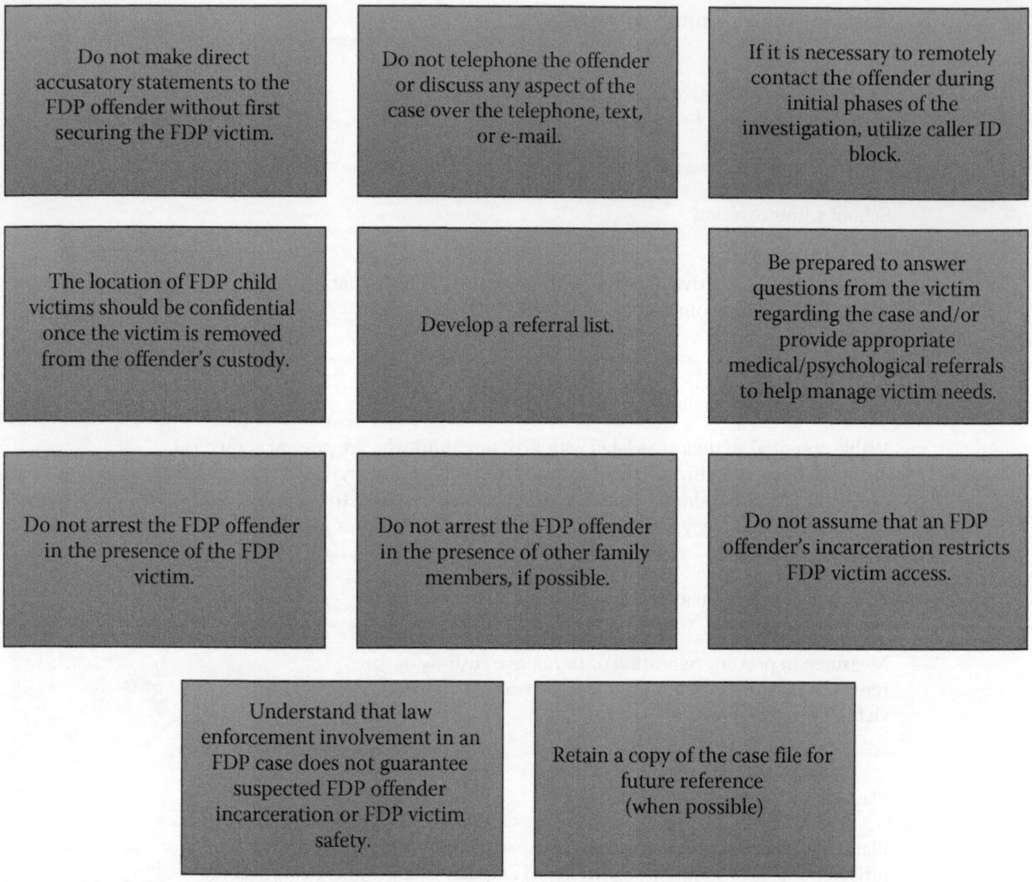

Figure 9.3 Intervention strategies in FDP criminal cases.

- Be prepared to answer questions from the victim regarding the case and/or provide appropriate medical/psychological referrals to help manage victim needs. *Inadequately prepared multidisciplinary team members may either cause irreparable harm to an FDP victim or ease the path of healing through appropriate intervention through understanding, action, and referral.*
- Do not arrest the FDP offender in the presence of the FDP victim. *Emotional and physical separation issues may arise if the FDP offender's custodial arrest is not secluded from the victim. The arrest is a visual representation of contact separation between the FDP suspect and victim that the victim may not be prepared to experience.*
- Do not arrest the FDP offender in the presence of other family members, if possible. *Abuse with an FDP factor is an insidious form of domestic violence. When law enforcement executes the physical arrest of the FDP offender in the presence of family members, physical and verbal retaliation is likely. The FDP offender may choose to resist the arrest simply because they do not want to go to jail or to elicit sympathy or assistance from family members. The presence of family members may empower the FDP offender to resist arrest through perceived familial strength.*

- Do not assume that an FDP offender's incarceration restricts FDP victim access. *Temporary custody orders or subsequent termination of parental rights actions are usually procured through juvenile courts (for FDP child victims). Dependency and custody matters are separate from criminal charges. There is often prevalent tendency within dependency court to reunify families, even in FDP abuse situations.*
- Understand that law enforcement involvement in an FDP case does not guarantee suspected FDP offender incarceration or FDP victim safety. *To address victim safety issues, the development of contingency plans is necessary. Some FDP cases fall short of criminal or medical provability standards causing an FDP offender's custodial release, arrest prevention, or the return of victim custody to a suspected FDP offender. Continued or reinstated exposure between a suspected FDP offender and victim is always a possibility. Situations that follow this route highlight the importance of retaining contact with FDP family members. Extended contact provides a mechanism to follow FDP suspect relocation choices and be alerted to FDP abuse recidivism. There is currently no known national abuse registry for known or suspected FDP abusers. Historical information regarding FDP offenders past conduct is generally difficult to access upon relocation.*
- Retain a copy of the case file for future reference (when possible).

FDP child victims may seek greater understanding of their victimization as they mature, especially if the FDP offender prematurely dies. The profound implication an intervention has upon the life of an FDP victim takes time to realize, and recall requests may personally be requested years after interaction. The potential need to recount a case for (much) later judicial review also requires retention of records. Recall may be impossible when records are discarded. Professionals involved in FDP cases should be guided by departmental rules and regulations regarding records retention.

Arguments for Termination of Parental Rights in FDP Cases

Classic versus Extreme FDP Abuse

Terminations of parental rights versus reunification standards are controversial and of primal concern in FDP abuse cases. Kinscherff and Famularo classify FDP abuse behavior into categories of extreme (production) and classic (simulation). They advocate that termination of parental rights in cases of extreme FDP abuse is essential for child protection. The basis for this view is found in the practical inefficiencies of judicial and child protective systems coupled with known risk patterns in extreme FDP victimization sequences. Extreme FDP is defined when an FDP offender places a victim at severe risk for death, disfigurement, invalidism, and massive impairment of psychological and social development by securing unnecessary medical interventions. Within the work of Kinscherff and Famularo, they conclude the following: "No evidence exists that their (offender) behavior is amenable to psychiatric treatment, or protective intervention is reliably effective short of severing physical contact and parental rights."[11]

Extreme FDP has infliction ranges that are derived from infliction means. The means or manner of FDP infliction has been identified as exaggeration of actual medical symptoms, presentation of a false history, description of factitious symptoms, mimicry of symptoms, and active induction of medical symptoms.[12]

Classic and extreme FDP differentiations are determined by the degree of immediate potential victim lethality produced from either means or symptoms acutely generated. Extreme FDP often aligns with an immediate high risk of death or permanent injury or produces the need for critical medical intervention that carries these same risks. Although the classic form of FDP may either equal or surpass the outcome of the extreme form, there is generally an elemental difference in required time to reach the same lethality level. In this view, FDP behavior seen within falsification of symptoms (without production of an overt offensive action) may be considered a classic or lesser form of abuse. However, the ability of an FDP victim to withstand any type of medical procedure is varied and often carries a significant risk of death or harm. This unknown risk factor applies to all forms of FDP abuse and easily transports a classic format with generally diminished risk of death to homicide.

FDP Strength despite Deterrents

Threatened harm to FDP victims by a custodial parent is effectively utilized as proactive argument when seeking termination of parental rights. FDP case literature review provides compelling testimony that FDP child abuse is so severe that termination of parental rights is the only relatively safe pathway to ensure victim protection. Four key risk points in FDP abuse cases illuminate issues courts should be aware of (Figure 9.4).

Hospitalization may not deter new or continuing FDP victimization. *One study of 48 FDP abuse cases found that 17% of the victims died as a result of nonaccidental poisoning. In at least 30% of identified FDP abuse cases, the parent continued to poison the child victim after hospitalization of the child occurred.*[13]

FDP offenders undergoing psychotherapy may not deter further FDP child victimization acts. *A study by McGuire and Feldman noted that of six FDP victims, five children continued to be abused after referrals were made to state protective agencies. All six children were abused while the suspected FDP offender (their mother) was undergoing psychotherapy.*[14]

Supervised visitation is not FDP victimization deterrent. *FDP child abuse victims have been victimized during state supervised parental visitation with an FDP offender. Children*

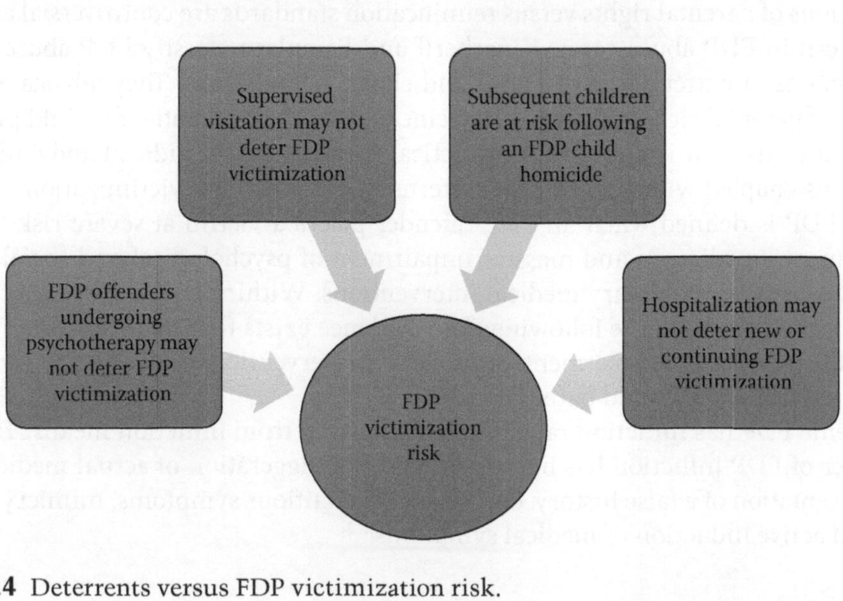

Figure 9.4 Deterrents versus FDP victimization risk.

have also been victimized in hospital settings after the FDP offender was advised that she was under video surveillance.[15]

Subsequent children may be at risk after the FDP-related death of a sibling. *When an FDP abuse victim gravitates to the status of an FDP homicide casualty, the victim's death does not mean that the FDP offender will stop abusive behavior. Risk of sibling FDP victimization has been identified.*[16] *Identification of a family in which a sudden infant death syndrome (SIDS) death occurs and an FDP abuse situation or homicide is detected suggests a possible link. A potential connection of child death as a result of SIDS should be reevaluated as a potential homicide as a result of FDP abuse or directed homicide.*[17]

Recidivism

Issues of recidivism relating to FDP victim safety may be introduced as further argument that termination of parental rights in FDP cases (with FDP abusers as custodial parents) is warranted. Although a "cure" status for FDP offenders is theoretically possible, there are many unknown factors surrounding the establishment of "cure validity." Chief among the concerns is the liability existing for dependent (child or elderly) victims if an FDP offender's portrayed behavior is not genuine and merely a continuation of honed deceptive practices. Documented case analysis of FDP offender treatment results provides questionable reliance on current rehabilitative endeavors. There also appears to be an absence of evidence that psychotherapy is effective in FDP abuse cases.[18]

Extraordinarily intense FDP offender denial of victimization responsibility, present in most cases, prevents effective psychotherapeutic intervention.[19] Typically, the FDP offender either refuses or flees therapy. If the FDP offender does admit responsibility for abusive acts (seen in very few cases) and agrees to therapy, FDP victimization may still continue.[20] One convicted FDP child abuser explained that although she had received therapy for her behavioral problem of FDP child abuse infliction tendencies, she would never be cured; therapy helped her understand and control FDP abusive behavior; she, however, often thought of reestablishing FDP abuse infliction patterns upon her child whenever she became "stressed out." McGuire and Feldman noted that the attempted treatment of FDP offenders has largely been unsuccessful.[21]

A significant issue germane to FDP child victims' custody is if apparently successful FDP offender rehabilitation is true or merely a continuation of demonstrated deceptive abilities. FDP offender rehabilitation success cannot be measured by conventional means because there is no physical or psychological test to prove therapy has produced a cure. There is no test to assure that FDP offenders will not reoffend or that the thought patterns/processes that allowed the FDP offender to abuse his or her victim have truly changed. FDP abuse is a thought process acted upon. This thought process includes obscurity, planning, deception, and a willingness to abuse another through systematic torture shroud process. Measuring the true status of an FDP offender is through the physical status of an FDP victim, and this should be unacceptable.

FDP offenders are often able to convince therapists of their innocence through compelling denial and rationalization of ongoing FDP victimization while the offender is in therapy.[22] The actions of a child abuser utilizing an FDP factor have been compared to the actions of a pedophile using a sexual/power factor. Both are child abuse! This FDP analysis suggests that any contact between an FDP abuser and victim carries with it significant risk. Death, physical/psychological victim harm, recidivism, family flight, and losing victims due to failure to adequately protect them from harm are concerns (Figure 9.5).

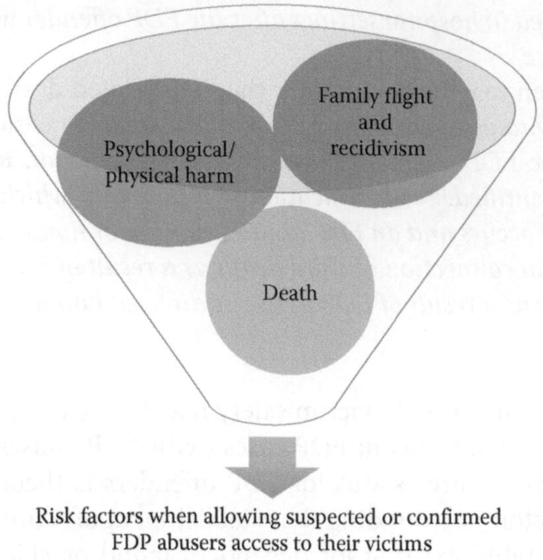

Figure 9.5 Offender–victim access risk.

Termination of Parental Rights: Prosecutorial Matters

To challenge the constitutionally protected right of parental responsibility, the court must find justifiable cause. Termination of parental rights takes away a parent's right of communication with or about the child and to participate in decisions regarding the child's development. Rights of parents, however, are not absolute and states have the power to protect their interests in child welfare when belief of abandonment, maltreatment, or neglect is present.[23]

Many states endeavor to preserve family unity by working to reunite children with their custodial parents even when abusive situations have existed. Statutory and case law formulates predicate for reunification measures whenever possible. This, once singular, view is changing, however, in favor of child protection. Recognized cases of premature or inappropriate reunification between child abuse victim and custodial parental child abusers have ended in further child victimization and slowly changed the public view on termination of parental rights.

Termination of parental rights requires that states show "clear and convincing evidence that a parent is currently unfit to further the welfare and best interests of the child." When considering parental rights termination, courts may not consider old or stale information[24] but may consider prognostic value of expert testimony[25] and the contrast of the FDP victim's health status as a result of victim/offender seclusion data.[26] The difficulty in FDP child abuse cases is that appearance is usually not reality.

The abuse continuum of FDP victimization allows for conceptualization that not all cases of FDP victimization may require termination of parental rights. Assessing FDP behavior on the FDP abuse continuum is predicated upon victim injury. In a straightforward abuse situation, victim injury is self-evident but in FDP abuse—results of either simulation or production may have delayed lethality consequences. Simulation (noninvasive) of medical illness takes longer than production (invasive or direct causation) to produce lethality. Extreme or produced forms of FDP are generally believed to require immediate intervention because the results of the FDP offenders act are often self-evident; victim protection needs are obvious. Noninvasive simulated signs/symptoms of illness (falsified medical charts, verbally alleged victim symptoms, reported illness) without substantiated medical abnormalities are often not provable because evidence may be lacking and diagnostic medical testing is underway. It is unlikely that substantiation for termination of parental rights will be attained in cases of isolated FDP simulation and FDP offender/victim access remains. Proving parental unfitness may be difficult.

Custody of FDP Victims and Their Siblings

Historical case review of known FDP abuse situations provides predicate that FDP abuse is not necessarily directed at only one child within a family. Predatory future abuse of an identified FDP victim's sibling(s) and/or historical chronic, yet undetected, FDP sibling abuse pose a realistic question of extended sibling threatened harm in FDP case situations. Siblings of identified FDP child abuse victims should be added to petitions of care and protective orders to allow investigative opportunity to evaluate protective need. Sibling inclusion also provides opportunity to question these children in neutral settings within societal defined familial norms (free from FDP abuse).

Hazard of Placing an FDP Victim with a Family Member

Abilities of a court-appointed caretaker (foster parent) for FDP child abuse victims and/or siblings require individuals with basic nurturing abilities and an understanding of FDP child abuse infliction processes and offender dynamics. Caretakers must have the ability to judge when actual medical care is needed and take appropriate action by summoning adequate assistance to address an FDP victim's legitimate medical need that has been enhanced or mutated by FDP offender actions. When an FDP abuse situation is discovered, FDP offenders may impart accusatory or distrustful attitudes toward medical staff as a prelude to defensive strategy. It is important that this attitude is not carried over to appointed caretakers. Realistic response to actual medical need is required.[27] Caretakers must be beyond reproach in their protection of children and able to recognize manipulation when presented.

Courts often strongly consider placing abuse victim custody within the family. Nonoffending parents in FDP abuse cases are generally considerations in custody placement. Nonoffending parents are generally not directly involved in FDP child abuse victimization,[28] but their role within FDP victimization may be seen as enabling and in some situations contributory within the FDP suspect's choices. Looking at interfamilial dynamics within known cases of FDP abuse provides child risk factors when considering FDP child victim placement with an FDP nonoffending parent. These concerns include the following (Figure 9.6).

In cases where surviving FDP child abuse victims or their siblings are placed into custody of the nonoffending parent, issues of child protection versus family loyalty are concerning and require verification. The wide range of behavioral possibilities within a nonoffending FDP spouse presents interdisciplinary victim risk issues as follows (Figure 9.7).

Family loyalty and a desire for family reunification or revenge/punishment by the nonoffending spouse onto either the FDP suspect or victim may be strong motivators regarding how a nonoffending spouse or other family member may behave if given custody of a surviving FDP abuse victim. Risk to the FDP victim includes physical and psychological harm.

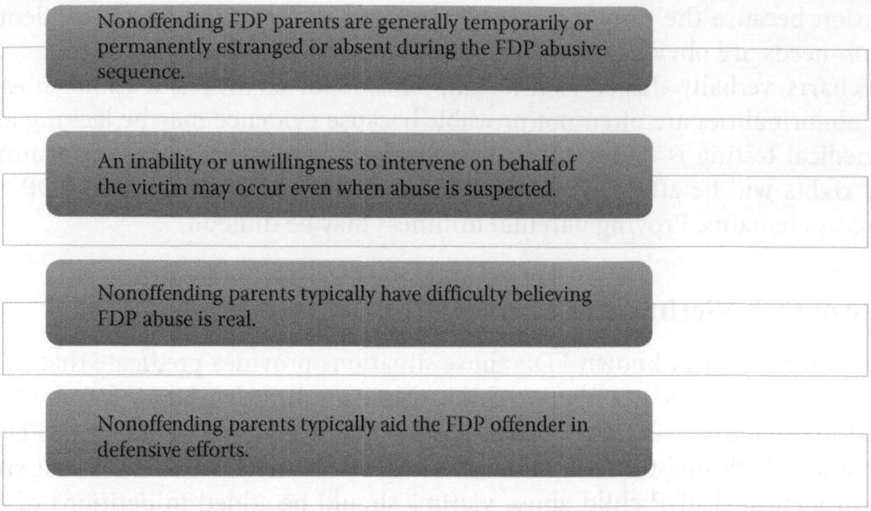

Figure 9.6 The nonoffending parent element.

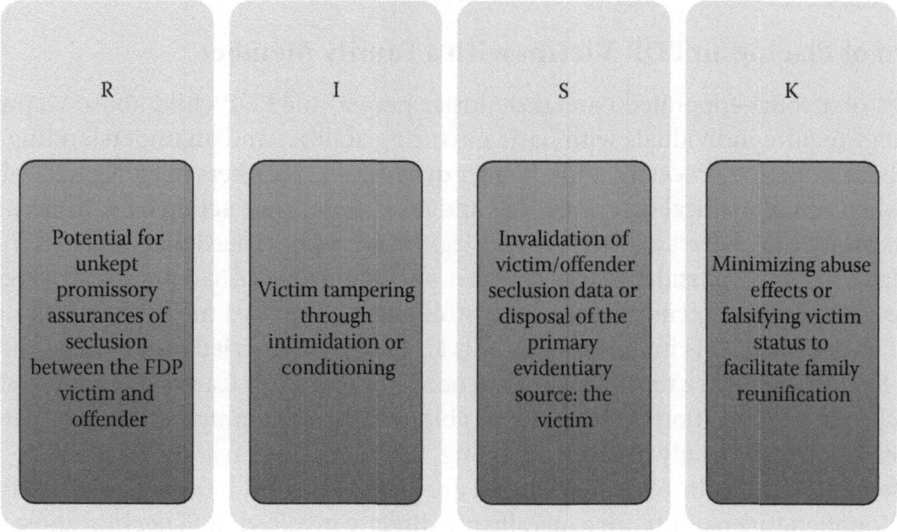

Figure 9.7 The nonoffending FDP parent potential response *risk*.

Examining the interaction (or lack thereof) between an identifying FDP offender and his or her spouse opens a window into the environment of abuse. Both spouses will view this environment from their own unique perspectives. The functionality of the family should be carefully considered as child custody (victim placement) is determined.

It is recommended that FDP victims and their siblings be initially placed in a neutral atmosphere free from the dangers associated with relative placement. A neutral atmosphere is defined as a location where the assigned caretaker has not formulated strong opinion regarding the guilt or innocence of the alleged FDP abuser. Neutrality is generally impossible within the home of family members, close acquaintances, or friends of the FDP-involved family. Locations that are not neutral provide heightened potential of disregard for child safety rules including reunification between FDP offender and victim. Unsupervised/unreported victim/offender reunification (contact) establishes further opportunity for victimization and may create conflict in victim/offender seclusion data evidence. The result may range from improper dismissal of a dependency petition facilitating reunification between the abuser and the abused.[29] The ultimate result may equate to victim death.

Guardian *Ad Litem*

It is highly recommended that a guardian *ad litem* be appointed by the courts in cases of FDP abuse to insure the welfare of the abuse victim. Custody issues are one aspect of advocacy the guardian may help to address. Court appointment of the guardian may provide a manner to ensure that appointees possess specialized knowledge regarding FDP abuse to address practicality concerns. Time constraints attached to complete background inquiries of potential temporary custody placement (foster care) do not necessarily allow for FDP specialty knowledge verification.

A guardian *ad litem* should be knowledgeable regarding the many facets of FDP abuse. A misinformed or uninformed guardian may easily misread the actual façade set forth by the FDP offender and become enamored with apparent reality orchestrated by an FDP offender intent on reclamation or retention of a victim. In some court situations, the ability of the guardian to accurately determine the verity of FDP familial suitability becomes a tedious task of investigatory splendor. The significance of the guardian's opinion of parental suitability is often of fundamental importance and weight to the court when determining temporary or permanent victim custody.

Visitation Issues

Court-mandated visitation between a suspected FDP abuser and a child victim must be strictly supervised. It is often difficult for the court to imagine the abusive creativity identified within various FDP victimization sequences; it seems reasonable for the court to assure victim safety with supervised visitation in place. This is a fallacy. There have been documented instances of physical victim abuse occurring during supervised visitation. Such abuse is not limited to physical infliction of harm onto a victim but extended to fabrication methodology formulated through verbalization technique alone. Child abuse victims and (generally) families do not understand the risk undertaken when allowable visitation with an FDP suspected abuser occurs.

Any required visitation occurring at child welfare agency location should be conducted under strict supervision. Visitation guidelines should be well planned and rules provided in writing to the suspected offender. A suspected FDP abuser should be required to acknowledge understanding of these guidelines after they have been read out loud by the caseworker then acknowledged by written signature to attest to understanding.

Protective Case Plan Development

Child abuse cases involving an FDP element involve child protection. Case plans are a tool to ensure standardized disposition relative to unsupervised or supervised visitation between an abuser and a victim or planned reunification. Internationally, individualized

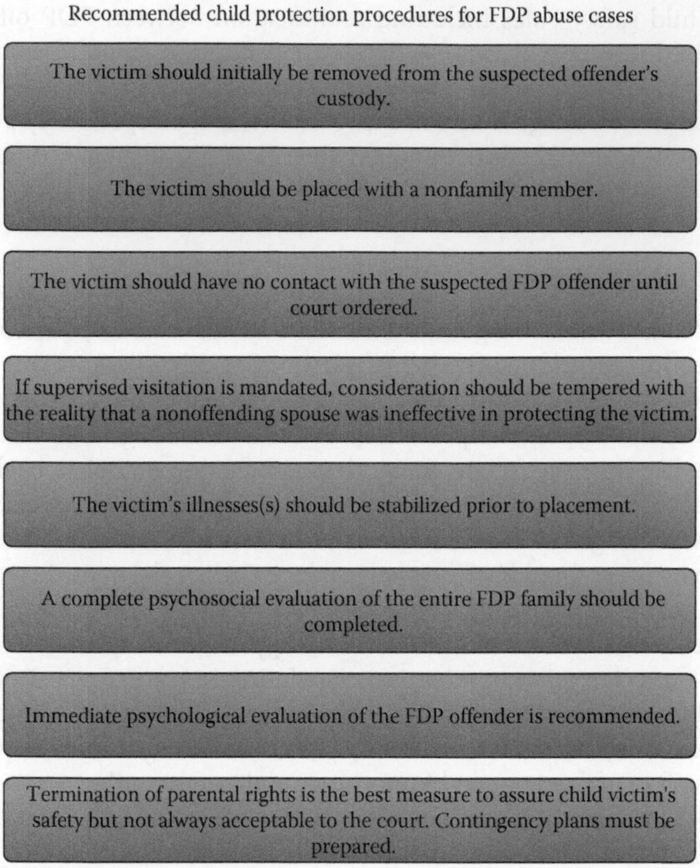

Recommended child protection procedures for FDP abuse cases
The victim should initially be removed from the suspected offender's custody.
The victim should be placed with a nonfamily member.
The victim should have no contact with the suspected FDP offender until court ordered.
If supervised visitation is mandated, consideration should be tempered with the reality that a nonoffending spouse was ineffective in protecting the victim.
The victim's illnesses(s) should be stabilized prior to placement.
A complete psychosocial evaluation of the entire FDP family should be completed.
Immediate psychological evaluation of the FDP offender is recommended.
Termination of parental rights is the best measure to assure child victim's safety but not always acceptable to the court. Contingency plans must be prepared.

Figure 9.8 Child protection for FDP victims.

agencies or disciplines have formulated specific environmental, logistical, and human factor contingencies to accomplish safe reuniting of families. Any case plan may be modified to accommodate particular victim safety needs to ensure the likelihood of safety. Within FDP abuse, there is no known reunification plan that will ensure victim safety because to do so requires reassurance that environmental factors, suspect primal thinking, and willingness to offend are permanently changed. The deceptive ability of FDP offenders makes this verification unlikely.

Termination of parental rights seems to provide the most reassurance of victim safety, but reluctance of the courts to unilaterally institute termination of parental rights as a standard in proven FDP child abuse cases is problematic. Termination is, therefore, only one possibility in long-term victim safety planning. One must acquiesce to the wisdom of the courts for final disposition of individual cases (Figure 9.8).

Conclusion

There is always something you can do to create change. In the realm of FDP child abuse victimization, identification of the problem and provability of FDP theory are the foundation for the initiation of protective intervention. Intuitive medical personnel generally initiate the process of FDP abuse or homicide identification/suspicion. Proving FDP abuse or homicide is a multidisciplinary group effort and victim protection is the universal link. Coordination and understanding within the multidisciplinary group facilitate positive case outcome.

Unique child protection issues found within confirmed FDP child abuse cases necessitate that variations of rudimentary protective procedures occur. Improper intervention has consequences that may affect the victim's viability. The sense of urgency to act within a child protective mode must be tempered with the reality that premature intervention may equate to ineffective action in halting a covert cycle of victim abuse; the potential for lasting change within a victim's life is contingent upon interdisciplinary team management.

Distinctive yet constantly evolving properties associated with FDP child abuse dictates that child protective caseworkers become educated regarding potential hazards associated with FDP abuse investigations. Hazards include risk factors and how those factors affect victim safety. The actions that a child protective caseworker institutes or omits directly affect victim protection outcomes and multidisciplinary team abilities to resolve a suspected FDP abuse case.

Setting behavioral limits for FDP abusers is only possible when FDP abuse identification and provability standards are met. FDP offender behavioral limits are dependent upon access to the victim that directly corresponds to child dependency issues and placement and deterrents (punishment predicated upon criminal justice standards or behavioral modification through social intervention). Deploying these limits provides the greatest victim safety measure for long-term and acute consideration.

Removal of victims from the custody of the FDP abuser requires evidence. FDP abuse is suspected to be multigenerational; family members are not considered appropriate sources of placement until vetted. Looking at the psychosocial history of an FDP family provides a source of social history and insight into family dynamic present that allowed FDP abuse to occur.

Suspected FDP abusers may not be criminally convicted, and the goal of dependency court may be family reunification. Social service agencies need to develop victim protection contingencies, and one way to accomplish that is by advocating that the FDP offender begins counseling as soon as practical. If the criminal justice system does not prevail through substantiated charges and the dependency court asserts authority to reunite the offender with the victim, there is a chance that further victimization may be lessened. There is also a chance that FDP offender knowledge will grow to exceed previous offense capabilities.

Notes

1. Jordan, K.S. and Moore-Nadler, M., Children at risk of maltreatment identification and intervention in the emergency department. *Advanced Emergency Nursing Journal*, January/March 2014;36(1):97–106.
2. Barlow, S., Freeborn, D., Cole, B., and Williams, M., Advanced practice nurse barriers to reporting child maltreatment. *American Professional Society on the Abuse of Children*, 2012;24:10–17.
3. Perman, C.M., Diagnosing the truth: Determining physician liability in cases involving Munchausen syndrome by proxy. *Journal of Urban and Contemporary Law*, 1998;54:267–290.

4. Meadow, R., Management of Munchausen syndrome by proxy. *Archives of Disease in Childhood*, 1985;60:385–393.
5. Dine, M. and McGovern, M., Intentional poisoning of children—An overlooked category of child abuse: Report of seven cases and review of literature. *Pediatrics*, 1982;70:32–34.
6. Wright, J., Munchausen syndrome by proxy or medical child abuse. *Journal of Rare Diseases*, 1997;3(3):5–10.
7. McGuire, T.L. and Feldman, K.W., Psychological morbidity of children subjected to Munchausen syndrome by proxy. *Pediatrics*, 1989;83(2):289–292.
8. Rand, D.C., Munchausen syndrome by proxy as a possible factor when abuse is falsely alleged. *Issues in Child Abuse Accusations*, 1989;1(4):32–34.
9. Rand, D.C., Munchausen syndrome by proxy: Integration of classic and contemporary types. *Issues in Child Abuse Accusations*, 1990;2(2):83–89.
10. See Note 2.
11. Kinscherff, R. and Famularo, R., Extreme Munchausen syndrome by proxy: The case for termination of parental rights. *Juvenile and Family Court Journal*, 1991;41–49.
12. Libow, J.A. and Schreier, H.A., Three forms of factitious illness in children: When is it Munchausen syndrome by proxy? *American Journal of Orthopsychiatry*, 1986;56(4):602–611.
13. Dine, M. and McGovern, M., Intentional poisoning of children—An overlooked category of child abuse: Report of seven cases and review of the literature. *Pediatrics*, 1982;70:32–35.
14. McGuire, T.L. and Feldman, K.W., Psychologic morbidity of children subjected to Munchausen syndrome by proxy. *Pediatrics*, 1989;83(2):289–292.
15. See Note 8.
16. Rosen, C.L., Frost, J.D., Bricker, T., Tarnow, J., Gillette, P., and Dunlavy, S., Two siblings with recurrent cardiorespiratory arrest: Munchausen syndrome by proxy or child abuse? *Pediatrics*, 1983;71:715–720.
17. Berger, D., Child abuse simulating apparent "Near Miss" sudden infant death syndrome. *Journal of Pediatrics*, 1979;95:554–556.
18. See Note 4.
19. Minford, A., Child abuse presenting as apparent "Near Miss" sudden infant death syndrome. *British Medical Journal*, 1981;282:521.
20. See Note 8.
21. Waller, D., Obstacles in the treatment of Munchausen syndrome by proxy. *Journal of the Academy of Child Psychiatry*, 1983;22:80–85.
22. Guandolo, V., Munchausen syndrome by proxy: An outpatient challenge. *Pediatrics*, 1985;75(3):526–530.
23. McGuire, T.I. and Feldman, K.W., Psychologic morbidity of children subjected to Munchausen syndrome by proxy. *Pediatrics*, 1989;83(2):289–292.
24. See Note 20.
25. See Note 18.
26. See Ind Code Ann. 31-3-1-6 (Burns 1987); Oregon Rev. Stat 109.324 (1984); Rhode Island General Laws 15-7-7(1981).
27. In Re Adoption of George, 27, Mass. App. Ct. 265, 537 N.E. 2d 1251 (1989).
28. Petition of the Catholic Charitable Bureau of the Archdiocese of Boston to Dispense with Consent to Adoption. 18 Mass. App. 656, 469 N.E. 2d 1277 (1984).
29. 395 Mass 180, 497 N.E. 2d 143 (1985).

Chronically Ill Child Caught in the Factitious Disorder by Proxy World

10

Unless someone like you cares a whole awful lot, nothing is going to get better. It's not.

Dr. Seuss

Mechanics

In a number of identified factitious disorder by proxy (FDP) abuse cases, victims have been abused while affected with a legitimate chronic illness. Legitimate victim illness symptoms may be enhanced or interspersed with factitious enhancements producing the following effects:

- Legitimate illness compounded by the actions of the FDP offender
- Factitious illness encircling real medical maladies

The complicated medical process of defining symptom origination of authentic biological origin versus those created by the actions of the FDP offender through factitious means is difficult. Entanglement occurs as a seemingly endless medical causation list to explain a victim's medical signs/symptoms of illness is encircled by an FDP abuser's extremely deceptive creativity and offense ability. Clarification of illness origin often does not become clear until the victim is separated from the suspected FDP abuser providing a true depiction of victim health status (Figure 10.1).

Prenatal Knowledge and FDP Offender Actions

Parents of children born with birth defects often contend with added parental stressors due to prolonged hospitalizations, medically necessary procedures, and required family adjustment. When a child is known to possess defects prior to birth, some mothers disassociate themselves emotionally from the fetus for personal reasons. Potential child death preparation or insulation from the reality of the child's health status upon birth may be attained through detachment. This reaction is not necessarily considered an abnormal response to a very difficult situation.

The personal quality of life for parents of a handicapped or special needs child sometimes forces parents to realize that the dream of a *perfect life* for themselves and their child is over before it has even begun. Most parents adapt to this realization, and if a pregnancy continues, parents envision themselves with their child at special functions such as the *Special Olympics*. They readjust preconceived ideals of perfection and opt for adjusted

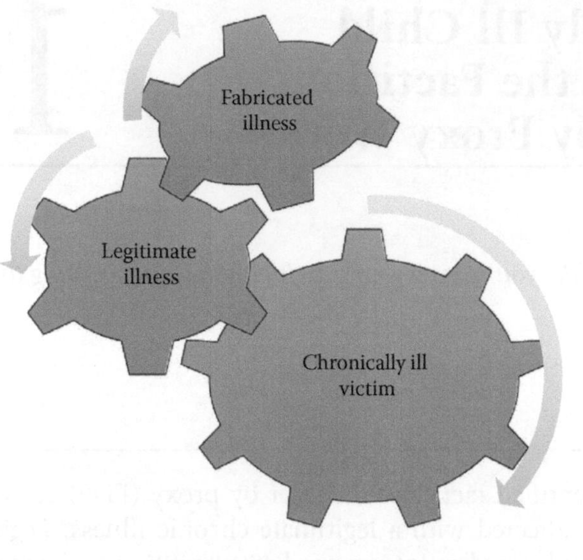

Figure 10.1 Chronic interactive mechanics of factitious disorder by proxy abuse.

reality predicated upon love for the infant. Loss of perfectionism does not necessarily mean a total loss—just an adjustment.

In cases of FDP, child abuse–perfectionism of life with a sick new baby, real or imagined, may die long before the child is born. Forcible reality and loss of perfectionism facilitate detachment. Detachment facilitates the ability of a mother to offend upon her own child with FDP abuse as the mechanism to maintain a connection with medical staff thereby relieving her of tremendous responsibility caring for an ill child. The reality of a lifetime of parental sacrifice to care for a handicapped child is replaced with hospital respite and a refocusing of importance upon the mother. The process takes normally occurring detachment to an extreme as life for the FDP offender becomes response to the infliction of harm upon her child—where there is a sense of belonging.

Fetal Murder Premeditation Potential in FDP Abuse Situations

Distancing and apathy may be seen in expectant females knowingly carrying handicapped children and be viewed as a normal reactionary response. Expectant FDP offenders who carry handicapped children may similarly be affected; however, the potentiality of contrived victim illness theoretically may exist before a child is born. Permanent disassociation between the FDP parent and her child pertinent to actual or contrived illness may be a realization that childbirth equates to transference of attention onto the child and away from the mother.

High-risk pregnancies (with handicapped children) generally garner enhanced medical staff attention upon the mother. Loss of enhanced attention at childbirth is an adjustment that FDP offenders may not navigate well. Clues that tell an FDP offender she will not remain the center of attention upon childbirth begin when the health status of the fetus seemingly becomes more important to medical staff than the health status of the mother. Whether or not this realization is accurate is irrelevant—the FDP offender's interpretation of situations becomes reality to her. When considering the likely pathway of a chronically ill child, although the initial response of the FDP offender may be delight, this response may change. Transference of attention onto the child may become a factor between life and death decisions with the knowledge that the child will likely be the prolonged attention center.

The FDP offender's inner justification for thought and action pertaining her chronically ill child's life may be indicative pre-birth. Warning indicators of factitious disorder may be revealed within the FDP offender's behavior during her pregnancy. Factitious disorder arises as the presentation of illness that is not provable. Associative symptoms possessed by the mother prior to the childbirth may be mimicked in parallel illness within the newborn. Self-infliction of illness by the FDP offender later linked to an equivalent illness in the child establishes knowledge of infliction basis. When a person inflicts or creates illness and experiences the consequences, they establish an intrinsic personal knowledge base. When that same infliction creates similar symptoms within a victim, there is a presumption that the offender understands the likely consequences of harm. Experience provides irrefutable knowledge. The following issues are relevant to signs/symptoms self-induced by a person (factitious disorder) that are later inflicted upon a proxy (FDP) (Figure 10.2).

Medical personnel characteristically view FDP abuse onto a fetus through the avenue of FD self-harm. The actions of pregnant FDP offenders through observable statements and actions create a question between self-harm and FDP abuse. Secondary gain, in the form of attention, provides specific offender benefit, but mothers who abuse their fetuses through the avenue of FDP may do so for direct harm reasons—especially if the fetus is known to be abnormal. FDP abuse case analysis of viable children provides insight into potential FDP activity *in utero*. The analysis of FDP offender observations during pregnancy and FD behavior provide interesting correlations that may illuminate a behavioral connection predicated upon action and suggest that FDP abuse upon a child may begin prior to childbirth.

The following FDP offender actions are considered:

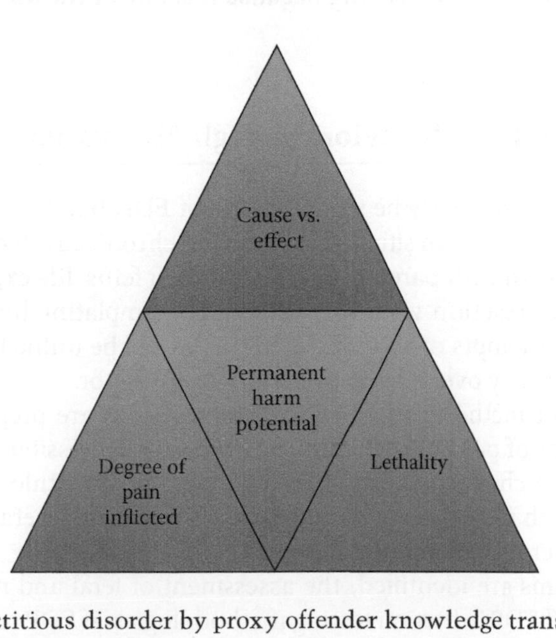

Figure 10.2 FD to factitious disorder by proxy offender knowledge transference.

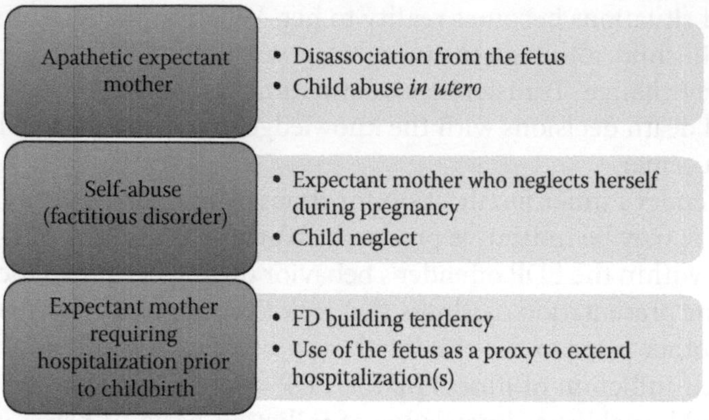

Apathetic expectant mother
• Disassociation from the fetus
• Child abuse *in utero*
Self-abuse (factitious disorder)
• Expectant mother who neglects herself during pregnancy
• Child neglect
Expectant mother requiring hospitalization prior to childbirth
• FD building tendency
• Use of the fetus as a proxy to extend hospitalization(s)

Figure 10.3 Factitious disorder by proxy offender action analysis.

FDP Offender Actions

FDP offenders who decide to utilize their children as FDP target objects may implement victimization thought process or action prior to birth. It is difficult to determine if an FDP offender's apathy toward a fetus is part of the FDP continuum or reactionary response to a perceived fetal condition (Figure 10.3).

Care should be extended regarding interpretation of an expectant mother's self-neglect as an early indicator of FDP behavior. Full exploration of potential causation for such neglect is necessary to rule out other forms of mental illness, poverty, or a general lack of education. FDP behavior as it relates to maternal/fetal neglect is complicated.

If an FDP offender is pleased to be hospitalized, it may indicate hospital preference to the reality of life outside the hospital setting (home or work). There are many possible reasons for this behavior including the presence of domestic violence, neglect, and adverse living conditions. Taking pleasure or acquiring an abnormal comfort level regarding hospitalization is concerning because it is one of the known characteristics of FD and FDP.

Linking Action to FDP Behavior through Motivation

FDP offender actions may clearly be symptomatic of FDP, but motivations are not necessarily classically FDP oriented in situations involving chronically ill children. When physicians are straightforward with parents, disclosing that a fetus' life expectancy is unknown, a classic FDP offender reaction would be delight, contemplating limitless hospitalization potential. Deliberate attempts of aborting the fetus would be unlikely in true FDP context unless homicidal tendency overrides the FDP attention factor.

FDP offenders act methodically. FDP offender actions are preplanned and executed with the least amount of possible detection. Although it is possible that an FDP offender who is the parent of a chronically ill fetus may hope for miraculous healing or lessened abnormality, childbirth focus is on situational reality. Reality generally equates to difficult parenting for an undermined amount of time.

When FDP victims are identified, the assessment of fetal and newborn development may reveal patterns of FDP infliction testing methodologies. If FDP coexists with homicidal tendencies, directed attempts of fetal abortion through disguised measures or directed murder through specific direct or indirect action may be found.

Stressors created by specialized care conditions for the handicapped or chronically ill child often affect parents' interpersonal relationship creating instability. When expectant parents fail to bond with their children, allowable abuse or orchestrated death may be facilitated. Parents who do establish bonding with their chronically ill child may view painful medical treatment endured by the child as a tortuous regime that tests their resolve; death may be seen as respite. In either situation, a parent may rationalize that mercy in death is better than a life of misery for the entire family. Private contemplation of death through the avenue of FDP abuse is a potentiality. FDP offenders understand that FDP abuse or homicide is difficult to detect and easily concealed.

When a chronically ill child is born and FDP abuse is suspected, care should be taken to fully realize the factor that directed homicide has upon the situation. Careless FDP infliction such as deliberate tubing disconnection causing excessive bleeding likely to cause death, repetitive life-threatening severe infections, or repeated cessation of breathing (suffocation) should create extreme suspicion. Overriding factors or directed homicide rather than classic FDP victimization sequences should be evaluated—even if the child has been repetitively hospitalized with apparently genuine medical conditions. Instances of child injury that appear carelessly induced or those that leave obvious evidentiary clues should not be automatically linked to FDP abuse through the victimization index. Covert ability and ingenuity possessed by the FDP offender should not be underestimated; obvious child injury may indicate directed homicide attempts within a window of FDP abuse.

Closely examining the hospitalization/illness cycle of a chronically ill child may reveal harm escalation associated with parental stress. Parents of chronically ill children may have a higher degree of frustration, and FDP parents are likely to have a lower coping threshold. Treatment ineffectiveness or a child's inability to progress in a manner hoped for may be motivators for parental behavior. Parents may wonder when *enough is enough* in terms of treatment and suffering and secretly hope for respite through death. For some parents, hope of this relief is not enough and homicidal thoughts occur. A small known number of parents act upon these thoughts and terminate the child's life. If that occurs through the avenue of FDP abuse, the difficulty detection factor is voluminous (Figure 10.4).

Threshold of Homicide

The existence of the FDP offender centers on the ability to covertly commit abuse while personifying magnificent caregiving ability. FDP deception is classically orchestrated to obtain an alternative reward that is not plainly evident to most people. The victim is the vehicle utilized to attain this intangible goal and preserved so long as the reward outweighs the risk or the victim's body is capable of absorbing the abuse. Deception skill may become easily transferable to highly complex schemes of ultimate elimination (death) of an unwanted victim under various circumstances.

There is a point when utilizing a victim as an FDP tool may become a detriment to the FDP offender and detection risk supersedes FDP offender gain. This point seems exasperated in victims who are permanently handicapped from either natural causes or FDP abuse

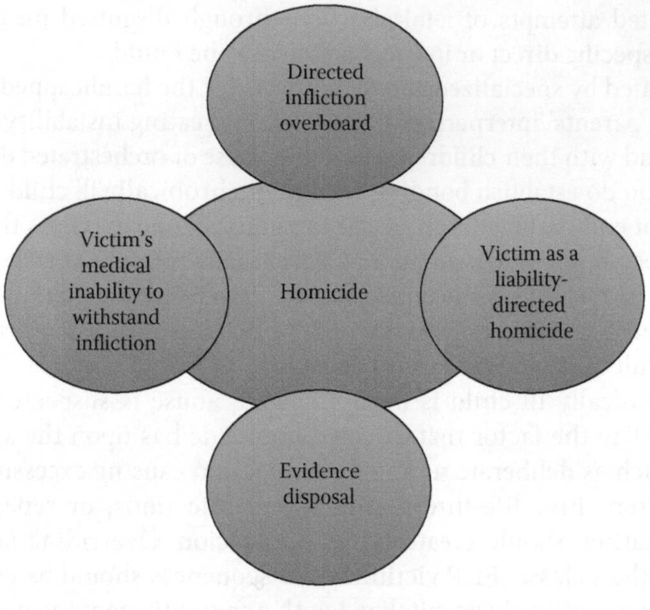

Figure 10.4 The pathway of factitious disorder by proxy homicide.

infliction. FDP offenders who move from by proxy infliction for self-gain attainment to directed homicide cross a threshold of willingness to protect their secrets. There is another, perhaps, unintended way that victim homicide occurs through the victim's inability to withstand medical treatments or upscale abuse at the hands of the FDP offender.

Measuring the unintended or intended death of an FDP victim is a complicated investigative examination of motive. FDP offender motive may be a realized self-gain goal commonly seen within FDP abuse situations or a directed homicide. Either intent may transpire at any point within the FDP abuse cycle or intermittently occur within a combination setting. When an FDP abuse victim is chronically ill (due to actual medical condition(s)) or permanently disabled, there will likely be factors that place extended pressure upon caretakers. The manner in which caretakers respond to this pressure predicates the likelihood of FDP abuse continuance or a decision to move toward directed homicide. Contributory stress factors are shown in Figure 10.5.

Nonoffending FDP Parental Contribution to FDP Homicide

Chronically ill FDP abuse victims abused by a custodial parent may also have a nonoffending parent in attendance. The nonoffending parent plays an intricate role within FDP offender choices pertaining to abuse or directed homicide. A nonoffending parent is easily caught up in the factitious world created by an FDP abuser and not necessarily aware of the ongoing abuse. The lack of suspicion by the nonoffending parent can be bolstered by blind trust for his or her mate, physical absence from the situation, emotional withdrawal from the given situation, and the weight of stress presented when caring for a chronically ill child (Figure 10.5).

Custodians of chronically ill or severely ill individuals often reach a place within medical treatment pathways that DNR (do not resuscitate) decisions emerge as mercy is considered. DNR is a normal part of ending life when recovery is hopeless and victim suffering

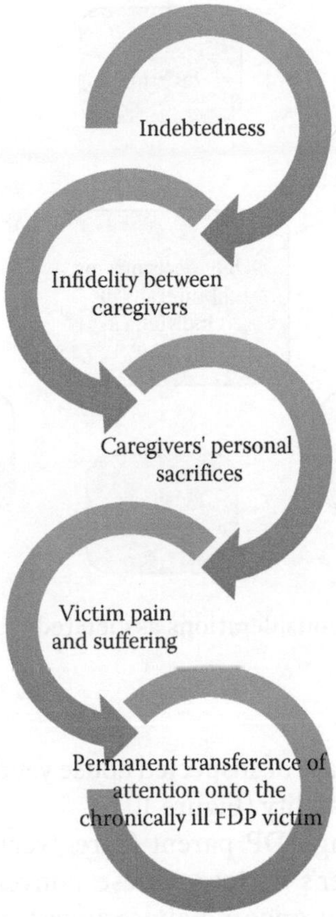

Figure 10.5 Homicidal decisions and contributory stress factors.

is profound. In FDP victimization cases that have progressed to the point of seemingly hopeless recovery, DNR status may be a consideration for the victim by the nonoffending custodian. When DNR status is actualized yet the victim is in reality an FDP abuse target, examining the sequence of events leading to the DNR decision is necessary to determine motive. DNR status determination by a nonoffending custodian may emulate from many sources: frustration with the medical staff's inability to heal the apparently ill victim, the victim's pain and suffering, permanent or irreversible victim injury, the emotional and practical toll caring for the chronically ill victim has upon the entire family, religious conviction, disassociation from the victim, total lack of awareness that the chronically ill individual is being victimized. Chronically ill individuals who are FDP abuse victims whose infliction pathway has led to severity are severely at risk from not only their abusers but from unknowing nonoffending associated caretakers.

DNR Decisions for Chronically Ill Individuals

Nonoffending FDP custodians of FDP victims should be evaluated to determine their relationship within the FDP abuse cycle. Role responsibility consideration relating to criminal facilitation of abuse stemming from nonoffending parental knowledge of ongoing victimization requires dialogue. Exculpatory statements of knowledge indicating that a

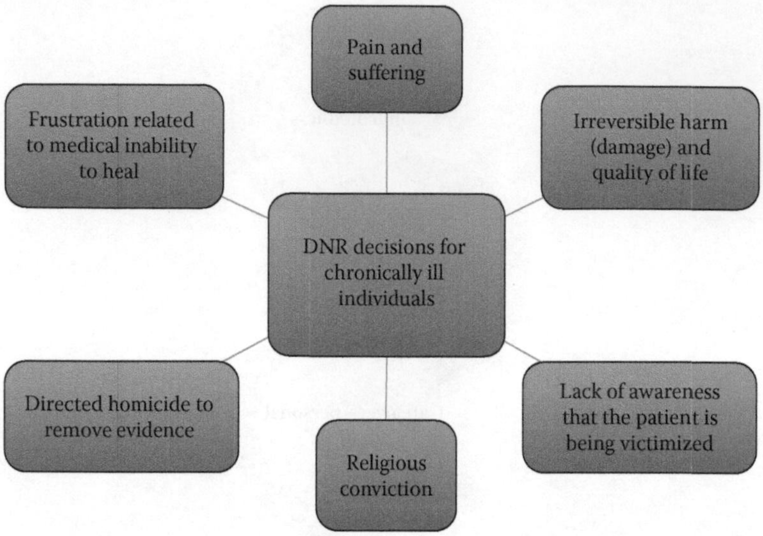

Figure 10.6 Do-not-resuscitate considerations associated with chronically ill factitious disorder by proxy victimization.

nonoffending custodian was aware of suspected abuse yet did nothing to protect the victim directly correlate to potential liability (Figure 10.6).

Speaking to a nonoffending FDP parent (caregiver) often validates circumstances surrounding the FDP offender's actions. These conversations originate from direct questioning stemming from an ongoing abuse investigation or from review of unsolicited conversations occurring between the nonoffending parent and family members, medical staff, friends, or other individuals. The FDP offender's ability to victimize is predicated upon access to the victim, motive and reward, and willingness. When FDP victimization occurs chronically, knowledge of the nonoffending parent is likely to be elevated. Theoretically, nonoffending parental status as an accomplice to FDP abuse is possible through the avenue of *failure to protect*. The point when a nonoffending custodian takes the initiative to express his or her concerns regarding suspicion of abuse is likely to reveal the degree of indoctrination within the FDP abuse cycle or the level of assumed responsibility for his or her part within the abuse. When suspicion is not acted upon, yet present, liability attaches. When suspicion is nonexistent due to indoctrination within the FDP abuse web, questions should arise regarding whether suspicion was present and ignored or absent because the nonoffending caretaker removed himself from the very difficult situation of caretaking attached to a chronically ill child. *Did the nonoffending parent walk away from responsibility*?

When a nonoffending caretaker is confronted with the reality of an FDP abuse scenario attached to their chronically ill dependent, disbelief is commonly expressed. Statements such as "This child gets all the attention in the world" or "My wife (husband) is a wonderful parent and would never do something like this" are prevalent. The shock of reality presented when FDP abuse is discovered seemingly hits the nonoffending parent hard. The remaining objective when confronting a potential nonoffending FDP caretaker requires the interviewer to understand that although nonoffending parents may not be responsible for direct victim harm causation, they may have enabled it to occur through denial of recognizable clues. Situational interpersonal relationship views held by the FDP offender and his or her nonoffending spouse and their relationships with the victim can be vastly different.

Nonoffending caretakers may view the challenges of a chronically ill child as a means of strengthening the relationship with their spouse. They may point out that whenever the child was hospitalized, the family rallied and supported one another and that care for the child required critical care dedication. Closeness described by the nonoffending parent occurs only when all family members are present, and this often occurs only when the child is hospitalized. The marriage between spouses may be in actuality a triangle that includes their chronically ill child as familial strength is forged through a bonding of medical need. The nonoffending parent may fail to recognize that his or her pattern of self-isolation when the chronically ill child was not hospitalized acted as a trigger (catalyst) for FDP infliction. Nonoffending caretakers may initiate isolation as respite through immersion into work or social endeavors that exclude the FDP offender.

Closely observing the *FDP marriage members* within a hospital setting is likely to negate a nonoffending caretaker's statement that "all is well within the family." Witness observations are likely to reveal estrangement between the parents as the nonoffending parent devotes needed attention toward the chronically ill child and away from his or her spouse. This estrangement supports one of the FDP identification elements—isolationism. When an FDP offender is isolated and not the center of attention, jealousy, discontent, or even hatred of the nonoffending spouse may erupt. Isolation not only occurs when the FDP offender is at home with a chronically ill child, but it also occurs in plain sight (in medical settings) when attention is bestowed upon the victim and away from the FDP offender. Although bringing a victim back into the hospital setting causes the nonoffending spouse to refocus attention upon the family and be present, it also provides the FDP offender with respite and reestablishes closeness between spouses that may be otherwise absent. There is concern within the infliction mode of FDP escalation that when recall of the nonoffending parent occurs in this manner, FDP offenders may view their victims as obstacles to their interpersonal relationship with their spouse due to attention shift. FDP offenders may feel that the nonoffending spouse cares more for the chronically ill child than for him/her, and this is sometimes accurate.

Nonoffending spouses may view themselves as supportive toward their spouses, but this view is often inaccurate. Factors of infidelity, suspicion of infidelity, or observed outright flirtation with medical staff by the nonoffending spouse may occur during prolonged victim hospitalizations. The nonoffending parents' blatant disregard for the FDP offender's feelings may not be acknowledged and contrarily viewed as *supportive perfection*. To further complicate this issue, when the FDP offender is asked to comment upon any existing interpersonal relationship such as marriage, outward portrayal is likely to be that her "marriage is wonderful and her spouse is supportive." Lies abound unilaterally when dealing with an FDP offender and a true reflection of the interaction occurring between the nonoffending spouse of an FDP offender will not be easily revealed from either source.

In situations where nonoffending spouses have abandoned their interpersonal relationship with an FDP offender (regardless of inherent knowledge of abuse), substitution has occurred. FDP offenders have substituted their nonoffenders support, love, and caring with medical staff enmeshment first as a coping mechanism then as a way of life. Nonoffending spouses have likely sought respite from intolerable conditions through work enmeshment or other relationships (including love and caring for the chronically ill child). The element of family support is awkwardly projected by both the FDP offender and nonoffending spouse when genuine family support dynamics are absent. In-place intrafamilial estrangement should be questioned during the FDP nonoffending spouse evaluation. Stressors created by the specialized conditions of a handicapped or chronically ill dependent upon the caretaker's relationship facilitate dysfunction. Dysfunction and the inappropriate FDP offender's response to that dysfunction help to facilitate FDP abuse.

Nonoffending Parental Reactions

Case Flow of FDP Abuse with a Chronic Illness Variable

FDP abuse cases involving a child who is chronically ill—either due to natural causes or as a consequence of FDP abuse infliction—may follow a progression as shown in Figure 10.7.

Evidence Management

Evidence collection in abuse or homicide cases that involve an FDP factor and a chronically ill person will be complicated due to the voluminous amount of medical data. Evidence collection and arrangement will be tedious and require organized review by competent professionals skilled in FD/FDP knowledge. Evidence should be organized and evaluated upon diagnostic levels that apply to medical and criminal platforms. These platforms overlap one another. (See Chapter 7 for details regarding evidence in FDP abuse and homicide cases.)

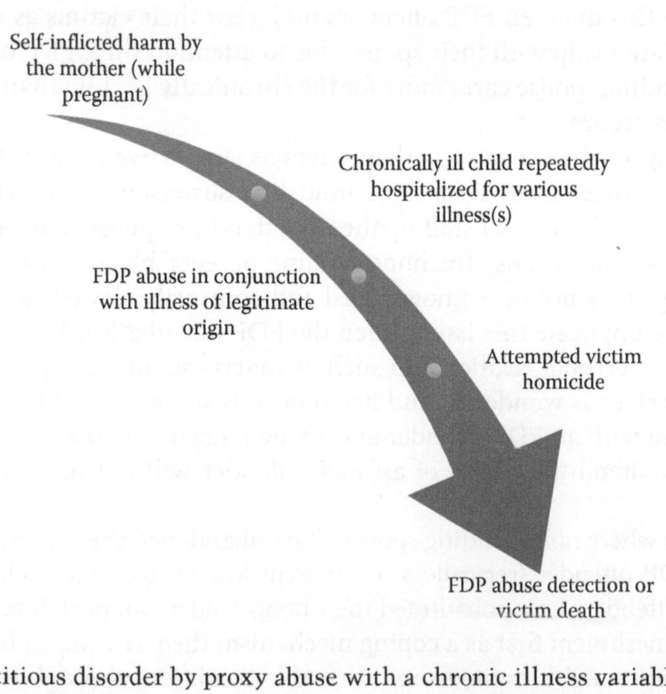

Figure 10.7 Factitious disorder by proxy abuse with a chronic illness variable case flow.

Homicidal Actions Involving Chronically Ill Children: Reviewed

When a child who appears to be afflicted with a chronic illness faces a pattern of near-death experiences, evaluation of potential (root) causation is warranted. Medical causation for death may include both natural causation and criminally linked abuse causes found within FDP abuse patterns. Individuals who die that are "chronically ill" may be undetected homicide victims with the following potential factors considered (Figure 10.8).

Death of a Chronically Ill Child: Causation Considerations

FDP victims are generally considered chronically ill. The lack of bond established or maintained between an FDP victim of homicide and his or her offender and subsequent disassociation by a nonoffending parent may be viewed as a predicate to euthanasia. Parents may inwardly conclude that mercy in death is preferable to a lifetime of misery for a chronically ill child and privately contemplate FDP homicide that is difficult to detect. Frustration due to ineffective treatment or an inability for a child's health status to improve may cause parents to wonder when "enough is enough." Treatment and suffering are often a constant factor in the life of a chronically ill child, and death brings respite. When hope of relief is not enough, homicidal thoughts may occur. Euthanasia relates to FDP abuse through the use of a DNR order when directed victim death is desired. Careful consideration pertaining to issues of DNR, euthanasia, and circumstances leading to that point are needed to determine homicidal culpability.

FDP abuse that is carelessly delivered may easily cause the death of a victim. Death may be intentional (directed homicide) or an unintentional consequence related to the victim's inability to endure abusive acts or the treatment applied to address inflicted symptoms or illness. Unintentional homicide has been identified through various means including deliberate disconnection of the chronically ill victim's medical intravenous tubing causing excessive bleeding, repetitive severe infections, or allowing potentially life-threatening medical procedures (usually surgeries).

FDP victims have a status of being chronically ill. Directed homicide or unintentional victim death may occur at any point during FDP abuse infliction and for many reasons. Extreme forms of FDP abuse likely to cause victim death include poisoning, manual suffocation, transplant procedures, a DNR status for FDP victims, direct physical abuse (throwing a child victim out of a window, breaking bones, etc.), and continuing the facade of victim illness after being advised by medical staff that if the child will likely die if his or her health does not improve.

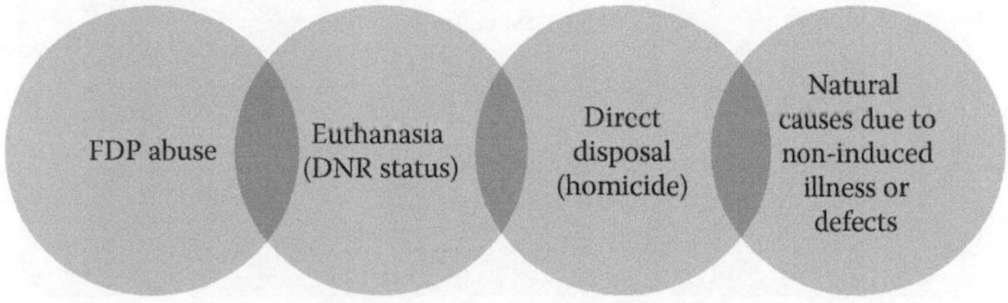

Figure 10.8 Death causation considerations for chronically ill individuals.

Injury to an FDP child abuse victim is not always covertly committed and is sometimes carelessly induced leaving obvious evidence or reasonable suspicion of wrongdoing. Infliction ability of the FDP offender is vast in terms of covert ability, lethality, and ingenuity, and the infliction method may change. When a chronically ill victim dies, FDP abuse rising to the level of homicide should be considered along with more conventional forms of homicide found within physical abuse. Death evaluation of a chronically ill person is complicated because it may occur in conjunction with verifiable illness whose origin is intermixed with organic (non-produced) illness.

Disassociation

Disassociation that may occur between caregivers and chronically ill children facilitates FDP victimization or homicide. Special stressors on caregivers of chronically ill children (regardless of justification) are important to understand because normal parental reactions to these conditions are also the vehicles of FDP infliction (Figure 10.9).

Disassociation between the FDP offender and the FDP victim provides the pathway for victimization as follows (Figure 10.10).

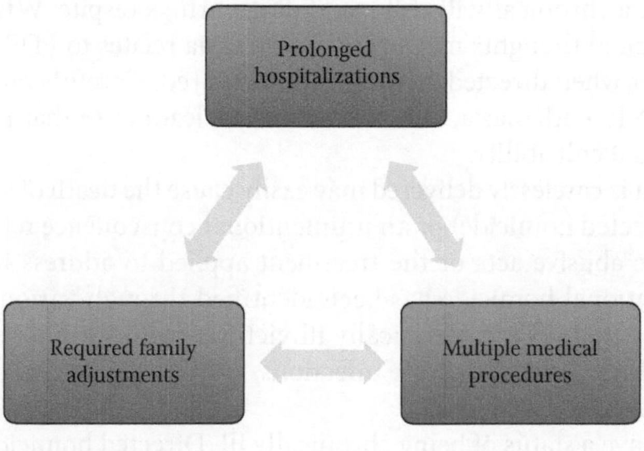

Figure 10.9 Family stress associated with the chronically ill.

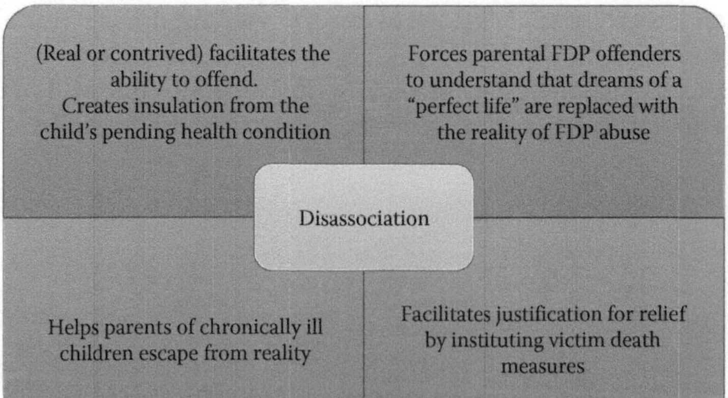

Figure 10.10 Disassociation facilitating chronic abuse.

The Unseen Murder of Victims 11

The dead cannot cry out for justice. It is a duty of the living to do so for them.

Lois McMaster Bujold

Factitious Disorder by Proxy (FDP) as a Homicidal Agent

Linking the cause of a person's death to the actions of an FDP offender is difficult to conceptualize and prove. Recognition of the presence of FDP behavior resulting in a death often occurs only after multiple FDP victims have endured chronic abuse. This abuse may have resulted in either permanent or temporary physical victim damage or risen to a lethal violence level. Evidence gathering in FDP death cases requires that uncommon investigative techniques are applied within standard investigative parameters relating to unresolved historical death investigations. As Vernon Geberth so eloquently noted, "an effective homicide detective is usually a person who has taken his experience and enhanced it with knowledge, flexibility and common sense." The investigation of homicide with an FDP factor will test the ability of seasoned investigators taking professional investigative ability to a new level of sophistication as detectives navigate the world of the FDP offender.

Child murder is an authentic problem infiltrating all walks of life on a global scale.

Filicide, child murder by parents, may occur as a result of child abuse, neglect, or FDP. Specific motives for filicide were initially described by Resnick, classified as (1) altruistic, (2) acutely psychotic, (3) accidental filicide (fatal maltreatment), (4) unwanted child, and (5) spouse revenge filicide. Altruistic filicide is murder committed out of love to relieve the real or imagined suffering of the child. Altruistic filicide may be associated with suicide.[1]

Resnick reported a "relief of tension" after altruistic and acutely psychotic filicides. The expulsion of energy after the child's death explains why some parents who had intended filicide–suicide did not complete the act of suicide. Conversely, other parents, "upon realization of the gravity of their act ... may attempt suicide even if it was not planned."[2]

Triangle Homicide Provability Standards (FDP Factor)

Homicide investigations involving an FDP factor require provability of three items:

- A death occurred.
- The death resulted from illegal actions of another.
- FDP abuse was the root cause of the death (Figure 11.1).

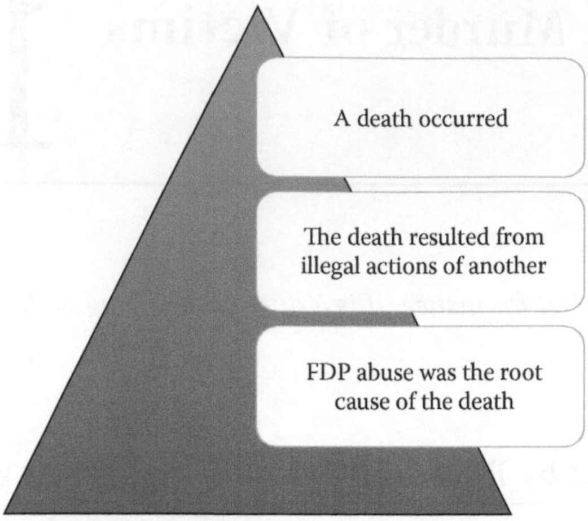

Figure 11.1 The basic facts of homicide.

Case Example

During 2004, a Virginia mother took her Baby (A) to a hospital nine times because Baby A stopped breathing. Baby A died after EMS was called to the family home and could not resuscitate the child. The cause of death was never determined (inconclusive) although Munchausen by proxy could not be ruled out. The mother garnering attention was thought to be fundamental in the cause of Baby A's medical visits. The autopsy showed there had been pressure on the infant's face but not enough to cause her death.

During 2005, Baby B was born to the same mother. Baby B visited the hospital emergency rooms 10 times because he stopped breathing. Child protective services placed Baby B into foster care where he suffered no further life-threatening events. Babies A and B experienced the same acute life-threatening events—with no medical explanation. The cause of death for Baby A was reopened. During 2007, a grand jury determined on that there was enough evidence for the mother to stand trial on charges of first-degree murder in the death of Baby A. The mother was arrested but was released on bond ($10,000.00) because she was pregnant and diagnosed with high blood pressure. The newborn was placed by social services at birth.

A plea agreement was agreed upon and the mother pleaded no contest to involuntary manslaughter/revocation, 1 year in prison, $651 in court costs, and 99 years probation.[3–5]

Intentional or Accidental Act

FDP behavior is not always provable in death investigations. When considering murder with premeditation and malice versus culpable negligence homicide FDP is a complication. Premeditated murder related to FDP abuse is complicated because murder is usually not the immediately evident goal of the FDP offender, and the pathway to FDP homicide is a long, twisting road.

A factor of premeditated homicide within an existing FDP abuse scenario involves an abuse sequence shift that teeters along the line between intentional and unintentional consequential victim death. Intentional homicide may occur when mitigating factors are indirect yet caused by the direct actions of the FDP offender. Mitigating factors include a victim's inability to accommodate medical intervention or directed FDP abuse application. When FDP abuse gravitates to homicide, looking at the case from a holistic homicide, methodology requires the examination of motive. Motive determination within an FDP-related homicide requires acknowledgment of FDP abuse and the educational background contained within.

Abuse with an FDP factor may rise to a level just short of victim death. Attempted murder is usually the substantive criminal charge when FDP abuse has severe victim consequences. Although victim harm severity is not predicated upon the mode of delivery in FDP abuse cases, when signs or symptoms of illness are simulated without direct application of inflicted harm, the general premise of victim injury is less and measuring victim harm may not rise to the level of attempted murder. Determination of this threshold is a prosecutorial decision predicated upon multidisciplinary review of victim harm status.

Recognizing that a death is related to FDP abuse does not necessarily occur at the time of victim death. FDP abuse and related homicide are generally well hidden, and when a singular victim death occurs related to FDP abuse, it is not always recognized. There have been cases whereby victim homicide attributed to FDP abuse is only recognized when subsequent FDP abuse or death victims are realized. This lays foundational predicate that whenever FDP abuse victims are identified, it is important to conduct an historical search looking for sibling death. If sibling death is found, regardless of stated causation, it is prudent to reexamine the circumstances allowing for potential causation as undetected FDP homicide. In FDP homicide situations, whether a child victim is biologically related to the FDP offender is irrelevant. The commonality is that FDP offenders have power and control over their victims—generally in caretaker roles.

When death is associated with an FDP abuse factor, examination of motive is pertinent. Death as an intentional act of aggression designed to eliminate evidence or control the likelihood of detection and death as an unintentional act of overindulgent abuse are the possibilities. FDP victim homicide does not occur from the singular hand of the offender as we see in other forms of homicide unless it is a directed action by the perpetrator for the specific reasons of evidence destruction. Absent directed action, many hands are involved but only the hands of the offender are unclean. Homicide with an FDP factor occurs as a by-product of chronic abuse compounded by a victim's inability to cope with the abuse or inability to cope with therapy initiated to treat resulting medical ailments. The indirectness of death caused by FDP abuse is difficult to recognize unless suspicion of FDP abuse precedes death. Recognition of potential FDP abuse patterns creates investigatory parameters and increased likelihood of victim survival. Potential witnesses in an FDP-related abuse or homicide case should not be limited to medical staff; witnesses include neighbors, friends, clergy, pharmacists, family, or any person(s) that had repetitive direct or indirect contact with the FDP offender. Linking abuse, death, or other criminal acts to FDP are not always accurately assessed.

Comportment of Murder

In the study *Murder in Families* by the U.S. Bureau of Justice (1994), specific child murder techniques were identified including beating, "shaken baby syndrome," arson, newborn disposed of in a toilet or trash can, drowning in a bathtub, use of firearm, suffocation/strangulation, neglect (dehydration, starvation, failure to use infant heart monitor), stabbing, poisoning, giving a lethal drug dosage, running over with a car, boiling, and placing in a freezer.[6]

Although easily recognized, specific murder techniques are often absent in FDP homicide investigations; an examination of direct and indirect FDP homicide causation reveals comparable correlations. FDP murder techniques must be indirect to be linked to an FDP delivery system, but the death of an individual within the scope of FDP infliction is murder.

A line of demarcation may exist between FDP victimization with unintentional related death and intentional FDP victim harm resulting in homicide. Intentional homicide is often viewed as a means to dispose of evidence. Unintentional victim death may occur through a victim's bodily inability to withstand medical procedures or the act(s) of orchestrated sickness (inflicted or verbally created) by the FDP offender. Inflicted harm is intentional, the result may not be. Intentional harm occurs when the FDP offender either inflicts bodily assault upon the victim or knowingly permits risky medical or invasive medical procedures to occur. The degree of bodily assault upon the victim gages a lethality assessment associated with a deadly force continuum. Homicidal intent should be evaluated based upon case specifics. Specific vehicles of identified FDP abuse include drowning, suffocation/strangulation, neglect, starvation, poisoning, lethal doses of drugs, intravenous injections of foreign matter, and lethal doses of common household items such as salt and dirt (see "FDP Continuum Escalation Scale", p. 100).

Case Example

Bobbie Sue Dudley was a nurse in Illinois during the 1970s, divorced, and spent time in a mental hospital. She was rehired as a nurse (in Illinois) during 1983 and had self-inflicted genital cuts, and her nursing license was suspended. Dudley obtained a nursing license in Florida during 1984 (not reporting the Illinois incidents) and obtained a nursing position in the St. Petersburg area working at various nursing homes where a number of patients died of apparent insulin injection. Twelve deaths and one near death of elderly patients occurred during a 13-day span at the facility where Dudley worked as the night shift supervisor.

On one particular night (when five patients were found dead), an anonymous woman called the police stating there was a serial killer "murdering patients at the nursing home." When law enforcement arrived, they found that Dudley had been stabbed allegedly by an intruder. The investigation revealed no evidence to support the theory that an intruder had been present.

During 1985, Dudley checked herself into a mental hospital and her nursing license was again suspended. Dudley applied workman's compensation from the nursing home where she was "allegedly stabbed" and underwent a full psych evaluation that indicated Dudley suffered from schizophrenia and Munchausen syndrome (FD). Dudley remarried. Dudley pleaded guilty to second-degree murder and first-degree attempted murder and was given a 95-year sentence. Dudley served 22 years of the sentence and died in prison during 2007.[7–10]

Exhumation Orders

The potential presence of hidden historical homicides within FDP investigations creates the potentiality of needed remains disinterment. Disinterment may become necessary when abuse or homicide victims are linked to an FDP factor, and it is realized that their subsequent sibling(s) have expired prematurely. The following is a generic example of an exhumation order that may be adapted to the specific needs of an agency. Legal review of this document is mandatory in all applicable situations.

GENERIC EXHUMATION ORDER

Agency Case #__________________________

Clerk's Case #____________________________

IN THE CIRCUIT COURT OF THE ___________JUDICIAL CIRCUIT IN AND FOR _____________ COUNTY, ____(STATE)________. IN THE MATTER OF ______________________________, A DECEASED PERSON, PETITION FOR ORDER AUTHORIZING DISINTERMENT OF REMAINS OF A DECEASED PERSON AND AUTHORIZING CORONER TO TAKE CUSTODY THEREOF FOR LAWFUL PURPOSES. (Health and Safety Code__________)

DATE:
TIME:
Petitioner, _________________________________, respectfully represents:

1. Petitioner is the duly elected Coroner of the County of _______________________.
2. Petitioner is informed and believes, and alleges thereon, that ____, a deceased person, died under circumstances either which should have been reported to the Coroner as required by law and/or which were such as to be of an unexpected and unexplained nature as to require the coroner's involvement.
3. The particulars concerning the death of ____________________, a deceased person, as well as the particulars in support of Petitioner's request for an Order Authorizing Disinterment, etc., are set forth in the attached Declaration of __________________________, Deputy Coroner.
4. A summary of the facts as they are known to Petitioner are hereinafter set forth: ____(State)____authorities contacted Petitioner in (Month and year) concerning a ______month old child at a (State) Hospital who was a suspected abuse victim by a Factitious Disorder by Proxy delivery process. The mother of the child made certain statements which led (State) authorities to learn about the death of another of the mother's infant children in ________(county) in __________(month and year). An investigation by Petitioner points to the likelihood that this latter child, _________(name), the subject of this petition, may have been the victim of Factitious Disorder by Proxy Homicide, and this would have direct bearing on the accuracy of the cause of death listed on the Certificate of Death.
5. Petitioner is requesting and Order of this Court authorizing him to disinter the remains of____________(Decedent's Name)__________, a deceased person, and to take custody of the remains so that an autopsy can be performed to more accurately

determine the cause of death and to facilitate any appropriate legal proceedings which may thereafter be appropriate.

6. Petitioner is informed and believes and alleges thereon, that although the father of the deceased would consent to disinterment and autopsy, the mother of the deceased, while not expressly objecting, has not given her express consent to disinterment and autopsy and had previously refused to authorize an autopsy by a local hospital at the time of the decedent's death in ___(month and year)____.
7. It is Petitioner's position that any objection to disinterment should be heard and determined by the Court.

WHEREFORE, Petitioner prays:

1. For an Order authorizing disinterment of the remains of __(Name of Decedent)__, a deceased person, and authorizing the Coroner to take custody thereof for lawful purposes; and
2. For such Order and further Orders as the Court deems just and proper.

Dated:_____________________ _______(Name of Coroner)_____________________

___________(Title)______________________________

By ________(Typed Name)_______________________
Deputy Coroner

____
County Counsel

By_________________________________
Deputy County Counsel

Attorneys for the Coroner

<Name>
Commission # 12345
<Jurisdiction County
My Comm. Expires Jan 1, 2025

_____________________ _____________________
Witnessed by: <Name> Notary Public

VERIFICATION

STATE OF________________________
COUNTY OF______________________

_________________________, Under penalty of perjury, says:

That _________________________, Coroner of the County of __________________, is the petitioner in the foregoing matter; that I am a Deputy Coroner of the County of _______________, State of ___________________, acting for and on behalf of the said ________________; that I have read the foregoing PETITION FOR ORDER AUTHORIZING DISINTERMENT OF REMAINS OF A DECEASED PERSON AND AUTHORIZING CORONER TO TAKE CUSTODY THEREOF FOR LAWFUL PURPOSES (*HEALTH AND SAFETY CODE)* and know the contents thereof; that the same is true of my own knowledge except as to matters therein stated on information and belief, and as to those matters I believe them to be true.

I declare under penalty of perjury that the foregoing is true and correct.

Executed at __(County and State)__, on the ___day of ___(month and year)__.

____
Affiant's Name

DECLARATION OF ___________________(Affiant)______

I, ________(Name)______, declare:

1. I am a deputy coroner employed by the office of the ________________ County Coroner
2. Our office was contacted in __(month and year)__ by the (Law Enforcement Agency) in (State) concerning a ____month old child at a __(State)__ hospital who was near death as a consequence of suspected factitious disorder by proxy child abuse. I am informed that the mother of the child had made certain statements that led ___(State)___ authorities to learn about the death of another of the mother's infant children in ___(County)__ in __(Date)__. Because of my knowledge and experience with factitious disorder by proxy and factitious disorder, I was assigned by coroner administration to investigate the death of _____(name of decedent)______.

3. Factitious disorder is listed as a recognized mental illness within the DSM-V. Factitious disorder occurs on a medical level when a person either inflicts or fabricates illness upon themselves then presents themselves to the medical community for treatment without disclosing the etiology of their alleged illness. Factitious disorder is listed within the DSM-V and the diagnostic criteria are:
    - Intentional production UPDATE HERE AND CITE

Whenever a person, regardless of whether afflicted with Factitious Disorder or not, utilizes another person in a replacement capacity for himself/herself for the purpose of assuming the sick role, the offensive action becomes abuse with a factitious disorder by proxy delivery factor (FDP). Determination of the presence or absence of FDP is predicated upon the examination of behavior. FDP offenders do not suffer from FDP; they inflict the behavior of FDP abuse upon their victims. FDP .....*This section needs reference work*

4. I am informed that relative to the __(State)__ case mentioned above, the mother __(her name)__ admitted to:
   (Describe any admissions made by the offender. Include all evidence to support the supposition of FDP child abuse in the most recently identified abuse victim. Include patterns of FDP behavior seen within the life of the decedent)

   All of this information makes both cases consistent with abuse relative to factitious disorder by proxy infliction methods. The attached certificate of death attributes __(name of decedent)__ death at age___ months to __(list original cause of death)__. I believe that no adequate explanation supports this causation and death should have initially been reported to the coroner or classified as ________________.

5. I am informed that law enforcement prosecutorial authorities in ___(state(s))__believe the cases show a pattern of abusive behavior that endangers other children of ___(Name of the Defendant)___ as well as

   suggesting that the cause of death attributed to the demise of __(decedent)__ is inaccurate and may have been due to abusive behavior.

6. I believe possible legal proceedings in __(county)__ could be initiated as a consequence of disinterment and autopsy, and __(name of state)___ proceedings already underway could be facilitated thereby.

I declare under penalty of perjury under the laws of the State of _____________ that the foregoing is true and correct, except as to matters stated on information and belief, and as to those matters I believe them to be true.

Executed on the day of _____(month)_____, __(year)__, at __(county and state)__.

____

Affiant's Name

<Name>
Commission # 12345
<Jurisdiction County
My Comm. Expires Jan 1, 2025

____________________ ____________________

Witnessed by: <Name> Notary Public

POINTS AND AUTHORITIES

I.

THE COURT IS EMPOWERED TO ORDER DISINTERMENT

Health and Safety Code section _______ gives the Superior Court authority to grant permission to disinter. Case law suggests that each case be considered in equity on its own merits, with regard for the interests of the public and decedent, the rights of those entitled to be heard by reason or relationship or association, and the rights of the institution, which granted the right to inter the body initially. In *re Keck* (1946) 75 Cal. App. 2nd 846, 171 P.2d 933; In *re Terra* (1952) 111 Cal. App 2nd 452, 244 P.2d 921.

In the instant case, the parents of the decedent have been given notice of the hearing on the Petition herein, as have local and __(state)__ law enforcement/ Prosecutorial authorities and the involved cemetery. The Petition and attachments thereto provide an ample basis for the Court to enter an Order Authorizing Disinterment.

II.

PERFORMANCE OF AN AUTOPSY AT THE DIRECTION OF THE CORONER IS A LAWFUL PURPOSE TO WHICH TO PUT THE REMAINS OF THE DECEASED

Government Code Section ______proved that the Coroner has a duty to inquire into and determine the circumstances, manner and cause of a number of types of deaths and that the Coroner has the right to exhume the body of a deceased person and undertake a variety of procedures when necessary to discharge his statutory responsibilities. Case law provides that the Coroner may order an autopsy without

Consent of the deceased family when in his judgment such is an appropriate means of ascertaining the cause of death. *Huntly v. Zurich General Accident and Liability Insurance Company* (1929) 100 Cal. App. 201, 280, P. 163.

In the case at hand, the Petition and attachments thereto support the propriety of the Coroner's intention to perform an autopsy to more accurately determine the cause of the decedent's death.

Dated:____________________ Respectfully Submitted,

__(Name of Counsel)_______

By ______________________________

Deputy County Counsel
Attorneys for the Coroner

SWORN TO AND SUBSCRIBED before me this _______day _________20__, in _____________County, __(State)__.

____
Judge

<Name>
Commission # 12345
<Jurisdiction County
My Comm. Expires Jan 1, 2025

____
Witnessed by: <Name> Notary Public

Sudden Infant Death Syndrome

Child abuse investigations positively linked to FDP have revealed the existence of deceased victim siblings whose deaths have been classified as sudden infant death syndrome (SIDS). Closer examination of these SIDS deaths resulted in overturned death rulings to homicide as a result of abuse. When children die under suspicious circumstances or as a result of unexplained illness/entity such as SIDS, undetected homicide is possible. The identification of FDP child abuse or FDP homicide should trigger a reexamination of death causation for previously ruled SIDS death cases.

The contradiction presented by FDP abuse within a SIDS death case is found within recognizable differences between the two. Understanding the differences provides definition. It is helpful to understand that generally, after the loss of a child, mothers may have feelings of being a "bad or inadequate parent." In actual SIDS situations, subsequent children within the family may inspire parents to be "super parents" intermixed with fear of loving a child too much. A need to portray oneself with remarkable parenting capabilities coupled with privately restrained emotion may create a falsified depiction of reality, and there is an insulation factor that is likely present. A most uncomfortable period for parents who have experienced loss of a child by SIDS is when a subsequent child reaches the age of the decedent. Parents of subsequent children who often overreact to normal situations are overprotective and tend to panic. It is common for parents of SIDS victims to mentally visualize their own reactions to potential tragedy involving their currently viable children.[11]

Potential SIDS Risk Factors

There are certain identified maternal risk factors thought to produce adverse results in fetal development that are reflected in newborn vulnerabilities.[12] These risk factors have not been proven to cause SIDS death but do provide insight when SIDS is found to be the cause of a child's death and FDP later becomes relevant. The vulnerability pretext a child has to SIDS varies and is thought to be related to a combination of physical and sleep environmental factors.

Physical factors associated with SIDS include the following:

- Brain abnormalities
- Low birth weight
- Respiratory infection
- Sleep environmental factors
    - Sleeping on the stomach or side.
    - Sleeping on a soft surface, lying face down.
    - Draping a blanket over a baby's head is also risky.
    - Sleeping with parents in the same bed. (Risk of SIDS is lowered if an infant sleeps in the same room as his or her parents.)

Investigatory Team Effort

Determination of hidden historical FDP-related homicide identified previously as SIDS often requires an associative effort between law enforcement officials and the medical examiner. Law enforcement officers have the capability of recognizing and investigating singular and serial FDP abuse through complicated investigatory processes correlated through a multidisciplinary team effort. Investigation involves evidence collection that may be shared with the medical examiner (coroner).

The medical examiner (coroner) is charged with evaluating information and evidence that originates from credible sources including the body of the decedent. When a historical FDP homicide is suspected, exhumation of a body contingent upon court order may be required for forensic medical evaluation. Decedents that have been cremated are not exempt from disinterment because all remains may provide some amount of toxin evidence via forensic testing.

If a medical examiner determines that historical decedents' cause of death was improperly labeled SIDS and reclassifies the death causation as FDP abuse, the death type changes from natural to homicide and a change in the death certificate is indicated. Reevaluating cause of death (regardless of the original finding) to homicide with an FDP abuse factor is predicated upon evaluation of FDP abuse evidence from a historical perspective from a viewpoint of knowledge bestowed by current victimization.

Deaths are generally classified as natural, accident, homicide, and suicide or pending investigation if determination cannot be made within the statutory time limit for filing the death certificate. Pending status is later changed to one of the other terms when causation is determined.

Deaths not due to external causes are identified as "natural." These are the only types of deaths a physician will usually certify. When the cause of death is impossible to determine, the cause of death is listed as "could not be determined."[13]

Death certificates list the chain of events leading directly to death, immediate cause of death, and underlying cause of death. Significant diseases, conditions, or injuries that contributed to death but which did not result in the underlying cause of death are the medical examiner's best medical opinion. A condition can be listed as "probable" even if it has not been definitively diagnosed.[14]

The terminal event is identified within the autopsy as well as the mechanism of death. Fatal injury, trauma, and impairment of function are also contained within the death certificate report. These items are specific within the FDP homicide analysis. Diseases or conditions contributing to death are also listed, but these do not result in the underlying cause of death in homicides with an FDP factor. The availability of additional medical information or autopsy findings may change the cause of death originally reported. The certifying physician then amends the original death certificate and a revised cause of death is sent to the State Vital Records Office.[15]

Linking a death to FDP factors means that the manner of death is homicide. The covert nature and complexity of FDP homicide lend itself to high probability that FDP homicide deaths are likely to be cold case death investigations. Unless a medical examiner is looking for FDP-related death causation at the time of death, FDP homicide linkage is likely to be missed and a person's death attributed to nonintentional means. When the manner of FDP homicide is linked to suffocation, little or no physical evidence may be left behind that further complicates detection.

Correlating FDP/SIDS Criteria

Reviewing a death that has been attributed to SIDS but is suspected to be FDP homicide is complicated. Considering root cause differentiations for FDP and SIDS illuminates differences (Figure 11.2). SIDS-related death usually occurs after an apparently healthy infant is placed in bed to sleep. The child is later found lifeless (silent death). EMS resuscitation is usually unsuccessful.[16] Death linked to SIDS involving apparently (chronically) ill children may be associated with genuine illness, mercy killing (euthanasia), and evidence disposal (directed homicide) or within the course of abuse with an FDP delivery factor. When this link is established, infanticide or child homicide with an FDP behavioral factor should be considered.

FDP utilizing a child proxy usually is seen as subtle (severe) child abuse. The infliction of harm upon the victim may increase to the point of death. There is an overlap within FDP behavioral analysis and known child abuse/homicide identification standards as follows:

Root Causes for FDP/SIDS Death Comparison

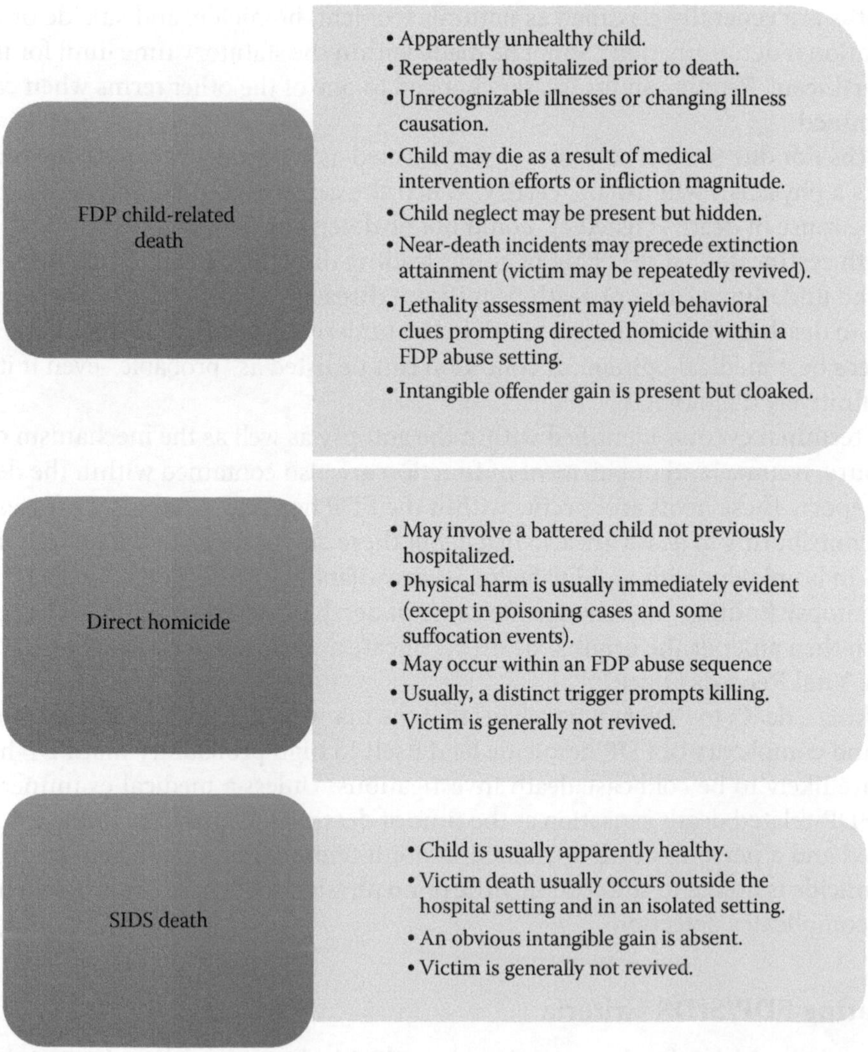
FDP child-related death
• Apparently unhealthy child.
• Repeatedly hospitalized prior to death.
• Unrecognizable illnesses or changing illness causation.
• Child may die as a result of medical intervention efforts or infliction magnitude.
• Child neglect may be present but hidden.
• Near-death incidents may precede extinction attainment (victim may be repeatedly revived).
• Lethality assessment may yield behavioral clues prompting directed homicide within a FDP abuse setting.
• Intangible offender gain is present but cloaked.
Direct homicide
• May involve a battered child not previously hospitalized.
• Physical harm is usually immediately evident (except in poisoning cases and some suffocation events).
• May occur within an FDP abuse sequence
• Usually, a distinct trigger prompts killing.
• Victim is generally not revived.
SIDS death
• Child is usually apparently healthy.
• Victim death usually occurs outside the hospital setting and in an isolated setting.
• An obvious intangible gain is absent.
• Victim is generally not revived.

Figure 11.2 A comparison of FDP death versus sudden infant death syndrome death.

Case Example

Nine of Marybeth Tinning's children died from 1971 to 1985; she was convicted of killing one of them. During 1986, Schenectady investigators questioned Marybeth regarding the deaths of the children, and she initially denied responsibility. During police investigation, Marybeth admitted she killed three of the children. "I did not do anything to Jennifer, Joseph, Barbara, Michael, Mary Frances, Jonathan," she confessed, "Just these three, Timothy, Nathan, and Tami. I smothered them each with a pillow because I'm not a good mother. I'm not a good mother because of the other children."[17]

The initial causes of death for the deceased children included SIDS (three children), acute pulmonary edema, Reye's syndrome, cardiorespiratory arrest (two children), acute meningitis, and acute pneumonia. A genetic flaw or "death gene" was thought to be responsible for the death of the children at one time.

Tinning was described as a "sympathy junkie"; "she liked the attention of people feeling sorry for her from the loss of her children." And her behavior was described by clinicians as a form of FDP. Tinning was tried and sentenced to 20 years to life in prison. Parole requests have been thus far denied.

There has been discussion regarding the implication of a serial child murderer's actions attributed only to the causation of FDP offender gain. Generally, many factors are present in the complex analysis of such cases. Knowing that FDP methodology exists and utilizing it as a potential factor in unexplained multiple deaths within a singular family may provide investigative insight and save the lives of futuristic victims.

Quandary of Uncertainty

Inaccurate labeling of a suspected FDP homicide could have significant implications. The interdisciplinary team concept expands in a significant way to include the investigative expertise of the medical examiner when a death is possibly linked to FDP abuse. All types of investigators are reminded that linking abuse or death to FDP requires medical collaboration. A case found in Missouri illustrates the potential outcome when death or abuse is mislabeled: *A woman was falsely accused of the death of her infant son who died as a result of apparent ethylene glycol poisoning. After a subsequent child was born, it was determined that the child had a rare disease labeled MMA that also resulted in the death of the first child.*[18] This case illustrates that all avenues must be explored when abuse or death is investigated. The importance of medical evaluation in abuse or deaths complicated with FDP suspicion is evident. Professional evaluation and the bridge that exists between FDP suspicion and the correct connection to abuse or death can be vast. No one wants to accuse a person of abuse or homicide and be wrong yet for FDP abuse victims; a failure to make an appropriate connection to FDP abuse may result in victim death. Gathering evidence to either support or dissuade the theory of FDP abuse/homicide provides credibility within the identification process.

Abuse through an FDP mechanism may be not only singularly present within a victimization sequence, but it may also exist in conjunction within other abuse formats including physical or sexual abuse. Although secondary FDP offender gain is attained only within the FDP victimization format, how the offender reacts to various pressures or how they choose to abuse a target victim includes possibilities. When injury to children is detected, suspected FDP offenders may have explanations for identified injury that include accidental or other causes. General investigative techniques should be used to eliminate alternative possibilities.

Case Summary

Over the 5-year life span of this child, his mother repeatedly posted on social media (Facebook, Twitter, MySpace) how ill the child was, professed her love for the child, and appeared dutiful. She also had a blog.[19] Repeated hospitalizations failed to produce a reason for the causes of the child's illness until a lethal amount of sodium was noticed in the child's body and he died. It was later determined that the mother of the child administered heavy concentrations of sodium (salt) to the child through his stomach tube. Craving attention, found within known factors of FDP, was presented as motive within the trial but not utilized as a defense.[20] The mother claimed that her child had celiac disease and other disorders.[21] The mother was charged with second-degree murder for poisoning her child and causing his death. She was convicted and sentenced to 20 years to life in prison.[22]

FDP in the Index of Homicide Causation

Understanding that FDP offenders do sometimes kill their victims provides implied categorization of FDP as a potential homicide methodology factor. A *Bureau of Justice Statistics Special Report (of) Murder in Families*, July 1994, did not isolate FDP methodology within the index. Generalized family murder statistics provide greater understanding of overall homicidal victimology. In this study, a parent was the assailant in the majority (57%) of murders involving victims under age 12, and offenders abusing the victim in 79% of the cases preceded deaths. This study provided reasons why parents murdered their offspring under the age of 12; one or more reasons were given for 62 or the 84 total child fatalities.[23] Victimization motives or known precipitating child fatality factors mirror homicide patterns found within known FDP abuse situations that have risen to the level of homicide. This study included the homicide factors as shown in Figure 11.3.

This comparative analysis illustrates a measurable connection between fatality data and FDP behavioral offense observations. The unspecified forms of child abuse category found within the study hold potential placement for FDP homicide statistics as they are recognized.

FDP offender typology provides concept differentiation within the scope of homicide pathways. The following correlations further define these points:

Definition Points

- *Physical Demeanor of the FDP Abuse Victim Does Not Necessarily Imply Homicidal Motivation*: An FDP abuse victim's bodily reaction to chronic abuse may lead to permanent disabilities. The weight of FDP offender discontent may be affected by required parental demands: time, commitment, risk versus reward, and increased potential for exposure as the child matures. This provides potential pathway for homicidal tendencies in chronic FDP victimization. It is reasonable that FDP offenders may impetuously offend upon their children but in a controlled forum through FDP methodology. Chronic FDP abuse is linked to prethought notions, tests, and applications. The ability of an FDP offender to perpetuate abuse grows as time passes and abuse continues. As an FDP child abuse victim matures, normal parenting challenges are complicated with abuse methodology and a chronically ill child. Required parental selflessness may be complicated with parental jealousy and/or hatred toward

BJS report on family murder 1994: factors	FDP abuse progressing to homicide potential factors
Unspecified forms of child abuse (18)	Unintended consequence in the commission of another crime
Victim's behavior, such as crying or misbehaving (15)	Victim's behavior age progression
Parent's emotional instability or retardation (9)	Unwanted child victim seen as a liability (threat detection)
Unwanted newborn baby (8)	Destruction of evidence
Unintended consequence in the commission of another crime (6)	Parent's instability
Neglect (5)	Difficulty in handling the responsibility of factitious harm infliction
Difficulty in handling the responsibility of child rearing (3)	
Child held hostage (1)	

Figure 11.3 Comparative analysis of family murder versus FDP homicide.

a special needs child garnering attention. The illusion created by the FDP offender (parent) of the "perfect life" within the FDP abuse mantra is destroyed as demands of the child victim supersede the wants of the FDP offender (parent).

- *Unwanted Children of FDP Offenders May Be Recognized as Abuse Victims Prior to Birth*: FDP offender actions may fit directly into behavioral activities within self-inflicted *f*actitious disorder when pregnant. When a pregnant female self-inflicts harm, the result may be directed abuse upon the fetus or fetal harm as an unintended consequence of self-inflicted factitious harm events. FD/FDP offenders are generally quite knowledgeable regarding actions that could be detrimental to a fetus and simply "do not care." Factors of disassociation/isolationism can be projected onto a fetus allowing harm. When FD offenders give birth, the projected interaction/bond between mother and baby should be carefully considered. What is projected may not be an accurate depiction of reality if it appears normal. Visible disassociation between mother and baby should create grave concern.
- *Flat Affect while Pregnant May Be Present*: Characteristics present within persons *exhibiti*ng factitious disorder include reliance upon medical personnel, repeated hospitalizations, multiple illness(s) of unknown cause, and changing symptomology basis. Medical concern regarding the effect treatment of the (FDP) mother may have upon a developing fetus may be met with apathy. The identification of associated potential fetal abnormality, perhaps caused by medical treatment of the mother, may further serve as an isolationism catalyst between mother and fetus.
- *Illness in the FDP Offender That Is Emulated in FDP Abuse Victim Is Considered 'Signature Illness'*: The signature provides a prosecution avenue based upon an FDP offender's demonstrated ability to offend *(on herself* and upon the victim) through

the establishment of inherent knowledge of consequential action versus affect. The premise for this inference is simply due to the offender's firsthand knowledge of abuse methodology, consequence, pain factor, and potential lethality outcome. Issues of intentional torture are relevant.

- *FDP Abuse May Escalate to Victim Death: Issues of premedicated murder versus* "excessive" injury resulting in unintentional victim death are always issues to be considered when determining causative factors in homicides and FDP delivery factor.
- *Victim Neglect within the FDP Abuse Continuum*: Victim neglect is often difficult to access within criminal investigations. Abuse or homicide investigations that involve an FDP factor generally involve an offender whose portrayal of motherhood is exemplary. Closer examination of interaction between an FDP offender and a victim may, however, reveal neglect through emotional and social venues. FDP victims are generally isolated from activities and normal developmental socialization because their time is largely spent within the hospital setting. An FDP victim is often diagnosed as "failure to thrive" during the hospitalization course of their victimization as their bodies cope with repeated infliction of harm. Looking for the root cause of "failure to thrive" will likely rest within a platform of intentional FDP abuse. Physical needs of the victim including the FDP offender may withhold food, exercise, liquids, and appropriate medication. Victim deprivation of necessities in conjunction with offensive FDP abuse infliction formulates predicate for neglect within the platform of FDP abuse methodology.
- *Inability of the FDP Offender (Parent) to Provide Adequate Parental Supervision*: Parenting inability of FDP offenders is often displayed within dependency court proceedings when FDP child victims are identified. Responsibility for child rearing becomes a "medical parenting partnership" in FDP child abuse situations that is generally not initially recognized by medical staff. This factor is present in all FDP cases involving child victims.
- *FDP Child Abuse Victims Are Held Hostage by FDP Offenders*: Hostages must be viewed as expendable if they are to be of value to the hostage taker; hostages do not have the physical or cognitive ability to walk away from the hostage situation. In this context, FDP abuse victims and offenders are disconnected from one another to effectuate the ability to offend. When an FDP abuse or homicide victim is uncovered, society often remarks that it is difficult to understand how an offender could commit such atrocious acts upon seemingly innocent victims. All FDP victims are either permanently or momentarily dependent and in the control of the FDP offender. The FDP offender disassociates himself or herself from the victim allowing abuse to occur. FDP victims cannot leave the custody of the offender and may not even be aware of the abuse. FDP victims, by literal definition, are hostages. They just may not be aware of it. FDP victims are subject to all unseen forces known to exist within hostage situations, including Stockholm syndrome. This may become relevant as FDP victims age and awareness of their abuse occurs.

Indirect FDP Offender Implications

When a suspected FDP abuse offender (mother of the victim) makes a statement that the victim is dying, the basis for this statement should be the cause for concern. No one knows a child better than the child's mother. Interpretation is correlated that the offender may believe the child is dying for specific reason(s). The offender's likely intent regarding FDP abuse victimization should be considered as review of use of a target child as a proxy is measured against intangible offender gain. Attention, verification of self-worth, making a home within the medical community, manipulation of family forces, and other intangible entities need to be closely scrutinized.

If a change has occurred within FDP victimization status and a quest for the victim's death has presented within the domain of the FDP offender's ability, directed homicide is likely. Homicide is an attainable entity within the FDP abuse process when there is benefit to the FDP offender in completing this task. Recognizing FDP offender benefit facilitating FDP victim death requires a wide scope of review. The multidisciplinary team may provide necessary viewpoint advantage within the victim protection venues or in review mode if victim death occurs.

An FDP child abuse victim's physical abnormalities, partially or totally attributed to FDP offender actions, may be permanent. When FDP offenders realize that an FDP child victim's injuries are going to be lifelong and their caretaking responsibility is likely to commensurate with the victim's permanent medical status, the FDP child victim's longevity may be threatened. Within the FDP offender's family, access to other living children or the ability to produce more children opens the avenue for FDP victim replacement. Victim disposal (or replacement) relieves the FDP offender of the hassle, responsibility, and detection threat represented by a child victim who has been permanently harmed. The decision an FDP offender faces regarding allowing an FDP child abuse victim to live is often linked to the escalation of a victim's legitimate illness(s), victim's advancing age, outside investigatory agency involvement, a realization that it was easier to offend upon the child victim when the child was younger, a plateau within family interaction, and available resourcing for subsequent victims. These factors and others provide a glimpse of motive and enhancement that may be present when a decision to kill an FDP abuse victim occurs. It is always a possibility that an FDP child abuse victim may one day just "disappear" or succumb to medical treatment for unresolved illness(s) (Figure 11.4).

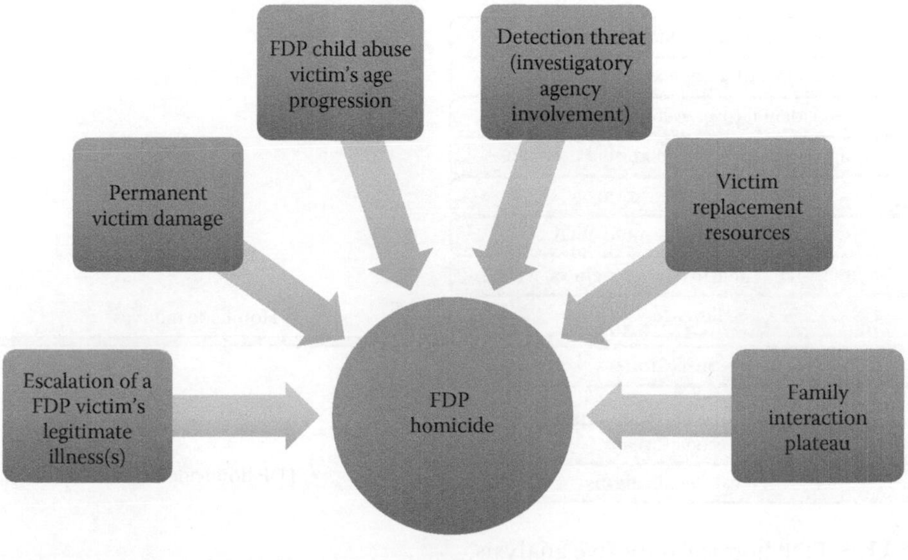

Figure 11.4 Homicidal decision factors for FDP murder.

Why Kill? FDP Homicidal Motivations

There are many potential factors present in an FDP homicide offender's life that may play integral roles in the overt decision to commit murder. Murderers have historically attempted to excuse their actions by providing the following behavioral explanations: protection/salvation, suffering relief (real or imagined), the unwanted child, mentally ill and unable to discern between right and wrong, revenge, and accidental (overzealous discipline) as a means to resolve situational problems.

In homicides linked to an FDP delivery factor, a shift from FDP abuse to directed homicide appears related to a very selfish individual decision acted upon by the FDP offender. This decision is thought to center on issues of detection, medical complication(s), convenience, and dissatisfaction with the results of FDP infliction, power, and control regarding interpersonal familial relationships. FDP-related homicides may also be aligned with unintentional death as FDP abuse exceeds a victim's capacity either directly or through medical treatment to address apparent illness.

Serial FDP Victimization

Analysis of Motive

When the death of multiple children occurs within one family and a potential FDP link is present, evaluating individual victim death commonalities tempered with an evaluation of known aspects of FDP abuse infliction is needed. Subsequent FDP victim deaths often appear neater than the first. Subsequent death causation(s) may be a variation of the original (first) death method or a completely new infliction mode. If a new method of attaining victim death or injury is presented, the effect and method of the first victim's

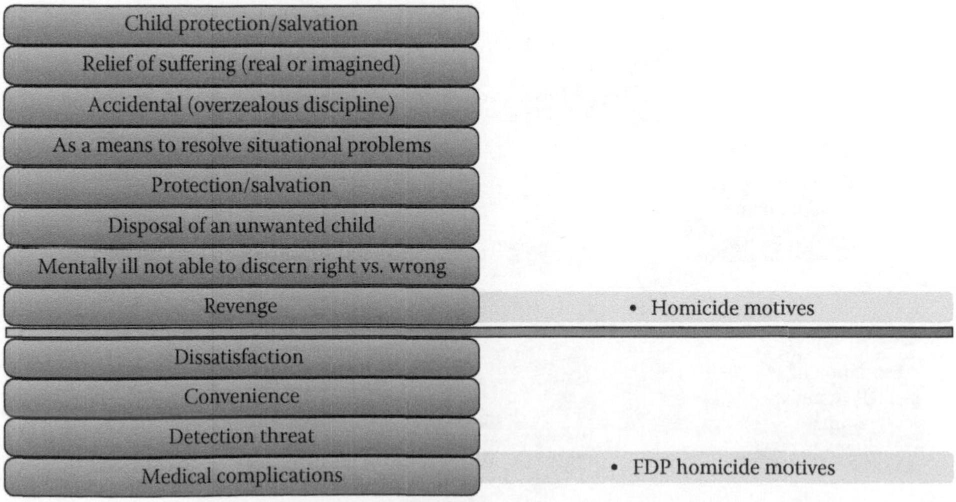

Figure 11.5 FDP homicidal motive analysis.

death may not have been optimal for the offender. Examination of potential offender dissatisfaction at the time of the original FDP homicide victim's death may be linked to the following: financial cost, low level of FDP offender benefit, high levels of inconvenience or harassment, extreme victim torture (pain and suffering), prolonged or quickness of the death process, influx of new key personnel (husbands), and a differentiation in the level of FDP abuse awareness among professionals associated with the victims. In most FDP cases involving multiple victim deaths, the old adage, "practice makes perfect," is perversely accurate. Subsequent FDP victim deaths within a family are often the result of improved abuse infliction methods of an initially concealed homicidal procedure (Figure 11.5).

When a Parent Is Suspected of Killing a Child but the Spouse Is Responsible

FDP Abuse: Serialization Methodology Factors

Most parents who endure the death of the child(ren) experience a grieving process that changes them. Normal emotional reaction(s) to a child's death include (but are not limited to) quietly crying at night, experiencing nightmares concerning the decedent, being overcome by grief, feeling angry at the world (displaced aggression), placing blame, feeling guilt, withdrawal, tremendous fear, apathy, and emotional extremes. After a period of time, acceptance of reality replaces emotion as the parent learns to block those thoughts/memories that produce pain and impair their ability to cope. A change in the parent occurs and strength emerges from survival and adaptation.

A parent whose child is killed by his or her spouse may react in a variety of ways depending upon circumstances. Denial is often prevalent because the nonoffending parent may be torn between love for the offender and the child victim; hate for the offender due to his or her actions and shame for the most grievous of family transgressions: murdering your own child. These factors complicate the process of nonoffending parents reporting known or suspected abuse or homicides within a family when the offender resides within (Figure 11.6).

Homicides occurring with an FDP factor generally involve a parent (mother), but caution is advised because mothers are not the only caretakers capable of FDP homicide. Paternal, intrafamilial, or other associative caretakers (babysitters) should be ruled out as suspects. If paternal responsibility for the victim's FDP-related death is proven, it is important to understand the likely factors exerted upon the mother during the process.

To further complicate this issue, FDP offenders may realize that thwarting suspicion away from themselves by placing it upon another family member provides confusion and therefore reasonable doubt regarding responsibility. Which parent is likely responsible?

It is plausible that the nonoffending spouse may only choose to see the offender in a more recent light of generosity or adulations and choose to pretend that offender is innocent of abuse or murder. The nonoffending spouse may have either been given or promised material things to increase dependence upon the offender by showing what

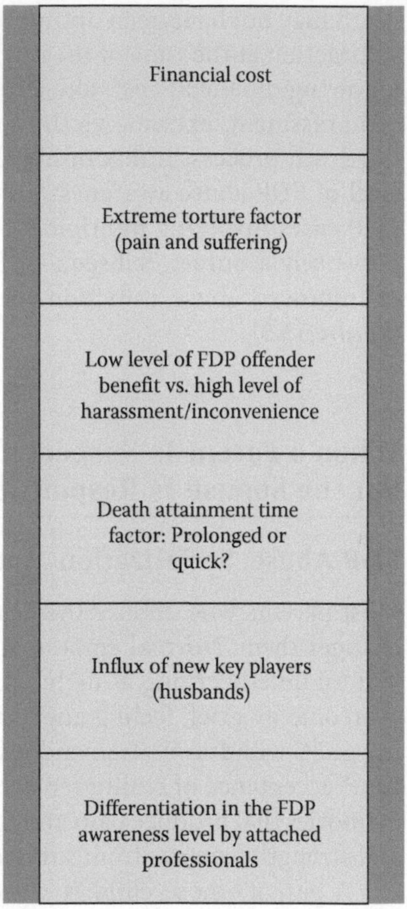

Figure 11.6 Serialized FDP homicide methodology factors.

could be lost if disclosure to authorities occurred. Items of material compensation for the life of the child victim might extend beyond monetarily based items to talk of a replacement child for both physical and emotional compensation—if the secret is maintained. The offender may also utilize threats of shared responsibility citing that the nonoffending spouse either failed to immediately notify/be truthful with authorities or was a bad parent due to failure to protect the child. A control combination of threat and negligence effectively imparts guilt and fear upon the nonoffending spouse creating a vacuum during a time of extreme emotion (child death). The result is likely to be silence.

In some cases, there may be an element of domestic violence present between spouses that cause an underlying fear in nonprimary aggressor. This fear is reinforced by knowledge or suspicion that he or she is likely cohabiting with a killer. Nonoffending spouses in familial murder investigations may be afraid that truth disclosure means loss of another loved one, loss of financial stability, and fear of reprisal and self-incrimination. It becomes far more palatable to remember the "good times" (wedding, vacations, holidays…) and block out horrific reality pertaining to a child's death. This coping method is often only a temporary solution to the looming ugliness of reality and a secret that is extremely difficult to keep.

Why Nonoffending FDP Parents May Not Be Truthful

To interview a nonoffending spouse effectively in a homicide investigation, you must relieve threats and impart the necessity of truth telling (Figure 11.7). If a subsequent child, either planned or present, is relative, addressing parental protective instinct is indicated. A nonoffending spouse must realize that forces present in the life of the FDP killer prior to the FDP child victim's death do not just magically disappear; there will always be a question of threatened harm to subsequent children of FDP offenders. An FDP offender that has crossed the threshold into homicide through the death of an FDP target victim has demonstrated a willingness to offend to a degree that is not manageable for potential subsequent victims. Pointing this out to a nonoffending parent provides reasonableness for eliciting the truth in the name of victim protection. In situations where intrafamilial dependents are not relative, all children or elderly persons that the FDP homicidal offender may engage in a custodial manner are potential abuse or homicide victims. This is a heavy weight for any nonoffending spouse to bear.

In FDP child homicide situations where it is believed the nonoffending spouse knows or suspects offender responsibility, there is likelihood that these suspicions have been shared with someone. If disclosure by the nonoffending spouse cannot be confirmed, he or she is a ticking time bomb and may invoke various coping methods in an attempt to control underlying emotion and attain respite. Reactions may include the

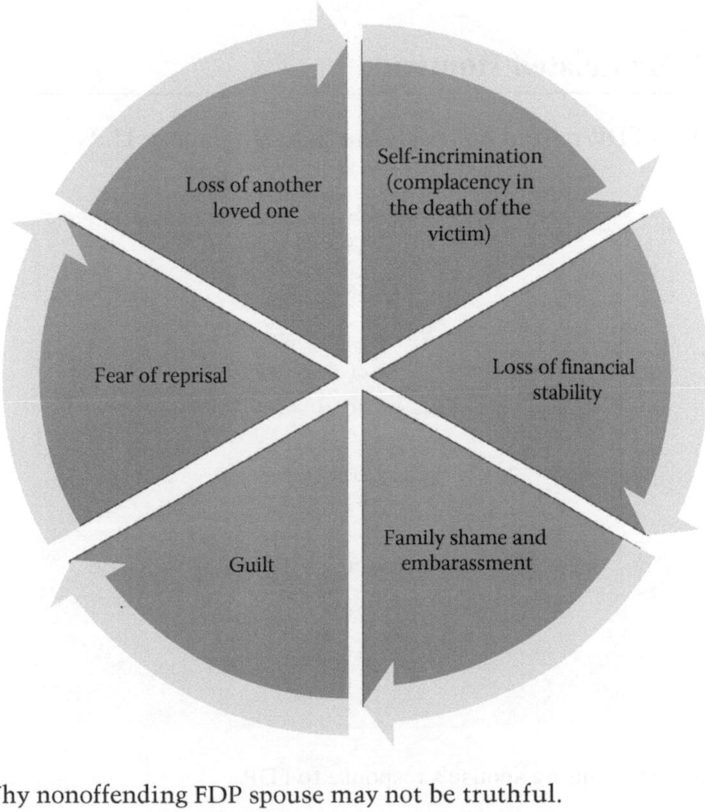

Figure 11.7 Why nonoffending FDP spouse may not be truthful.

use of drugs or alcohol, living in a fantasy world devoid of the reality of a dead child or other family member, work immersion producing withdrawal from family, or rage toward the FDP offender. Family withdrawal through work immersion allows the nonoffending spouse safe responsibility distance regardless of actual or suspected knowledge of FDP abuse/homicide.

FDP Nonoffending Spouse Reactionary Behavior

Detectives are cautioned to carefully impart tact when interviewing potential nonoffending FDP spouses. Inward instability may either immediately or with delay, explode through avenues of suicide or homicidal behavior by the nonoffending FDP spouse as confrontation with the truth commands potential human reaction. When speaking to a nonoffending spouse, it may appear that shock is present and it is impossible to determine genuine thought process. Nonoffending FDP spouses may demand atonement from the FDP offender that may result in FDP offender homicidal death by the spouse (Figure 11.8).

Nonoffending spouses are also at risk of death because they are likely witnesses to the FDP offender's behavior, and elimination of witnesses is also a concern based upon demonstrated offender behavior through FDP victimization pathways. Protective measures are suggested for the nonoffending spouse of an FDP offender.

Methods of FDP: Related Homicide

Specific methods of FDP-related homicide are shown in Figure 11.9.

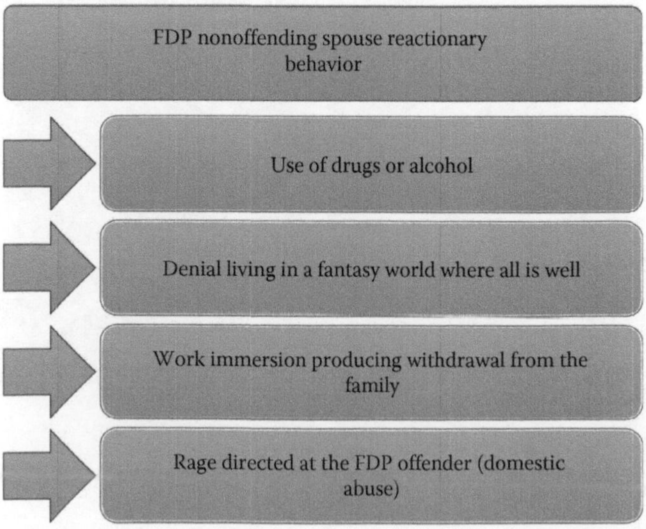

Figure 11.8 The nonoffending spouse's response to FDP.

Specific methods of FDP-related homicide
• Drowning • Suffocation/strangulation • Neglect • Starvation • Poisoning • Lethal drug doses • Intravenous injections of substances • Salt poisoning • Introduction of common household items into the blood stream of the victim (dirt, fecal matter,...) • Lying (verbal illness fabrication) • Medical treatment to address fabricated illness symptoms

Figure 11.9 Homicidal methods within FDP victimization.

Notes

1. Susan Hatters Friedman, M.D., Hrouda, D.R., Holden, C.E., Noffsinger, S.G., and Resnick, P.J., Filicide-suicide: Common factors in parents who kill their children and themselves. *American Academy of Psychiatry Law*, 2005;33:496–504.
2. Resnick, P.J., Child murder by parents: A psychiatric review of filicide. *American Journal of Psychiatry*, 1969;126:73–82.
3. http://hamptonroads.com/2008/05/smithfield-mom-pleads-guilty-babys-death.
4. http://www.whsv.com/home/headlines/18764854.html. Accessed on November 1, 2013.
5. http://hamptonroads.com/node/243781. Accessed on November 1, 2013.
6. Murder in Families. U.S. Bureau of Justice Statistics Special Report, July 1994. Accessed on November 1, 2013.
7. http://articles.orlandosentinel.com/1986-03-31/news/0210170086_1_nurse-dudley-horizon.
8. Linedecker, C.L. and Burt, W.A. *Nurses Who Kill*. Kensington Books, 1990. Accessed on November 1, 2013.
9. http://crime.about.com/od/serial/a/bobiiedue-dudley.html.
10. scholarcommons.usf.edu/cgi/viewcontent.cgi?article=2379&context. Accessed on November 1, 2013.
11. *The Subsequent Child, Part 2*. http: sids-network.org subch2, html.
12. http://www.mayoclinic.org/diseases-conditions/sudden-infant-death-syndrome/basics/causes/con-20020269.
13. *Medical Examiners' and Coroners' Handbook on Death Registration and Fetal Death Reporting*. Department of Health and Human Services Centers for Disease Control and Prevention Nation Center for Health Statistics, 2003, p. 72. Accessed on November 1, 2013.
14. http://www.cdc.gov/nchs/data/dvs/blue_form.pdf.
15. http://www.cdc.gov/nchs/data/dvs/DEATH11-03final-ACC.pdf. Accessed on November 1, 2013.
16. Reece, R.M., Fatal child abuse and sudden infant death syndrome: A critical diagnostic decision. *Pediatrics*, 1993;91(2):423. Accessed on November 1, 2013.
17. *People v. Tinning*. 142 AD 2d 402—NY: Appellate Div., 3rd Department, 1988.
18. *Patricia Stallings v. State of Missouri*, 1989. https: //univ.law.umich.edu.
19. http://www.usatoday.com/story/news/nation/2015/03/02/lacey-spears-verdict/2462509/.
20. http://www.washingtonpost.com/news/morning-mix/wp/2015/03/03/the-rare-disorder-experts -say-. Accessed on November 1, 2015.

21. http://www.emaxhealth.com/12410/murder-trial-involves-celiac-disease-and-munchuusen-proxy. Accessed on November 1, 2015.
22. http://www.usatoday.com/story/news/nation/2015/03/02/lacey-spears-verdict/2462509/. Accessed on November 1, 2015.
23. See Note 1.

12 Alternative Victimization

A wise man proportions his belief to the evidence.

David Hume

Alternative Victimization with an FDP Factor

The life path of the factitious disorder by proxy (FDP) offender is centered on a cause and effect rationale with a seemingly disposable tool—the life of the FDP abuse victim. There is a general multidisciplinary professional consensus, based upon known abuse situations (with an FDP factor), that FDP offenders primarily target children; the children are exploited as tools utilized for acquiring secondary offender gain. Although other abuse or homicide victims have been categorized clearly with an FDP abuse factor, child victims are most prevalent. Patterned FDP child victimization parallels unique indicators of alternative victimization identified through FDP case analysis.

Understanding the distorted potential of an FDP offender's abusive thoughts and rationalization enables criminal investigators to recognize and comprehend alternative bases of FDP victimization. FDP alternative victimization includes medical personnel, hospital establishments, insurance companies, public trust, celebrity causes, media, elderly persons, pets, and professionals (law enforcement, fire services). FDP offenders' deceptive ability hides the reality of abuse through complex, organized deceit while portraying the illusion of innocence. For child abuse victims, the illusion is "perfect parenting." Abuse with an FDP delivery system requires FDP offender skill and control (dominion) over the victim at the time of the abusive act. Acts of victim abuse with an FDP factor are viewed as criminal infractions of American Law.

Medical Staff

Outside the border of an FDP offender's family, medical personnel are generally first contact. The relationship between the FDP offender and medical staff grows from remote to enmeshed. The FDP offender weaves a web of misconceived personal alliance between herself and medical caregivers. The medical world becomes the FDP offender's world as the proxy victim is utilized to gain and maintain medical staff access through the establishment of illness. Any threat to the stability of the relationship between medical staff and the FDP offender may directly affect the viability of the FDP abuse victim.

Threats of access interruption or discontinuance of interaction between the FDP offender and the victim may undermine perceived stability between medical personnel and the FDP offender. FDP offenders seem to somewhat base their identity upon interaction with medical professionals. A betrayal of trust between the FDP offender and medical staff occurs during abuse with an FDP factor as the "goodness of medicine is utilized as a self-serving FDP offender destruction vehicle."

Medical staff is otherwise victimized within FDP abuse/homicide situations during the course of multidisciplinary investigation. The characteristic response of FDP offenders accused of FDP abuse is to thwart suspicion by accusing others. It is common for medical staff to be the objects of accusations of wrongdoing. Allegations of improper medical services/treatment become part of the defense with abuse/homicide cases, and civil litigation is generally expected from surviving family members.

The Premier Attention Medium

In most FDP abuse situations, the FDP offender's premier medium is the FDP victim's physician. Closeness between the FDP offender and the physician (to the victim) creates a factitious vacuum that tests medical alliances. Independent observations by non-enmeshed medical personnel often contradict closely involved medical staff's beliefs of reality perception. It is as if the physician is so convinced of FDP offender's behavioral correctness that the ability to question the truthfulness of the entire abuse sequencing is absent.

Physicians and nurses closely involved with the treatment of an FDP abuse victim may have difficulty maintaining objectivity once the bonding process is complete between the FDP offender and primary medical staff personnel. Differentiation between the FDP offender's outward actions seen as genuine by the "viewing public" and actualization of abuse inflictions is difficult (if not impossible) to recognize. Medical staff that express suspicion of victim illness etiology may attempt to point out discrepancies between logical illness cause and illogical medical effect. These concerns are often met with inaction or dismissal by medical staff close to the case, and a defensive posture emerges within those most likely to realize that abuse is occurring.

Subsequently, primary care physicians who believe that medical intervention actions are justified facilitate the emergence of an adversarial relationship within the medical realm due to conflict of opinions. Believing that a person is ill within the context of FDP abuse is predicated in part or whole upon the testimony of the FDP offender. It is also based upon the effects of victim abuse imparted by the behavioral choices made by the FDP offender. This conflict creates confusion surrounding victim treatment and is theorized to be part of the FDP offender's master plan that allows the infliction of abuse to remain undiscovered for as long as possible.

A review of FDP cases often reveals the presence of numerous specialties within an FDP victim's treatment progression. Specialty physicians treat individual victim symptoms or illness, and they look at the victim from a particular viewpoint. The primary care physician is often little more than a vehicle to access specialty physicians, and if he or she is not actively reviewing specialty physician findings, then FDP recognition is unlikely. Medical treatment of an FDP abuse victim is generally a chronic examination of changing reasons why a person is apparently ill. The complexity and confusion of an FDP victim's illness pathways and systematically ingrained belief that the FDP offender's character is what she portrays facilitate abuse. The FDP offender often seeks out numerous physicians' opinions as she searches for desired medical intervention for the proxy creating a maze of medical (mis)information. The complexity of medical documentation including victim treatment(s) creates medical ailment situations often not clearly evident. The primary care physician acts as the conductor within the orchestration of specialists, but once entrenched in a case, it is difficult to flex between the mode of caregiver and that of investigatory suspicion regarding the origin of an FDP victim's illness(s). Belief that an FDP victim is legitimately ill is evident. This belief is not always untrue as legitimate illness commonly coexists with fabricated illness or the fabrication of illness produces legitimate (real) symptoms. Looking for the root cause of an FDP victim's maladies within a medical realm is complicated, indeed.

Nursing staff must deal with specific issues when confronted with a potential FDP abuse or homicide situation. Nurses are expected to provide continual emotional support for patients and their families or provide others that may be substituted in that role. Nurses provide for the physical needs of the patient while documenting family interaction within the official medical records; they are observers and care providers. Issues of maintaining confidentiality may conflict with obligation to report suspected abuse.[1]

Hospital Deception and Insurance Fraud

Hospitals provide treatment facilities for ill people and allocate space for that purpose. The availability of treatment testing, location, and staff is limited. FDP abuse victims may be ill as a result of inflicted abuse, in whole or in part, from the actions of their abusers or they may not be ill at all. Over a period of time, an FDP child victim is often described as having "resident status" due either to repeated or to continual hospitalization. During the time that an FDP victim is hospitalized, space availability for other patients is nonexistent.

Public awareness and professional awareness of abuse through the FDP pathway have increased over the years. Repeated FDP victim hospitalizations are generally part of the abuse or homicide sequencing. Documentation of medical situations that are linked to FDP steadily increased and so have criminal abuse cases. These cases are not contrived or the subject of any one person's work. The cases have been identified over various locations, methodologies, and circumstances. It is quite difficult to accept the notion, by some, that FDP abuse or FDP-related homicide is not real; reality is documented.

Health insurance providers are the U.S. national vehicle of opportunity for fraud perpetrated by the FDP offender. Caretakers who utilize FDP child abuse as a means of end-goal attainment access a medical system that is largely funded by health insurance payment. The majority of known FDP abuse/homicide cases have health insurance payment connections. National healthcare or private medical insurance may both be victims, when chronic FDP abuse is in play. Through medical treatment, FDP child abusers intensify their monstrously devious actions against the FDP abuse victim by incorporating a seemingly genuine, often unidentifiable, child illness into the realm of the hospital setting. In FDP abuse situations where no health insurance exists, victim treatment costs within a medical setting generally revert back to the hospital where the treatment occurred or onto singular medical service providers. It is unknown if either the hospital or medical service providers are ever able to collect this medical debt. When FDP offenders are incarcerated, debt collection is highly unlikely.

FDP abuse sequencing has resulted in overwhelming medical costs that are either absorbed by the hospitals in which they are accrued or billed to the medical insurance foundation that binds the family at that given time. Health insurance carriers historically had few options other than to render payment for services. FDP abuse and homicide are criminal acts. Inflicted symptoms within an FDP abuse scenario are part of a scheme to defraud. Medical treatment that addresses these symptoms should be considered payment for medical fraud. Insurance companies have no test or screening feature that can predict or identify FDP behavior before it occurs and currently rely on intuitive medical personnel and law enforcement intervention. Review of identified possible or confirmed FDP abuse/homicide situations sets into motion medical fraud reviews within risk management divisions of hospitals.

Monetary loss to a hospital, insurance carrier, or specific medical care provider is voluminous within the scope of chronic FDP abuse and factitious disorder (FD) pathways. Cost factors are associated with diagnostic testing that includes invasive surgeries, technical expertise (radiology testing parameters, lab work, consultation), medical personnel costs (specialists, nursing, home healthcare, primary care, etc.), and hospitalization costs (supplies, space, services, etc.).

Medical care costs do not immediately cease when an FDP abuse case or FD situation is uncovered. Medical costs continue to build, as necessary follow-up care is sought to resolve chronic conditions of created illness(s). Counseling and/or psychological treatment is usually part of the postidentification cost package that is not only applied to a surviving victim but also usually extended to an entire family. Medical follow-up care may be necessary for years or a lifetime after a true medical diagnosis is linked to FD/FDP. Follow-up care needs are predicated upon abuse infliction severity–associated victim damage(s). The time range of allowable exposure between the FDP victim and offender enhances the chronic nature of abuse. The amount of time an FD offender self-inflicts prior to detection may also correlate to injury severity (Figure 12.1).

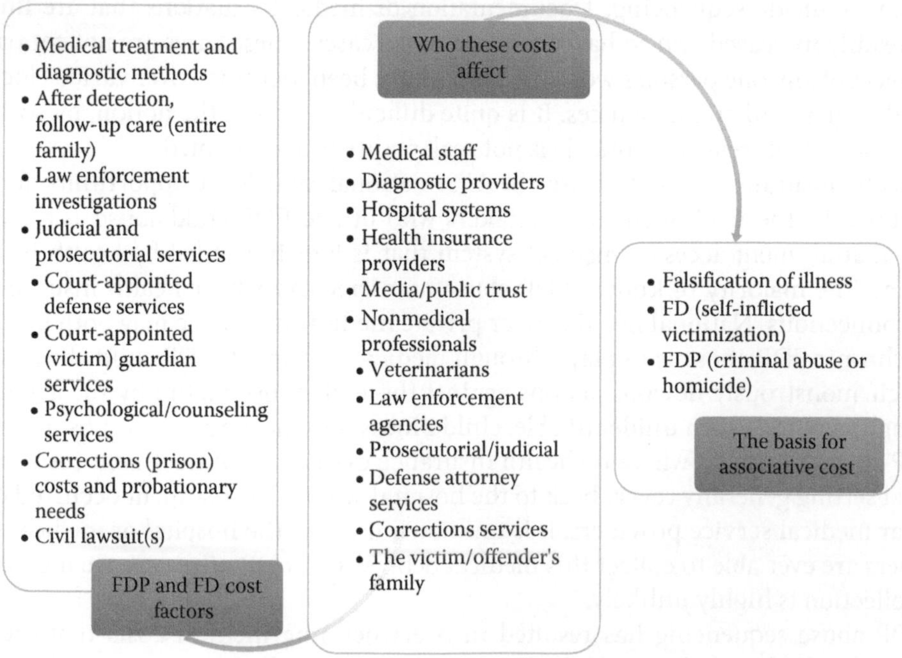

Figure 12.1 Cost analysis of factitious disorder/factitious disorder by proxy behavior.

Health insurance representatives may find that multidisciplinary staffing requests (FDP abuse cases) for continued observation of a suspected FDP victim (patient) or FD participant (self-imposed victim) are requested. Discussion regarding responsibility for payment of medical services under such circumstances has spurred debate. Managed care or health insurance representation should be informed that early discharge or denial of payment for medical services before confirmation of FD/FDP may continue a pattern or repeated hospitalization and render further financial burden to the insurance provider.[2] Establishing cooperation between a health insurance provider and interdisciplinary team regarding FD/FDP case management requires an understanding of potential financial cost when potential FD/FDP cases are not proven through sufficient investigation when the opportunity is presented. Identification and tracking of suspected FD/FDP abuse situations have increased. Medical testing sophistication to determine illness cause has expanded and with this expansion, associative costs have risen proportionately.

In FD/FDP cases, suspicion of covert deception generally occurs only after significant medical testing or procedures have occurred. The diagnosis of FDP is usually not placed until most other causes have been ruled out for an FDP abuse victim or person exhibiting factitious self-inflicted illness. Characteristically, only upon FDP abuse methodology exposure resulting in law enforcement intervention or recognition and intervention within an FD self-imposed illness scheme will abusive actions of the FD/FDP offender cease. The recidivism rate for persons suspected or convicted of FDP child abuse is believed to be extremely high if their actions remain hidden/not exposed. Exposure often rests upon the combined initial efforts of the multidisciplinary team followed by prosecutorial effort than judicial ramifications related to criminal statutory convictions. FDP child abuse cases not recognized allow FDP offenders to linger within an at-will mode of victim abuse. These cases show clear victimization patterns of multiple hospitalizations within multiple hospitals at multiple locations.

In rural areas, it is common for a total lack of knowledge regarding FD/FDP to be present within all aspects of multidisciplinary case intervention. At times, only one professional member of the group may be slightly aware of FD/FDP existence. Knowledge within the professions is not restricted to any one particular profession. Conversely, when an abuse or homicide case is linked to FDP or an FD situation is uncovered within a particular geographical area (usually within the media reporting range of an abuse location), knowledge may be significant. To some, it appears that the same particular professionals tend to "find" the presence of FD/FDP within medical or criminal cases. There have been attempts to link these professionals to improper accusatory statuses. One must consider that professional ability is built upon experience and education and evaluate such accusations on an individual basis. Just because a professional sees the potential of FDP abuse or homicide within a case does not mean that they are correct or incorrect. Full case evaluation predicated upon the establishment of evidence is required. Professional opinion is only one part of a multidisciplinary case evaluation.

Public Trust: Fraud, Money, and Know-How

Deceptive actions of the FDP offender violate general public trust. Why is it so difficult for society, in general, to believe that abuse or homicide with an FDP element exists? There is disbelief seen with sentencing trends of FDP offenders charged with aggravated child abuse, murder, fraud, and other criminal charges. A trend completely disavowing the FDP delivery element within an abuse or homicide case has become standard practice within the criminal realm of prosecution for FDP behaviorally related cases because abuse or homicide is just that. How it is delivered is secondary to the fact that it is a crime.

FDP is a complex abuse entity that occurs within a format of disguise; the main role player is the FDP offender who is a master of deception. Perhaps the lack of believability attached to abuse or homicide attained through an FDP delivery system rests within general credibility and societal expectations of mothers (FDP offenders). General acceptance of "seeing is believing" is not accurate within the world of FDs because what is seen is exactly what an FD/FDP offender wishes and not reality. Realism is portrayed fantasy for the FDP offender who dwells in a sphere of singular contentment as she secretly revels in the aftermath of FDP abuse infliction. For most people, this concept is difficult to understand. For the FDP offender, pretending that the world is something other than what it actually is becomes more palatable than assuming actual responsibility (Figure 12.2).

Hospitalization of the FDP abuse victim and associated shift in family responsibilities and interaction play an important role in the management of the FDP offender's stress. Interpersonal relationships may take a "back seat" to the more predominant issue: health of the victim. Over prolonged time periods, it is inevitable that persons external to the family will notice family struggle and sympathize. General principles for many include the belief that we are here to help those less fortunate. In FDP abuse situations, for altruistic right reasons, the public may become involved in the life of the FDP abuse victim, offender, and family. Charitable work is the most likely avenue of interaction and often occurs through fundraising and direct monetary donations to the "less fortunate." Public trust dictates that most people generally govern charitable donations with proper discretion; U.S. laws designed to enforce this belief demand it.

An FDP offender is generally characteristically above suspicion of wrongdoing, which sets the stage for an almost limitless avenue of public deception and fraud within the framework of FDP abuse methodology. What usually begins as unsolicited public assistance may quickly become active collection and collaboration of charity as the FDP offender revels in the attention surrounding notoriety and benefits from monetary assistance. The effect of monetary contribution to the FDP offender and specifically how that affects the interpersonal relationship with her spouse—in a positive manner—are powerful. Consideration of the FDP abuse victims' well-being is overridden with a conscientious decision of the offender that secondary gain associated with the continued deception (exploitation of the victim)

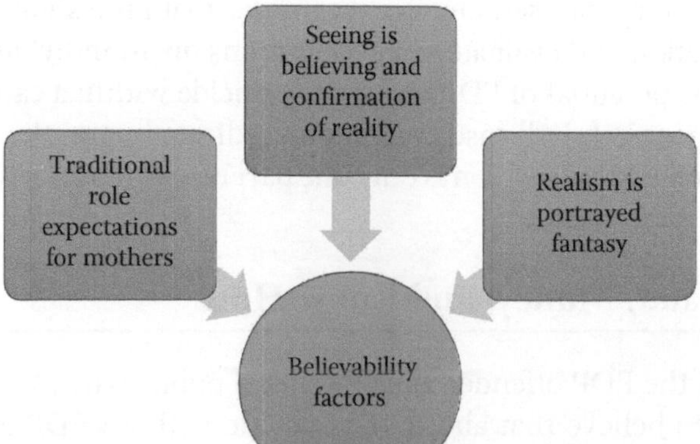

Figure 12.2 Twisted reality.

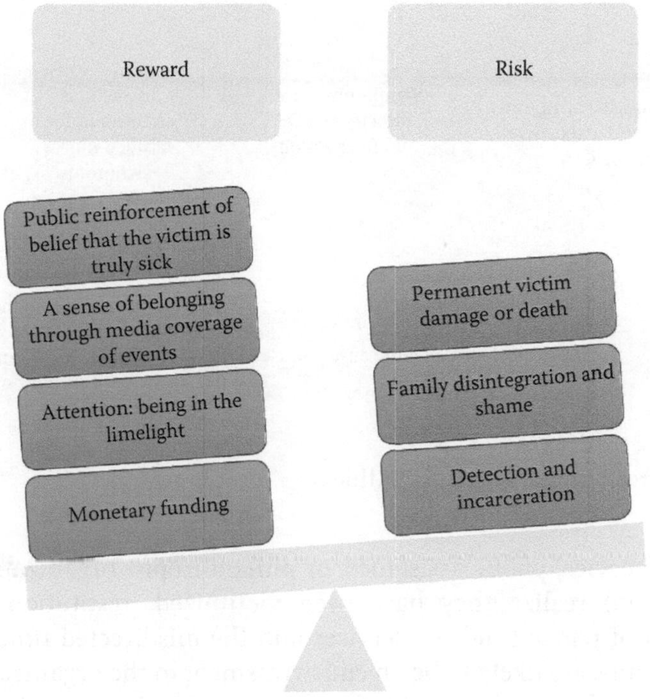

Figure 12.3 Factitious disorder by proxy victimization: reward versus risk.

outweighs the risk. Risk factors include detection, permanent victim damage or death, family shame (if detected), incarceration, and disintegration of the family (Figure 12.3).

Justification of an FDP victim's illness is reiterated over and over again as the FDP offender's public appearances with the apparently ill victim by her side reinforce the FDP offender's expressed belief that the illness is real. It often becomes difficult to differentiate victim symptoms caused directly by the criminal actions of the FDP offender, symptoms caused by medical treatment initiated to treat falsified symptoms, and actual illness that develops from a combination of the two. There are potential complications of bona fide illness (chronic conditions naturally occurring) coexisting with factitiously created symptoms. Perhaps illness symptom sourcing becomes FDP offender internal justification and deniability of responsibility for FDP victim illness or death. FDP victim illness may have multiple outlets but only one root cause: abuse.

Root Cause of Factitious Illness

FDP offenders who choose to access public sympathy through charitable organizations may embark upon a campaign of media glitz and involvement as the polish and skill of deception is directed toward the usage of the media as a proxy. A new pathway may develop for the FDP offender within the attention of media as an aggressive campaign of active collaboration ensues with public involvement. The media is used in a deceptive manner through the ongoing abuse of the FDP victim in ways that add extortion to the list of criminal acts. All the while, FDP victims are replaceable pawns in a dangerous game of complicated deception (Figure 12.4).

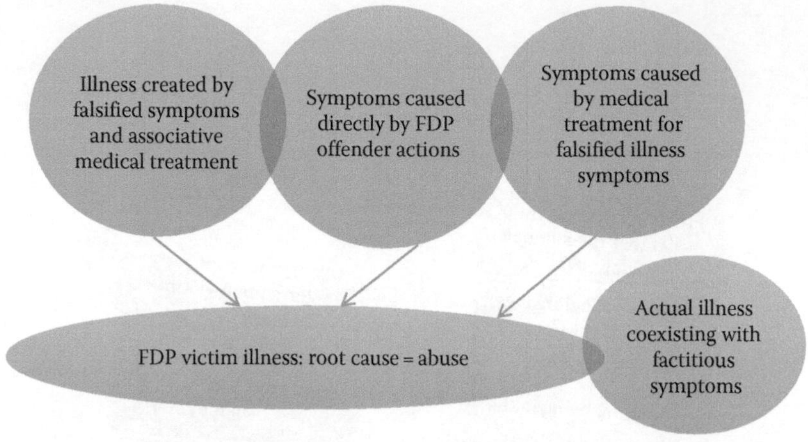

Figure 12.4 The root cause of factitious illness.

When social service, public assistance, or philanthropist organizations (used within the FDP deception) realize they have been victimized, restitution may be sought. Misappropriation of public funds or services and the misdirected fundraising efforts of philanthropist groups are likely to be an embarrassment to the organization. Holding the FDP offender and/or family accountable for organized fraud in accordance with criminal activity and/or through civil litigation measures is tenuous. The process is often long and tedious with no guarantee of judgment for the organization or company defrauded. There is also no likely monetary resource to repay criminal or civil judgment in favor of the fraud victims.

FDP Offender's Relationship with "Celebrities"

The primary driving force behind FD/FDP behavior is believed to be the correlation or need for attention that once attained provides validation of self-worth to the FDP offender. It is a center-stage way of life that suggests something is missing within the normalized life of the offender when heightened sensation or drama is absent. The chronic nature of FD/FDP activity illuminates a very practical aspect of life within a medical setting under the pretext of FDP abuse or FD self-inflicted harm. Funding to support medical needs of the FDP victim or the FD self-inflicted offender is needed; funding needs affect the entire FD/FDP family.

Within an FD/FDP setting, the offender generally attains attention through medical or other professional venues (law enforcement or fire service staff) initially. The focus of attention may later extend to the media who become aware of the plight of an FDP victim. Media coverage regarding an apparently chronically ill child draws significant attention to viewers that include celebrity champions for various causes. The scope of media interaction with the FDP offender includes an elevation of higher entity when media communication is established as the FDP offender acts as guardian and spokesman for the FDP victim. Media staff is often considered of celebrity stature. FDP association with celebrities provides enhanced offender attention and often generates increased monetary gain in the form of donations/public assistance/reduced or waived medical fees or other.

The FDP offender personifies the FDP child victim as the "star of the show," but careful examination of this dynamic reveals that the FDP offender is the true benefactor of celebrity contact. FDP offender benefit is derived from media attention surrounding the celebrity contact that places the FDP offender into the glare of notoriety. Theoretically, FDP offenders may attain belief that they are "above" common people as the aurora of "stardom" as celebrity is woven into the network of usable FDP offender actions that produce attention.

Situations or events (seen as an upsurge in an FDP victim's medical crisis or symptoms) may prompt celebrity involvement within the plight of the victim. It is suspected that when this occurs the FDP offender orchestrates escalated victim abuse (seen within the FDP abuse infliction severity scale) to produce response. This is most likely when prior media attention has occurred relating to the FDP situation. FDP child victims are, again, utilized as objects by the FDP offender without regard for death or injury potential. The involvement of celebrities within an FDP abuse situation silently reinforces to the FDP offender and the rest of the world that the FDP victim is truly ill. High-profile celebrity presence validating an FDP victim's status of illness indirectly reinforces entrenched mothering mechanisms of the FDP offender. FDP victim abuse produces measurable results and tells the FDP offender that infliction is worth the risk of detection or permanent victim harm/death. The twisted usage of celebrity benevolence by FDP abusers does not appear to occur in every FDP abuse/homicide scenario; the defrauding of celebrities in this manner appears relatively small in comparison to the majority of legitimately chronically ill children aided by caring humanitarians of celebrity status.

Assistance of the Media

Child abuse or child homicide cases involving an FDP factor carry high media coverage appeal. The dramatic manner that FDP cases tend to unfold incorporates audience participation as witness to the events; these cases are always high profile. Within the scope of a criminal investigation, keeping media case coverage to a minimum is preferable. Minimization of media coverage surrounding FDP-related violence is unlikely; even the most downscaled FDP abuse/homicide event is newsworthy and a media sensation.

The media, although generally unaware, may become the FDP offender's instrument to elicit public sympathy, support, and monetary relief through organized charitable contribution by telling the story of the FDP victim's plight with authorities. In many cases, once the FDP victim's story is aired, public opinion and private opinion of the suspected offender are favorable, FDP victimization is difficult to understand, and the FDP offender's manipulative skill often elicits empathetic public response.

Prolonged and repeated FDP offender abuse toward an FDP victim has shown that the skill to offend is perfected through practice. For an FDP offender to diversify "attention gathering" techniques, he or she must be avid in the task of indirect goal attainment. Goal attainment methods (victimization pathways) used by FDP offenders do not always include media and celebrity use within the primary mode of repetitive victim-fabricated or victim-induced medical symptomology.

Media and celebrity use by FDP offenders do appear to be linked to repetitive undetected victimization perfection and associated FDP offender confidence. The repetition of victim harm, without detection, provides skill set and confidence levels within the FDP offender. An offender testing and evaluating methodic FDP victim abuse while weighing the result of that abuse compared to the risk of detection is thought to occur. Theoretically, FDP offenders make decisions to continue offensive victim abuse knowingly and willingly and in an informed manner without regard to the consequence to the victim.

Although the FDP offender may fear exposure when confronted with medical suspicion of an FDP victim's illness causation or by law enforcement within a criminal context, this fear is accompanied by other factors. Exposure means the end of the FDP abuse benefit of medical staff attention through victimization, but it opens the door to a greater degree of attention or notoriety contained within media coverage. When an FDP abuser is accused of the heinous crime of (child) abuse or homicide with an FDP factor, the contained deception of abuse or homicide explodes into the limelight of public awareness through media exposure. The attention afforded the FDP offender is direct and notorious but significant. Perhaps this attention is in a format unfamiliar to the FDP offender, but the result is intense and poses the question regarding whether or not the notoriety is enjoyed. Personnel charged with the investigation of FDP abuse/homicide should be aware of the high-profile status of all FDP-related cases and likelihood that media coverage will occur during their investigation. Media coverage is evidence that may later be utilized by a prosecutor as the criminal case unfolds within the court system and should be properly collected.

When abuse or homicide with an FDP factor is uncovered, the FDP offender is placed into an extremely defensive position that must be maintained to continue his or her chosen lifestyle within the FDP abuse continuum. The newsworthiness of FDP abuse/homicide cases causes the media to seek out the FDP offender; it is often difficult for the FDP offender to resist the temptation of media coverage and walk away from the glare of significant attention. Taking a safer route of "no comment" produces isolation and determining preference is based upon many factors. Subsequently, many FDP offenders become guests on talk, tabloid, and news shows presenting themselves as victims of the criminal justice system claiming unsubstantiated systematic prosecution and their innocence.

FDP offender reactions exhibited when in front of an audience are sometimes mirrored within criminal interrogation situations. Vulnerability exhibited "on camera" or in the public domain is very different than "off camera" comportment of strength, cunning, and self-assurance. When no one is (apparently) looking, the truism of FDP offender character may be found. Image portrayal "on stage" or in the glare of the media should be considered within the context of FDP offender motive and gain. A behavioral transformation appears to coincide with media utilization as a vehicle for FDP offender benefit. What you see is not necessarily an accurate depiction of reality.

The FDP offender, through the use of the Internet, may also utilize media directly or indirectly. Public and private response to posted calls for personal or cause funding have become commonplace. The amount of money generated from a particular posting has a wide range depending upon public generosity and circulation of the post. Investigators should monitor Internet sites such as GoFundMe as potential avenues of extended fraud within the scope of FDP chronic child abuse or homicide situations (Figure 12.5).

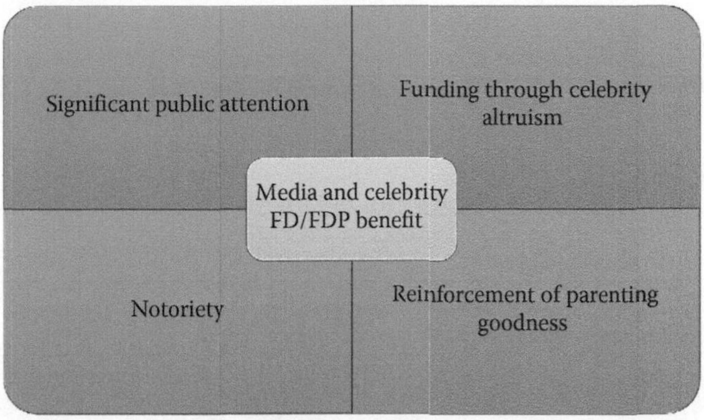

Figure 12.5 Media and celebrity as factitious disorder/factitious disorder by proxy benefits.

FDP Offender Skill versus Caution of the Law

Presumptive FDP offender ability often tests the skill and rationalization abilities of medical personnel. This triggers personal havoc for intuitive medical staff that question FDP offender's behavior because they suspect foul play. An FDP offender's mask of deception may transform to aggression as the offender seeks to sway suspicion away from him/herself and "place blame" onto the accusers. Havoc is often viewed in the form of either threatened or instituted lawsuits that equate to potential loss of revenue and reputation for the FDP offender's "accuser." It appears that for the FDP offender, a win/lose rationale becomes far greater than a truth/deception concept in a high-stakes game of virtual reality through the deceptive thwarting of suspicion. Control and the definition of reality often seem to rest within "rules of engagement" established by the FDP offender. It is a power and control deployment.

Lawsuits

To maintain control of the game, the FDP offender modifies the "rules." If medical professionals involved in the case are not attuned to established research concerning the likelihood of FDP offender's lawsuit threats, then hesitation and retreat may occur. What may result is FDP victim's lingering in a prolonged period of willful torture without the hope of intervention until they die. Exposure of the truism surrounding victim abuse or death through the inflictive causative factor of FDP abuse may never be attained when the threat or institution of a lawsuit is allowed to affect professional judgment.

The instigation of a lawsuit by a suspected FDP offender may reveal a premeditated defense and/or an attempt to thwart successful intervention. Medical personnel response and tenacity pertaining to the belief that FDP abuse is occurring coupled with a directed path of investigation may alter preconceived FDP offender plans causing an amendment to the agenda and abuse delivery mechanism or type changes. Shifting an FDP offender's MO often produces increased abuse to the victim in both severity and frequency. FDP offender's fear of permanent loss of her safety net (the target child victim) may also predicate the action of temporary reprieve for the victim and/or flight of the offender. Both situations

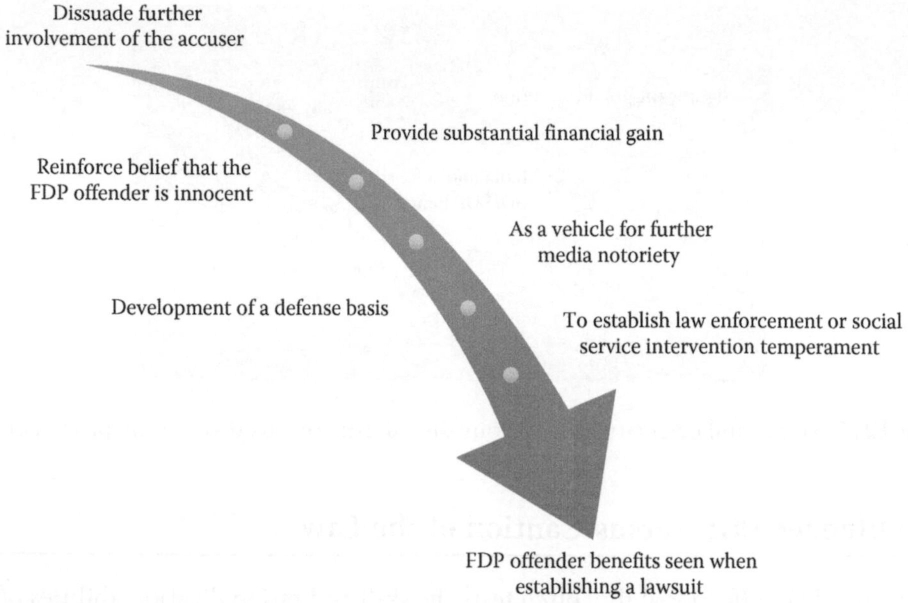

Figure 12.6 Factitious disorder/factitious disorder by proxy lawsuit diversions.

mandate the need for meticulous investigative case building (protocol) prior to allowing the FDP offender awareness that intervention is forthcoming or suspicion has been aroused.

It is commonplace for FDP offenders to either threaten or initiate lawsuits in part, as a response to FDP abuse allegations. Vehement denial of allegations will coincide with professed innocence. Lawsuits are utilized by the FDP offender as a tool in attempts to acquire specific results as shown in Figure 12.6.

Actuality and/or lawsuit threat is theorized to temper pending actions of social service agencies considering custody separation court actions between a suspected FDP offender and a victim. The judiciary may view an FDP victim's threatened harm as tentative until abuse with an FDP factor is proven within the criminal investigative realm. Dependency issues are often determined prior to or unofficially contingent upon criminal case disposition. Social service agencies that have a history of FDP victim intervention and have experienced public scrutiny for either FDP victim custody removal or a lack thereof may be affected by those experiences. The exhibition of caution regarding potential FDP child abuse victim's custody removal from a suspected FDP offender follows a pathway generated by the evaluation of evidence on a custody platform. This is the same evidence that criminal cases and medical decisions are also predicated upon. The time that social service agencies require to make a determination of child extraction from a family or the decision of dependency court to prematurely return an FDP abuse victim or siblings to the custody of a suspected FDP offender has direct implication upon the victim's survivability. These decisions are based upon evidence gathering and establishment, and during the time of indecision or consideration, an opportunity for an FDP offender to upscale victim infliction or move toward directed victim homicide occurs. The weight of decisions regarding FDP abuse–child custody for social service agencies and the judiciary is formidable.

Civil Lawsuits

In civil litigation, physical complaints and symptoms are common. People may calm occupational disability, emotional suffering, and loss of ability to fulfill marital, occupational, and other social roles as a result of physical damage. Physical damage translates into reimbursable injuries.[3]

When a person uses an illness, injury, or symptom originating from a factitious base, there is a conscious production of signs and symptoms of disease. Recognizing that such a person is utilizing a factitious factor within a civil claim is important because it may involve a significant amount of money and if the false claim is not recognized, the internal processes ongoing within the claimant are likely to continue as medical costs continue unabated.[4]

Case Examples

During 1982, a 63-year-old woman came to a large teaching hospital complaining of uncontrollable hip pain, and a host of medical tests and treatments ensued. The patient later sued the hospital for malpractice, stating that when a nurse injected her with Demerol, paralysis resulted. The patient retained a hand surgeon and surgical nurse as experts. The experts opined that the hospital was negligent when the nurse utilized an incorrect technique during the injection.

Pursuant to the lawsuit, research revealed that the patient had more than 50 lengthy hospitalizations during her lifetime, and more than 180,000 pages of medical records were revealed. The patient had undergone more than 500 invasive procedures and tests in multiple organ systems without any definitive results.

At the age of 41, medical staff found the patient manipulating her thermometer to fake raised temperature and manipulating her urethra to place blood in her urine and was evaluated by a psychiatrist but refused therapy. Hospitalizations and testing continued.

At the age of 42, the patient was admitted to a new hospital, failing to disclose her history, and was diagnosed with thyrotoxicosis that was spontaneously resolved.

At the age of 43, the patient was admitted to a large medical center, and her medical history was revealed. A multidisciplinary team evaluation produced a diagnosis of Munchausen syndrome (FD), but the patient continued to hospital hop without disclosing this finding.

This case went to trial and the judge refused to allow the issue of Munchausen syndrome to be heard by the jury citing that to do so would constitute an improper comment on the plaintiff's credibility and usurp the function of the jury. The jury awarded damage to the patient in the amount of $1,300,000.00 and granted a remittitur of $500,000.00.

The defense appealed. The appellate court reversed the trial court finding that a discussion of Munchausen syndrome would not have usurped the jury function (*Cohen v. Einstein*),[5] and a new trial was ordered. The court noted evidence of mental illness that impairs a witness's credibility to "perceive, remember and narrate perceptions accurately is invariably admissible to impeach credibility, even if not adequate to demonstrate competency."

The patient dropped the suit, and a retrial was not pursued.

A 36-year-old man sustained a hand injury while working as a restaurant chef in Pennsylvania and went to the emergency room for sutures and antibiotics. The care was covered by workman's compensation. After 14 days, he returned to the ED because the wound had developed necrosis and was referred to a plastic surgeon. Month after month, the injury failed to respond to various antibiotic and other treatments and the condition worsened. Testing revealed no abnormalities.

This man also had an old burn injury on his other hand and advised the plastic surgeon that the injury was caused by napalm during the Vietnam War. He also advised that he had been exposed to Agent Orange infected with malaria and had been on combat patrol.

The patient relocated to Alabama and began treatment at a new hospital without condition improvement. Five months later, he relocated to Florida and sought treatment at another hospital. In Florida, the patient was allowed to change his own dressings supervised by clinical staff and consistently relayed his Vietnam experiences. The patient's condition significantly worsened, and his surgeon requested a psychiatric evaluation that revealed the presence of FD.

The patient's former employer's workman's compensation carrier referred the case for forensic psychiatric evaluation. The evaluation found that the patient fabricated his educational, work, family, and service records; the patient had never been exposed to combat, Agent Orange, or napalm and had suffered no service-related injuries. The workman's compensation carrier stopped paying for medical care. The patient was not heard from again.

Munchausen syndrome was first suspected 3 years after the initial injury. The patient was confronted and denied that he was producing symptoms.[6]

Looking at a case from a risk management viewpoint when people have a long history of multiple unexplained or unresolved illnesses and/or hospitalizations and their employment, familial, and medical histories are either omitted or proven false utilizes a forensic and current review factor. These cases cross the threshold between clinical diagnostic and criminal entities. The falsification of injury and subsequently obtained medical treatment is a costly entity and scheme to defraud. Hospitals, workman's compensation agencies, or medical insurance companies bear the greatest weight in terms of monetary loss in treating falsified injury found within FD applications.

Betrayal of Man's Best Friend

FDP abuse is not limited to child or elderly victimization or indirect alternative victimization groups. There have been identified abuse situations with animals used as proxy target victims through the avenue of FDP methodologies. Household pets may become victim surrogates when FDP offenders choose to utilize veterinary professionals in the same role seen within medical professionals.[7] The animals assume the role traditionally held by children and veterinarians assume the role traditionally held by physicians. It is important to recognize that many people regard their pets as their children and the bond is no less. Within this understanding, the use of pets within the FDP abuse process is clarified.

Conclusion

The existence of abuse or homicide with an FDP delivery methodology is evident. The choice to include the FDP factor within the criminal justice aspect of prosecution for abuse or homicide is dependent upon individual case evaluation. Notoriety associated in most abuse or homicide situations where the element of FDP delivery exists has attuned the public and professions to the potential deviancy of the FDP offender. This notoriety is generally immediate but not necessarily long term.

A distortion of FDP offender moral/primal thinking occurs during FDP victimization; established societal norms related to acceptable custodial care of dependants (FDP victims) are warped or bent to suit the needs of the FDP offender. The ability of the FDP offender to modify the delivery mode or injurious range of abuse to a victim seems to evolve and is based upon mitigating factors.

It appears that peripheral factors such as media usage and alternative victimization, once considered unusual, are regularly experienced in FDP abuse pathways. It is also clear that abuse and homicide with an FDP delivery factor occur nationally and internationally with reporting of these cases predicated upon the educational level of involved professionals and, to some extent, the general public. Education provides an increased likelihood of FDP victim survival, but the line that exists between education/suspicion and intervention is complicated with liability surrounding potential error.

Abuse or homicide with an FDP factor remains complicated.

Notes

1. Weber, S., RNC. Filicide-suicide: Common factors in parents who kill their children and themselves. *Journal of Pediatric Nursing*, February 1987;2(1):50–53.
2. Eminson, D.M. and Postlewaite, R.J., Factitious illness: Recognition and management. *Archives of Disease in Children*, 1992;67:1510–1516.
3. Eisendrath, S.J. and McNiel, D.E., Factitious disorders in civil litigation: Twenty cases illustrating the spectrum of abnormal illness-affirming behavior. *Journal of American Academy of Psychiatry and the Law*, 2002;30:391–399.
4. Powell, R. and Boast, N., The million dollar man: Resource implications for chronic Munchausen's syndrome. *British Journal of Psychiatry*, 1993;162:253–256.
5. *Cohen v. Einstein*. 592A:2d720 (Pa. Super. Ct. 1991).
6. Janofsky, J., The Munchausen Syndrome in civil forensic psychiatry. *The Bulletin of the American Academy of Psychiatry and the Law*, 1994;22(4).
7. Sheridan, J.S., MSBP in Context II, in: *MSBP: Issues in Diagnosis and Treatment*, Levin, A.V. and Sheridan, M.S. (Eds.). New York: Lexington, 1995, pp. 90–92.

FDP Behavior as Defense Application

13

Everyone here has the sense that right now is one of those moments when we are influencing the future.

Steve Jobs

Behavior of FDP within Sexual Battery Cases

Child molestation is often described as a societal taboo that causes extreme emotional upheavals with affected families. Child molestation may provoke bias within people directly or indirectly associated with child molestation situations that include intervention efforts. Child sexual abuse (CSA) situations involving very young children are among the cases that tug at a person's heart producing anxiety and uneasiness externally and internally. Sex is perhaps the most powerful force known to man; sexual abuse of young children is perhaps the most powerful manipulator of individual emotion and reaction and a veritable threshold between right and wrong behavior in most cultures.

Persons convicted of sexual crimes against children are usually severely dealt with by the criminal courts. Sexual abusers acting in a custodial capacity during the victimization, when caught, are likely to secure eternal severance of (custodial) rights. CSA, like child abuse or child homicide with a factitious disorder by proxy (FDP) factor, is a crime of family shame that, on societal and personal levels, is difficult to witness, verbalize, or understand. Both situations are perversions of culturally defined, behaviorally accepted norms. Public response to both FDP abuse/homicide and CSA is shock followed by repulsion. In most CSA or FDP abuse situations once criminal justice and dependency issues are settled, child victimization may be selectively overlooked by the family and forgotten by society. Selective prolonged recognition omission for extreme child abuse or homicide situations may occur because remembering the horror of such crimes within the forefront of daily living is emotionally taxing. The identity of CSA and FDP child victims is shielded from public sight in the name of child protection through mandated anonymity that affords child abuse victims the opportunity for a greater degree of life normalcy and prevents further exploitation and damage. Anonymity, however, also allows society to selectively view severe child abuse situations (CSA or FDP) minimizing impact and questioning the reality of victimization occurrences.

Convicted CSA offenders (pedophiles) experience public accountability for their actions. Convicted pedophiles are forever labeled as such, and their behavior is monitored, seemingly forever, through established CSA offender registration services that are publicly posted for all to see. In the United States, CSA is not tolerated. In some states, residents in communities where CSA offenders reside are entitled to be notified of the CSA offender's presence. Restrictions on employment and housing are placed upon the convicted CSA offender, and monitoring by corrections in situations occur. After a convicted CSA offender is released from the criminal justice penalty of a prison sentence, the civil commitment process found within Jimmy Ryce hearings ensues further limiting the ability of the CSA offender from contact with society. When a person is convicted of CSA, it is a lifelong sentence because society has learned that the behavior of one (pedophile) can affect the lives of many (people). The education of society gleaned from repetitive patterns of child victimization, the unreliability of permanent offender rehabilitation, and the gravity of victim abuse underscore the magnitude of potential threatened harm in CSA abuse situations.

Examination of the likelihood of reoffense by a CSA offender is an element in societal view and this includes a fear factor based upon fact. Fear is a powerful force that affects people in positive and negative ways simultaneously. Fear tends to create demand upon those it affects by directing action, clouding judgment, or pressuring resolution without considering all potential factors. Fear may project people into states of hypervigilance motivating change or work product in a positive (or negative) manner.

The difference between how society views the heinousness of CSA abuse that may lead to the death of a victim and FDP abuse that may also lead to the death of the victim is relativity. The anonymity potential of CSA-related crime means that all children within society are potential victims. The established pattern of custodial presence within FDP-related crime means that the primarily targeted child victims are kept within the smaller resource pool of specified families. The death of either a CSA or an FDP child victim is homicide, but potential consequences are dissimilar.

Professionals encountering potential CSA situations should be skeptical when everything looks "normal" within the scope of CSA investigative parameters. When parents of CSA victims appear ideal yet their behavior is aligned with FDP warning signs/indicators, further investigation within the scope of FDP abuse victimization is needed. These case types are not prevalently recognized with the basis of known CSA situations but are possible. Managing factors of fear and emotion within the community and within oneself are critical in maintaining objectivity required to dissect a true case of CSA from that of indirect FDP-related abuse.

Describing FDP behavior through the type of abuse the victim experiences has provided thought-provoking theories of FDP differentiation and classification among professionals.

Rand described FDP within the context of falsified sexual abuse allegations and as "contemporary type" FDP with a heavy emphasis on emotional abuse.[1] False sexual abuse accusations may occur "when a parent or other adult caretaker fabricates or induces the idea that a child has been abused and then gains recognition from professionals as the protector of the abused child." This behavior may occur in divorce situations—especially when child custody is disputed.[2] In cases of child custody dispute and/or divorce, there are many reasons why the allegation of abuse, in any form, may be presented. Within the context of FDP, a false allegation of sexual abuse should be examined through the evidence presented. It is a complicated issue that is affected by potential witness maneuvering and/or active collusion.

False Child Sexual Abuse Accusations: Victim Consequences

Not every alleged case of child molestation has a factual basis. False accusations of child molestation may occur in situations including child custody disputes, divorce proceedings, and revenge scenarios, as a defense by those convicted of CSA, and in FDP cases as a

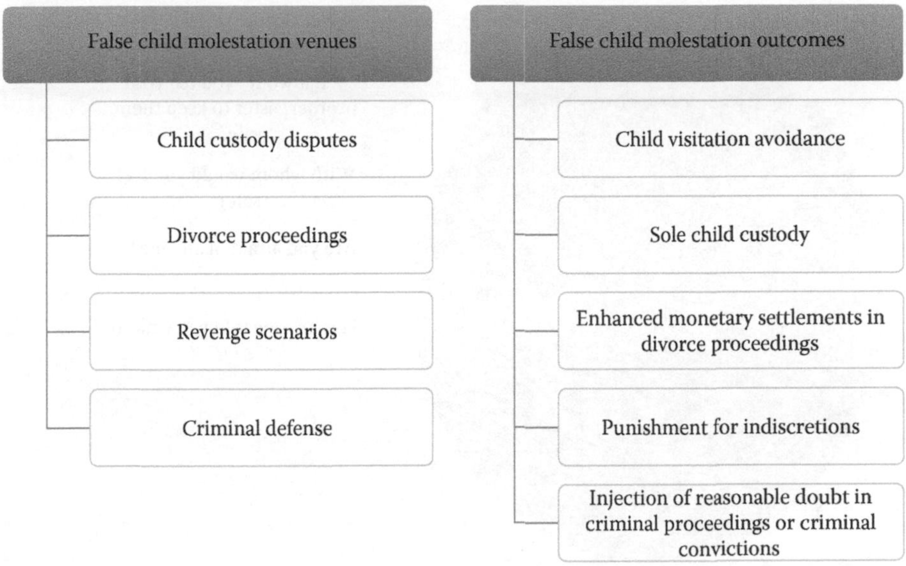

Figure 13.1 False claims of child molestation: venues and outcomes.

mechanism of thwarting suspicion. Likely effects of instituting false molestation charges include avoidance of child visitation privileges that include joint or shared child custody, the attainment of sole child custody, enhanced monetary divorce proceedings, punishment for a partner's indiscretions, a means to inject reasonable doubt within criminal court proceedings, or to overturn criminal convictions (Figure 13.1).

Forced separation between a child and parent emulating from sexual impropriety allegations has potential effects upon the child. Emotional consequences include personal depreciation that may progress to brainwashing depending upon the situation and the emotional consequences linked to medical exams, testing, and interviews. Alienation and victim contamination toward an accused parent may appear irreversible even when a child is later reunited with a falsely accused parent.

When children are utilized as dispensable objects in modes containing false accusations of molestation, their existence is often enveloped in a fantasy world. Within this sphere coaching by the accusing parent, probing by therapists, detectives, and their courts provide the basis for their understanding and confirmation of reality. Separation of truth and fantasy is often not easily attained. When children are inaccurately portrayed as CSA victims, their testimony is usually inconsistent, incredible, or fantasized. Physical evidence to support CSA allegations is usually nonexistent or inconclusive.[3]

Interviewing children that believed to be objects of falsely reported CSA is difficult. These children may genuinely believe their victimization status due to conditioning that includes an element of applied external attention related to their status. CSA victim may be either nonverbal or not qualifiable due to physical/cognitive maturity or a lack of understanding regarding fact versus fiction. If the detective believes that a false CSA situation is presented, generalized questioning may aid in determining the accuracy of situational assessment by the potential CSA victim (Figure 13.2).

Children that are subjects of false CSA accusations that originate from a caretaker should be removed from the accuser's custody. There is an assumption that the child's

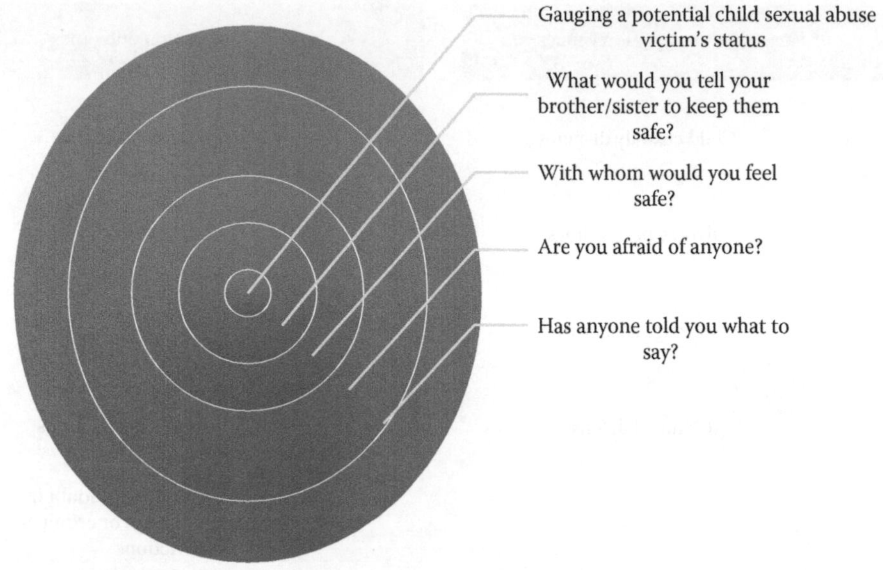

Gauging a potential child sexual abuse victim's status
What would you tell your brother/sister to keep them safe?
With whom would you feel safe?
Are you afraid of anyone?
Has anyone told you what to say?

Figure 13.2 Generalized questioning for child sexual abuse investigations.

needs have been disregarded while the accuser's desire has been indulged when the child is utilized for secondary gain attained from the false allegation. The ability of the accuser to adequately parent is compromised, and the child is neglected when a willingness to subject a child to CSA protocol supersedes protective custody expectations.

FDP as a Sexual Abuse Defense

FDP has become a defense for persons accused of CSA. Male defendants have raised the issue of false accusation claiming that a child victim's mother has "planted lies" and fabricated CSA evidence for the purpose of attaining attention in a manner directly linked to FDP methodology profile criteria. CSA evidentiary issues are rationalized or surmised by the accused, or convicted, CSA defendant in the manner notated in Figure 13.3.

Preparing for a potential FDP defense in CSA cases includes recognizing that a CSA defendant asserts that a nonoffending CSA parent is in actuality an FDP child abuser, the purpose of the falsified CSA claim is systematic gain through attention and/or sole custody of an FDP target victim, and CSA allegation is being utilized as a means to thwart suspicion of FDP child abuse.

Negating CSA defense assertions may involve relieving the specter of (juror) doubt that FDP abuse insertion produces. This may include proving that a nonoffending parent of a CSA victim (usually the victim's mother) is NOT an FDP offender and focusing on physical case evidence. Case review of the CSA victim's pathway prior to CSA allegations should be carefully evaluated for FDP patterns. In the absence of FDP methodologies, pathways, and FDP offender secondary gain, the reasonableness of abuse through an FDP delivery system is compromised and FDP allegations are unlikely to be true. Care should be taken to guard against premature assumptions when evaluating FDP within a CSA

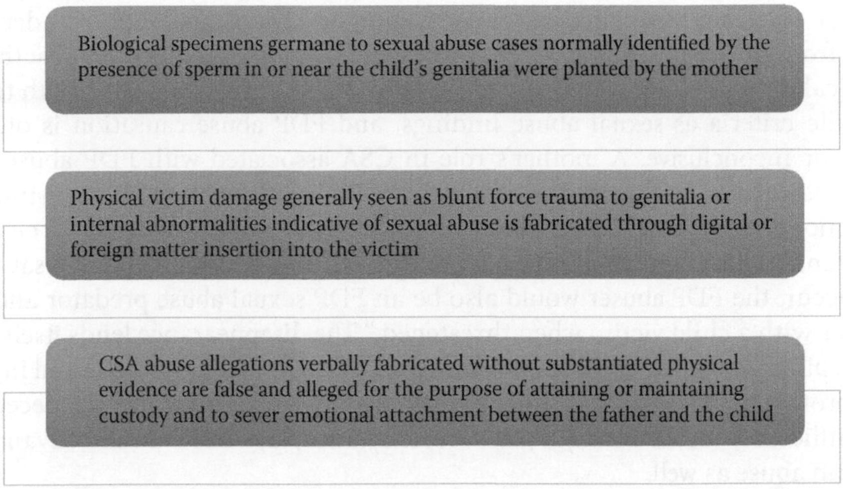
Biological specimens germane to sexual abuse cases normally identified by the presence of sperm in or near the child's genitalia were planted by the mother
Physical victim damage generally seen as blunt force trauma to genitalia or internal abnormalities indicative of sexual abuse is fabricated through digital or foreign matter insertion into the victim
CSA abuse allegations verbally fabricated without substantiated physical evidence are false and alleged for the purpose of attaining or maintaining custody and to sever emotional attachment between the father and the child

Figure 13.3 Child sexual abuse defense platforms.

format. The child victim may simultaneously fill the role of targeted victim within both abuse forums and be victimized by both parents. This is unlikely, but possible.

Parental Abduction, Sexual Abuse Allegations, and Factitious Disorder by Proxy

CSA allegations are not always true. The issue of child custody as a motivator for false accusations of CSA has been known for some time; CSA allegations as a potential means for an FDP offender to thwart suspicion and maintain sole custody/control of an FDP abuse victim are new. Child custody in FDP abuse situations represents the ability of an FDP offender to maintain his or her chosen lifestyle. The critical role an FDP abuse victim has within the FDP offender's life is significant in terms of verification of an FDP offender's self-worth. FDP abusers threatened with loss of child (victim) custody, from any venue, will react. The reaction may include flight, relocation and continued abuse, upsurge in victim abuse, directed homicide, and attempted thwarting of responsibility by various means. The importance the FDP child victim has within the FDP abuse role enmeshes with the offender's lifestyle and self. To lose child custody of an FDP victim might be viewed as the loss of oneself (to the FDP offender) because such loss represents the cessation of attention.

In true cases of FDP child abuse, the FDP offender may exhibit generalized FDP offender profile traits including the use of a target child for repeated hospitalization access. Lack of causative victim illness determination is sometimes interspersed with numerous claims of varied reasons why a victim is ill. One of these claims is CSA, usually directed at the nonoffending parent. Cases of falsely reported CSA within an FDP abuse parameter have included stranger as well as custodial named suspects. The *stranger* suspect element occurs when no paternal factor is immediately present within the FDP offender and victim relationship and is seen as a means to thwart suspicion away from the FDP offender for victim injury or illness. Paternal absence may be related to family abandonment (temporary or permanent), divorce, or separation or because the FDP offender is hiding the child from the nonoffending parent through relocation or underground activity.

Medical determination of a CSA victim's physical ailments may align with traditional FDP profile criteria as sexual abuse findings, and FDP abuse causation is often undetermined or inconclusive. A mother's role in CSA associated with FDP abuse has been described as "driven by the need to establish credibility through medical justification for her allegation that the child is being victimized." FDP offenders who falsely accuse other of CSA may inflict harm representative of sexual abuse to substantiate the accusation. If this were to occur, the FDP abuser would also be an FDP sexual abuse predator and likely to "disappear with a child victim when threatened." The disappearance lends itself to parental kidnapping depending upon circumstances justified by claims of abuse and in the name of child protection. Defense may posture that custody is the catalyst in the deception that rises to inflicted CSA victim injury, but custody also plays a role in the advancement of FDP victim abuse as well.

Factitious Sexual Harassment

Falsely acquiring victim status through an FD methodology may occur on a vast victimization platform including sexual abuse and sexual related acts.[4] Thoroughly investigating alternative incentives for a person to self-portray as a victim is recommended. Reasons why a person might claim to be a victim include revenge, validation of self-perception, eliciting emotional support, opportunity to release anger, and repetition compulsion.[5]

Differentiation and Commonalities: Factitious Disorder by Proxy Abuse and Child Sexual Abuse

Critical differentiation between FDP and CSA is the presence or absence of FDP protocol and measurable secondary FDP offender gain indirectly resulting from victimization. When the presence of secondary gain, warning signs, and FDP abuse pathways are absent, the reason for FDP victimization is questionable; it makes no sense. Factitiously creating CSA situations for purposes other than those listed within known FDP offender benefits is false reporting but for other purposes (Figures 13.4 and 13.5).

Reasonable Doubt: FDP and Criminal Case Building

When criminal court evaluates abuse or homicide with a link to FDP, they must consider the reasonableness associated with case evidence and weigh the merits of criminal statutory violations based upon facts. The reasonableness or likelihood of planted evidence in CSA cases within the context of FDP abuse methodology is generally considered highly unusual but theoretically possible. Those accused of CSA have attempted to thwart suspicion by claiming that they are victims of FDP in a way that produces attention for the FDP offender by falsely claiming that a child (in common to both the alleged CSA and FDP offender) is falsely portrayed as a CSA victim. There are many questions that should be asked if this situation presents to clarify linkage specifically addressing interfamilial

FDP	CSA
☐ Offender is usually female and the victim's mother (female guardian)	☐ Offender is usually male
☐ Method: Surreptitious abuse and in a medical setting	☐ Method: surreptitious abuse and in a privatized setting
☐ Victim's behavior is generally not indicative of knowlege of abuse	☐ Victim's behavior is generally indicative of abuse awareness
☐ FDP victims may die as a result of direct or indirect abuse; deaths are offender driven	☐ CSA victims infrequently die as a result of CSA(only) victimization
☐ Victim removal from an FDP offender's custody is the most common method of victim protection	☐ CSA offenders' removal from the victim's home or custody is the primary means of victim protection
☐ Appears unusual that FDP victim abuse occurs during custody or visitation dispute situations	☐ CSA occasionally occurs during custody/visitition dispute situations
☐ FDP offenders may have mental illness conditions but are generally not found to be insane.	☐ CSA offenders do not usually exhibit overt mental illness
☐ Young FDP victims are generally unaware they are being abused; coercion is not needed to maintain secrecy	☐ CSA victims are often coerced into maintaining secrecy and are aware of their victimization status
☐ There is no specifically targeted victim gender and no gender prevalence	☐ Female CSA victims are more prevalent than male
☐ FDP abuse is concealed but committed in plain view	☐ CSA is concealed and committed in seclusion
☐ Physical evidence is abundant but often not recognized	☐ Physical evidence is not always abundant or present
☐ FDP victims who realize they have been abused historically do not disclose the abuse to anyone.	☐ CSA victims may realize their abuse long after abuse has stopped (when victims feel safe). Disclosure may occur.
☐ Medical personnel and law enforcement generally conduct investigations	☐ Child protective services and law enforcement generally conduct investigations
☐ The criminal setting is usually within the confines of a medical facility	☐ The criminal setting is usually within the confines of the home

Figure 13.4 Factitious disorder by proxy/child sexual abuse comparative checklist.[6][7]

relationship, profile factors, allegation origination, historical review, active collusion, reasonableness, and opportunity. The following interactive fact finding questions are suggested (Figure 13.6):

When the first law enforcement related to FDP case was publicized in the United States during 1991, communication from a prison inmate convicted of CSA followed. The inmate

Notes

1. Rand, D., Munchausen syndrome by proxy as a possible factor when abuse is falsely alleged. *Issues in Child Abuse Accusations*, 1989;1:32–34.
2. Rand, D., Munchausen syndrome by proxy-a complex type of emotional abuse responsible for some false allegations of child abuse. *Issues in Child Abuse Accusations*, 1993;5:135–155.
3. Child sexual abuse, assault and molestation issues, Report by the 1991–1992 San Diego County Grand Jury.
4. Feldman, M.D., Ford, C.V., and Stone, T., Deceiving others/deceiving oneself: Four cases of factitious rape. *Southern Medical Journal*, 1994;87:736–738.
5. Feldman-Schorrig, S., Factitious sexual harassment. *Bulletin of the American Academy of Psychiatry and the Law*, 1996;24(3):387–392.
6. Levin, A.M.D. and Sheridan, M., *Munchausen Syndrome by Proxy. Issues in Diagnosis and Treatment*. New York: Lexington Books, 1995, p. 237.
7. Artingstall, K., *Practical Aspects of Munchausen by Proxy and Munchausen Syndrome Investigation*. Boca Raton, FL: CRC Press, 1998, pp. 295–297.
8. See Notes 2 and 3.

Significance of Fire in Factitious Disorder by Proxy and Factitious Disorder Cases 14

Nothing makes us so lonely as our secrets.

Paul Tournier

In an increasing number of abuse cases with a factitious disorder by proxy (FDP) factor and in some adult factitious disorder (FD) false accusation cases, the element of fire has been identified. Often, more than one fire is found to have occurred during the FD/FDP offender's lifetime. These fires are generally not immediately associated with death causation of FDP victims or significant human injury but are increasingly recognized as a significant factor within an overall potential FDP investigative behavioral analysis.

Detectives assigned to investigate abuse or homicide with an FDP factor would be astute to prepare for the potential need for arson-related investigations. A broad understanding regarding cases involving children within fire situations may provide an essential investigative edge as officers are confronted with the additional element of arson within FDP-related investigations. Keeping in mind that fire not only serves to hide criminal evidence, it is also a motivational factor spurred by revenge and monetary compensation or a source of thrill/notoriety, vandalism, fraud, sabotage, pyromania, and others (Figure 14.1) is wise.

Arson Detectives and Criminal Investigators: The Mini Team Concept

When criminal detectives and arson investigators form a team, a formidable investigative alliance occurs. This liaison is needed from time to time within the course of criminal investigations involving the FDP factor. Fire-related investigations require determination of origin and cause. Criminal detectives may lack the scientific technical analysis investigative ability to conduct advanced analytical inquiries within fire-related FDP situations. Fire causation determination involves the analysis of environmental, involved equipment, and human factors. Technical skill of a trained arson investigator is needed to rule out fire causation agents regularly found within arson and fully explore environmental and technical issues that differentiate accidental versus intentional fire causation. Looking for motive and linking an arsonist's motivation to the criminal conduct found within FDP applications is an investigatory specialty. When the element of fire is present within a known or suspected FDP abuse/homicide entity, the results of arson and criminal investigations are not mutually exclusive.

Investigative/interview capabilities of the police detective, skilled in the methodology of FD/FDP mechanics, are often necessary to accurately assess schematic arsonist behavioral totality as related to the FDP investigation. Police detectives, within the scope of the multidisciplinary team, may fully explore the human element visualizing secondary

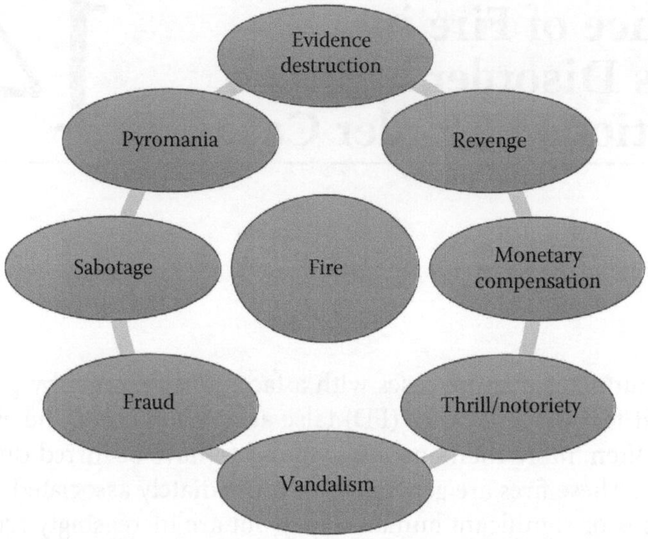

Figure 14.1 Motivations in FDP arson.

FDP offender benefit and evidentiary parameters. Benefit is usually only recognized following prolonged and complicated victim abuse and is dependent upon environmental, circumstantial, and educational processes. Fire destructiveness enables physical evidence elimination.

Within the context of the multidisciplinary team approach to crimes involving an FDP element, the subset of a mini detective team formulated by the joining of arson and police detective may serve to expedite the investigation and determine causative fire origin. Working together toward a common goal, members compliment one another as shared investigative experience is revealed. A team concept allows cohesively prepared criminal case development. Team members that anticipate and compliment one another without tension factors are most successful. Primarily, the arson investigator should assume physical evidence examination at fire scenes; primarily, the trained criminal detective should assume witness interviews.

As individual team members apply their skill during the case management investigative process, associative multidisciplinary team members should observe for verification, input, learning, and support. Multidisciplinary team concept protocol providing individual discipline contribution solidifies within a common goal format. Communicative understanding between team members is attained through organizational meetings that may be formal or informal according to specific case needs. The welfare and protection of surviving FDP abuse or homicide victims should be foremost on the agenda. Multidisciplinary organizational meetings may directly serve child protective needs yet fail to extend protective measures through criminal sanctions. If the origin of a death from fire or fire-related injury is unknown or suspected to be linked to abuse or homicide with an FDP delivery factor, the investigative multidisciplinary team should include the following (Figure 14.2):

A point person or leader should be established at the initial team meeting. Team members represent individual case tracts; the ultimate team goal is constant, and focus should be on (surviving) victim protection followed by criminal justice. Personal attitude, conflict, and ego have no place on the team (see Chapter 8 for details).

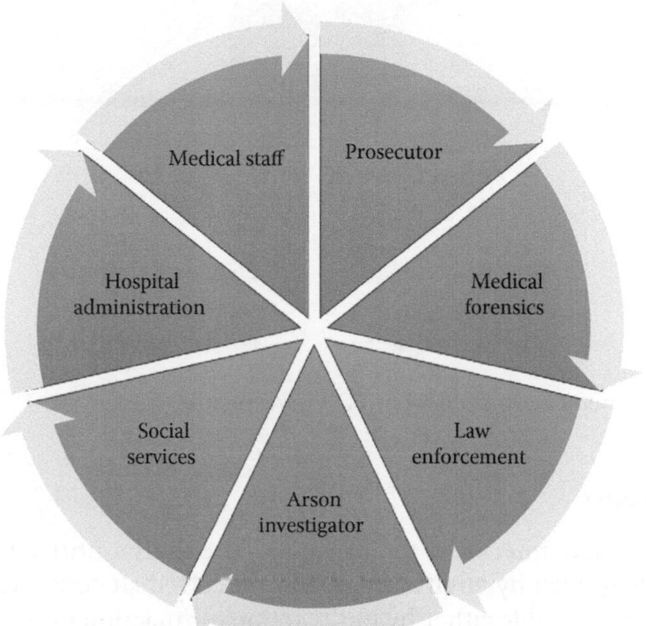

Figure 14.2 Multidisciplinary teams: FDP investigations and arson.

Investigative Interviews: Children and Fire

Arson is defined as follows: "The illegal burning of a building or other property: the crime of setting fire to something."[1] It has been said that arson is the easiest crime to commit but the most difficult to detect and prove.[2] Arson is generally considered a crime of violence. Arsonists generally commit arson by intruding into the privacy of a dwelling, but there are situations when arsonists dwell within their targeted areas as well. The sphere of FDP-related crime and FD behavior have been identified as internal targeted areas where arsonists sometimes dwell.

The red glow and warmth of a fire is usually a pleasing positive sight—when such fire is contained, fire is useful in many aspects. The destructive force that fire possesses is powerful on extreme levels of application bases. Not all uses of fire are good and in the hands of a criminal, fire is potentially lethal and may be utilized in heinous ways. The determination of fire origination involves consideration of the following: culpable negligence and accidental or intentional origination. Pinpointing origination requires investigative technical and interview skill.

Children who have suffered accidental or intentional fire-related injury either physically or emotionally require specialized care and handling within the context of criminal investigations and associated interviews. Investigative ability, versatility, and flexibility are foundational needs during an interview with a suspected FDP-related criminal offender. A frequently seen high threshold of significant child injury found within FDP cases that involve an element of fire often exerts a heavy emotional toll upon investigative professionals. Communication barriers between the interviewer(s), victim, and parent(s) of the victim have to be overcome and interview challenges have to be conducted. One or more of the victim's parents may also be suspects or defendants in the case (Figure 14.3).

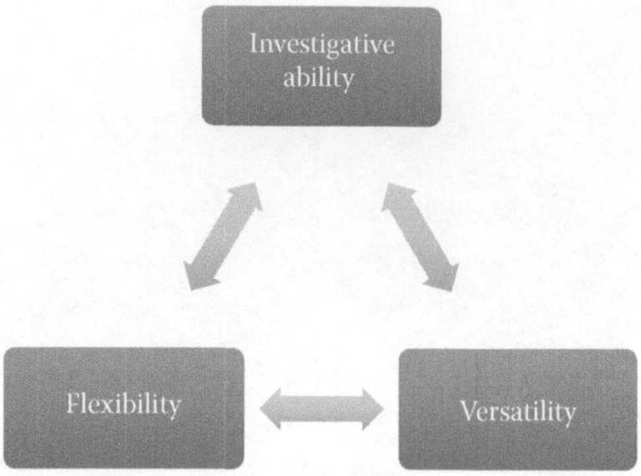

Figure 14.3 Fundamental concepts as an FDP investigator.

Children and Trust

Within an investigative interview, the process that children utilize to determine trust within an adult is guided by environment and perceived sincerity. Children who perceive that they are *in trouble* either by guilt, action, or inaction become threatened and cannot or will not necessarily disclose difficult experiences (i.e., abuse). Threats produce fear in the child and may allude to punishment, embarrassment, sorrow, or shock (Figure 14.4).

Fear can be manifested in displaced aggression, introversion, or shock. To obtain access to information possessed by a witness or victim, threats must be relieved. Tapping into a victim's or witnesses' courage to facilitate verbalization of abusive experiences requires victims or witnesses to overcome their fears. Conquering fear is facilitated when an interviewer establishes trust within an interview through bonding that predicated upon an open dialogue beyond the reproach of insincerity. Interviewers who lie to interview subjects risk total incapacitation if untruths are discovered because credibility and associated trust is eliminated. Positive communication between the interviewer and subject is possible even in dire situations but requires elemental investigative masking skill to achieve a productive interview while maintaining honesty. The confidence held by the interviewer is key and a testament to skill usually achieved through experience.

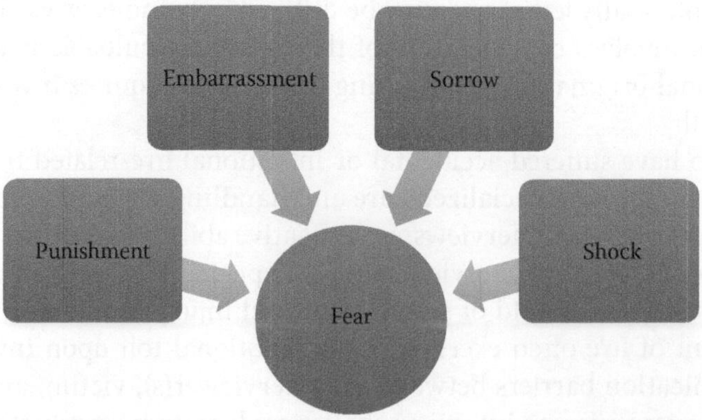

Figure 14.4 Victim response to fire victimization.

Young children may not possess necessary cognitive skills to verbalize traumatic events they have witnessed or participated in. A child's communicative level may be measured through preliminary assessment and be revealed through playacting, drawing, observation, or interaction. Adaptation of specialized interview skills should be gauged to the child's maturity level. The interviewer should speak to the child in the language of the child at the level demonstrated. Some situations involve great physical injury either experienced or witnessed by the child, and traumatization may affect the child's communicative ability due to shock, fear, or shame. The interviewer must judge and utilize the appropriate communicative level needed and be flexible to adjust interview protocol accordingly.

Environment of the Interview

Environment and timing are primary concerns when accessing interview locations for victims or witnesses involved in fire-related FDP situations. At fire sites, a successful interview requires forethought. It may not be enough to visually remove the fire scene from a victim's or witnesses' view because the smell of fire permeates and overshadows everything. When human beings are involved in a fire, the smell is unmistakable and unforgettable. For children involved in fires, fire scene sight and smell perpetuate fear and prevent a needed bond establishment required to produce an effective interview outcome.

Persons in or near a selected interview site are distractions to child witnesses who may not possess the ability to focus on more than one thing at a time. An area that is least intimidating to a child witness is one that affords visual and audio privacy without instilling fear. Specialized interview rooms designed for children such as those located within many police departments or child protective agencies are optimum. If this type of facility is not available, the interviewer must evaluate what is available and select an area deemed most conducive to conduct an interview. Locations that have produced successful interview results with children at the site of fire scenes include the following: vacated spare bedrooms, interiors or vehicles, and open outdoor areas away from the fire scene such as public parks. Child interview locations not recommended include closets, rooms with many toys, and areas of high people concentration (malls, theme parks, movie theaters). Traumatized children may deem isolation with an interviewer threatening or as punishment. To minimize misinterpretation, locking or tightly closing interview room doors should be avoided. Within the seclusion of an interview, reassuring the child of intentions and explaining the process of the interview is recommended.

Parents of Adolescent Burn Victims

Observation Demand

When children are interview subjects, parents generally tend to be quite concerned and may demand to be present during the interview process. The decision to allow or disallow a parent within sight of a child during an interview encompasses legal and social factors. Facilitating physical parental presence while interviewing children creates interview quality concern and affects potential interview outcome. Nonverbal control exerted by parental presence may cause a child witness to withhold, fabricate, or falsify information. If the parent is also a suspect within the criminal investigation at hand, extreme factors of fear and manipulation to the child interview subject are presented.

The use of specialized interview rooms containing surveillance or observation mirrors are excellent alternatives to the physical presence request often presented by the parent(s) of child interviewees. Allowing parents to observe the interview of their children in this manner alleviates their concerns and preserves the integrity of the interview. For most law enforcement and social service agencies, established interview protocol provides unilateral guidance regarding child interview locations and procedures.

Emotional Factors

Burn injuries and associated treatment are painful. If you have ever experienced a body burn, you clearly understand the pain component associated with even the slightest burn injury. Adults who encounter a child burn injury victim may experience emotional instability commensurate with understanding of burns and in accordance with the visual victim damage they may witness. A person's emotional response to appalling injury, especially in a child, is typically unpredictable and varied. Genuine caretaker reactions may indicate sincerity but gauging validity within those reactions is difficult to assess. An FDP offender is a master at disguising or hiding the truth—in all forms including reactionary response. When the parent of a burn victim is also a suspected abuser utilizing an FDP delivery system, astute observation is required; are you seeing genuine parental reaction or a carefully orchestrated deviation of reactionary norm?

Keeping an open mind is important for interviewers addressing the magnitude of child burn injury cases especially those containing a potential FDP element. Parental reaction to children critically burned can be contrary to what is expected. Reaction alone does not establish the element of guilt. Witness or parental reaction is also affected by potential participation level in arson situations, shock regarding fire outcome, continuation of FDP methodologies, anger to the point of homicide toward persons responsible for the child's burn injury (nonoffending parents), guilt to the point of suicide for failure to prevent the child's burn injury, or total apathy related to withdrawal altogether from the situation (Figure 14.5).

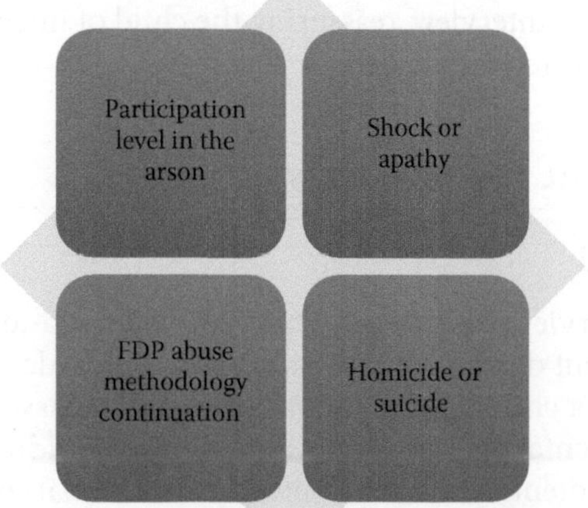

Figure 14.5 Parental reactions to FDP victim burn injuries.

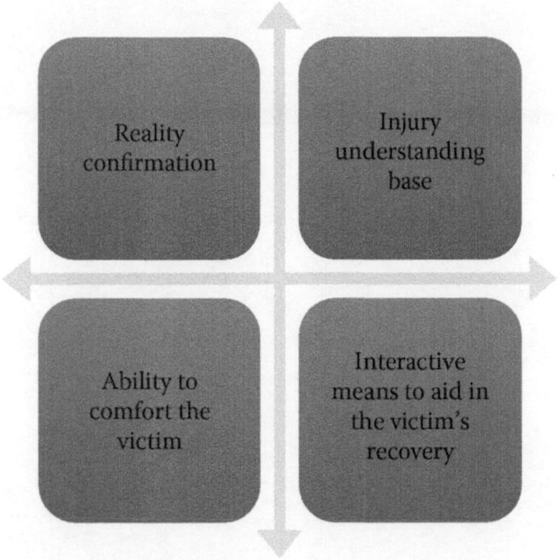

Figure 14.6 Visualization of FDP victim burn injuries.

When parents are culpably negligent for children's injuries, demonstrated extreme emotional initial responses may be followed by total shut down. Parental realization that a child has been either critically or fatally burned normally elicits a desire of the parent to be with the child to visually understand what has happened and to comfort the victim. Visualization of a child's injuries provides confirmation that the injury and medical condition is real, an understanding base of the victim's medical condition, the ability to comfort the child, and interactive means to aid in the victim's recovery (Figure 14.6).

If a parental reaction to a child's injury is abstinence then suspicion regarding injury responsibility should be considered. Parental absence from a child burn victim may include direct refusal to see the child, (feigned) physical illness that would preclude child access, overwhelming concern for matters other than the health status of the child, or abandonment. Intentional or unintentional fire origin may directly or indirectly link to parental culpability after thorough investigations. Fact-finding linked to evidentiary procurement is often a prolonged process within fire investigations embellished with an FDP factor and incorporates intricate spheres of investigative collaboration (Figure 14.7).

Accepted Norms and Media Influence

Media generally provides community education regarding fire details when children are involved in fires. Investigators often overlook the opportunistic tool the media represents within potential criminal case resolution. Fire cases involving child death or injury are noteworthy media events viewed by the public often producing public opinion and the identification of unknown event witnesses.

When the suspected abuse of a child is linked to questionable parental actions found within the FDP methodology continuum and case law regarding those action types is new or undeveloped, public opinion matters greatly. Law guides the manner of child abuse or child homicide prosecution, but there is a human element within case direction for unique or new situation types. The human element is prosecutorial stance, and it is affected by public or community standards. The issue of culturally acceptable behavior may play a role

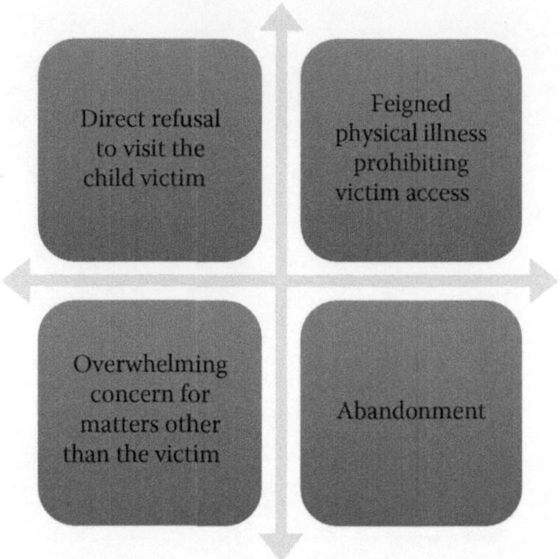

Figure 14.7 Suspect (offender) behavior in child burn cases.

in final case outcome and be kept within a closed circle if a case is not publicized. People have opinions regarding the abuse of children in any format. When child abuse or child death is heinous and caused by the actions of an individual, the public often demands restitution and people come forward to aid in that endeavor crossing cultural, familial, ethnic, and social boundaries in the process. Standards of culturally accepted norm within individual communities may ultimately allow criminal behavior to go unpunished but tolerance levels vary by location, person, and prevalent cultural attitude.

Parents criminally charged with child abuse or death generally elicit sympathy from familial individuals and judgment from strangers. The closer the community, the greater the likelihood of extended *familial* boundaries. In this sense of *familial contact*, individuals not biologically related to the suspect are connected through association or cause. Publicizing questionable actions or inactions of a suspect unlocks citizens' mouths—generally through anger—creating a personal inability to abide by former community or cultural standards. Pressure is exerted on the criminal justice system to act as the gravity of criminal acts upon a child victim tug at the hearts of strangers and family alike.

Media coverage of FDP child abuse or homicide cases has produced witnesses that have come forward advising on previously unreported child abuse and child-involved fire situations. These situations have been germane to the current event being analyzed. The existence of unreported abuse may become elemental in determination of present case direction and disposition. Residents in close proximity to the child abuse/death location (neighbors) often observe neglect or other behaviors that they do not associate as important. Through media coverage of a child injury event, these same neighbors may step forward voluntarily because they are angry. A community's level of acceptance, and therefore silence, commonly seen in child burn injury investigations fluctuates but has been known to become a driving force in criminal case prosecution.

Additional Witnesses in Burn Injury Investigations

Adolescent burn injury victims and their siblings are potential witnesses. Information provided by siblings of burn victims is often insightful in the context of present and historical family information. In burn injury cases where child neglect is suspect, there is a likelihood that social service agencies interacted with the family prior to the present event and records associated with potential contact should be reviewed.

For child burn injury, fire injury investigations whose origin is initially unknown, careful documentation of witness or suspect activity is required. When determining the cause of the fire requires prolonged investigative analysis of evidence or sustained/repetitive witness interviews, initial observations are important to document. An investigative interview stance is developed from collective review of all case aspects. When the cause of victim harm is unknown, origin of causation theory is the first step in proving causation and establishing an investigative stance. The stance or angle of the investigation may change during the course of the inquiry as adjustments provide modification within case development. Interviewers are required to maintain flexibility to address the unique nature of each developing case investigation.

Case Report

A police department in a large midwestern city received a series of complaints from a young married couple who had two preschool-aged sons. Jeff, the husband, worked the night shift at a local company. Mary, his wife, did not work outside the home and was not pleased with her husband's work schedule.

Just after Halloween, Mary reported a residential burglary. Some of Mary's clothes were reported missing including lingerie. Mary later reported to the police that a large red heart had been drawn on the windshield of her vehicle. A week later, while the family was in church, a burglar apparently once again burglarized the family home, entered through a broken window, but nothing was taken. After this burglary, Mary began finding red hearts all around the house that were drawn in lipstick, red marker, and crayon. The hearts were in notebooks, blouses, and panties.

Mary continued to report strange events to local law enforcement approximately every 10 days. These events included a small doll with red markings found on the porch, a doll with an attached noose found hanging from a bunk bed, and teddy bears with the words "dead" or "die" written on them and found in the yard.

A police detective was stationed in the family residence during Jeff's working hours for 10 days and no events occurred. While at the residence, the detective noted that if he mentioned a like for a certain food, when he returned to the residence, Mary would offer her homemade version of the item. The couple received counseling from the police who considered them crime victims. Valentine's day arrived and Mary received chocolates in the mail containing razor blades.

A fire started in the residence during March and the fire department was called to the residence four more times in the following weeks. Without the residents' knowledge, a sophisticated surveillance camera was deployed for exterior monitoring. Detectives had previously informed the residents of all investigative measures relating to this case. Within a week, Mary was observed on camera dropping mutilated dolls, stuffed animals, and threatening notes on the front porch. She was also observed starting a fire at the front door.

Mary was arrested and interviewed by the detective who was previously stationed at the house. Mary stated that she started the fire and dropped items on the porch because the police were losing interest in the case. She later admitted to placing all evidentiary items at the house and committing the first arson. Mary pled guilty and received probation with mandatory counseling. The police had spent 5 months and many thousands of dollars investigating 30 separate victimization reports. After completing probation, Mary and her family relocated. Shortly after relocation, a physician contacted suspecting that Mary was giving her child large amounts of laxatives. The result of that matter is unknown.

Please note that when police began to suspect Mary was making factitious reports, inquires revealed that Mary had reported being the recipient of threatening calls and notes while in college. Mary's domineering father removed her from the school when the police failed to solve the case.[3]

Ritualistic Abuse by Fire

Fire injury involving ritualistic child abuse occurs. The motive for an offender to harm a child through the medium of fire is difficult to conceptualize and more difficult to address once revealed. When a child is injured through the medium of fire, in-depth inquiry into the social/religious background of the suspect and an evaluation of the regular behavioral activities are required.

What is revealed from the accumulation of facts related to historical fact-finding from the platform of a current criminal case investigation will help determine potential causation and aide in formulating the investigative case plan. Known parameters of FDP abuse found within historical evaluation of a suspect in fire-related child injury or involvement may indicate abuse with an FDP factor. Looking at background factors from a religious view may illuminate a totally different motivation platform and/or one that is interlinked within the FDP abuse continuum. Ritualistic child abuse containing a fire element that is committed during the execution of a religious rite or at the direction of a religiously backed belief system may result in intentional or unintentional child harm. The investigative interview is preeminently important to determine the reason(s) why a perpetrator's actions leading to child burn injury occurs.

The difference between a child burn injury produced within the FDP continuum versus child burn injury intentionally or unintentionally attained within the scope of a religiously backed action plan requires specialized investigatory background and technical expertise. The interviewer should be aware that within fire injury child abuse cases, identified warning indicators should be an alert of suspect involvement. The presence of a victim's chronic illness history of unknown etiology and prior multigeographical, residential, and hospitalization history are FDP abuse indications. When the examination of variant locations link to geographic areas of known alternative religious practices, inquiry into the intricacies of identified variant faiths is warranted. Some religious views and culturally specific attitudes reflect a view that ill children are expendable or treatable within the parameters of a faith that is contrary to U.S. law. Caretakers of chronically ill children within this grouping may seek unconventional means in order to heal their children through religious rites involving the use of fire as a cleansing agent. The development of intentional homicidal actions may also result. The intentional or accidental infliction of fire-related child abuse by a caretaker within the scope of religious freedom could be present. Motive determination is critical in the establishment of causative origin.

Gauging Parental Response

A suspect's age and cultural exposure should be considered as background factors during the investigation of fire-related child abuse or death. An interviewer needs to understand that in most situations (non-FDP related), children are usually *manageable* unless they are ill. Ill children place greater stress on caretakers that often requires unlimited extraneous parental dedication, especially when the illness is chronic. People tend to place value on objects or other people that often reflects attitude regarding the value of life itself. A mother who bears a child at a very young age may later feel resentment and lament that her own childhood was taken away. Extreme resentment focused toward the child may become evident and reflected in various abuse-related situations. Of hatred for a child may be repressed while open expressions observations outside remain clouded. As a young mother experiences the stress of parenthood while observing the lifestyle of peers, many feelings occur including an understanding that her life is different, feeling that the lifestyle of her peers is unattainable, isolation, fear, entrapment, and anger. Demonstrated child neglect may result and precipitate a critical abuse incident. Certainly, in-place support systems affect the likelihood of this progression, but it is important to recognize that these pathways can exist (Figure 14.8).

Stress associated with single parenthood (real or perceived) is astronomical for a young parent of an ill child. The responsibility of parenting usually falls to the mother of the child for many reasons that include mate abandonment prior to birth, or thereafter, or in-place emotional mate abandonment (stress related).

The mother of an ill child may be under distress and find it difficult to admit her true feelings toward the child. Resentment may be prevalent but unstated, and she may blame the child for perceived wrongs within her life. Society will not normally sanction the abdication of parental responsibility of a child through avenues of abandonment/neglect or homicide. The result may be perceived parental entrapment that manifests resolution through the creative means of FDP abuse or disguised child abuser within a forum of fire-related injury. Invention of socially acceptable explanation for a child's illness or demise

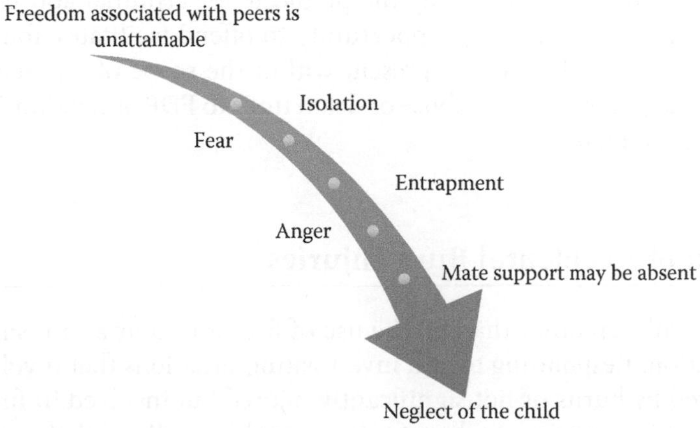

Figure 14.8 The pathway to FDP child victimization.

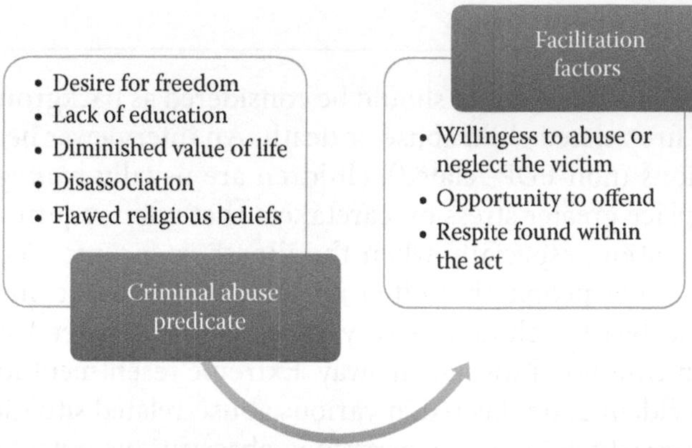

Figure 14.9 Criminal abuse and facilitation factors.

when it is fabricated or otherwise criminally linked is a creative process. Interviewers should review the totality potential of criminal abuse or death situations against the reasonableness of injury explanations to determine the likelihood of deception. A parent torn by the desire to gain personal freedom and parental love may justify harm and child injury in the name of parental discretion by fabricating causative factor or denying knowledge altogether.

When explanations are absent or causation undetermined regarding fire origination and subsequent victim injury or death, suspicion factors should escalate. The maturing process of a healthy child gradually adds parental responsibility that theoretically diminishes over time. Parental responsibility of a permanently ill child begins and remains constant over the lifetime of the parent. The origin of the permanent illness (real or fabricated) is irrelevant. FDP offenders who create signs/symptoms of illness in their victims that gravitate to permanent victim abnormality or parents who are responsible for children permanently abnormal naturally will understand exactly how that personally affects them. A desire for freedom, lack of education, lack of respect for the life of the child, disassociation, and flawed religious beliefs lay the predicate for criminal abuse. Willingness to neglect or abuse the victim and the opportunity to offend facilitates abusive acts. When predicate and facilitation factors are present within the scope of a potential abuse case, looking deeply into possible victim abuse or death links to FDP or religiously based assaults is warranted (Figure 14.9).

Investigation of Accidental Burn Injuries

The burning of children other than by the use of fire can occur as a result of intentional or accidental action. Responding to and investigating situations that involve children that have been injured by burns or not significantly injured but involved in fires encompasses many components. Interviewers benefit from understanding distinctive symptomology that exists between burns caused by deliberate abuse and burns of accidental nature. The key component within either causation type is found within interview dialogue of witnesses, victims, and suspects and the ability of the interviewer to recognize verbal and nonverbal statements. The ability of the victim to disclose the nature of the burn is often nonexistent due to ability, injury, or fear (of retaliation).

Suspected burns of water origin require specific investigatory steps to substantiate offender culpability. Water becomes the vehicle of injury, and water temperature is paramount in criminal linkage.

When children sustain painful and disfiguring injuries and the origin is suspected criminal behavior, interviewers are required to control their emotions. Personal ability to control the eagerness to arrest the perpetrator or an agency-promoted desire to swiftly conclude a case must be tempered with the reality of evidentiary required element. Once a crime has occurred, the case detective has the ability to control case quality through investigative ability, emotional containment, and the application of patience. The timetable for case investigations is predicated only by the statute of limitations.

Using Fire within the World of FDP

Most fire(s) associated with FD/FDP are not initially classified as arson. Victim injury in FDP cases is a result of direct and indirect actions, and criminal cases are built upon both circumstantial and pathological elements. Arson classification generally occurs after FDP victim identification following prolonged abuse or the recognition of repetitive FD false criminal reporting. Direct victim injury in fires emulates from the measurable elements of smoke and heat and the effect of flames, but in FDP situations, circumstantial versus pathological evidence is analyzed as fire causation is sought. The evaluation of evidence provides clarity to concealed yet direct cause versus effect when fire is the medium used by an FDP offender. The time factor involved in fire-related FDP abuse is realized within FDP offender benefit examination as it relates to victim hospitalization. When FDP victims are involved in fire-related injury or situations and no link is made to arson, the FDP abuse continuum proceeds unabated.

Significance of Fire

The presence of household fire situations within the life of an FDP offender or FD-related situation has been repetitively identified. Case review indicates that one or more fires may precipitate FDP abuse events, and warning indicators were present but not recognized by assigned arson investigators. In all identified cases of FDP with a fire element, the offender's life was actually or perceived as less than optimal for various reasons.

When something is burned, it either disappears or is discarded due to damage. Fire occurring before or after associated FD/FDP behavior has tangible and intangible results. Tangible benefits include the destruction of evidence (which may include the victim) and a visual reaffirmation of injury or criminal victimization. Intangible benefit includes public sympathy and aid, refocused spousal attention, perceived improvement of a domestic relationship, and hospitalization of the victim (FD or FDP attention continuation).

FD/FDP Offender Benefits Resulting from Fire

Fires that occur within the realms of FDP may be viewed as attempts to cleanse an imperfect or undesirable domestic situation by erasing its memories and/or as a directed victim injury or homicide vehicle (Figure 14.10).

People who experience a household fire may experience property loss but usually feel fortunate if personal injury is averted. This *norm* is often not accurate in the life of an FDP offender. When property is viewed with priority status rather than the life of a child, indications of a potential FDP offender's misguided value system is presented. Specific items that take on significant value, such as a baby book or photos that appear more important than a child victim, may be an indication of reality versus fantasy confusion. The *perfection and sterility* of a photo cannot be replaced with the reality of a live child and all associated challenges. Placing primary value upon *things* within the setting of a household fire diminishes the value of survivors or of lost life. The significance of the loss of a *baby book*, the FDP offender places extremely high value upon, can be telling. When a mother looks at a baby book, she sees the *perfectness* of her child in a sanitized environment, it is like looking at a child through a looking glass. Reality is not necessarily contained within a baby book yet this loss is often significant to FDP offenders. Loss of this book may represent the loss of perfectionism utilized by the FDP offender to bridge a gap between reality and fantasy. An FDP offender's decision to inflict victim harm is possibly made at the point of fire institution because perfectionism yields to harsh reality and choices are made.

Gratification Scale of FDP Arson

Fire can be viewed as cleansing in many applications. When forests are burned, there is an ending of life that later produces the foundation of rebirth. People who are involved in fires often see it as the ending of a portion of their life but a beginning of the next. Practical

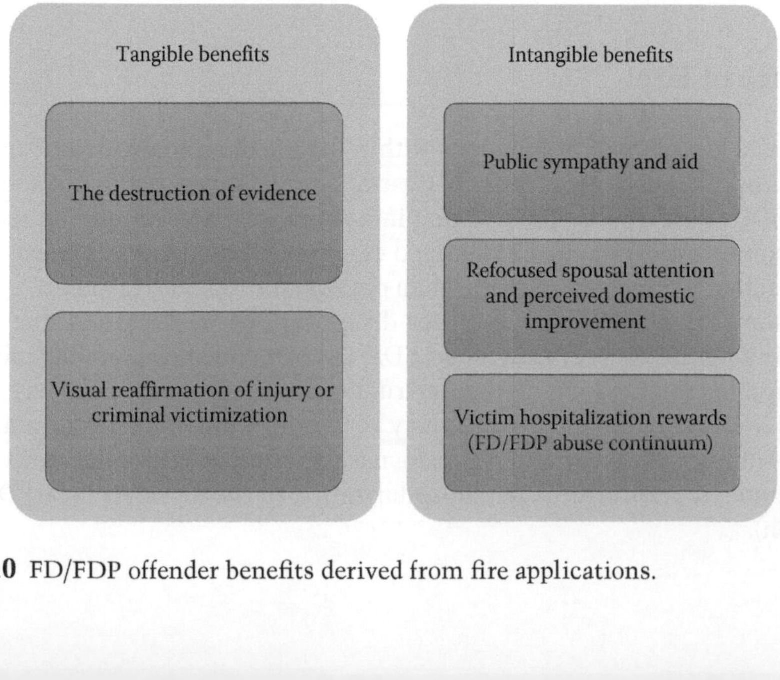

Figure 14.10 FD/FDP offender benefits derived from fire applications.

people view their involvement in a fire as devastation producing financial and emotional hardship; not all people are practical. In FD/FDP situations where offenders are arsonists, testing and modification occur in much the same manner as seen in the FDP abuse continuum. Initial fires may be viewed as a test of the offender's ability to utilize fire as a tool. Secondary fires are likely improved versions of initial testing. The continued pattern of fire use within an FDP setting appears to be a building process of offender skill.

Measurement of fire results in an FDP mode seems to reinforce justification for setting them and provides an offender the element of abuse infliction confidence. Confidence is amplified over time when the offender's actions remain undetected. Careful examination of primary and subsequent fire offender benefits is likely to reveal a pattern of indirect or intangible rewards. Infliction versus reward is an elemental system within FDP abuse. Reward within FDP abuse or FDP abuse associated with arson is *subtle and indirect.* Reward is personal rather than public and valuable only to the offender usually in the form of attention and verification of self-worth. Recognition of the presence of this reward may be difficult to establish unless awareness of potential existence and knowledge of the FDP continuum are tools in the investigator's belt. The following gratification scale provides examples of FDP arson offenders and anticipated personal gain (Figure 14.11):

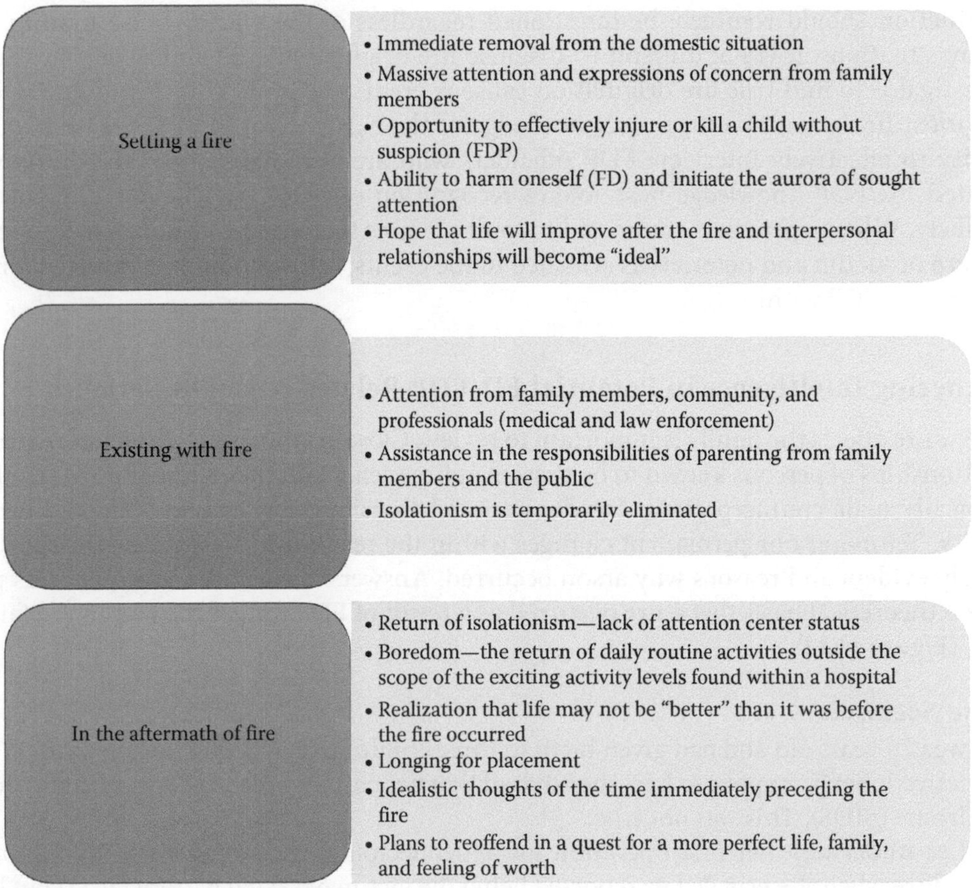

Figure 14.11 Gratification scale for FDP arson offenders.

By the Hand of God

When an FDP offender is challenged regarding fire origination, explanations generally have a wide range that include environmental and inorganic sourcing. Lightning strikes, faulty electrical equipment, and the actions of mysterious unidentified arsonists are some explanations given by known FDP abusers utilizing arson.

Lightning strikes carry a particular inference relating to application by a higher entity associated with an act of God by persons of various religious backgrounds. When FDP offenders possess apparent strong religious backgrounds, family members are generally also religiously attuned. Lightning is sometimes viewed as God's way of communicating with believers. From this understanding, offenders and their family members may view the *lightning* that allegedly started a fire as God's way of directly communicating with believers. This belief may become the basis for an FDP offender's justification for victim abuse. The validity of the belief is irrelevant. Lightning has been historically described as "white fire" due to appearance. The color white is associated with purity and perfectionism.

Factor of Repetition

When families are involved in more than one fire in a relatively short time period, fire origination should routinely be questioned regardless of the *official* cause finding. For many situations, it is not difficult to disguise fire origination. The ability of a fire/arson investigator to find true fire origination cause is predicated upon ability and knowledge. For most fire arson investigators, knowledge of the existence of FD/FDP is limited; the ability to effectively interview FDP offenders who are also arsonists is also limited. A limited FD/FDP knowledge base makes recognition of FD/FDP behavior difficult and unlikely. When a person is connected to multiple fires that involve children in a capacity of *hero* or victim and notoriety is attached to the events, cases should be evaluated for the element of FDP within.

Gathering Intelligence in Potential FD/FDP-Related Arson Situations

How a fire affects the family is important to review. Close examination of the interpersonal relationships of persons known to be present at fire scenes and their close family members (typically male counterparts in the domestic relationship) may provide offender benefit clarity. Temporary or permanent changes within the relationship may either be subtle or clearly evident and reasons why arson occurred. Answers to the following questions provide a theoretical basis that a fire occurred as a result of FDP influences within the family unit (Figure 14.12):

Case Scenario

Lee was 26 years old and had given birth to three children, two of which were dead. When Detective Joliet first spoke to Lee, she advised that her children died of sudden infant death syndrome (SIDS). This was not true.

Lee underwent her first operation for appendectomy when she was 13 and another procedure when she was 17. Lee reported being the victim of sexual battery (at 17) but later recanted the allegation. Six months later, Lee's sister—Fran—gave birth to an apparently

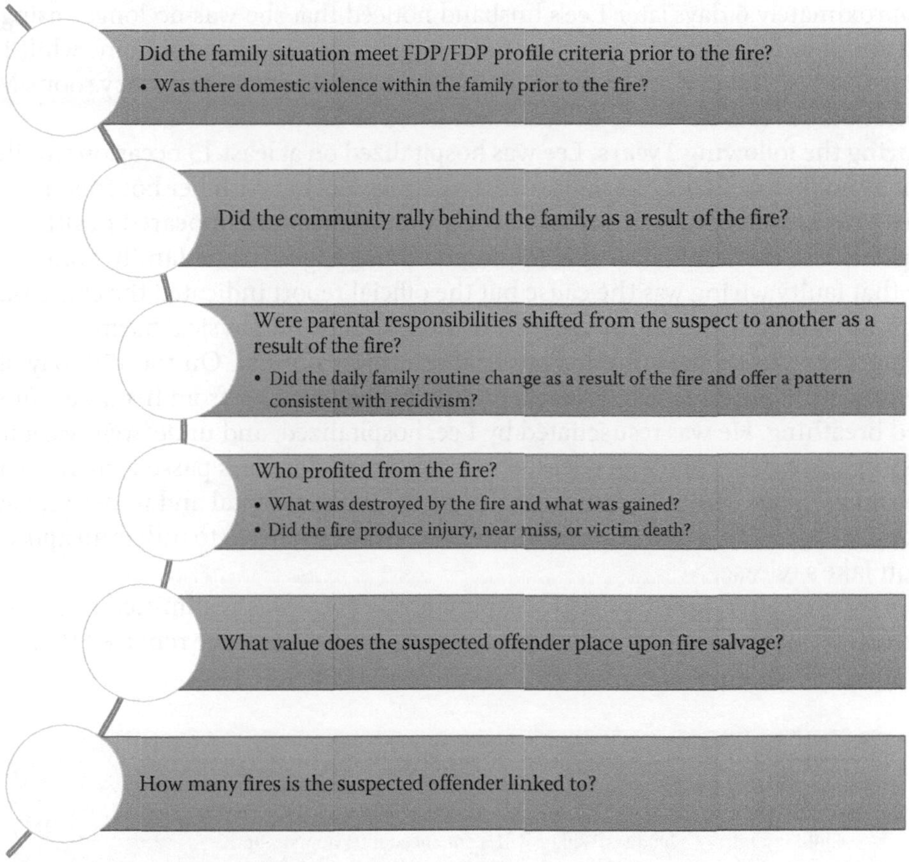

Did the family situation meet FDP/FDP profile criteria prior to the fire?
• Was there domestic violence within the family prior to the fire?
Did the community rally behind the family as a result of the fire?
Were parental responsibilities shifted from the suspect to another as a result of the fire?
• Did the daily family routine change as a result of the fire and offer a pattern consistent with recidivism?
Who profited from the fire?
• What was destroyed by the fire and what was gained?
• Did the fire produce injury, near miss, or victim death?
What value does the suspected offender place upon fire salvage?
How many fires is the suspected offender linked to?

Figure 14.12 FD/FDP arson intelligence gathering.

healthy son (Joel). From birth to 5 months, Joel repeatedly stopped breathing for no apparent reason. Joel died during the fifth month of his life. Fran committed suicide but Lee told everyone that Fran had been murdered.

Over the next 3 years, Lee was hospitalized approximately 25 times for various ailments of known and unknown causes.

When Lee was 22, she gave birth to her first child, Melanie, who appeared healthy at birth. When Melanie was 20 days old, she stopped breathing and was resuscitated by Lee. Melanie was hospitalized for 3 days and discharged. Twelve days later, Lee reported that Melanie had a high fever and was rehospitalized. The existence of the fever could not be verified. Within the hospital, in the sole presence of Lee, Melanie's IV became disconnected and she stopped breathing. Melanie was transferred to a larger prominent teaching hospital. Four days passed and no further problems occurred; Melanie was discharged to home.

Melanie had been home with Lee for approximately 10 days when Melanie's bedroom caught on fire. The cause of the fire appeared to be a defective light. Lee and her husband were experiencing domestic difficulty at the time of the fire and planned to relocate. Lee was treated for chest pain. Three days following the fire, Lee reported that her husband had abused her. Ten days later, Lee appeared at her doctor's office with visual signs of facial battery.

Approximately 6 days later Lee's husband noticed that she was no longer using a prescribed apnea monitor for Melanie. The following day, Melanie died at home while in Lee's care. Postmortem lividity was present when Melanie reached the emergency room. Melanie was 3 months old and her cause of death was listed as SIDS.

During the following 2 years, Lee was hospitalized on at least 15 occasions for illnesses that could not be verified. Lee established a new relationship with her boyfriend and when she was 24 years old gave birth to her second child (Jake). Jake appeared healthy at birth. During the first weeks of Jake's life, a household fire engulfed the family home. Lee told people that faulty wiring was the cause but the official report indicated the cause was a fire ignited in a trashcan. The family escaped without significant physical harm.

When Jake was 16 days old, his physical exam was normal. On the 17th day of Jake's life, he was at home alone with Lee, reportedly began bleeding from his mouth/nose and stopped breathing. He was resuscitated by Lee, hospitalized, and underwent various invasive testing procedures and was released into Lee's care. Ten days passed when Lee reportedly found blood in Jake's stool; he was readmitted to the hospital and underwent surgery. At 34 days of age he then was released into Lee's care. Lee refused to utilize an apnea monitor upon Jake's release.

Shortly thereafter, Jake reportedly experienced apnea, was readmitted to the hospital, had no further apnea episodes, and was released. The next day, Lee reported that Jake was

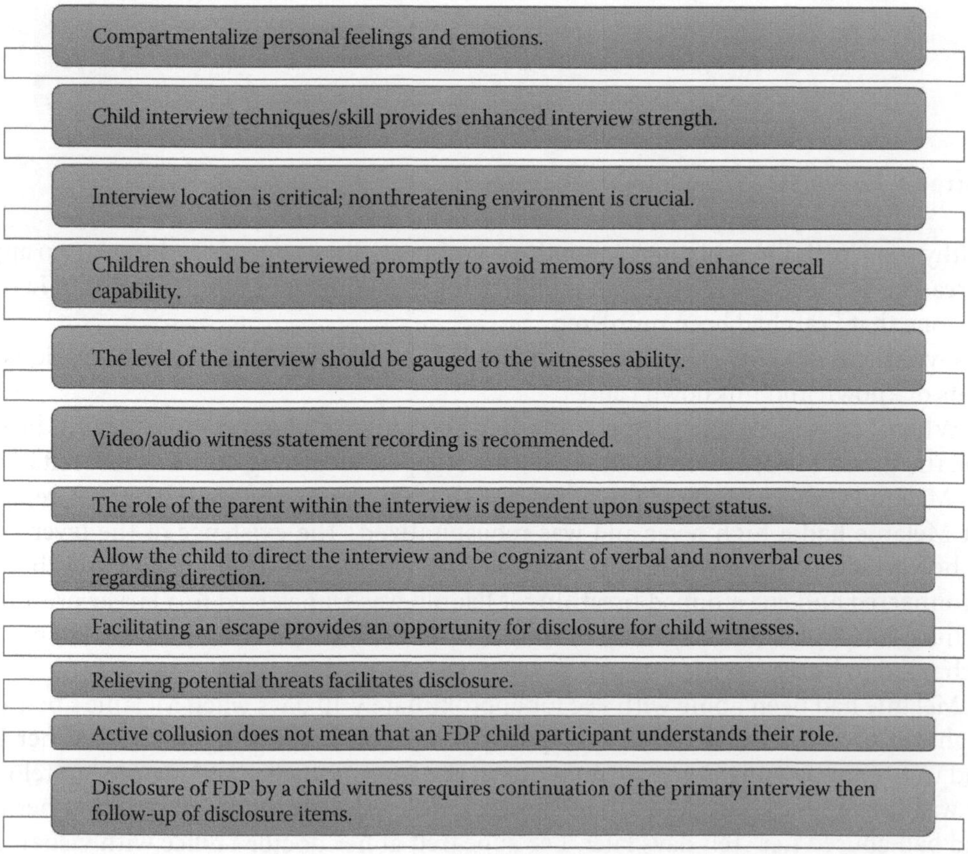

Compartmentalize personal feelings and emotions.
Child interview techniques/skill provides enhanced interview strength.
Interview location is critical; nonthreatening environment is crucial.
Children should be interviewed promptly to avoid memory loss and enhance recall capability.
The level of the interview should be gauged to the witnesses ability.
Video/audio witness statement recording is recommended.
The role of the parent within the interview is dependent upon suspect status.
Allow the child to direct the interview and be cognizant of verbal and nonverbal cues regarding direction.
Facilitating an escape provides an opportunity for disclosure for child witnesses.
Relieving potential threats facilitates disclosure.
Active collusion does not mean that an FDP child participant understands their role.
Disclosure of FDP by a child witness requires continuation of the primary interview then follow-up of disclosure items.

Figure 14.13 Children and fire: interview tips.

having choking spells. Days later, Jake's continuing medical problems were reported by Lee, and Lee reported recent multiple miscarriages and underwent medical testing.

Thirteen days later, Jake appeared normal at his 2-month checkup. Twenty-eight days after that Lee reported that Jake stopped breathing and resuscitated him. Lee then rushed him to the doctor's office. This was the 1-year anniversary of Melanie's death.

During the next 4–5 months, both Lee and Jake were hospitalized for various illnesses. Jake was approximately 7 months old when Lee remarried. Six days after the marriage ceremony, Jake was found dead. The official cause of death was undetermined.

Four months after Jake's death, Lee stated that she attempted suicide but this could not be verified. Following that, she reported that her new husband raped her; this could not be substantiated.

Approximately 18 months passed when Lee gave birth to her third child, Renay, who was removed from the custody of Lee and appeared to be healthy. Lee was subsequently charged with the murder of Melanie and Jake (Figure 14.13).[4]

Conclusion

Not all repetitive fires within singular families will be connected to directed acts of arson. Not all arson that involves families with ill children will have an FD/FDP connection. When fire situations become suspect, an evaluation of the fire scenario should be linked to an FD/FDP investigative review; established links are indicative of arson. Reviewing fire origination causation within an FD/FDP context does not always occur at the time of the initial fire investigation and is initially dependent upon the education level of the arson investigator; a liaison between criminal and fire investigative units provides clarity.

Notes

1. Merriam-Webster.com., *Merriam-Webster*, n.d. Web. September 22, 2015. http://www.merriam-webster.com/dictionary/arson.
2. Café, T. and Stern, W., Is it accidental fire or arson? *Chemistry in Australia Magazine*, April 1989.
3. Artingstall, K. and Brubaker, L., Munchausen syndrome related offenses. *Law and Order Magazine*, October 1995:83–90.
4. Gentleman, G. and Hanon (Artingstall), K., Children in fire investigations. *Fire Engineering*, June 1991:12–14.

Criminality of FDP Abuse-Prosecutive Stance

15

No matter what people tell you, words and ideas can change the world.

Robin Williams

Criminality of FDP Actions

Complexity of FDP within Criminal or Civil Case Preparation

When people are crime victims, they generally know it. Criminal activity involves the breach of an intangible definitive line that has been crossed, and those on either side of that line generally understand that once the threshold is breached, there will be consequences. Criminal charges of murder, kidnapping, assault, fraud, sexual offenses, drug violations, federal criminal acts, and many others, which are all well defined statutorily, rest within this understanding. The same premise applies to the violation of a person's civil rights and associated litigation to address those alleged violations.

American laws and commensurate criminal sentencing guidelines exist to provide behavioral guidance and associated punishment for rule breaches. This premise could be black and white or gray. The concept of misbehavior and punishment may provide an amount of victim respite as the notion of criminal justice intercedes victimization pathways. Police agencies, prosecutors, and the forward extension of law through judiciary (on all levels) entwine themselves as stewards of justice on behalf of victimization and rely on a fundamental understanding of human behavior for effectiveness and fairness as they examine situations exacting accountability. A typical juror is the epitome of unbiased fairness, but jurors are human and their educational levels vary. The complexities of crimes, which occur circumscribed via a factitious disorder by proxy (FDP) factor, require juror education if the concept is brought forth and it is very confusing to the general public.

When a person has a clearly defined mental illness such as schizophrenia or depression or others and they commit a crime, people generally presume that the person afflicted is unable to control their behavior and therefore not responsible for their actions. Psychologists, psychiatrists, and a host of social work experts readily opine this very principle and it is a defensive posture in the arena of the judicial system. When this occurs, it may become a judicial or jury matter to apply responsibility judgment. Jurors make decisions based upon their understanding of human actions, the concept of right vs. wrong, acceptable vs. unacceptable behavior, and their understanding of law violation.

What people do to one another within the platform of harm, whether it be physical, emotional, or financial and what they fail to do whether it be failure to protect or neglect in vulnerable populations (such as children or the elderly) may offend and shock the core of generally acceptable human conduct. Behavior involving a factitious factor often distresses investigators (police and social service staff) and shocks the public. Interactive disbelief surrounding known facts and veiled actions may encompass the courtroom as each juror, judge, prosecutor, defense attorney, and media representative or observer views unspeakable horrors. Many ask how the defendant sitting in front of them, appearing stellar in all ways, could possibly have committed such atrocious acts upon often-helpless victims. Confusion is complicated with one's own emotions as determination of a defendant's responsibility for actions collides with the often-attempted relief defense of that responsibility due to a defendant's claimed mental status.

Understanding how the concept of factitious behavior collides between the psychological realm and the legal realm requires foundational background on both sides. *The Diagnostic and Statistical Manual of Mental Disorders* (Fifth edition; DSM–5; American Psychiatric Association, 2013) is the most widely accepted nomenclature used by clinicians and researchers for the classification of mental disorders.[1] Within the DSM-5 is found clinical concept definitions of behaviors—some associated with criminal conduct under certain conditions. When a person's conduct crosses the threshold of singularly defined mental illness into an intentional and therefore criminal behavior modality, the divide between these definitional behaviors becomes muddied. Criminal or civil case preparation requires expansive knowledge of both clinically defined abnormal behavior and criminally recognized illegal behavior. Differentiation is often shrouded in subtle nuances, confusion, and strategic options.

An argumentative question, often preliminarily associated within the suspicion stage of an FDP investigation, is whether or not the offender is mentally ill and thus absolved from the responsibility of their actions. In some cases, psychiatric disorders such as hysteric personality, borderline personality, narcissistic personality, depression, or others may be present, which does not necessarily mean that a person's actions are excused. In most situations involving an FDP factor, the offender seems to have an understanding of right vs. wrong.

I used to say unequivocally that "I had seen it all" and little would shock me. That is not true because as criminals learn what works for them and adapt to how system and law changes in their favor, crimes become more sophisticated and the mechanisms of cover-up or deception expand in complexity and severity. This requires anyone sitting in positions of judgment, investigation, or prosecution to have a vast array of education and conception while maintaining a keen sense of justice, as what is readily seen may not necessarily be indicative of the truth. Holding people responsible for covert actions entails understanding secondary pawn elements and the art of cover-up.

Defense attorneys have the most difficult job as advocates of person's accused of criminal behavior. Sometimes, the accused are honest with their defense attorneys and sometimes they are not. Guilt and the defense attorney's knowledge of that guilt may have little to do with justice as client-attorney privilege enters the equation. The standard for criminal arrest of an offender is probable cause that a crime has been committed. The bridge to a successful prosecution of that same individual is proof beyond a reasonable doubt. Sometimes, the bridge can seemingly be over an ocean.

In a civil trial, plaintiffs have the burden to prove each and every element of a civil case by a preponderance of the evidence (more likely than not or greater than 50% standard of certainty). In criminal trial, plaintiffs must prove someone guilty "beyond a reasonable doubt" or by nearly 100%. An issue of proximate cause—a defendant's actions or failure to act make possible foreseeable actions of another third party within the scope of victimization—may be at issue. The indirect result of a defendant's action or inaction causes a subsequent criminal act to occur that causes damage to the plaintiff.[2]

Prosecuting criminal acts shrouded in the deception of factitious behavior is complicated. Prosecutors often find that they must lay groundwork of psychological, medical, and legal understanding for jurors and the judge. Factitious-type behavior complicates and confuses people, and this confusion sometimes becomes a defensive posture as behavioral accountability is intertwined with responsibility relief due to alleged mental incapacity. The factor of intentional choice viewed through demonstrated action and cover-up is a crucial element in the assignment of accountability and subsequent punishment. Understanding concepts of factitious disorder, factitious disorder by proxy, mental illness, insanity, criminal acts of abuse, fraud, and others becomes a necessary task. A prosecutor simply not addressing a factitious factor in a criminal or civil case is a strategy call that may easily become a defensive posture.

When an abuse or homicide case has an FDP element, criminal prosecution of the offender occurs. To ensure effective prosecution, broad-spectrum FD/FDP knowledge is required to facilitate prosecutorial direction and anticipate likely defense strategies. FD/FDP knowledge allows the following: latitude to anticipate obstacles and provide the victim with his/her entitlement of a competent prosecutor; the ability to connect established offender criminal behavior within the format of known FD/FDP methodologies; and the ability to effectively anticipate the defense strategy of FD/FDP. A cognizance of potential victim lethality within the scope of FDP abuse is mandated because victim fatality potential is present in all abuse situations that are linked to the FDP abuse delivery factor (Figure 15.1).

The most effective criminal investigative procedures in FDP abuse or homicide cases are also the cornerstones of effective abuse or homicide criminal prosecutions that possess an FDP factor. Investigative procedures are tools that yield evidence substantiating or nullifying criminal prosecution. The most compelling evidence in criminal cases involving an FDP factor includes: video documentation of actual abuse events; toxicology screens; victim/offender separation data and analysis; and investigative interrogation results (Figure 15.2).

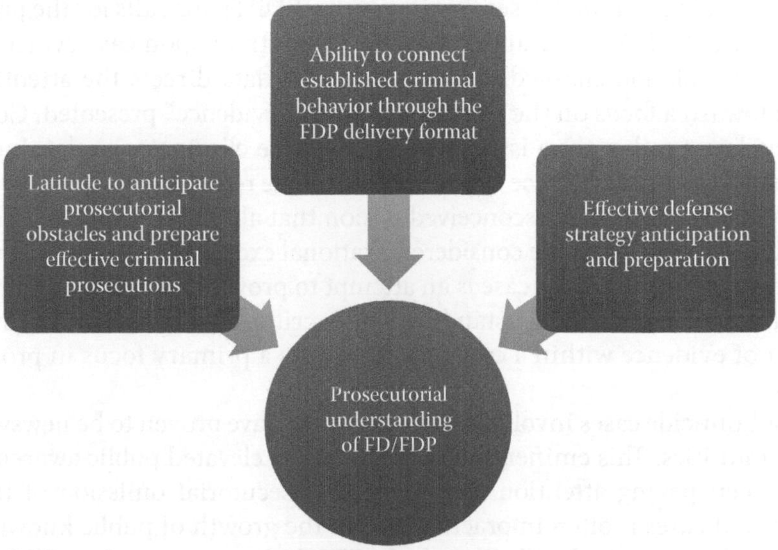

Figure 15.1 FD/FDP criminal prosecutorial strategy.

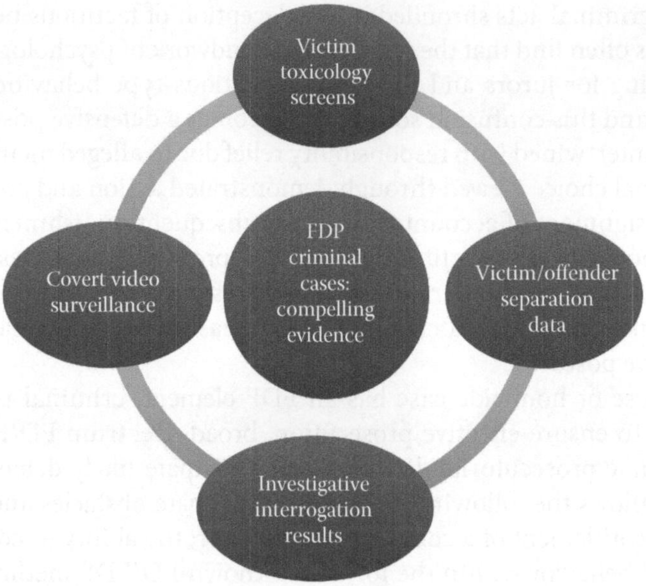

Figure 15.2 Criminal-law violations primary evidence.

Record review and FDP profile linkage help provide FDP case alignment that adds fuel to the prosecutorial position but like all other criminal cases, effective prosecution is based upon the establishment and presentation of evidence. In criminal cases of abuse, homicide, fraud, elder abuse, a medical scheme to defraud, or others, FDP is the method or mode of delivery utilized by the offender. FDP is not a criminal charge within itself.

Status of Exclusion

Suggested protocol in criminal cases that involve an FDP factor calls for the prosecution to generally exclude the FDP issue altogether and concentrate upon case evidence pertinent to the criminal violation charged. Exclusion of FDP data directs the attention of court deliberation toward a focus on the value of "definitive evidence" presented. Concentration upon case evidence rather than issues of FDP presence eliminates explaining situational FDP case complexity. An evidence-dominated rationale redirects focus onto victimization and away from the generally misconceived notion that all FDP offenders suffer from psychological illness(s) that could be considered a rational excuse for abusive behavior. A focus on FDP in an abuse or homicide case is an attempt to provide reasoning or explanation for why an offender victimizes. Understanding why is critical background information in the development of evidence within a case but not always a primary focus in prosecuting the criminal act.

Abuse or homicide cases involving the FDP factor have proven to be newsworthy items in most communities. This eminence has facilitated an elevated public awareness, and the defense has been paying attention. Preferential prosecutorial omission of the FDP element in criminal cases is often impractical due to the growth of public knowledge. Often, criminal cases that possess the likelihood of a FDP link are centered on FDP as a defense strategy. Justification for criminal acts or an alternative reasoning for false accusation by

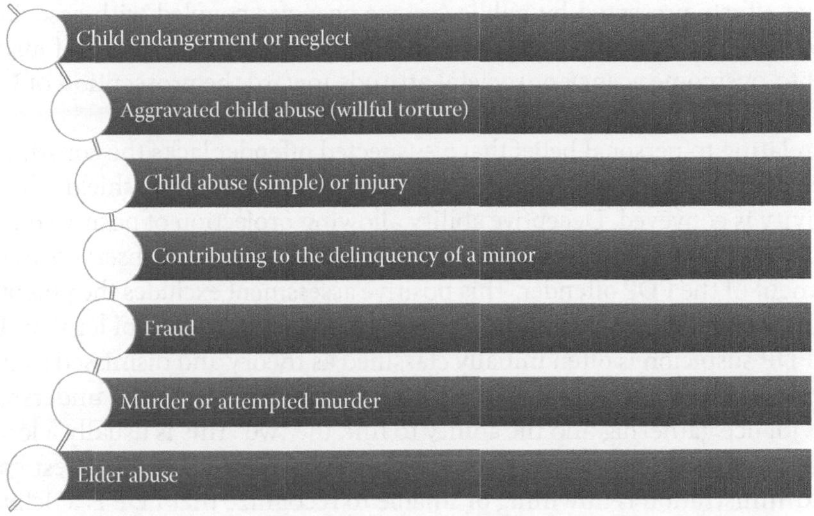

Child endangerment or neglect
Aggravated child abuse (willful torture)
Child abuse (simple) or injury
Contributing to the delinquency of a minor
Fraud
Murder or attempted murder
Elder abuse

Figure 15.3 Criminal-law violations linked to FDP behavior.

a nonoffending parent within civil/custodial litigation proceedings are ways that potential FDP abuse is bent. Abuse or homicide trials with an FDP factor may easily become deliberations regarding the FDP factor rather than the substantive charge as the central issue of offender accountability for abuse or homicide is lost in the process.

The issue of parenting ability relating to child dependency and custody may simultaneously be raised within criminal proceedings involving an FDP factor. Rationalization for termination of parental rights (when the parent is the suspected FDP offender) within the forum of dependency court may be laterally connected informally to criminal case proceedings. Dependency outcome often precedes criminal disposition enabling FDP influential factors in dependency court to authenticate defensive posture or prosecutorial stance in criminal court.

Dependency findings do not necessarily determine criminal case disposition but may affect outcome. It is incumbent upon criminal prosecutors to prepare for the potential influx of FDP as defense strategy emulating from various angles. Case clarity is attained by establishing a wide knowledge base and emphasizing the evidence of criminal conduct present rather than facilitating FDP as a predominant focus within trial by ignoring it altogether. The qualifier of domestic violence is present when the FDP offender is also the parent of the victim.

Criminal statutory law violations that have been identified or linked to an FDP delivery mode include those given in Figure 15.3.

Barriers to Effective Prosecution

There are many identified obstacles associated with the investigation of FDP. One of the most distressing issues is related to generalized societal attitudes regarding the value of children. Overcoming ingrained thinking that subconsciously or consciously places or detracts from the value of life due to a victim's age can be monumental. In some situations, the economic or social standing of a victim or victim's family reflects placement value.

Investigative efforts presented by public service agencies coupled with associative investigative cost factors fluctuates by case and location. Individual opinions of justice may be insufficient to overcome agency or societal attitude toward the prosecution of FDP offenders when (agency) managerial and/or community support is lacking.

Issues relating to personal belief that a suspected offender lacks the constitutionality to offend often create a barrier that the offender utilizes as a protective shield when suspicion of FDP activity is conveyed. Deceptive ability allowing projection of positive outward traits reinforced by apparently positive measurable deeds often entrench observers in their favorable assessment of the FDP offender. This positive assessment excludes the potential for suspicion or limits the effectiveness or possibility of a successful medical or legal probe into this suspicion. FDP suspicion is often initially classified as theory and dismissed as irrelevant.

Determination of the existence of FDP requires basic elemental understanding followed by evidence gathering and the ability to link the two. This is usually a long, arduous process that requires administrative support on medical and criminal investigative levels. If agency administration is unwilling or unable to recognize that FDP is a delivery system within a criminal context, they are also unlikely to view a suspected FDP offender as a potential threat, making victim intervention improbable.

The practical basis and positive resolution of legal intervention in FDP abuse or homicide cases emanates from knowledge. Procurement of knowledge provides detectives and prosecutors the power to achieve effective victim intervention. Knowledge also creates a crucial pathway of FDP understanding essential to sufficiently, properly, and expeditiously resolve criminal investigations with an FDP delivery factor in terms of victim justice (Figure 15.4).

A prosecutorial barrier is found in FDP reporting tendencies. Although statutorily mandated reporting of suspected child abuse by medical personnel is law, the medical community typically hesitates to report suspected FDP victimization until after abuse has persisted for quite some time. Fear of civil liability and an insufficient understanding of FDP appear to facilitate reporting reluctance. It is usually only after a victim crisis has arisen that suspected abuse with an FDP factor is reported. Evidence is often either stale

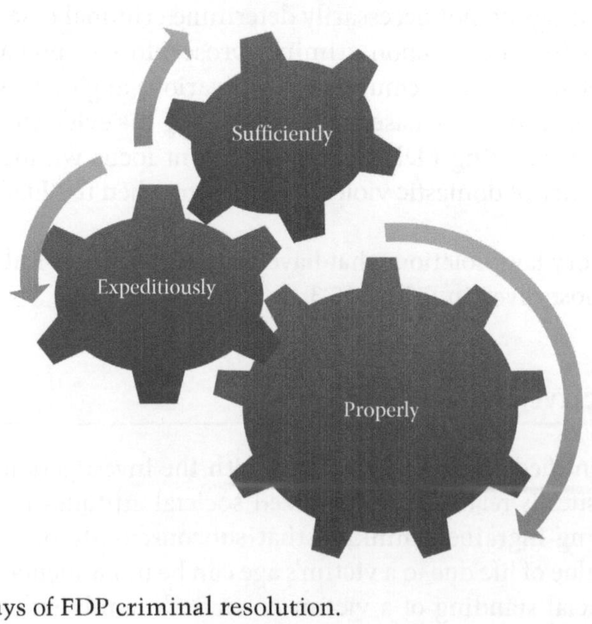

Figure 15.4 Pathways of FDP criminal resolution.

or lost as a result of reporting delay and the opportunity for covert surveillance prior to suspect awareness is diminished.[3]

Restricted information flow and facilitated manipulation of medical specialists by FDP offenders occur within the FDP continuum. Prosecutors may find that specialists do not communicate effectively with one another resulting in confusion, overlap, and excessive medical treatment for the victim. Review of the total patient medical package is critical in suspected cases of abuse or homicide with a FDP factor because confusion is a hallmark of FDP offender ability that facilitates the continuation of victim harm. Use of the multidisciplinary intervention team helps to provide necessary connective oversight.

When physicians actively assume the investigative role of an interrogator in abuse or homicide cases with an FDP factor, they cross into the domain of a law enforcement investigator. Subjects within the investigation may respond in a variety of ways including total shutdown, continued falsification of events, upsurge in victim illness, and other. When FDP offenders realize that their behavior is suspect by the acknowledgment of medical staff inquiry, they are afforded reactionary preplanning preparation-time for the likely next step—the involvement of law enforcement. Physicians are trained to listen to the parent and care for the child—they are neither inherently skilled in interrogation nor skeptical as most law enforcement investigators are. When a physician attempts to interrogate a suspected FD/FDP offender, their investigative skill is about as effective as the Officer's medical skill. Role reversal is not recommended.

Offender Accountability

The belief that FDP offenders victimize only their own biological children is false. Documented cases of FDP victim abuse when the offender acted in the capacity of a temporary custodian (babysitter or other caregiver) have occurred. The existence of these cases illuminates a *public safety domain threatened harm status* whenever FDP offenders are granted access to children.

FDP offender behavior has been likened to the actions of a pedophile through the apparently common existence of ingrained offender rationalization that permits child abuse or death to occur. Pedophilia and FDP are each considered behaviors—not mental health conditions of the offender or victim; these behaviors are not publicly viewed as excuses for victimization nor condoned. There is a presumption in abuse orchestrated by a pedophile or an FDP offender that both offenders possess an underlying understanding that their behavioral choices are unacceptable and criminal as defined by the laws of the United States. Common defensive stance that either offender may not be aware of the illegality of their actions is considered meritless. Lacking knowledge of the law is not a defense, and the fact that the actions of both pedophiles and FDP offenders occur within a shroud of secrecy tells us that there is an offender understanding that both abusive behaviors are not acceptable within society; these are crimes of shame.

The behavior of sexual pedophilia toward children is considered predatory and presented as an extreme threat to public safety. A predator is one who plunders or abuses other people for his/her own profit.[4] Registration of sexual predators is required in most states. The predatory status of pedophilia is so concerning that community notification is often mandated when convicted sexual predators (pedophiles) relocate or reside within communities. Judgment regarding a sexual predator failure to comply with statutory registration requirements is often severe. The notion that a pedophile should receive leniency rather than stern judicial handling is unheard of. Attempted rehabilitation of a pedophile through therapeutic means does not generally take precedence within the sentencing guidelines and is usually viewed as futile. Rehabilitation, although theoretically possible, is overshadowed by the atrociousness of the crime and provided as a means to minimize the risk posed to potential future victims.

The predatory pattern of child abuse within pedophilia and FDP are similar in terms of covertness, long-term victimization harm, unacceptable societal standards, and lethality potential. However, there is a marked difference regarding how these two abuse methods are viewed and disposed of by the courts.

Courts seem to recognize that the thought process of a pedophile cannot permanently, truly, and verifiably be altered through therapy. This notion is supported by the fact that once a pedophile serves his criminal sentence, a civil process of indefinite containment found within the Jimmy Ryce Act ensues.

Courts generally recognize that segregation between FDP offenders and children is warranted because of a continued victimization risk factor, yet often fail to ensure that the FDP offenders' own children are segregated permanently. FDP offenders often play upon the emotions of the court as the consequences of taking a mother away from all existing children vs. the risk to allow access is weighed. Promises of access overview, psychological therapy (that has no definitive cure), and sometimes the lack of offender admission affect the court decisions regarding FDP offender access to surviving children.

Termination of parental rights in cases of FDP victim abuse by a parent is complicated with factors of leniency. The majority of FDP offenders are female (mothers of the victims) while the majority of identified pedophiles are male (may or may not be related to the victims). In FDP situations, the diminishment of offender punishment and deferral to various rehabilitation programs coupled with criminal probationary provisions sets a standard of concern for unabated FDP abuse tendencies. The rationalization for this compromise is that incarceration would not "cure" the FDP offender's engrained behavioral pattern and willingness to offend; yet, family reunification is generally desired.

The reflection that society would be better served through probation, thereby lessening perceived continuance of victim punishment by maintaining separation from the offender (mother) is often present. FDP offenders may be portrayed effectively as victims who are unable to control abusive actions because of their own needs. These needs, however, are attained at the expense of another person who cannot resist or defend him/herself.

It is interesting that similar atrocities of child abuse seen within the actions of pedophiles and FDP abuse offenders are sometimes scrutinized so vastly different by courts and by society. Judiciary views regarding abuse or homicide with an FDP factor currently do not reflect enhanced penalties found in other premeditated victimization and willful torture cases. Criminal sentencing and dependency rulings do not always reflect the differentiation between the degree of victim injury and the abhorrence of the criminal act.

Criminal Prosecution Strategies

Abuse or homicide cases that involve the FDP factor should be argued as straightforward cases of maltreatment to avoid asserting mental illness as a primary defense. FDP-related abuse is preplanned willful torture and a scheme to defraud. The risk of facilitating victim/

offender contact contingent upon psychotherapy is a concern when focus is not on the primary offense. When FDP is introduced within a criminal abuse or homicide trial, stressing the foundational factors of FDP as a delivery system within the scope of abuse or homicide is recommended. FDP is a classified factitious disorder in which production of symptoms is voluntary and consciously perpetrated.[5] When this action is upon another, it is an abuse method.

Typically, there is no evidence of significant mental illness present within the FDP offender other than the behavior of FDP itself.[6] Please note that there is a huge lack of evidence to support the theory that psychological treatment of an FDP offender will produce a cure to behavioral thinking that facilitates abuse or homicide actions within an FDP forum. A dependent person (child, elderly, or otherwise compromised) is often the target of a FDP offender's pathological conduct of complicated abuse, and victim injury risk is extreme.

Abuse through an FDP conduit is willful torture shrouded in secrecy and usually committed through the veil of the sanctity of motherhood. FDP offenders intend for their victims to become ill; they allow and inflict injury upon them while claiming no knowledge of the source of injury/illness. The victim is totally devalued and an object utilized for offender gain. FDP abuse victims sometimes die, and those who survive may be permanently injured physically and psychologically.

Hospitals, medical treatment centers, police/fire departments, and pharmacies in the surrounding area where the FDP abuse is uncovered or historical residential locations of the family should be blanket subpoenaed for medical treatment or contact evidence. The FDP offender (defendant) may need to be notified if required by state law, and so this investigative step should occur after the offender is taken into custody.

In many cases of FDP, the alleged offender may elect to testify in court. Prosecutors may benefit from understanding that the FDP offender could consider testifying in court a new form of attention. The courtroom, in a sense, becomes symbolic of a stage facilitating a pathway for the FDP offender to a "star" when all eyes are focused upon him/her. Testifying may internally validate or justify the offender's actions as a measure of uncontrollable need or act as a means to portray innocence to observers and self. Prosecutors should prepare carefully for cross-examination of a suspected FDP offender recalling the potential for extremely deceptive, convincing, and manipulative testimony—all projected, as sincere portrayal of actual reality as a cornerstone in FDP methodology. FDP offenders are so confident in their acting ability that courtroom testimony may be considered a challenge or simply a continuation of a game already played.

Case Preparation

Criminal cases involving an element of FDP/FD are voluminous. It is the responsibility of the prosecutor to arrange a "mountain of complicated information into a nutshell" so that it can be understood. Evidence management alone often tasks the prosecutor's office resources as the allocation of manpower is diverted toward case preparation. Additional elements of controlling and compacting vast amounts of paperwork (medical records) that generally are not easily understood in layman's terms add to case demand. The requirement for recognition of evidence and total case comprehension may often seem overwhelming.

Clear, concise visual aids large enough to be easily seen by the judge and jury are helpful within the courtroom. The complexity of FDP victimization precipitates the need for presentation information on an appropriate level for each juror to grasp. It is recommended that a comprehensive, yet condensed, reference portfolio of the case be acquired by the prosecutor and presented to jury members. Victim photo(s) at the time the abuse occurred then selectively presented to jurors provides clarity of the abuse and humanizes victimization.

Refutable Defense Standards

The modern upsurge of FD/FDP elements found within abuse and homicide situations originates from standards of knowledge and the ability to recognize hidden abuse. Innovative, but often ineffective, criminal defense strategies have been displayed within the realm of identified cases and are listed in Figure 15.5.

Prosecutors should prepare to address these potential defense issues and others during trial preparation and link these to trial strategy preparation.

Expert Testimony Usage in FDP-Related Litigation

FD and FDP as elements in any type of criminal, civil, or dependency court case establish a standard of complexity and associated confusion to most people bearing witness to the proceedings. The complexity factor is one reason why moving toward a focus on substantive underlying abuse charges is preferred; explanation of FDP as an abuse delivery system seems to place the FDP element in proper perspective so long as the perspective is credible and understandable.

It is recommended that a medical expert(s) be consulted and case evaluation conducted for later courtroom presentation. Local general physicians often lack necessary knowledge

- The victim suffers from legitimate medical illness that accounts for victim harm or death
- Improper treatment caused victim damage
- The victim's "system" was "deficient," which made him/her susceptible to illness or infection
- The victim's health improved due to "spontaneous remission"
- The defendant intentionally made the victim sick due to fear of untreated legitimate illness
- The defendant is mentally ill
- FDP is not real

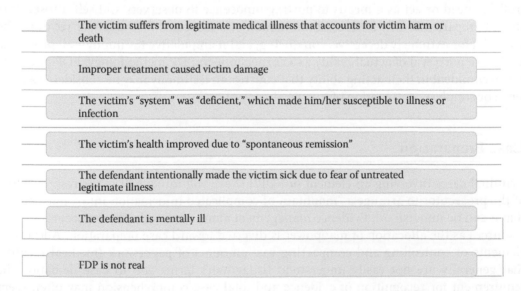

Figure 15.5 FDP criminal defense strategies.

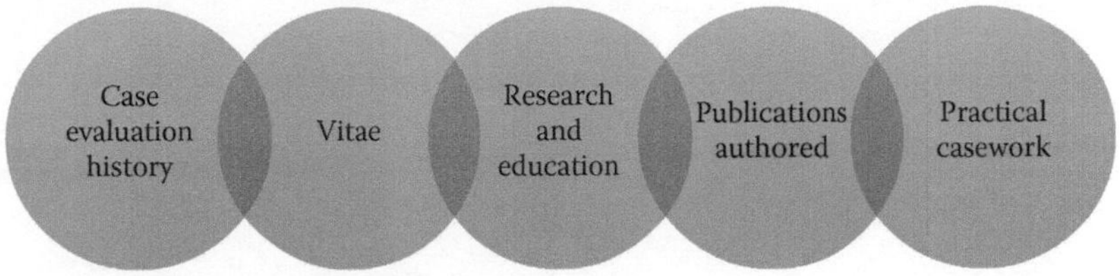

Figure 15.6 FDP expert witness fundamentals.

required for effectively testifying in FDP abuse cases but this is dependent upon individualized experience, awareness, and education.

Prosecutors should consider usage of experts based upon their training and experience and the ability to effectively communicate. Individuals who are truly field experts do not necessarily promote that status, and financial gain is not the primary goal of consulting on a case. The status or label of "expert" is one that is generally attached to a person by others—not promoted from within. It is also helpful to realize that most people would like to be considered an expert at something, and a natural tendency toward self-promotion regardless of ability is sometimes evident. Caution should be extended and consideration given when selecting experts for courtroom presentation.

When attorneys attempt to qualify witnesses as experts, it is important that the witness understand his/her own ability as an expert vs. the ability of the general population. Credibility of an expert witness is subject to judicial consideration or perceived qualifications, including training, experience, and demonstrated "special" ability. Attorneys should remind potential expert witnesses that the following items may facilitate verification of their abilities: keeping good notes, vitae; list of books studied and research conducted; publications authored; practical experience (casework); and current collaboration within the field. This information should be presented in deposition and later to the court within qualification testimony (Figure 15.6).

In jury trials, expert witnesses are usually qualified with the jury excluded. When the jury re-enters the courtroom and questions are repeated, repetition must be consistent. Opposition to attempt discrediting the expert status qualification may be offensive, abusive, and attempt to provoke emotional response. Presenting attorneys should review qualification questions with a prospective expert witness and ensure that case documents are reviewed prior to court time. Negating the validity of an expert witness status is created by distraction formulating reasonable doubt that an individual possesses needed qualifications. Expert testimony is offered as a service to the court in the following manner (Figure 15.7):

The expert may testify to his/her opinion of physical condition/abnormality of the victim; behavioral considerations including action/interaction between the defendant and victim; excited utterances and confessions (post-Miranda if custodial). Experts may also testify without first-hand knowledge of the case when hypothetical scenarios are posed that resemble actual case facts. When a witness is qualified as an expert, his/her opinion is generally allowed.

Expert testimony should not be offered as exclusive evidence of guilt or innocence of the defendant. Expert testimony should be one ingredient in the total case package. Care should be exercised that expert witnesses do not overstep their own qualifications and render opinions they are not licensed nor qualified to convey. Expert testimony is extremely effective in criminal, civil, and dependency cases that involve an FDP factor and carefully controlled by the courts.

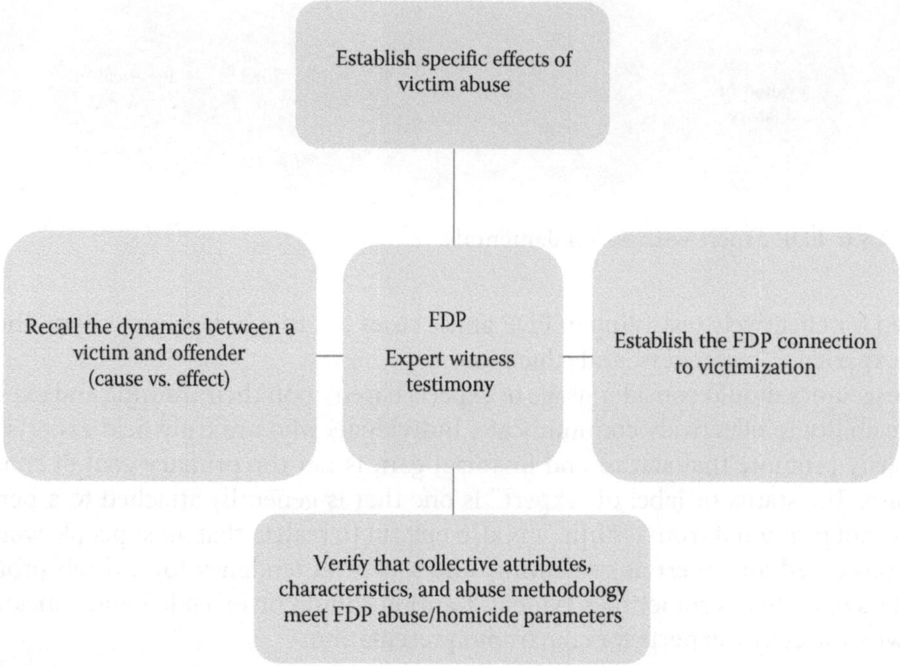

Figure 15.7 Testimonial presentation of the FDP expert witness.

Landmark cases (*Daubert* and *Frye*) provide guidance to the court regarding the definition and qualification standards of "expert witnesses."

Evidence-Based Medicine

The use of scientific evidence to make diagnoses is similar to the way courts use evidence to make judgments. Looking at medical vs. legal reasoning enlightens this topic. Validating illness through diagnosis is an essential role of physicians.[7] Doctors assume that parents will accept medical findings and comply with advice given; doctors assume that what patients or their parents tell them is true.[8] When patients or young patient's parents actively deceive doctors regarding illness, the normal patient–doctor relationship changes by placing physicians into the role of a possible crime investigator where suspicion is required.[9]

> When all investigations for all possible causes of illness have been performed, whatever explanation is left after all others have been excluded must be the cause.

When the cause for illness (suffocation, poisoning, or fabrication) is a crime, not a diagnosis, the multidisciplinary team addresses the actions of the FDP offender on multiple levels. Detectives investigate crime; doctors investigate symptoms of diseases. FDP offenders who smother, poison, or otherwise abuse their victims have demonstrated harmful behavior. It cannot be said that they are suffering from smothering/poisoning or abusive behavior. It makes little sense when courts accept the notion that an FDP offender is "suffering from FDP," and there is no predisposition that a person who inflicts victim harm through the avenue of FDP covert behavior is necessarily mentally ill.[10]

Expert Testimony

When cases are emotionally charged because they involve children, it is important that the expert witness remain objective and truthful especially when evidence is circumstantial. Expert witnesses are permitted to opine on the matter at hand but should ensure that all other reasonable explanations for the victim's death or abuse have been explored and excluded. When the protection of vulnerable victims is at stake, there is a danger of experts becoming identified with their view in a way that reduces objectivity.[11]

Experts in cases involving FDP child victims may be met with hostility because they accuse defendants who are idealized among society (generally mothers of small children). The notion that a mother could kill or harm her child within the covert venue of FDP abuse is a difficult concept for people (in general) to grasp. It is important that experts have both expertise and control of their prejudices. When expert testimony is overturned upon appeal, how does that affect credibility?

Daubert v. Merrell Dow Pharmaceuticals, Inc., 509 U.S. 579, 113 S. Ct. 2786, 125 L. Ed. 2d 469 (1993)

Supreme Court decision whether the *Kelly/Frye* standard for admitting the results of new scientific techniques should be modified (hereafter *Daubert*) held that *Frye* was abrogated by rule 702 of the Federal Rules of Evidence (28 U.S.C.). Concluded that the *Kelly/Frye* formulation (*Kelly* formulation) should remain a prerequisite to the admission of expert testimony regarding new scientific methodology.

Such factors include (1) whether a theory or technique has been or can be tested; (2) whether the theory or technique has been subjected to peer review and publication; (3) the known or potential rate of error; and (4) whether the technique has been accepted by a relevant scientific community.

Daubert has been applied in the following manner:

- A district court must "ensure that any and all scientific testimony or evidence admitted [at trial] is not only relevant, but reliable."
- It is "the trial judge['s] ... task ... to ensure that an expert's testimony both rests on a reliable foundation and is relevant to the task at hand"
- "Vigorous cross-examination, presentation of contrary evidence, and careful instruction on the burden of proof are the traditional and appropriate means of attacking shaky but admissible evidence."
- The trial court must make "a preliminary assessment of whether the reasoning or methodology underlying the testimony is scientifically valid and of whether that reasoning or methodology properly can be applied to the facts in issue."
- To determine the admissibility of expert testimony, a court must consider, among other factors, whether the methodology is generally accepted within the scientific community

Frye v. United States (D.C. Cir.1923) 293 F. 1013, 1014 [*54 App.D.C. 46, 34 A.L.R. 145*]

(*Frye*), and (2) whether a police officer without scientific expertise is qualified to give an opinion concerning the results of the HGN test. The Court of Appeal answered both questions in the negative and reversed defendant Leahy's convictions for driving under the influence of alcohol.

Frye has been applied in the following manner:

- While courts will go a long way in admitting expert testimony deduced from a well-recognized scientific principle or discovery, the thing from which the deduction is made must be sufficiently established to have gained general acceptance in the particular field to which it belongs.
- Expert opinion based on a scientific technique "is admissible if it is generally accepted as a reliable technique among the scientific community."
- When a scientific principle or discovery crosses the line between the experimental and demonstrable stages is difficult to define.
- The court in *Frye* ruled that scientific evidence, such as the results of a polygraph examination, may not be admitted into evidence unless the test has achieved "general acceptance" in its field.
- The restrictive *Frye* test allowed scientific expert testimony only with regard to concepts that had "general acceptance in [a] particular field."
- In *Frye*, the court held that for an expert witness' testimony to be admissible, the testimony must be based on scientific principles that are generally accepted in the relevant scientific community.

Levels of Certainty

There are levels of certainty of expert opinion that include conclusive, probable, possible, and suspected thresholds (Figure 15.8).[12]

Prosecutors should be aware of the level the expert witness intents to opine with prior to testimony presentation. Expert witnesses often provide a necessary element of education to all in the courtroom including attorneys and should disclose to the presenting attorney what their expert opinion will represent.

Expert Testimony

The use of expert testimony is often a central component in FDP criminal case building. Criminal abuse/homicide cases involving an FD/FDP component have been made or lost as a result of expert testimony. The difficulty in establishing FD/FDP case identification and required educational understanding transcends the boundary between legal and medical fields due to complexity, awareness, identification, and the air of uncertainty created

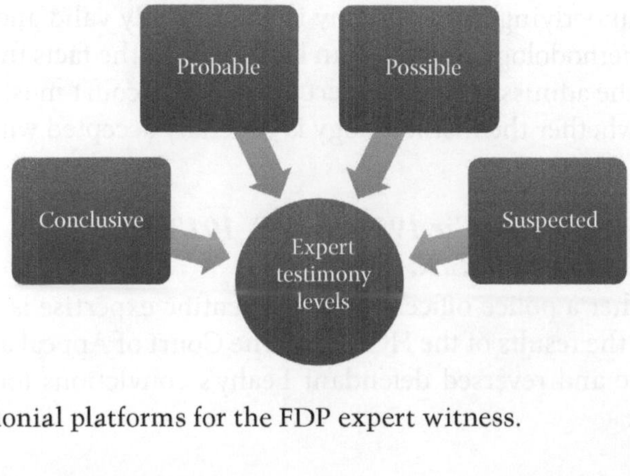

Figure 15.8 Testimonial platforms for the FDP expert witness.

by the FD/FDP offender. There have been FDP child abuse/homicide cases that also involve elements of legitimate victim illness or active victim collusion in which medical experts utilized by the same investigating agency could not reach consensus. If expert medical consensus cannot be attained, prosecution of the case as a criminal entity may be affected and intervention impeded. The identification of qualified experts skilled in application and knowledge of FD/FDP is critical in criminal case preparation.

Issues of the uncertainty of FDP recognition have been challenging on a multidisciplinary level. Medicine has been described as an art that implies fluidity, mold ability, and influence. Medical schools teach raw skills (history taking, note writing, disease process). Medicine viewed as art finds artists within the physician and the patient who work together toward diagnosis and treatment. For very young or old patients, caretakers often become artists on behalf of the patients.[13]

Uncertainty is part of medicine and may fall into three categories: technical, personal uncertainty, and conceptual uncertainty. In child abuse cases, technical uncertainty is linked to expertise and evidence; personal uncertainty is nearly a universal component in child abuse work; conceptual uncertainty occurs when abstract information is applied to concrete scenarios.[14] For FDP child abuse situations, all of these factors are amplified because nothing is straightforward.

Experts have been categorized into two distinct groups: local and national. Local experts are persons in the geographic location of FD/FDP victimization events and/or criminal prosecution who have experience working with situations involving FD/FDP. Local experts should be evaluated based upon the degree of involvement they have had within the case at hand. Simply conferring upon a suspected abuse case with an FDP attachment does not necessarily qualify a physician to be an expert in FD/FDP case evaluation. Medical professional notoriety and associative liability connected with FD/FDP case involvement has been an issue seen within historical FD/FDP cases.

National experts skilled in FD/FDP testimony have usually been involved in numerous case evaluations with suspected inference of FD/FDP directly or indirectly. Most of national experts on the subject of FD/FDP have added the element of research to their resume, and many have published on the subject. Experts who are authors sometimes cite their literary work(s) as evidence of expertise and testament to their expert ability. Care should be taken to evaluate the quality of publication(s) and the study or research behind what is printed. Prosecutors who elicit the use of expert testimony should consider the use of both local and national expert resources within case building and prosecution efforts. Local experts may provide direct observed testimony related to victimization while national experts may support a local expert's observations, conclusions, and opinions while expounding upon the case from a research perspective. National expert testimony may provide enhanced credibility within a criminal case.

Insanity Defense

An individual that utilizes FDP as a delivery system for abuse or homicide is not automatically considered to be mentally ill, although other psychiatric disorders may or may not be present (see Chapter 1). FDP offenders who realize their behavior is being scrutinized for abuse and have not been physically arrested may voluntarily self-admit to a mental facility as a means of securing an insanity defense. This action may be at the direction of their attorney or self-initiated. If this occurs, emphasis should be placed upon the fact that

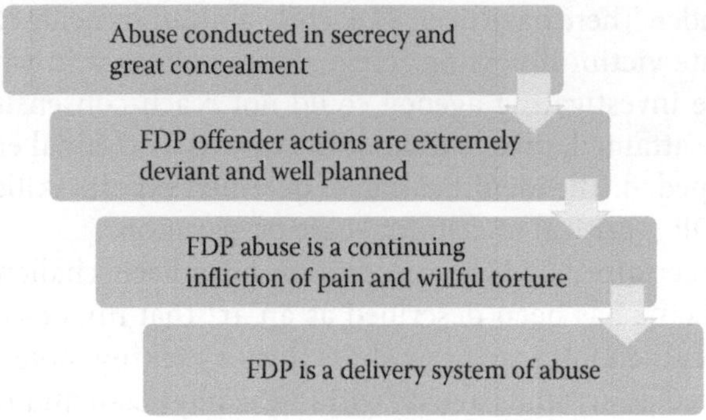

Figure 15.9 FDP abuse methodology.

abusive act(s) with an FDP delivery factor were conducted in secrecy and often with grandiose concealment effort; FDP abuse is extremely deviant, well planned; and FDP abuse is a continuing infliction of pain and willful torture (Figure 15.9).

In averting the defense strategy of insanity, prosecutors may be aided by examining the psychological/psychiatric records of the defendant and victim. FDP upon minor victims is considered child abuse and an exception to the therapist privilege rule in most U.S. states. In most known cases of child abuse with an FDP delivery factor, the offender appears psychologically normal and may effectively convince mental health professionals of their innocence only to later be convicted of criminal acts. FDP offenders are experts at manipulation and have been able to convince persons of all backgrounds that their child(ren) are legitimately ill when the reality is the children are abuse victims at the hands of the offender. FDP offenders have also demonstrated a working ability to elicit sympathy from all professions without exclusion (Figure 15.10).

Why Is FDP Behavior Criminal Abuse? (Figure 15.11)

Case Law

Case law provides a basis of understanding regarding abuse and homicide with an FDP delivery system. The following is a summation of pertinent cases presented within the U.S. courts that possess an element of FD or FDP. This list is a snapshot of cases and represents only a fraction of known criminal, civil, and dependency cases involving an FDP factor. Further details may be found by accessing these cases in totality:

State v. Lumbrera, 845 P.2d 609, 252 Kan. 54 (1992).
State v. Lumbrera, 257 Kan. 144, 891 P.2d 1096 (1995).

Victim A was a 4-year-old boy. A telephone call was received by a Kansas hospital from a woman who did not identify herself, stating that her son's lips were blue and that he was not moving. Shortly thereafter, the defendant carried the lifeless body of the victim into the hospital emergency room. The child had petechiae (small purple spots on his face and eyelids); no obstruction was present in the child's airway; and food was present in his stomach. The presence of petechiae is an indication of asphyxia. The cause of death was initially determined to be asphyxia by smothering. The results of the subsequent autopsy were consistent with the preliminary finding of death by smothering.

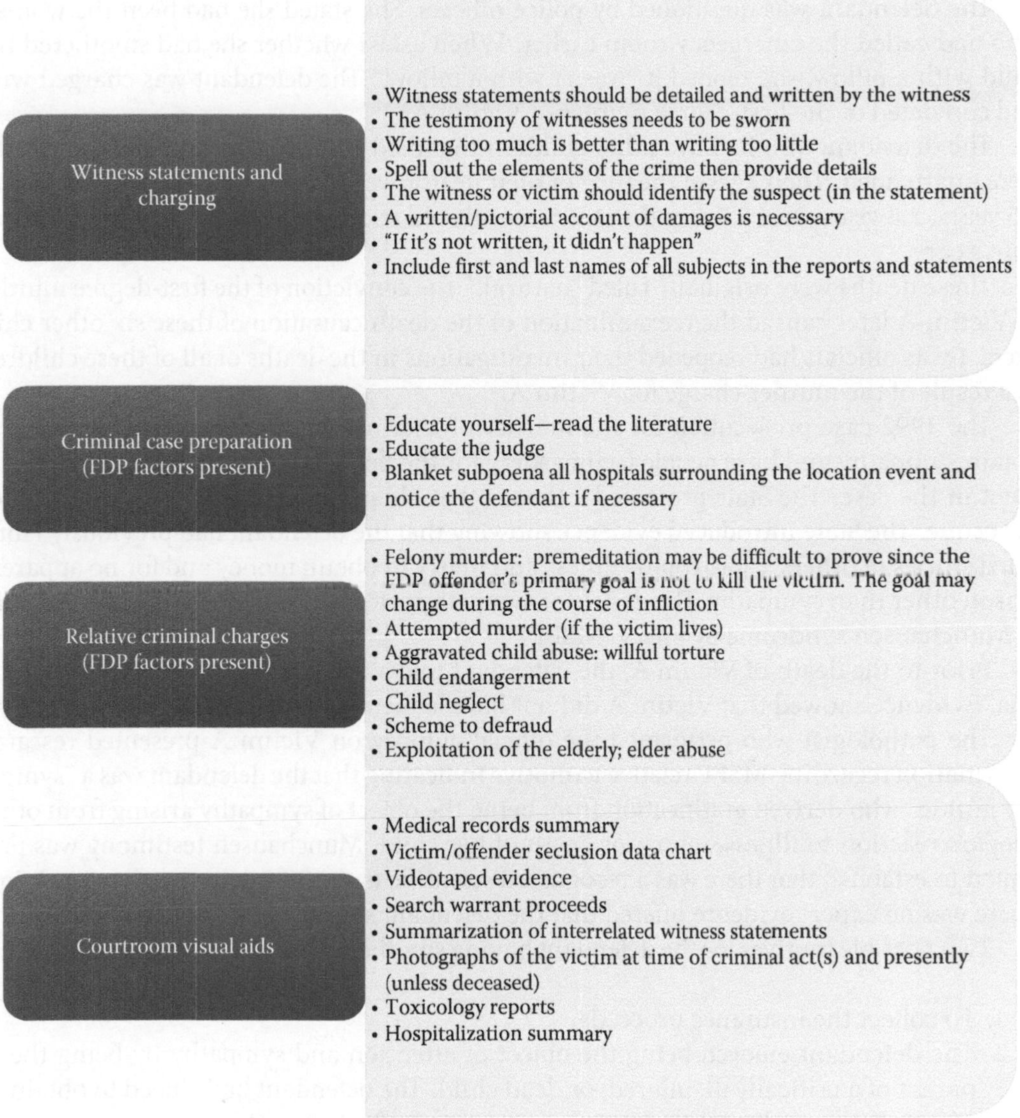

Witness statements and charging
• Witness statements should be detailed and written by the witness
• The testimony of witnesses needs to be sworn
• Writing too much is better than writing too little
• Spell out the elements of the crime then provide details
• The witness or victim should identify the suspect (in the statement)
• A written/pictorial account of damages is necessary
• "If it's not written, it didn't happen"
• Include first and last names of all subjects in the reports and statements
Criminal case preparation (FDP factors present)
• Educate yourself—read the literature
• Educate the judge
• Blanket subpoena all hospitals surrounding the location event and notice the defendant if necessary
Relative criminal charges (FDP factors present)
• Felony murder: premeditation may be difficult to prove since the FDP offender's primary goal is not to kill the victim. The goal may change during the course of infliction
• Attempted murder (if the victim lives)
• Aggravated child abuse: willful torture
• Child endangerment
• Child neglect
• Scheme to defraud
• Exploitation of the elderly; elder abuse
Courtroom visual aids
• Medical records summary
• Victim/offender seclusion data chart
• Videotaped evidence
• Search warrant proceeds
• Summarization of interrelated witness statements
• Photographs of the victim at time of criminal act(s) and presently (unless deceased)
• Toxicology reports
• Hospitalization summary

Figure 15.10 Law enforcement criminal case submission standards—FDP abuse/homicide.

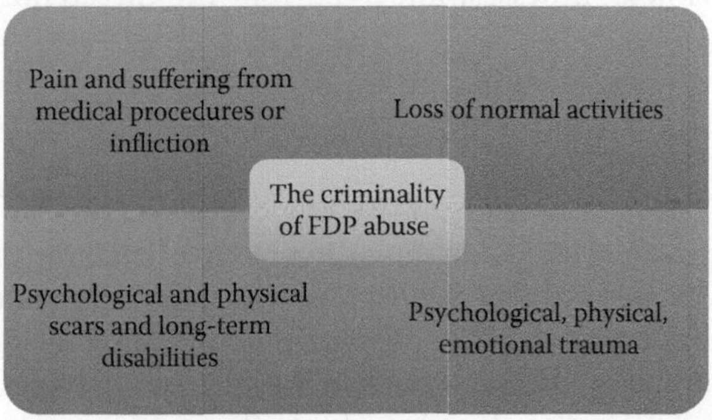

Figure 15.11 The criminality of FDP abuse.

The defendant was questioned by police officers. She stated she had been the woman who had called the emergency room earlier. When asked whether she had smothered the child with a pillow, she replied it "wasn't with a pillow." The defendant was charged with and convicted of the first-degree murder of Victim A.

The defendant also had five other children that died young in Texas, and their deaths were unattended. Their ages at the time of their deaths were listed as 3 months, 1.5 months, 3.5 years, 2.5 years, and 5.5 months. A 2.5-month-old relative also died while in the defendant's care.

These deaths were originally ruled "natural." The conviction of the first-degree murder of Victim A later caused the reexamination of the death causation of these six other children. Texas officials had reopened their investigations in the deaths of all of these children as a result of the murder charge for Victim A.

The 1992 case prosecution for the murder of Victim A emphasized that the need to obtain sympathy and have people feeling sorry for the defendant was an instrumental element in the case. The State presented a theory that obtaining sympathy was a motive for the crime. The State introduced evidence showing that the defendant had previously fabricated stories of others' catastrophic illness and injury to obtain money and for no apparent reason other than sympathy. The desire for sympathy is termed as a motive for the behavior of Munchausen syndrome by proxy (MSBP).

Prior to the death of Victim A, the defendant told a witness that Victim A had leukemia. Evidence showed that Victim A did not have leukemia or other cancer.

The pathologist who performed the official autopsy on Victim A presented research information regarding MSBP relative to motive indicating that the defendant was a "sympathy junkie" who derived gratification from being the object of sympathy arising from other people's reaction to illness, injury, or death of her child. Munchausen testimony was presented to establish that there was a recognized scientific name afforded to such a condition. There was no expert evidence offered that the defendant suffered from such a condition.

Two possible motives for the defendant having smothered her son, Jose, were presented:

1. To collect the insurance proceeds.
2. The defendant enjoyed being the object of attention and sympathy by being the parent of a critically ill, injured, or dead child. The defendant had a need to obtain sympathy, a need to obtain people feeling sorry for her, and her problems commensurate with Munchausen syndrome. The manner of obtaining the needed sympathy was through the avenue of MSBP by presenting her child as afflicted with terrible sickness, illnesses, and recurrent life-threatening and debilitating problems.

Evidence included testimony indicating:

- Approximately 1 year prior to the death of victim Jose, the Def. advised her work supervisor that Jose had leukemia. Jose did not have leukemia or any other cancer.
- British medical journal entitled *Suffocation* was entered as evidence.
- The case pathologist described the defendant as a "sympathy junkie" who derived gratification from being the object of sympathy arising from other people's reaction to illness, injury, or death of her child. The state presented a motive for the crime as the attainment of "sympathy."

- Munchausen testimony was provided to establish that there was a recognized scientific name afforded to such a condition. There was no expert evidence offered that the defendant suffered from such a condition.
- Evidence showing that the defendant had previously fabricated stories of others' catastrophic illness and injury to obtain money and for no apparent reason other than sympathy was to be presented but all evidence relative to either Munchausen syndrome or MSBP was stricken, and the jury properly admonished to disregard.

The jury was instructed that statements, arguments, and remarks of the counsel are not evidence, and statements made that are not supported by the evidence should be disregarded. All evidence relative to Munchausen syndrome or MSBP was stricken, and the jury was admonished to disregard it. On appeal, the judgment of the district court was reversed due to trial errors and the case remanded for a new trial.

During 1995, a retrial occurred regarding the death of Victim A. While awaiting this trial, the defendant pled nolo contendere to first-degree murder of two of her other children (while in Texas). This information was admitted into the retrial for the death of Victim A, and the conviction of first-degree murder of Victim A was affirmed. A pecuniary profit was established for the defendant by the death of each child. Medical forensic evidence was presented relating to the official cause of death of Victim A: asphyxiation probably due to suffocation. MSBP was not an element in the 1995 retrial.

Diana Lumbrera received two life sentences for the deaths of her two children in Texas.

Opinion filed on March 10, 1995.

- The concept that a mother would intentionally kill her own young child is so repugnant that such a theory places a heavy burden on the State.
- Evidence that the defendant had been previously convicted of two chillingly similar crimes and shortly before each child's death the defendant had sought medical attention for the child. The state asserted that seeking medical attention prepared an official record of health problems that made the subsequent unexplained death less suspicious.
- The defendant had obtained life insurance on each of the children and financially benefitted from their deaths.
- No expert testimony attempting to prove that the defendant suffered from the disorder MSBP was presented.
- The prosecution met its heavy burden of proving the "repugnant" theory that the mother intentionally killed her child, when it presented evidence of the defendant's prior trips to the emergency room with the child.

The defendant appealed her conviction for the murder of her child, Victim A. She received two life sentences for two other child murders in Texas—subject to a plea of nolo contendere.

Cooney v. Rossiter, 583 F.3d 967 (7th Cir. 2009)

After an Illinois state court found that Cooney suffered from MSBP, she lost custody of her two sons. Cooney sued the state court judge, children's psychiatrist, and children's representative in federal district court, charging constitutional violations. The district court dismissed the suit.

Judges are absolutely immune from suit, when acting in judicial capacity in ruling. Guardian *ad litem* and court-appointed experts, including psychiatrists, are absolutely immune from liability for damages when they act at the court's direction.

Matter of Jessica Z., 135 Misc. 2d 520, 515 N.Y.S.2d 370 (Fam. Ct. 1987)

Jessica (born November 10, 1985) was hospitalized between March–July 1986 with diarrhea. She underwent surgery and came close to death. During August 1986, a 14-day trial occurred and Jessica's mother (M) was charged and later convicted, by preponderance of credible evidence, for causing Jessica to ingest laxatives for a period of 4 months, resulting in her diarrhea, surgery, and near death. Twenty-one witnesses testified, including 12 doctors, 1 psychologist, respondent, and her husband, Jessica's father.

A presentation of MSBP research and characteristics and subsequent assignment of this behavior to the appellant was bolstered by the following case observations:

Persistent diarrhea, no satisfactory diagnosis hospitalizations, and surgery: Jessica was referred to a pediatric gastroenterologist due to dehydration caused by diarrhea and vomiting. After receiving intravenous (IV) feeding, she improved and returned home, only to be readmitted shortly thereafter with the same symptoms. Exhaustive tests revealed no explanation for her condition, and Jessica underwent her first major surgical procedure, which revealed unexpected congenital abnormalities. Shortly thereafter, both the vomiting and diarrhea returned. A second major surgical procedure was undertaken to determine whether Jessica's continuing diarrhea was due to adhesions from the first surgery; nothing was found and Jessica's gastroesophageal reflux was repaired. A gastrointestinal tube and Broviac catheter were inserted.

After the second surgery, Jessica's vomiting stopped but her diarrhea continued. More tests were done and medical experts were consulted—without answers. "Every conceivable possibility, from AIDS to cystic fibrosis, was considered and rejected—except for one"—that Jessica was being poisoned.

After 55 days of hospitalization, Jessica returned home, with diarrhea, attached to two tubes, which were attached to two pumps to regulate the speed of her tubal feeding. One week later, she was readmitted to the hospital intensive care unit (ICU), in critical condition, shock, and with a 106° fever having developed bacteremia. Jessica responded to treatment in ICU while under nursing observation and rapidly improved. Jessica was transferred to a private room where her parents assisted in her care and her diarrhea returned.

A chemical test on Jessica's stool revealed the presence of phenolphthalein (a chemical found in Ex-Lax and other laxatives). The test was repeated with the same result.

Reactions of the parents to accusations of abuse: The respondent and her husband were told that Jessica had ingested phenolphthalein and they calmly denied responsibility. The mother cried. Child Protective Services (CPS) was notified of suspected child abuse, and Jessica was placed in the care of the Department of Social Services.

The following day an incident occurred that was later linked to the respondent's credibility and was reported by two nurses who were on duty that day. The respondent requested the nurses accompany her to the pantry (an unlocked room on the pediatric floor where babies' formulas and other equipment are kept) to check the formula because she suspected someone was poisoning Jessica. The respondent urged them to accompany her and stated: "just humor me." When the refrigerator door was opened, the respondent spotted something dark in one of the partially opaque plastic formula containers. Upon examination, a large bar of Ex-Lax was found in the formula of another hospitalized child. The nurses described the respondent's reaction as "elated." She said, "this should prove that mom didn't do it," but "please don't tell Dr. N. it was my idea to check the formula." The respondent denied making these statements.

Laboratory analysis of the stool of the baby whose formula was contaminated revealed no phenolphthalein. There were no reports of any babies, other than Jessica, suffering from suspicious diarrhea, or of any findings of phenolphthalein in any adult or infant stools.

After removal from the respondent's care—diarrhea stopped: After discovery of the chemical in the Jessica's stool, when the respondent's contact with Jessica was strictly supervised—her condition improved. All feeding tubes were eventually removed, and Jessica started to thrive and she gained weight.

The respondent exhibited characteristics typical of MSBP mothers: Training in medically related fields, the respondent had been employed as a dental assistant and most recently as a medical secretary. The respondent had medical terminology knowledge and an impressive ability to articulate Jessica's complicated medical history.

- Jessica was found to be an abused child, pursuant to Family Court Act § 1012 (e) (i), in that the respondent caused her to ingest sufficient quantity of laxatives from March 1986 to July 19, 1986, so as to cause her serious illness, hospitalization, and surgery.
- Jessica was placed in the care and custody of her father.
- The Department of Social Services (DSS) structured and monitored a plan to coordinate efforts and communication between the respondent's psychiatrist, Jessica's pediatrician, her father's therapist, Dr. N, and the DSS caseworker and arranged for psychiatric treatment for the respondent with a board-certified psychiatrist on no less than a once-a-week schedule.
- DSS arranged for therapy for Jessica's father and arranged for Jessica to be examined once a month and conducted announced or unannounced bimonthly visits to the home.
- In the event, DSS found that this order was violated, or if, in the opinion of any one of the above physicians or therapists, Jessica appeared to be at risk, DSS had authority to remove Jessica from her parents' home without necessity of first obtaining a court order.
- The court applied the doctrine of *res ipsa loquitur* to explain the cause of Jessica's injuries and held that by preponderance of evidence, the mother was guilty of child abuse.

People v. Phillips, 64 Cal. 2d 574, 414 P.2d 353, 51 Cal. Rptr. 225 (1966)

Malice is implied when the killing is proximately caused by "an act, the natural consequences of which are dangerous to life, which act was deliberately performed by a person who knows that his conduct endangers the life of another and who acts with conscious disregard for life."

A physician could be criminally liable for failure to provide care that could have extended the patient's life, even if the underlying disease that the physician failed to treat immediately caused death.

In RE MM, Cal: Court of Appeal, 2nd Appellate Dist., 8th Div. 2013

The mother of two boys was identified as an FDP abuser. A restraining order was issued and appealed by the mother. The restraining order was upheld, and custody of the boys was given to the father.

MM1 was born in November 2007. Before he was 18 months, he was admitted to hospital three times for gastrointestinal issues and brought to the emergency room on three other occasions. MM2 was born during June 2009 and began having medical issues as MM1 stopped having medical issues. During May 2011, a social worker at a hospital where MM2 was being treated noted that FDP was likely a factor in MM2's illnesses after a positive glucose output was found in MM2's surgically placed feeding tube only after the mother was alone with him. The mother was fixated on different symptoms, and a high number of doctor visits occurred. The mother "fired" doctors, and the father had asked DCFS for help. The referral was unfounded.

During May 2011, the mother apparently gave MM2 apple juice elevating his glucose output; MM2's feeding pump then mysteriously turned off several times during the night when the mother was the only other person in the room. The mother claimed that MM2 must have turned the machine off himself. MM2 was 2 years old at the time.

On July 18, 2011, MM2 was readmitted to Children's Hospital for dehydration and fever (eighth admission to that hospital) and had a history of previous additional admissions to other area hospitals. A physician at Children's Hospital believed that FDP was a factor in MM2's illnesses. MM2 was released to the mother's custody and returned shortly thereafter to the emergency room with new alleged symptoms. MM2 was readmitted, and no new symptoms observed.

The mother and father of MM1 and MM2 received court-ordered monitored visitation only. The children were eventually released to the father only, and a temporary restraining order was issued for the mother preventing contact with the children outside the scope of supervised visitation.

The mother wrote a letter to the court suggesting the babysitter was a sexual predator and was hitting the children and the father was punishing the children by putting chili peppers in their mouths and had threatened to kill her. These allegations were unfounded. The restraining order was converted to a 3-year term on December 12, 2011. The mother appealed, and the ruling was upheld. The court noted that the children were at substantial risk of future harm based upon substantial evidence.

MM2's health improved once placed into the father's custody.

Miller v. Newport, No. CV-12–540-RHW (E.D. Wash. June 9, 2013)

During 1983, Plaintiffs (PBM and DM) alleged that ("DSHS") employees and physicians unconstitutionally removed children from their custody, as a result of dependency proceedings. DSHS employees suspected Plaintiffs of child abuse and neglect.

On November 17, 2005, a petition for dependency alleged that JG (then age 8) and RB (then age 6) were being abused/neglected, due to the concerns reported by the medical care team. A 72-hour administrative hold was placed, and then the minors were returned to the Plaintiff's custody on November 17, 2005, after the Superior Court found insufficient reasonable cause to believe that shelter care was necessary.

Approximately 2 months after the CPS investigation, DSHS/DCFS social worker asked a Seattle pediatrician who specializes in child abuse, to review RB's medical records and evaluate the prior reports of FDP/MSBP. The pediatrician reported to DCFS on January 17, 2006, opining that RB was a victim of pediatric condition falsification (PCF), having reached that conclusion after a 9-hour review of medical records.

February 10, 2006, PBM contacted CPS and requested that RB and JG be placed with their biological father (Mr. B). On March 14, 2006, PBM relinquished the custody of JG and RB in a stipulated order of dependency and agreed to their placement with Mr. B. PBM was granted supervised visitation after new findings of physical abuse involving JG surfaced. Eventually, Mr. B disappeared and the girls were placed into foster care.

On June 6, 2007, PBM and DM gave birth to a daughter (AM). On June 8, 2007, a petition for dependency as to AM was filed based on concerns that PBM reported to family members that her baby would be unhealthy, prior to the birth. DSHS/DCFS alleged that AM would be at risk of imminent harm by her mother who created false medical conditions in her other children. On June 8, 2007, pursuant to an *ex parte* order of protection, AM was taken into DSHS custody. On June 13, 2007, a shelter care hearing was held, wherein the court granted PBM the custody of AM. PBM was ordered to not have any unauthorized contact with AM.

On August 5, 2007, CPS received a report that DM and PBM had fled to Canada with AM. On August 15, 2007, CPS was advised DM was incarcerated in Canada. Thereafter, PBM turned herself in. A DSHS/DCFS courtesy supervisor then drove to the Canadian border and picked up AM who was then placed into shelter care.

DM and PBM were charged with kidnapping in the first degree. On September 25, 2007, DM pled guilty to attempted custodial interference in the first degree and received 38 days' custody; PBM pled guilty to the latter charge on December 11, 2007, and received 32 days' custody.

On August 27, 2008, AM was returned to DM and PBM. On April 13, 2009, JG and RB were reunited with PBM. The dependency of JG and RB was dismissed on October 12, 2009. DM and PBM relocated to another state.

A CPS employee, an administrator, doctor, or law enforcement officer shall not be held liable in any civil action for the decision for taking the child into custody, if done in good faith under this section.

Munchausen syndrome by proxy definition: *Roska ex rel. Roska v. Peterson,* 328 F.3d 1230, 1238 n. 2 (10th Cir. 2003); *see also Yuille v. State Dep't of Soc. & Health Servs.,* 111 Wn. App. 527, 530 n. 2 (2002).

MSBP is known as FDP or PCF. *See* Feldman Decl., ECF No. 42 at Ex. 3.

Reid v. State, 964 S.W.2d 723 (Tex. App. 1998)

On February 7, 1984, Emergency Management Services (EMS) personnel were summoned to the appellant's home because her infant daughter (MR) had suffered an apnea episode. Upon arrival, the appellant was attempting to resuscitate MR. MR was transported to a hospital where efforts to revive her were unsuccessful; MR was declared brain dead and was removed from the ventilator. MR died approximately 14 hours later. After an autopsy, MR's cause of death was determined to be brain death secondary to cardiorespiratory arrest of undetermined etiology.

MR was born on May 17, 1983, and died on February 8, 1984. MR suffered approximately 13 apnea episodes prior to her death. Apnea episodes were similar: they usually occurred on weekdays between 1:00 and 4:00 p.m.; MR was usually awake before the episodes began; the appellant was the only one present who observed the onset of an apnea episode; and she was the one who had to revive MR by the use of mouth-to-mouth or cardiopulmonary resuscitation. MR had undergone tests without a satisfactory physiological explanation for the apnea episodes.

The appellant and her husband also had another child, RM, who had apnea episodes from 1985 to 1988. RM was adjudicated a child in need of assistance, removed from the custody of the appellant and her husband, and placed in foster care. After that time, RM suffered no further apnea episodes.

RM was born on May 2, 1985. RM experienced his first of approximately 15 apnea episodes 26 days after birth. The appellant was the only one who witnessed the onset of severe apnea episodes; they only occurred when RM was awake; the appellant performed mouth or cardiopulmonary resuscitation upon RM; RM underwent numerous tests without a satisfactory physiological explanation for the tests. RM never had another apnea episode after he was removed from the appellant.

The appellant was convicted of murder for the death of MR and sentenced to 40 years confinement in the Institutional Division of the Department of Corrections. The sentence was appealed based upon the following:

- Trial court abused its discretion in admitting testimony regarding MSBP because
  - MSBP is not relevant and not scientific knowledge
  - MSBP is not relevant and would not assist the trier of fact
  - The probative value of the evidence is substantially outweighed by its prejudicial effect
  - The presentation of MSBP is impermissible character evidence under Rule 404(a) of the Texas Rules of Criminal Evidence.
- The appellant claimed that the trial court abused its discretion in admitting evidence including an error in admitting expert testimony regarding MSBP to prove the appellant committed the extraneous offenses against RM and MR.

The judgment of the trial court was affirmed.

This case has been applied in the following manner:

1. Determining that expert testimony on MSBP was relevant in murder trial to explain the mother's alleged conduct and show the mother's motive for allegedly causing death of her infant child.
2. The court of appeal provided a thorough analysis of the scientific reliability of expert testimony on MSBP. The court concluded that "the trial court did not err in determining the scientific reliability of the MSBP testimony."
3. Describing how the children of MSBP parents are also "victimized … over the years in an ongoing pattern of … diagnostic tests which are in themselves …, abusive because they involve invasion into the body … [and] that carries with it … a fatality risk."
4. "Although a prosecutor ordinarily need not prove motive as an element of a crime, the absence of an apparent motive may make proof of the essential elements of a crime less persuasive."
5. A doctor testified that the syndrome is diagnosed by further testing or removing the child from the alleged perpetrator, at which time the signs and symptoms will resolve themselves if the alleged perpetrator was the cause.
6. The Texas Court of Appeals in Amarillo upheld a trial court decision allowing prosecutors to present evidence that a young victim's sibling had also suffered the same unexplained apnea symptoms from 1985 to 1988 before he was removed from his mother's care, when the symptoms disappeared.

IN RE ZS, 2014 Ohio 3748 (Ct. App. 2014)

On August 24, 2012, SS was found to be a victim of child medical abuse, and his two brothers were at risk. Specifically, his mother had established a pattern of misrepresenting and exaggerating (SS's) symptoms to his various doctors, who then performed several unnecessary and invasive medical procedures on him. When a doctor became unwilling to agree to his mother's demands regarding (SS's) treatment for fictitious illnesses or conditions, she simply went to another doctor and misrepresented his symptoms to obtain medical treatment.

The mother's description of (SS's) symptoms and various ailments was inconsistent with the observations and diagnoses of the doctors and other medical professionals who treated him. The doctors reported that although SS had several verifiable conditions they were non-life-threatening and did not seriously affect his well-being but the mother maintained that SS was suffering from several rare and fatal conditions. Medical tests proved conclusively that SS was generally healthy. Medical record review noted that the mother's two other boys, ZS and MS, had experienced similar treatment from their mother though not to the extent that she had with SS.

During August 2013, a hearing was conducted. The mother dismissed her counsel on the first day of the hearing claiming that he was not acting in her best interests and was incompetent. The dismissed attorney was the fifth attorney providing representation and at least three of the five had been "fired." The juvenile court informed the mother that she could retain private counsel; however, no other attorneys would be appointed to represent her and no further continuances would be granted. The mother ultimately chose to continue pro se during the adjudicatory and disposition hearing.

The juvenile court found that it was in the boys' best interest to grant temporary custody and a first extension of temporary custody to MCCS.

On appeal, all of the mother's assignments of error were overruled and the judgment of the juvenile court was affirmed.

"Medical child abuse" is a form of child abuse that occurs as a result of a caretaker providing false or misleading medical information about his or her child to medical providers. Medical child abuse can occur when a caretaker exaggerates or fabricates information about the child's symptoms. It can also occur when a caretaker directly causes the child to exhibit certain symptoms, for instance, by having the child ingest a substance that will make him or her nauseous and then claiming the child is suffering from another condition entirely.

IN THE MATTER OF DM, 2014 Ohio 2160 (Ct. App. 2014)

DM was born on February 17, 1996, and AD was born on January 13, 1999. Both are the biological children of the appellant ("mother"). The complaint alleged that the mother violated a county court order by trying to have DM placed on mental health medication, that the mother abused marijuana, and that domestic violence occurred in the home.

A psychologist testified that the mother was fixated on DM and his issues and the mother stated that DM was very violent with severe emotional problems. The psychologist's evaluation was that the mother was diagnosed with FDP, cannabis abuse, and borderline personality disorder.

The psychologist noted inconsistencies between what the mother reported was wrong with DM and other documentation or evaluations of DM and opined: "when a child has a mental health condition, the primary source of information a professional relies on to diagnose such issues is information from the child's caregiver. As the child gets older and starts to relay information to the professional himself or herself, the reports are inconsistent with the previous information provided by the parent." The psychologist opined that the situation in this case likely mirrored this sequence and that the mother's behavior with regard to DM was emotional abuse. The psychologist further stated that the mother's ability to care for AD was compromised because if the mother did not have access to DM, she would likely shift the fabrication of symptoms to AD.

The trial court ruled that DM was an abused child and AD was a dependent.

The appeal ruling found that the trial court did not err in finding DM abused and in finding AD dependent. The appellant's first and second assignments of error were overruled, and the judgment was affirmed.

IN RE DD, No. C069766 (Cal. Ct. App. May 16, 2013)

Mother took DD to the "crisis unit" after consulting with the child's pediatrician and claimed that DD had bipolar disorder. The crisis unit disagreed, and DD expressed that he feared his mother. A referral was made to social services that was deemed "unfounded" for physical abuse and "inconclusive" for general neglect.

Two days later, social services received a second referral alleging general neglect. The reporter stated that the mother "refused to accept the diagnosis that there was nothing wrong with her child," was "medication and diagnosis seeking," and gave the minor medication "even though clinicians and psychiatrists saw no evidence of reported behaviors." The reporter stated the mother had "slapped" DD and took DD to the emergency room "three or four times for heart palpitations." Before this referral was resolved, social services received a third referral.

On April 1, 2011, the department received a report that the mother may be suffering from MSBP, placing DD at risk. The mother claimed that DD would become violent or manic and would "rage," putting himself and his mother in jeopardy. None other than his mother, however, had witnessed these episodes. Based on [mother's] reports of symptoms and behaviors, the child was diagnosed with bipolar disorder, attention deficit hyperactivity disorder, oppositional defiant disorder, and nonspecific cardiac arrhythmia by a series of physicians and prescribed at one time or another the following: Seroquel, Depakote, Abilify, Ativan, Concerta, Ritalin, Topamax, Lamictal, clonidine, Tenex, and Intuniv.

The Department of Social Services alleged the mother failed to protect the minor.

On approximately April 2, 2011, the child was admitted to a hospital to rapidly be weaned off all his medications while monitoring his heart, in order to determine the correct required medications.

The specific falsifications in this case are described as follows:

- Mother reported the child was severely allergic to a wide range of foods resulting in the child complaining of hunger due to his very limited diet. Allergy testing during hospitalization revealed only allergies to egg whites, bananas, and seasonal allergy to pollen.
- Mother repeatedly reported she was fearful of the child due to his aggressive, "raging" behaviors toward her.
- Mother refused services that potentially could have resulted in the child returning to the home in a safe environment.
- During the child's hospital stay over 6 days, he was noted to comply with staff requests and played with only a couple of minor incidents of hyperactivity where he was easily redirected.

- Various professionals, including (but not limited to) school personnel, behavioral health, police, emergency medical technician staff, and ER staff involved with the child on a frequent basis neither observed nor documented any out of control/raging like behaviors as described by the mother.
- Mother has a history of moving the child from the care of one doctor to another and has changed the child's school several times.
- The child's father has not maintained a relationship with the child.
- The mother was instructed to not return to the hospital but returned and told the child that he was being taken away from her because he was a bad boy at home, she was losing her parental rights, and he will possibly never see her again. This caused the child's heart rate to increase to 140 beats per minute resulting in the monitoring company calling the nurses' station to ask what was going on to cause the rapid increase in the child's heart rate.
- DD's diagnoses were based solely on the mother's reporting

The court found by preponderance of evidence that the child was at risk and reasonable visitation discretion for the mother was to be decided by social services. The court ordered the mother not to bring items to her visits with DD including food and ordered appointment of a court-appointed special advocate and authorized psychological evaluations for the mother and DD.

Social Services recommended continued foster care for DD and reunification services for the mother. Based on its investigation, the Department concluded that DD was at risk if he was returned to mother's care because the mother had not made significant changes to her behavior since DD was detained.

The orders of the juvenile court were affirmed.

State v. Montano, No. 2 CA-CR 2013–0367 (Ariz. Ct. App. Apr. 29, 2015)

After a jury trial, the appellant was convicted of intentional abuse of a child under the age of 15 years with death or serious physical injury likely, a class two felony. The trial court sentenced the appellant to a slightly mitigated term of 13 years' imprisonment. Conviction was affirmed.

The appellant gave birth to D. in August 2010. In late February 2011, D. was hospitalized due to bloody diarrhea and fever. Two days later, she was moved to the ICU to obtain treatment for multiple blood infections, which caused her to enter a state of "septic shock." She remained there until early April 2011. During her 2-month stay, D. contracted several additional life-threatening infections that required different courses of antibiotics. She acquired the infections "sequentially"—she would become infected, receive treatment, and then a new infection would arise. While D. was in the ICU, the appellant rarely left her hospital room.

D.'s infections were found in her blood and were either fecal- or water-borne. Tests were conducted to determine the infection source. Test results revealed no indications of an underlying condition that could have caused multiple infections. There was no medical explanation for the number and type of D's infections. Hospital staff suspected that someone was intentionally infecting D. by introducing bacteria into her central IV line (I.V.).

Based on this suspicion, the hospital installed a video camera in D.'s hospital room.

Three days after the camera was installed, the appellant attempted to obstruct the camera view by placing an alcohol wipe in front of the lens. Later that day, the camera revealed the appellant emerging from the hospital bathroom and approaching D.'s crib with one hand hidden in a sweatshirt. While (located) beside the crib, the appellant grabbed D's IV tubes, triggering the I.V. alarm.

The following day, the appellant was confronted regarding concerns that she had been "intentionally putting things" into D.'s I.V. The appellant was described as having no "emotional response" or "reaction" to the accusation. The appellant admitted obstructing the camera lens because she was concerned about the infant's "privacy." The appellant learned the hospital intended to notify CPS of their suspicions and responded, "I'm surprised that you haven't called CPS before now."

The appellant was prohibited from visiting D. and not allowed back in her room, and no new infections occurred. All existing infections resolved and D. was discharged from the hospital a few weeks later.

- The appellant was in D.'s room constantly, and often exhibited strange behavior and asked "bizarre" questions.
- The appellant was repeatedly asked to stop putting blankets over the side of D.'s crib and closing the blinds, which interfered with staff observation of D.
- The appellant was described as detached, emotionless, and "not participating in D's care."
- The appellant shared with one nurse that she had not been "excited" about being pregnant with D.
- The appellant could have received 17 years on the child abuse conviction; the judge considered and sentenced the appellant to 13 years in the Department of Corrections.
- Prosecutors believed that the appellant made her baby sick to get the attention of the child's father and "win him back."

State v. Butler, 1 So. 3d 242 (Fla. Dist. Ct. App. 2008)

On numerous occasions between 1999 and 2002, the appellant brought her young daughter (Child A) to a Florida hospital emergency room and reported the child was suffering from seizures. The child's physicians could not diagnose any clinical disorder or disease that would have caused the reported symptoms, despite extensive examinations and diagnostic testing. On February 5, 2002, the appellant brought Child A to the emergency room, reporting that Child A had suffered another seizure and that she was unresponsive. Medical staff was unable to revive Child A, and she died at the age of two. An autopsy suggested that Child A died of asphyxiation and did not identify a natural cause of death. Criminal charges were not immediately filed, and, in 2003, the appellant moved with her family to another state, where she gave birth to another child (Child B).

Shortly after Child B's birth, the appellant began to bring him to a hospital reporting symptoms similar to those she reported with Child A in Florida.

The cause of Child B's reported symptoms could not be medically determined and suspicion arose that the appellant was abusing the child. In accordance with hospital policy, an assistant prosecutor was contacted. The assistant prosecutor obtained court permission to conduct video surveillance of Child B while he was hospitalized seeking an explanation for any actions that would indicate how the purported signs of illness were occurring and "To take immediate custody of the child … if the child is deemed to be in imminent danger." Four hidden cameras were fixed on the child's hospital bed and an adjacent recliner and linked to a closed-circuit television, which the hospital security continuously monitored.

The appellant was not aware of the camera installation. During the night, the hospital security officer saw the appellant "place something over Child B's nose and mouth" and summoned nursing staff.

The appellant was later arrested and prosecuted for child abuse.

In 2006, the appellant was charged (in Florida) with one count of second-degree murder and one count of aggravated child abuse in the death of Child A. The state filed notice of its intent to introduce, at trial, surveillance footage from Child B's hospital room. The appellant moved to suppress that evidence which was granted by the court finding that "the surveillance was conducted not for the purpose of treating the child, but for the purpose of investigating whether his mother was abusing him," and that "the surveillance never would have occurred but for the court order authorizing the same." Likening a hospital room to a hotel room, the court concluded that the appellant had a reasonable expectation of privacy in the room.

The State appealed the suppression order, and the decision was reversed with the court stating that the appellant did not hold a reasonable expectation of privacy standard in a hospital room.

State v. Hocevar, 7 P.3d 329, 2000 M.T. 157, 300 Mont. 167 (2000)

After a jury trial, the appellant (Mother) was convicted of criminal endangerment regarding her son's (Victim W) ingestion of an overdose of Benadryl. An appeal was filed. The appellant exemplified MSBP and smothered her sons and claimed that considering the conduct in sentencing in the criminal endangerment conviction was double jeopardy.

The conviction was affirmed in part and reversed in part.

On May 21, 1992, the appellant's then 4-year-old son (Victim W) complained to his mother that his head hurt and so two children's Tylenol tablets or Tylenol Elixir were placed on the coffee table in the living room by the appellant. There was allegedly no water on the table. The doctor later testified that Victim W was not able to swallow capsules without water. The appellant testified at trial that Victim W had a cup of water. Also on the coffee table was a bottle of Benadryl capsules without a cap. The appellant stated that she habitually removed the plastic wrappers from Benadryl capsules and put them in a bottle so that she would have quicker access to them at the onset of an allergy attack. The appellant then told Victim W to take his medicine and resumed baking cookies in the kitchen.

A neighbor came and went, and then the appellant noticed that her Benadryl was gone. The children's Tylenol was still sitting on the coffee table. Victim W confirmed that he had eaten the Benadryl capsules. The appellant testified that Victim W had tried to take other people's medicine on other occasions and that he had previously tried to take more vitamins than he was supposed to take.

The appellant unsuccessfully tried to phone her husband and then instructed the neighbor who had just visited to pick up the husband from work, called the emergency room, and tried unsuccessfully to reach a particular physician. The husband arrived home, and he and the appellant took Victim W to the emergency room.

The hospital called Dr. P; Victim W's stomach was rinsed and he was given activated charcoal and a laxative to quickly remove the Benadryl from his system. The appellant and her husband stated that Victim W ingested 250–300 mg of Benadryl; 480 mg is considered a lethal dose for the weight of Victim W at that time. Dr. P testified that the symptoms of a Benadryl overdose include a fast heart rate, dilated pupils, hallucinations, combativeness, agitation, and hyperactivity and that she observed hallucinations in Victim W. Victim W was placed in the ICU for observation overnight and was released on the following day.

Dr. P was concerned that Victim W's Benadryl overdose might not have been accidental, partly based on her prior experience with Victim W's brother, Victim M.

Victim M died in December 1991 at the age of 10 months. Dr. P first saw then 6-month-old Victim M in August 1991 shortly after the family had moved to Montana from California where Victim M had been on an apnea monitor because another of the appellant's children, Victim Z, had died of sudden infant death syndrome (SIDS). Victim M appeared normal to Dr. P, but she decided to prescribe another apnea monitor for him.

After the August office visit, Victim M was hospitalized several times and brought in for office visits several times, for problems including seizures, viral infections, and diarrhea. Victim M's last office visit on December 5, 1991, was normal. On December 19, 1991, Dr. P was summoned to the emergency room for a code blue (a child undergoing cardiopulmonary resuscitation) involving Victim M, who was unable to breathe on his own and died the following day.

Dr. P feared that the appellant exhibited the symptoms of MSBP and consulted with specialists about the situation. Social Services removed Victim W from home on May 22, 1992, the day he was released from the hospital following the overdose and placed him in a foster home for several weeks followed by reassignment with the paternal grandparents. After an investigation, Victim W was returned to the custody of the appellant and her husband during November 1993.

The appellant gave birth to a girl (D), in April 1993, who was also placed in a foster home until being returned to the appellant and her husband in November 1993. The appellant and her husband parented another biological female child after that.

In the case of the death of Victim M, the state contended that MSBP caused the defendant to engage in a common plan whereby she injured her children. Moreover, the expert witnesses on the subject of MSBP whom the state called provided testimony to that end.

State v. Davis, 519 S.E.2d 852, 205 W. Va. 569 (1999)

The defendant appealed her convictions for the attempt to injure her infant son by poison and first-degree murder of her infant daughter and subsequent sentence to life imprisonment without parole for the murder conviction and to a consecutive sentence of 3–18 years' imprisonment for the attempt to injure by poison conviction was in error. The appeal assigned the following errors: (1) insufficiency of evidence to support the convictions, (2) failure to dismiss for pretrial indictment delay, (3) failure to instruct jury on malice, (4) failure to instruct on lesser included offenses, and (5) prosecutorial misconduct.

The convictions were affirmed.

Records indicated that the defendant was married, and two children were born to the marriage. The first child (Victim T) was born on February 27, 1979. The second child (Victim S) was born on July 18, 1981. The defendant was a registered nurse.

On September 30, 1981, the defendant and her husband rushed Victim S to the hospital after he appeared to have a seizure. Blood testing revealed a normal blood sugar level of 72 but spinal fluid testing revealed an abnormal low reading of 11. Victim S's condition was grave, and he was flown to another hospital where an abnormal and dangerous level of insulin was found in his body. The treating physician concluded that someone had injected Victim S with insulin and reported this suspicion to another physician who failed to make a child abuse report to authorities. As a result of the large quantity of insulin in Victim S's body, he sustained massive brain damage and severe retardation and lives in a state of vegetation.

On March 10, 1982, the defendant rushed Victim T to the hospital stating he had been vomiting and complaining of burning of the urine. Victim T was admitted to the hospital. During the late evening hours of Victim T's hospital admission, a nurse observed the defendant injecting something into Victim T. and confronted the defendant. The defendant told the nurse to chart the shot as a thiamine injection.

On the morning of March 12, 1982, Victim T was being transferred by ambulance to another larger hospital and died in the ambulance before it reached the hospital.

Victim T's autopsy result was that death was a homicide caused by caffeine overdose. In Victim T's stomach, "beads" of caffeine pills that had been contained in pill capsules were found. On the evening of Victim T's death, an empty blister pack, which had contained diet capsule pills, was found by the defendant's husband in a tied-up garbage bag on his back porch.

Law enforcement officials began an investigation into Victim T's death in 1982 but halted it at some point prior to 1985. The case was reopened in 1995. In November of 1996, a grand jury returned an indictment charging the defendant with attempting to injure Victim S by poison and the first-degree murder of Victim T. The defendant was subsequently convicted and sentenced on both charges.

There was evidence that the State became cognizant of a medical theory, which could establish the motive for the crimes. The theory, MSBP, appears to have been discovered in 1977 but was not widely known until the late 1980s. The substance of MSBP is that a parent will harm a child in order to bring attention and sympathy to the parent. Insofar as this theory relates to the motive, and the motive is not an element of an offense, we are not persuaded that this evidence supports the delay in bringing charges.

State v. Cutro, 618 S.E.2d 890, 365 S.C. 366 (2005)

The appellant and her husband operated a home daycare. Between January and September of 1993, two infants died at the home. A third infant, AM, became ill while at their home and was subsequently diagnosed with serious brain damage.

The State produced evidence that all three infants were victims of shaken baby syndrome. The appellant was convicted of two counts of homicide by child abuse and sentenced to concurrent life sentences for killing the two infants; she was acquitted of the assault and battery charge regarding AM.

The State's theory of the case was that the appellant's actions were motivated by MSBP, which the State's medical experts defined as a form of child abuse in which the perpetrator harms a child in order to garner sympathy and attention for herself.

On appeal, the case was affirmed.

Other Notable Cases

In re Hope L., 775 N.W.2d 384, 278 Neb. 869 (2009).
Austin v. State, 222 S.W.3d 801 (Tex. App. 2007).
Starks v. City of Waukegan, No. 09 C 348 (N.D. Ill. May 21, 2013).
Cooney v. Casady, 735 F.3d 514 (7th Cir. 2013).
MATTER OF MARIA S., 2014 N.Y. Slip Op 50690 (Fam. Ct. 2014).
Arnett v. Colvin, No. C2: 13-CV-01996-MJP-JLW (W.D. Wash. Aug. 22, 2014).
People v. Kranz, 197 N.W.2d 276, 39 Mich. App. 69 (Ct. App. 1972).
LESLIE O. v. Superior Court, 231 Cal. App. 4th 1191, 180 Cal. Rptr. 3d 863 (Ct. App. 2014).

People v. Spears, 2015 N.Y. Slip Op 81690 (App. Div. 2015).
Jones v. State, 751 S.W.2d 682 (Tex. App. 1988).
Jordan v. Ct. of App. for Fourth Sup. Jud. Dist., 701 S.W.2d 644 (Tex. 1985).
Jones v. State, 716 S.W.2d 142 (Tex. App. 1986).
People v. Hoyt, 210 A.D.2d 786, 620 N.Y.S.2d 520 (App. Div. 1994).
United States v. Woods, 484 F.2d 127 (4th Cir. 1973).
People v. Tinning, 142 A.D.2d 402, 536 N.Y.S.2d 193 (App. Div. 1988).
Buchanan v. State, 69 P.3d 694, 119 Nev. 201 (2003).
Byrom v. State, 863 So. 2d 836 (Miss. 2003).
Matter of Jordan, 616 N.E.2d 388 (Ind. Ct. App. 1993).
In re Greene, 568 S.E.2d 634, 152 N.C. App. 410 (Ct. App. 2002).
Yuille, 111 Wn. App. at 529.
Newell v. Colvin, No. 12-cv-480-SM (D.N.H. Feb. 10, 2014).
R v. Folbigg, 2003 N.S.W.C.C.A. 17 (2003).
Ware v. Moe, Civil No. 03-2504 ADM/JSM (D. Minn. Apr. 19, 2004).
England-Case Against Beverley Allitt.

Education of Judges

The most eloquent, factually correct or obvious case compilation of abuse or homicide with an FD/FDP element may ultimately become worthless within the forum of criminal prosecution or dependency court if the presiding judge lacks a knowledge base regarding FD/FDP methodology, research, and background case law. The ability of a judge or jury to differentiate between forms of abuse with an FDP factor and associated victim risk may be the only difference between effective and ineffective intervention within a family network affected by FDP abuse.

In due course of the prosecution of abuse or homicide with an FDP factor, education of the prosecutor, jury, and judge seems relevant to the verdict vs. sentence relationship. FDP offenders displaying their roles as "great pretenders" within court situations often further confusion surrounding their actions. Judicial sentencing decisions often reflect the courts' exposure to the defendant's manipulative abilities coupled with personal belief or disbelief of the accusatory case standards.

The actions of an individual utilizing an FDP factor as a means of abuse or homicide delivery defy a standardized moral code and appear so unnatural that some justices may find difficulty levying sentences that "punish" the offender's behavior when the behavior itself is often not fully understood or aligned with other similar offenses such as pedophilia. FDP behavior is shrouded in a medical illness variable. The seriousness of abuse with an FDP factor is often unstated and minimized by both the defense and prosecution when the victim survives the abuse. Minimization is affected by the natural desire of society and victims to reunite parent with child. Unconditional love expressed by a child toward a parent (who is also a child abuser through the FDP delivery mode) is a powerful force to ignore and must be dealt with through educational factors to ensure that justice and victim protection needs are met.

Charges levied against a defendant utilizing a FDP methodology are often reduced with provisions placed for rehabilitation and proposed reunification of the family. The direct actions related to FDP delivery ranging from abuse to homicide become masked in societal pressure for family reunification. This entity is especially prevalent if multiple children are present in the family and the defendant is their mother. A judge must decide the balance between what is in the best interest of the children and dissemination of justice. Looming is the question of true rehabilitation vs. feigned rehabilitation with the actual outcome leaving the lives of children hanging in the balance. Many courts hold that family reunification efforts outweigh potential victim risks with certain safeguards in-place but the question of certainty remains quite elusive. Authentic offender rehabilitation is measured and evaluated over time. The courts often overlook the relativity of time in FDP abuse situations as child victims are anxiously reunited or not segregated from the FDP child abuse offender. The reunification between the FDP offender and victim will always produce a certain level of undetermined risk, as victimization recidivism remains possible with no guarantee that the FDP offender will not revert to past practice. FDP offenders' unrestricted access to children or other dependent individuals could easily facilitate another FDP abuse scenario and who would know?

Sentencing Tendencies

FDP offenders have a demonstrated ability to convince people that FDP abuse allegations are false or that an FDP victim would be safe if restored physical custody of victims or their siblings to defendants was conditional upon psychotherapy. Many courts have developed a standard seeking to reunite FDP offenders and their (surviving) child victims while leaning on a relative safety net that includes supervised visitation/monitoring coupled with psychotherapy treatment. A lack of judiciary understanding of potential risk factors in FDP abuse cases, even with admissions by the offender, allows leniency to pervade. An assumption is that psychotherapy is an effective treatment to correct associated FDP offender thinking but there is a lack of evidence to support this assumption. It is unclear if psychological counseling/intervention will ever be sufficient to prevent an FDP abuser from reoffending and no one will say that it does without incurring significant liability.

In all cases of abuse or homicide with a confirmed FDP factor, extensive victim protection measures should be incorporated into the criminal sentencing and dependency rulings. Reunification or permitted access between an FDP offender and surviving children is likely to occur at some future point, and victim safeguards are the responsibility of the court. Conditions given in Figure 15.12 should be considered.

Conclusions

Increased frequency of abuse or homicide with an FDP delivery factor has produced a common defense of FDP abuse as an involuntary misguided response to a greater need of attention and self-worth verification. The defense attempts to portray the FDP offender as a victim, unable to help himself/herself or control his/her actions toward the victim. Judges and juries should be reminded of the descriptive status of FDP and FD found within the current DSM-V (see Chapter 1) and be clear that FDP is abuse—not mental illness that excuses offender behavior. FDP is intentional and repetitive torture that runs a gamut from abuse to homicide.

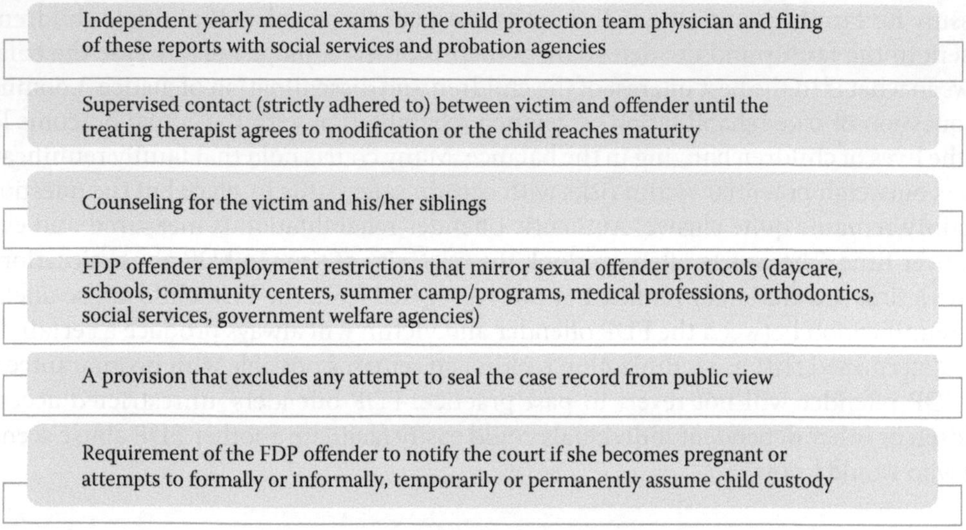

Figure 15.12 Court ordered FDP victim/offender reunification and access.

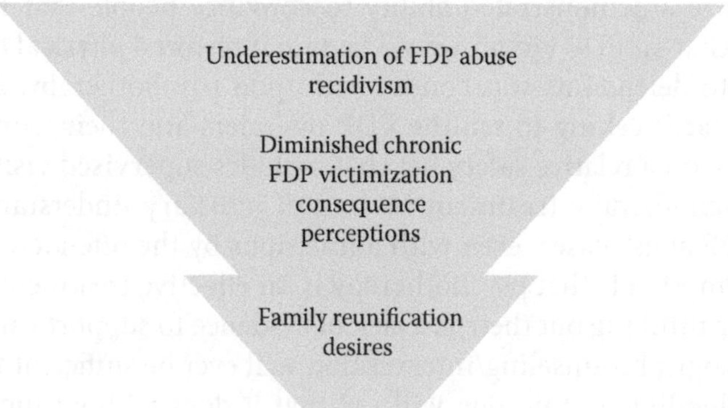

Figure 15.13 Predicate challenges for FDP offender sentencing.

Abusive actions of an FDP offender are often admitted as offenders are portrayed by the defense as individuals in need of help—not as the criminals they are. The result has been sentencing leniency by the courts facilitating family reunification and placing children right back into a status of threatened harm. Family reunification tendencies, diminished chronic victimization consequence perceptions, and an underestimation of recidivism that facilitates the American Justice System are challenges within the criminal and dependency aspects of sentencing predicate found within abuse or homicide cases with an FDP factor (Figure 15.13).

Historically, we can say with certainty that incarceration is not an effective deterrent in FDP abuse cases, even when the victim perishes as a result of inflicted harm. The question remains how best to protect the vulnerable victims of FDP abuse in the long term while balancing the fundamental need of criminal justice within the scope of FDP victimization.

Notes

1. American Psychiatric Association, *Diagnostic and Statistical Manual of Mental Disorders* (5th ed.). Washington, DC: Author, 2013.
2. International Association for Healthcare Security and Safety, *Supervisor Training Manual for Healthcare Security Personnel* (3rd ed.), IAHSS, Glendale Heights, IL, 2012, p. 95.
3. Personal Interview with Dennis NiceWander, ASA, Broward County, FL.
4. The American Heritage®, *The American Heritage Dictionary* (2nd college ed.). Boston, MA: Houghton Mifflin, 1985, p. 975.
5. Meadow, R., Management of Munchausen syndrome by proxy. *Archives of Disease in Childhood*, 1985;60:385–393.
6. See Note 3.
7. Campbell, J., Scadding, J., and Roberts, R., The concept of disease. *British Medical Journal*, 1979;2(6193):757–762.
8. Adshead, G., Evidence-based medicine and medicine-based evidence: The expert witness in cases of factitious disorder by proxy. *Journal of the American Academy of Psychiatry and the Law*, March 2005;33(1):99–105.
9. Rogers, D., Tripp, J., Bentovim, A. et al., Nonaccidental poisoning: An extended syndrome of child abuse. *British Medical Journal*, 1976;1(6013):793–796.
10. See Note 8.
11. See Note 8.
12. Café, T. and Stern, W., *Chemistry in Australia Magazine*, April 1989.
13. Moles, R. and Asnes, A., Has this child been abused? Exploring the uncertainty in the diagnosis of maltreatment. *Pediatric Clinics of North America*, 2014;61(2014):1023–1036.
14. Beresford, E.B., Uncertainty and the shaping of medical decisions. *Hastings Center Report*, 1991;21(4):6–11.

Epilogue

Factitious disorder by proxy (FDP) is an abuse delivery system within a context that ranges from simple abuse to homicide. FDP offenders' behavior is shrouded in secrecy and generally masked within the medical world of diagnostic uncertainty. FDP abuse/homicide victims are often vulnerable children or the elderly, and the victimization has secondary tentacle results affecting socioeconomic and professional realms.

To engage individuals who victimize using an FD/FDP factor basis, we must venture into their lives, but by doing so we also allow them to venture into our own. The result will invariably change the observer's life views, but more importantly looking in will open the door of hope for a victim who might otherwise perish unnoticed. Child abuse with an FDP delivery factor has cast skepticism and doubt upon the sanctity of motherhood, and through this revelation, the naiveté of the world is no longer a silent partner to that facade. We now understand that there are no limits to a person's behavior and no protected class of either victim or offender. It is both a sad and hopeful realization.

There are many reasons to blindly believe that criminal actions with an FDP factor are contrived; just because we may want this to be so does not mean that it is. FD/FDP situations continue to be identified in the medical realm internationally, and linking those actions to criminality has evolved in many countries including the United States. Evidence is firm and facts are facts.

We have moved beyond the days when FD and FDP abuse was considered a theory rather than an existence, and that is one of the fundamental changes between the first edition of this series and the present. Initially, there were limited amounts of reported cases and a lack of definition/direction from the psychology viewpoint and legal realm. Now, we have qualified clarity.

The rewrite of this book originated because the entity of FD/FDP is not a common occurrence, and the criminal aspect of FDP victimization is challenging to law enforcement officials who are charged with the intricately complex criminal investigation of crimes related to FDP abuse. The relative rarity of these situations requires that new generations of investigators, prosecutors, judges, defense attorneys, social service agencies, medical, psychological, and law enforcement professionals be aware. To be uninformed of FD/FDP is a disservice to victims and simply unacceptable.

> Now this is not the end. It is not even the beginning of the end. But it is, perhaps, the end of the beginning.
>
> **Sir Winston Churchill (1874–1965)**

Index

D

E

W

* 9 7 8 1 4 9 8 7 3 2 2 1 5 *
#0015 - 090816 - C0 - 254/178/20 [22] - CB - 9781498732215